You're Read
the Wrong Di

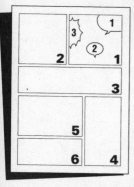

Whoops! Guess what? You're starting at the wrong end of the comic!

...It's true! In keeping with the original Japanese format, Akira Toriyama's world-famous **Dragon Ball** series is meant to be read from right to left, starting in the upper-right corner.

Unlike English, which is read from left to right, Japanese is read from right to left, meaning that action, sound-effects, and word-balloon order are completely reversed...something which can make readers unfamiliar with Japanese feel pretty backwards themselves. For this reason, manga or Japanese comics published in the U.S. in English have traditionally been published "flopped"—that is, printed in exact reverse order, as though seen from the other side of a mirror.

By flopping pages, U.S. publishers can avoid confusing readers, but the compromise is not without its downside. For one thing, a character in a flopped manga series who once wore in the original Japanese version a T-shirt emblazoned with "M A Y" (as in "the merry month of") now wears one which reads "Y A M"! Additionally, many manga creators in Japan are themselves unhappy with the process, as some feel the mirror-imaging of their art alters their original intentions.

In recognition of the importance and popularity of **Dragon Ball**, we are proud to bring it to you in the original unflopped format.

For now, though, turn to the other side of the book and let the adventure begin...!

—Editor

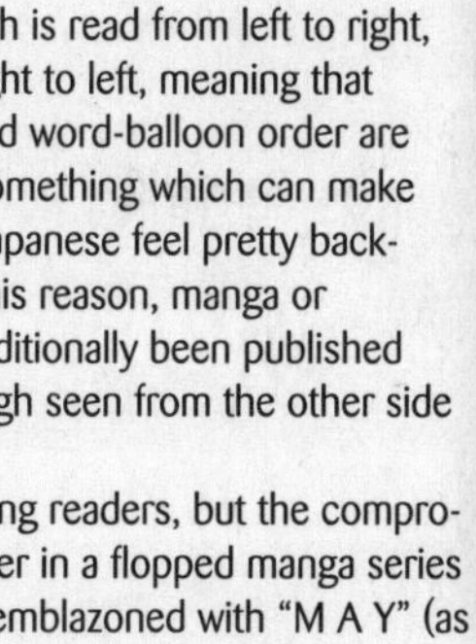

SHONEN JUMP MANGA

Vol. 15

DB: 15 of 42

STORY AND ART BY
AKIRA TORIYAMA

THE MAIN CHARACTERS

Tenshinhan

A martial artist who trained under Tsuru-Sen'nin, brother of the assassin Taopaipai. Tenshinhan renounced the path of evil and narrowly beat Goku at the last *Tenka'ichi Budôkai.*

Son Goku

Monkey-tailed Goku has always been stronger than normal. His grandfather Gohan gave him the *nyoibô*, a magic staff, and Kame-Sen'nin gave him the *kinto'un*, a magic flying cloud. Most recently, he has spent three years training with Kami-sama, the deity who watches over the world of Dragon Ball.

Yamcha

A student of Kame-Sen'nin, and Bulma's on-and-off boyfriend.

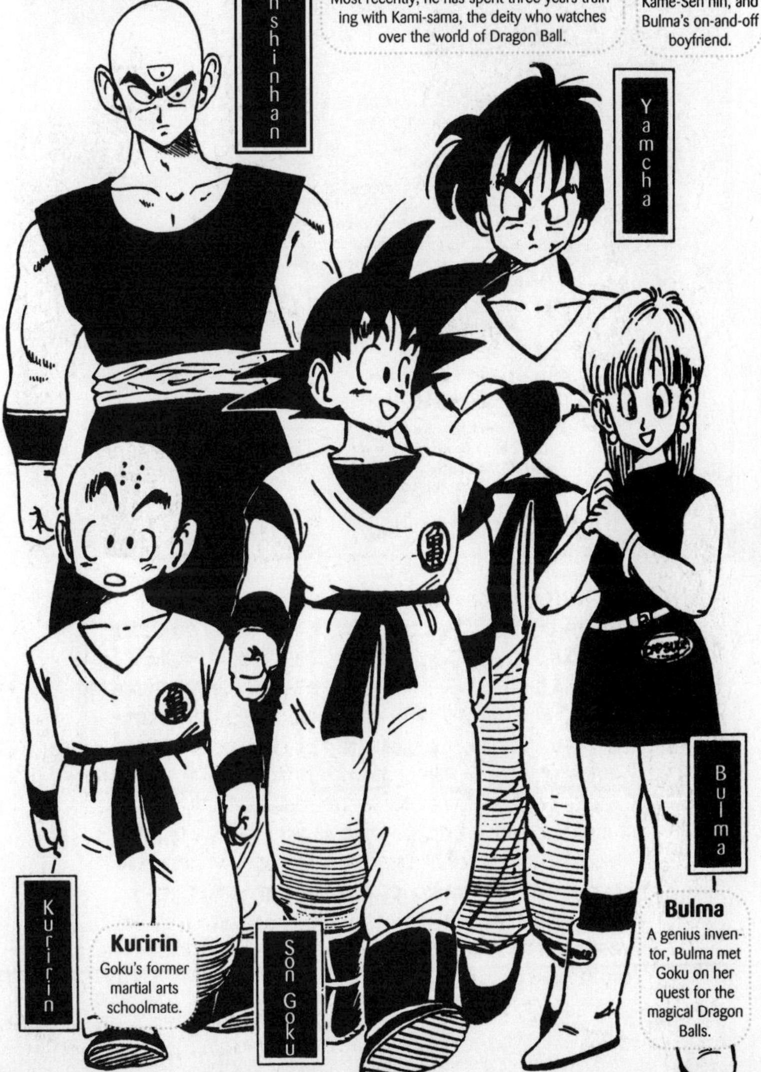
Yamcha
Tenshinhan
Bulma
Son Goku
Kuririn

Bulma

A genius inventor, Bulma met Goku on her quest for the magical Dragon Balls.

Kuririn

Goku's former martial arts schoolmate.

Shen

An incompetent martial artist who seems to have made it to the final rounds by blind luck.

Shen

Piccolo

Piccolo

Created from the sinful thoughts cast off by the divine Kami-sama when he ascended to god-hood, Piccolo is evil incarnate. The current Piccolo is a clone of the original, and possesses all the original's memories. He has entered the tournament under the name "Demon Junior."

Kame|Sen'nin

Kame-Sen'nin (The "Turtle Hermit")

A lecherous but powerful martial artist, the rival of Tsuru-Sen'nin (the "Crane Hermit"). He trained Goku, Kuririn and Yamcha.

Legend says that whoever gathers the seven magical "Dragon Balls" will be granted any one wish. Son Goku, a powerful young martial artist, first started his adventures by searching for them. As he grew older, he competed in the *Tenka'ichi Budôkai* ("Strongest Under the Heavens") fighting tournament, winning second place two times in a row. When the Great Demon King Piccolo tried to conquer the world, only Goku was strong enough to defeat him. But Piccolo used his dying energy to create a clone of himself, vowing that the clone would return in three years to get revenge. Now three years have passed, and the reborn Piccolo, and all Goku's old rivals, have come to the *Tenka'ichi Budôkai* to see who is the strongest in the world...

DRAGON BALL 15

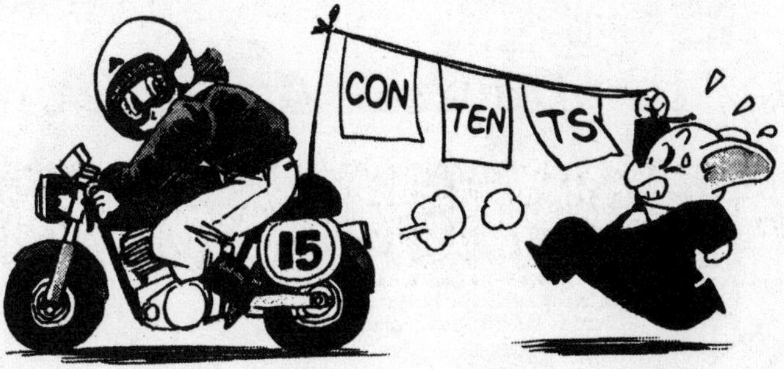

CON
TEN
TS
15

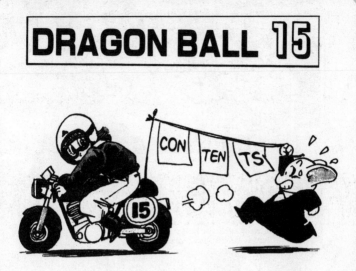

Tale 169 · Tenshinhan vs. Taopaipa

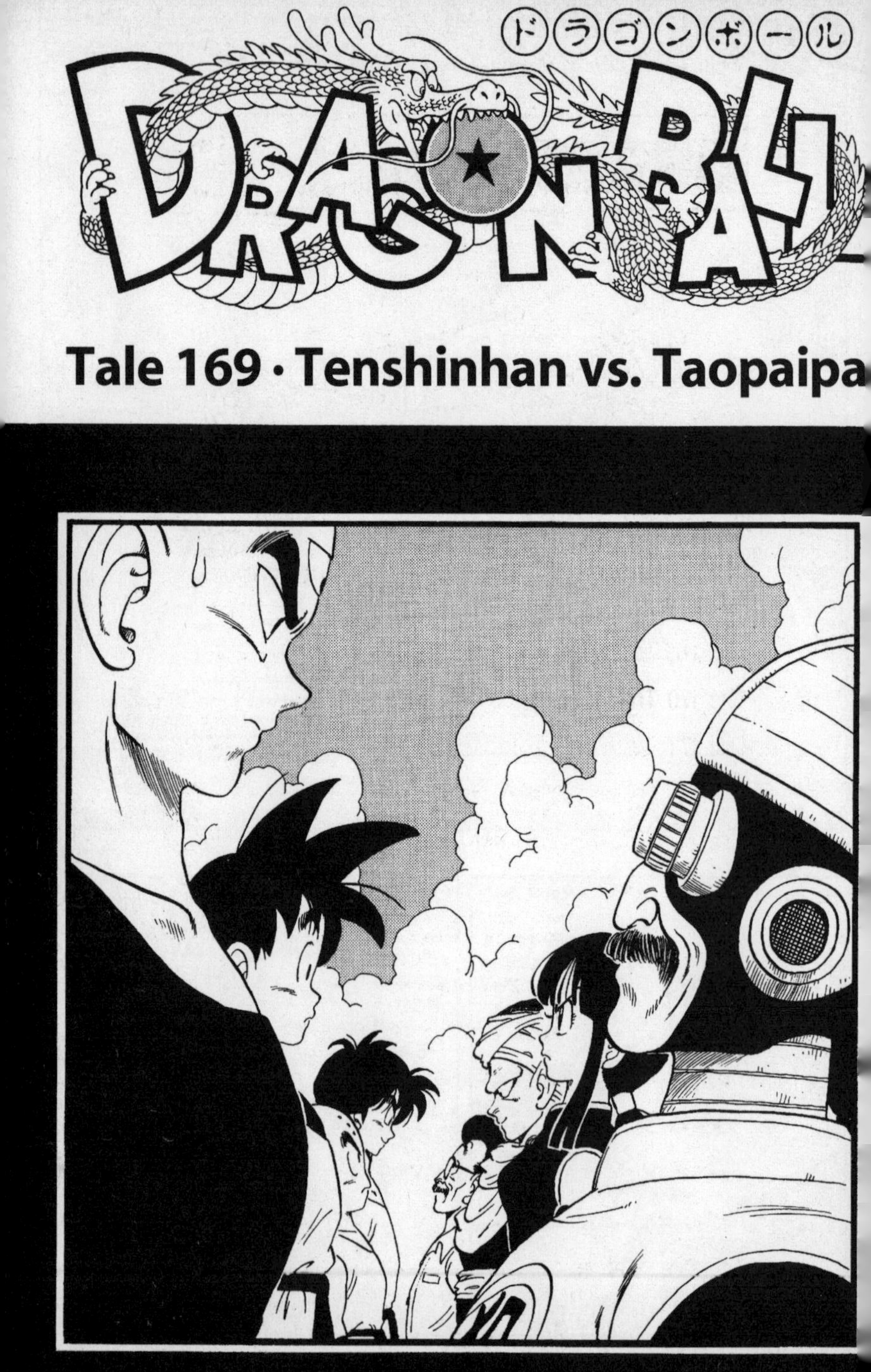

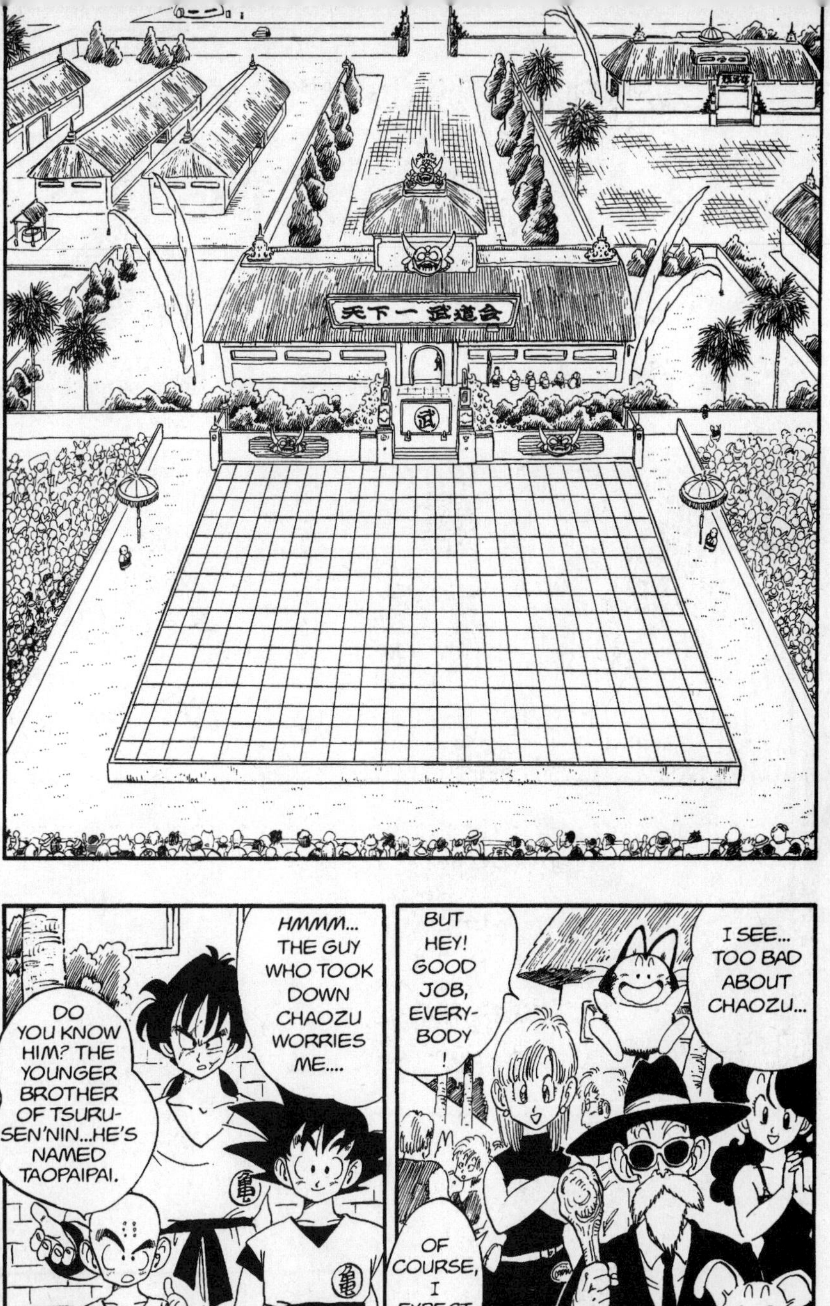
天下一武道会
武
I SEE... TOO BAD ABOUT CHAOZU...
BUT HEY! GOOD JOB, EVERYBODY!
OF COURSE, I EXPECT NO LESS!
HMMM... THE GUY WHO TOOK DOWN CHAOZU WORRIES ME....
DO YOU KNOW HIM? THE YOUNGER BROTHER OF TSURU-SEN'NIN...HE'S NAMED TAOPAIPAI.

READ THIS WAY

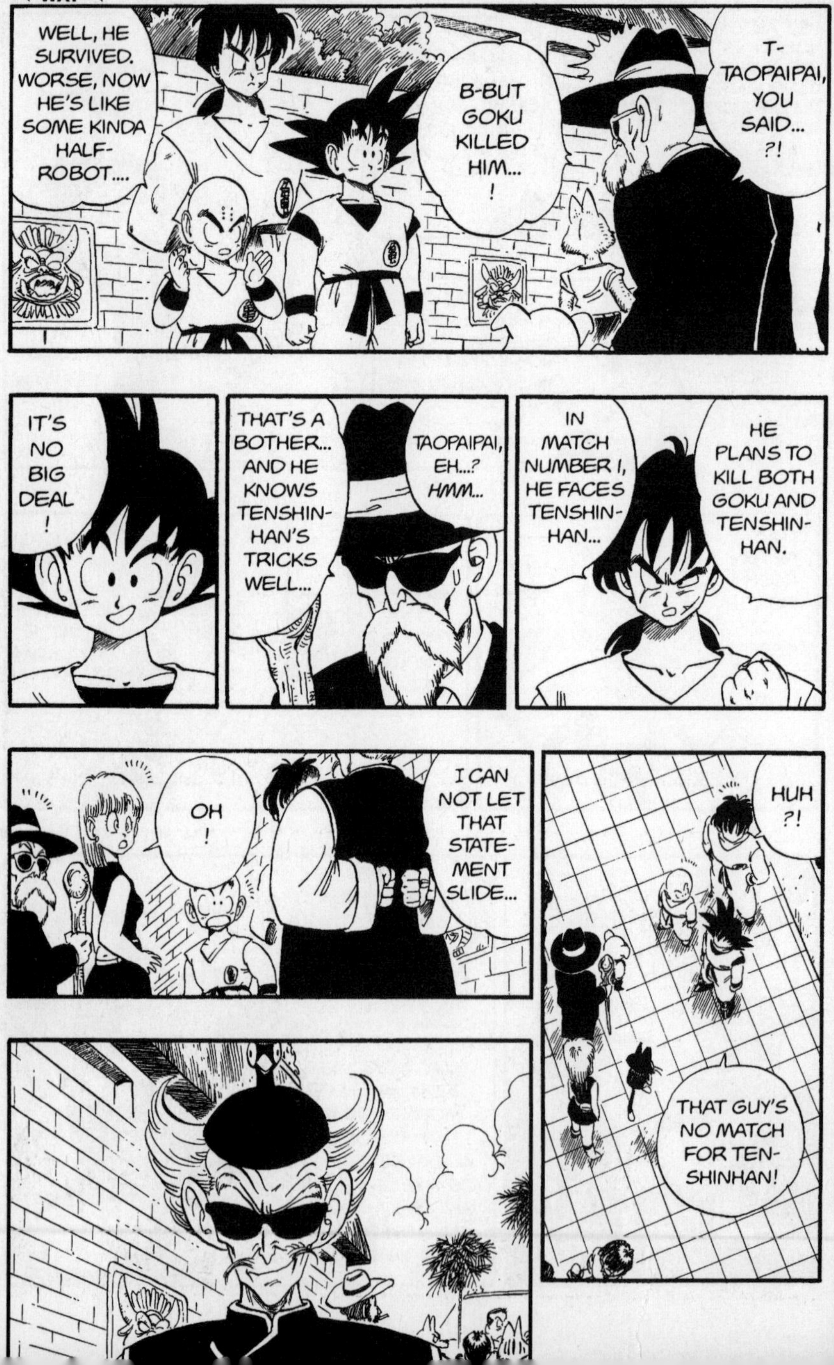
T-TAOPAIPAI, YOU SAID...?!
B-BUT GOKU KILLED HIM...!
WELL, HE SURVIVED. WORSE, NOW HE'S LIKE SOME KINDA HALF-ROBOT....
HE PLANS TO KILL BOTH GOKU AND TENSHIN-HAN.
IN MATCH NUMBER 1, HE FACES TENSHIN-HAN...
TAOPAIPAI, EH...? HMM...
THAT'S A BOTHER... AND HE KNOWS TENSHIN-HAN'S TRICKS WELL...
IT'S NO BIG DEAL!
HUH?!
THAT GUY'S NO MATCH FOR TEN-SHINHAN!
I CAN NOT LET THAT STATEMENT SLIDE...
OH!

READ THIS WAY

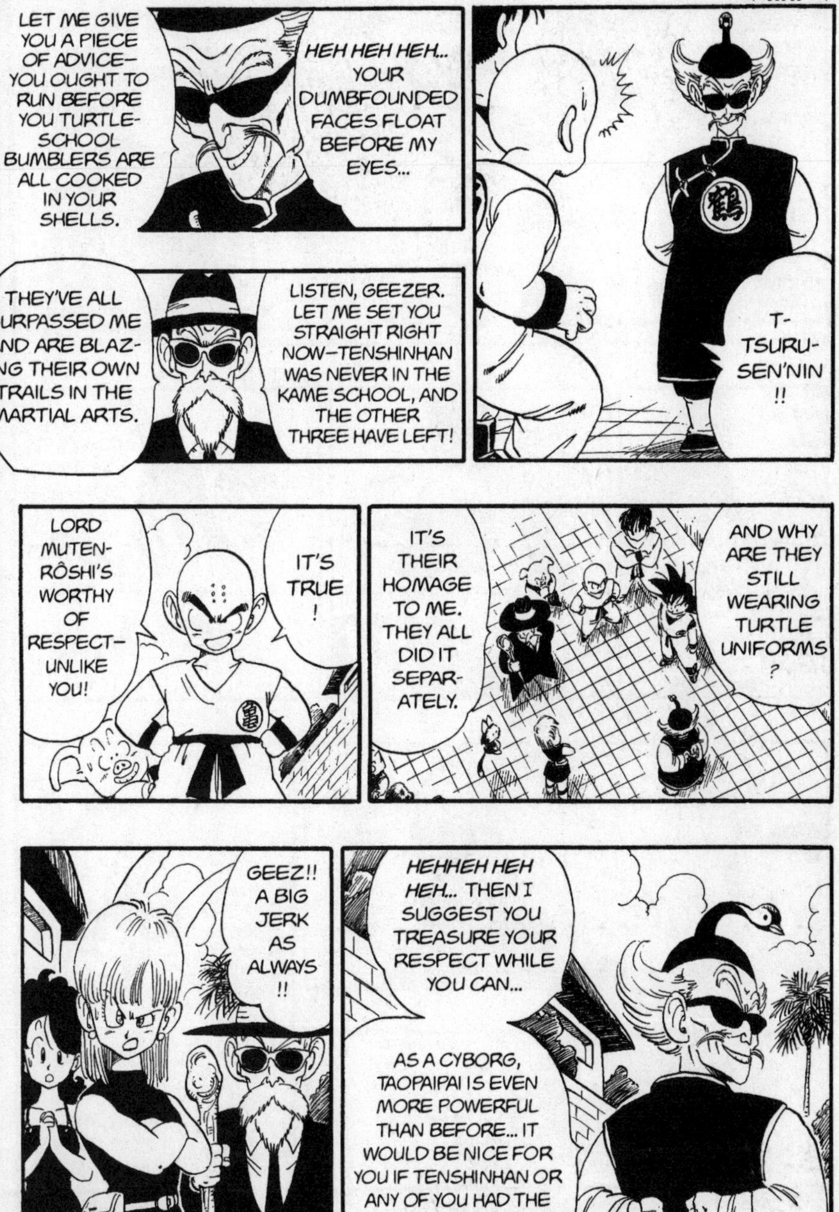

T-TSURU-SEN'NIN!!
HEH HEH HEH... YOUR DUMBFOUNDED FACES FLOAT BEFORE MY EYES...
LET ME GIVE YOU A PIECE OF ADVICE— YOU OUGHT TO RUN BEFORE YOU TURTLE-SCHOOL BUMBLERS ARE ALL COOKED IN YOUR SHELLS.
LISTEN, GEEZER. LET ME SET YOU STRAIGHT RIGHT NOW—TENSHINHAN WAS NEVER IN THE KAME SCHOOL, AND THE OTHER THREE HAVE LEFT!
THEY'VE ALL SURPASSED ME AND ARE BLAZING THEIR OWN TRAILS IN THE MARTIAL ARTS.
AND WHY ARE THEY STILL WEARING TURTLE UNIFORMS?
IT'S THEIR HOMAGE TO ME. THEY ALL DID IT SEPARATELY.
IT'S TRUE!
LORD MUTEN-RÔSHI'S WORTHY OF RESPECT— UNLIKE YOU!
HEHHEH HEH HEH... THEN I SUGGEST YOU TREASURE YOUR RESPECT WHILE YOU CAN...
AS A CYBORG, TAOPAIPAI IS EVEN MORE POWERFUL THAN BEFORE... IT WOULD BE NICE FOR YOU IF TENSHINHAN OR ANY OF YOU HAD THE SLIGHTEST CHANCE OF WINNING...
GEEZ!! A BIG JERK AS ALWAYS!!

READ THIS WAY

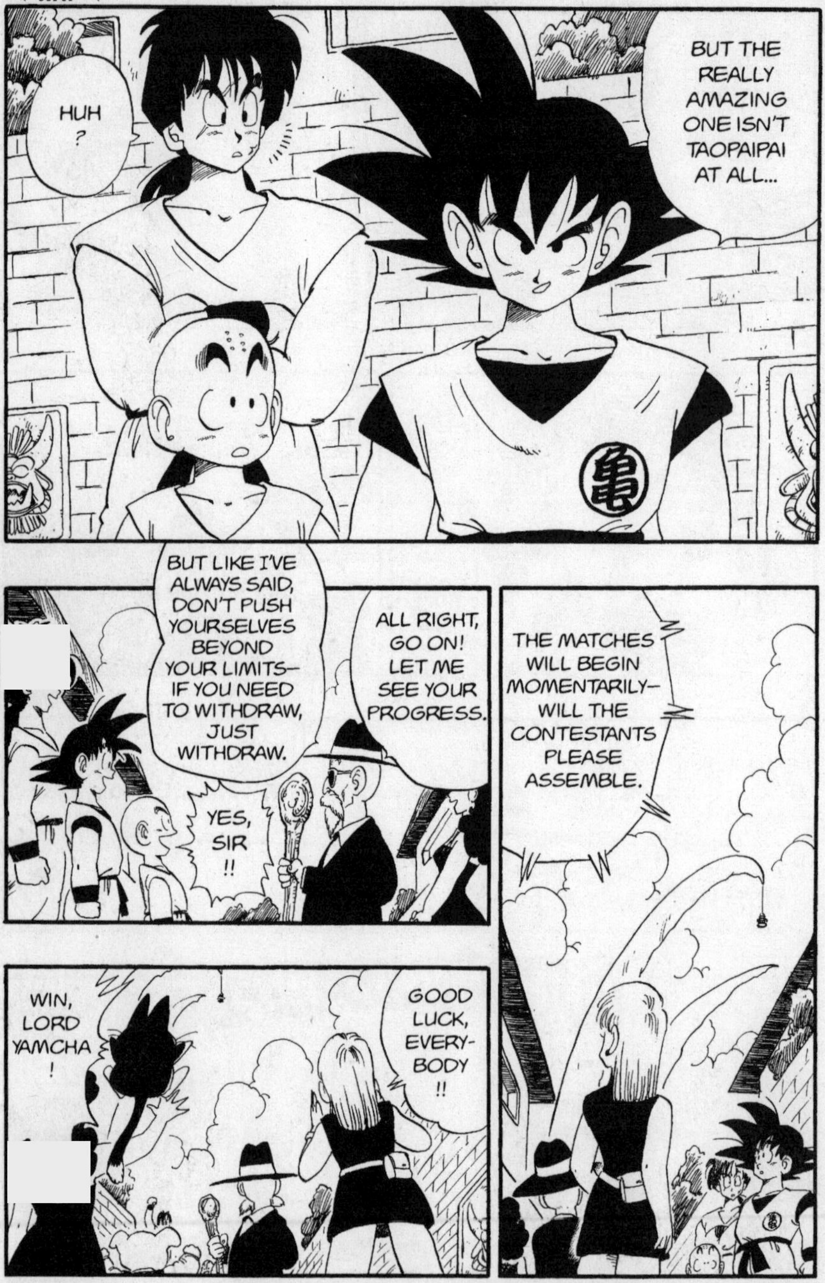
BUT THE REALLY AMAZING ONE ISN'T TAOPAIPAI AT ALL...
HUH ?
THE MATCHES WILL BEGIN MOMENTARILY—WILL THE CONTESTANTS PLEASE ASSEMBLE.
ALL RIGHT, GO ON! LET ME SEE YOUR PROGRESS.
BUT LIKE I'VE ALWAYS SAID, DON'T PUSH YOURSELVES BEYOND YOUR LIMITS—IF YOU NEED TO WITHDRAW, JUST WITHDRAW.
YES, SIR !!
GOOD LUCK, EVERY-BODY !!
WIN, LORD YAMCHA !

READ THIS WAY

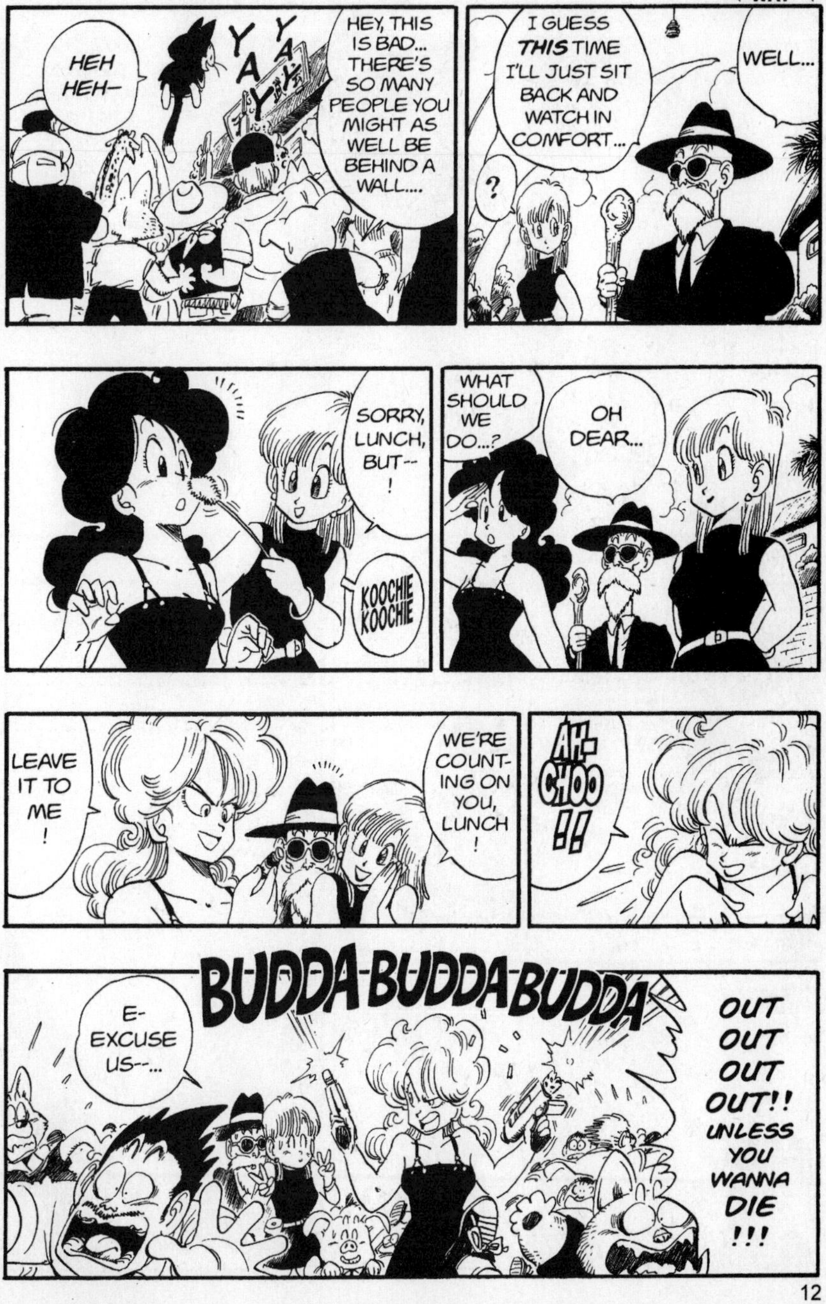
WELL...
I GUESS THIS TIME I'LL JUST SIT BACK AND WATCH IN COMFORT...
?
HEY, THIS IS BAD... THERE'S SO MANY PEOPLE YOU MIGHT AS WELL BE BEHIND A WALL....
HEH HEH-
OH DEAR...
WHAT SHOULD WE DO...?
SORRY, LUNCH, BUT--!
KOOCHIE KOOCHIE
AH-CHOO!!
WE'RE COUNTING ON YOU, LUNCH!
LEAVE IT TO ME!
OUT OUT OUT OUT!! UNLESS YOU WANNA DIE!!!
BUDDA-BUDDA-BUDDA
E-EXCUSE US--...

READ THIS WAY

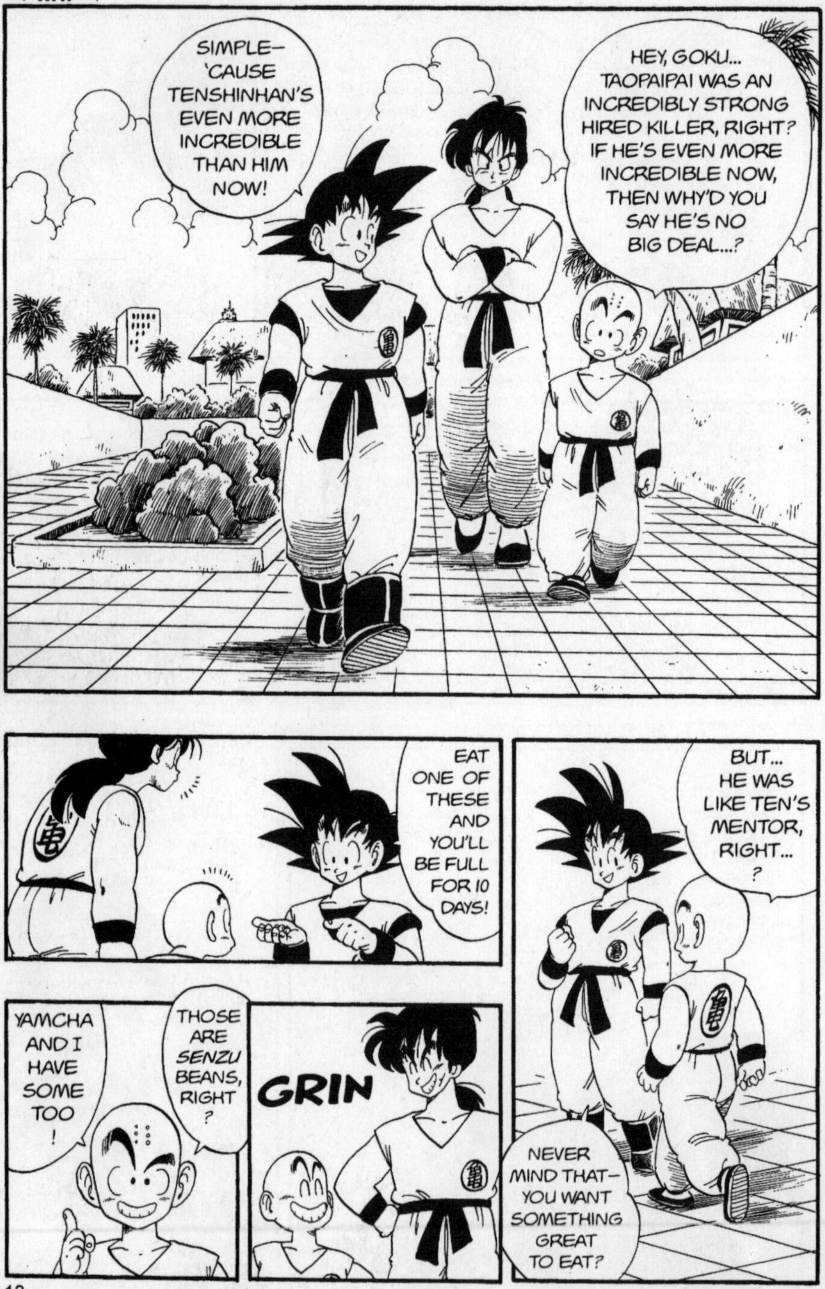

HEY, GOKU... TAOPAIPAI WAS AN INCREDIBLY STRONG HIRED KILLER, RIGHT? IF HE'S EVEN MORE INCREDIBLE NOW, THEN WHY'D YOU SAY HE'S NO BIG DEAL...?
SIMPLE— 'CAUSE TENSHINHAN'S EVEN MORE INCREDIBLE THAN HIM NOW!
BUT... HE WAS LIKE TEN'S MENTOR, RIGHT...?
NEVER MIND THAT— YOU WANT SOMETHING GREAT TO EAT?
EAT ONE OF THESE AND YOU'LL BE FULL FOR 10 DAYS!
GRIN
THOSE ARE SENZU BEANS, RIGHT?
YAMCHA AND I HAVE SOME TOO!

READ THIS WAY

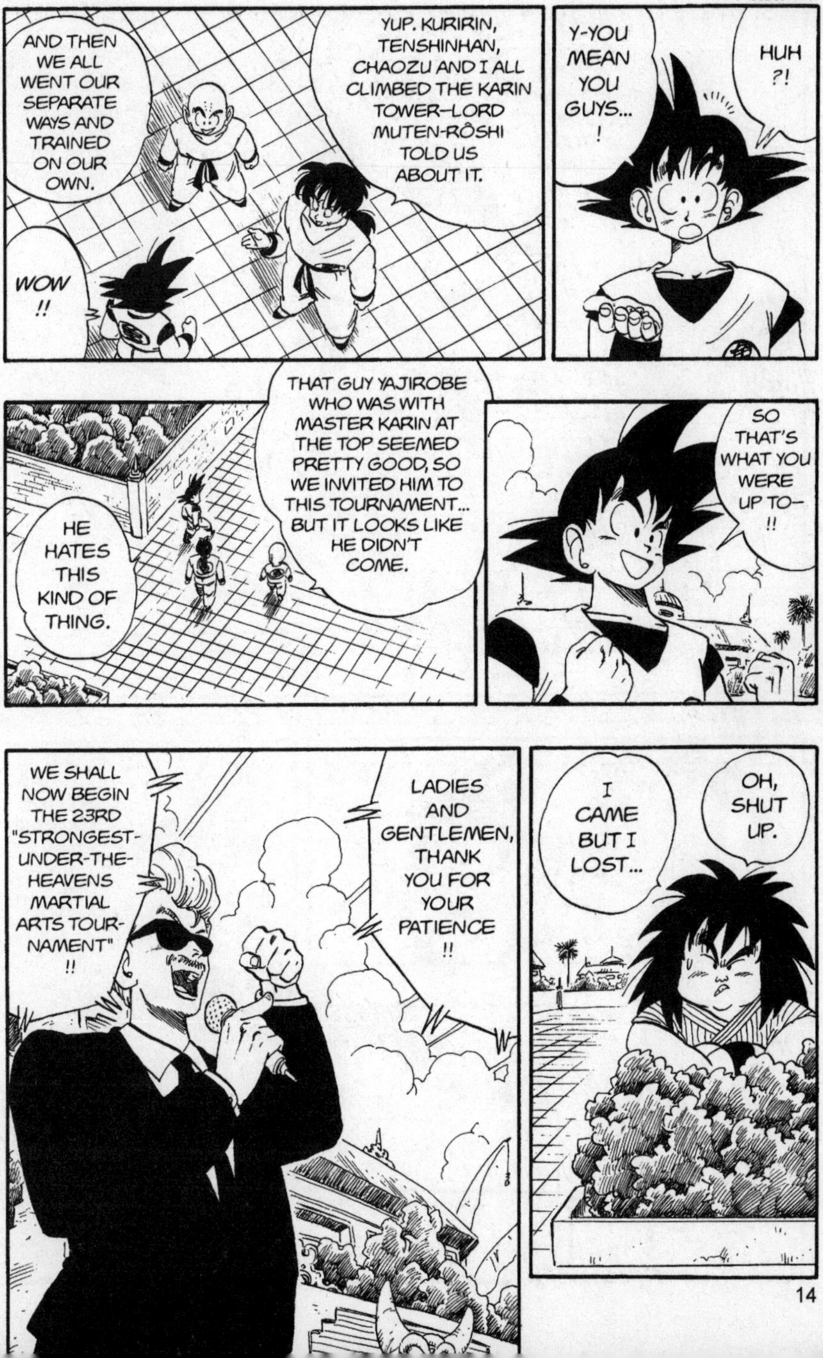

HUH ?!
Y-YOU MEAN YOU GUYS... !
YUP. KURIRIN, TENSHINHAN, CHAOZU AND I ALL CLIMBED THE KARIN TOWER—LORD MUTEN-RÔSHI TOLD US ABOUT IT.
AND THEN WE ALL WENT OUR SEPARATE WAYS AND TRAINED ON OUR OWN.
WOW !!
SO THAT'S WHAT YOU WERE UP TO— !!
THAT GUY YAJIROBE WHO WAS WITH MASTER KARIN AT THE TOP SEEMED PRETTY GOOD, SO WE INVITED HIM TO THIS TOURNAMENT... BUT IT LOOKS LIKE HE DIDN'T COME.
HE HATES THIS KIND OF THING.
OH, SHUT UP.
I CAME BUT I LOST...
LADIES AND GENTLEMEN, THANK YOU FOR YOUR PATIENCE !!
WE SHALL NOW BEGIN THE 23RD "STRONGEST-UNDER-THE-HEAVENS MARTIAL ARTS TOURNAMENT" !!

READ THIS WAY

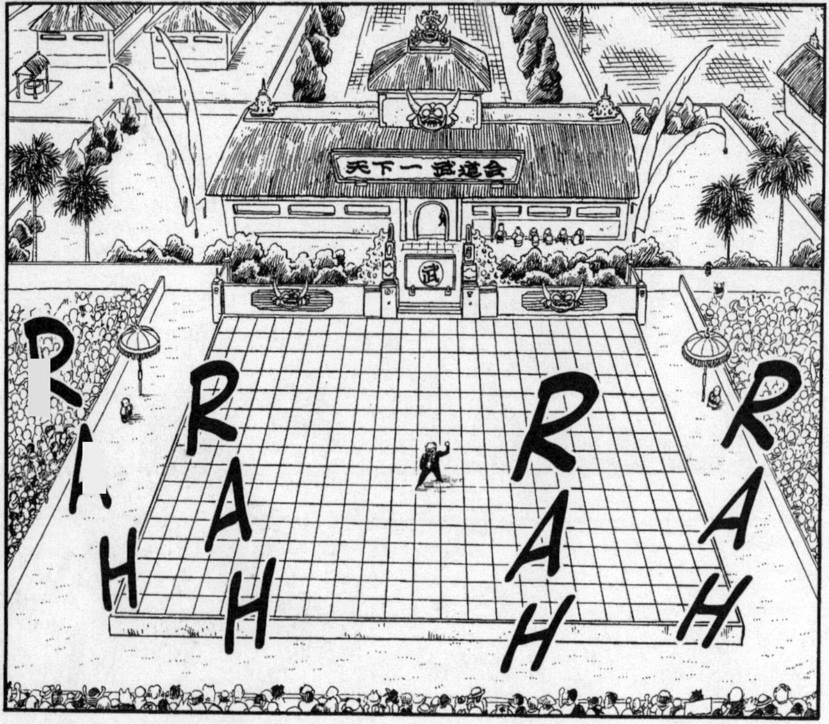
天下一武道会
武
RAH
RAH
RAH
RAH

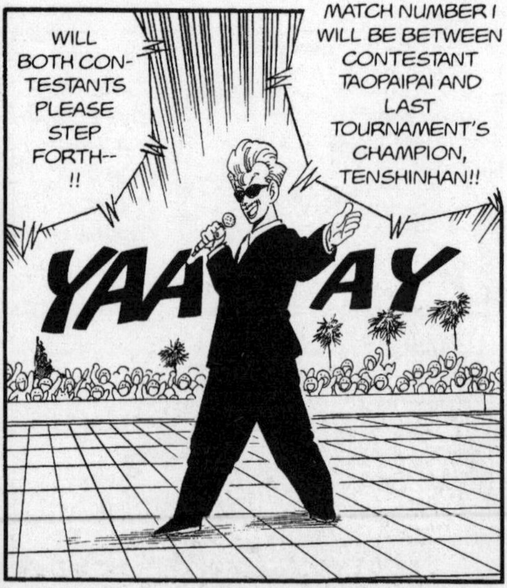
MATCH NUMBER 1 WILL BE BETWEEN CONTESTANT TAOPAIPAI AND LAST TOURNAMENT'S CHAMPION, TENSHINHAN!!
WILL BOTH CON-TESTANTS PLEASE STEP FORTH--!!
YAA AY

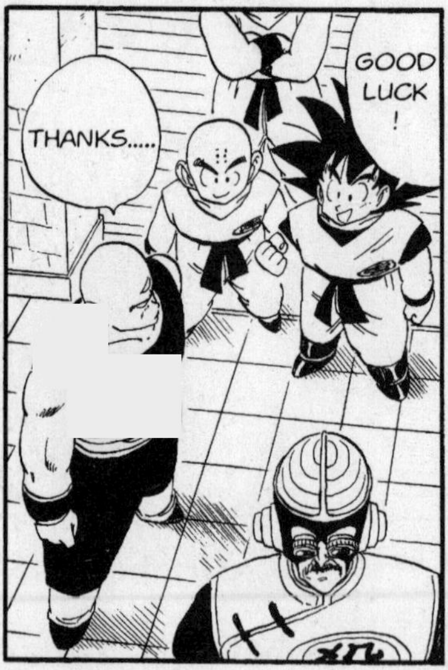
GOOD LUCK !
THANKS.....

READ THIS WAY

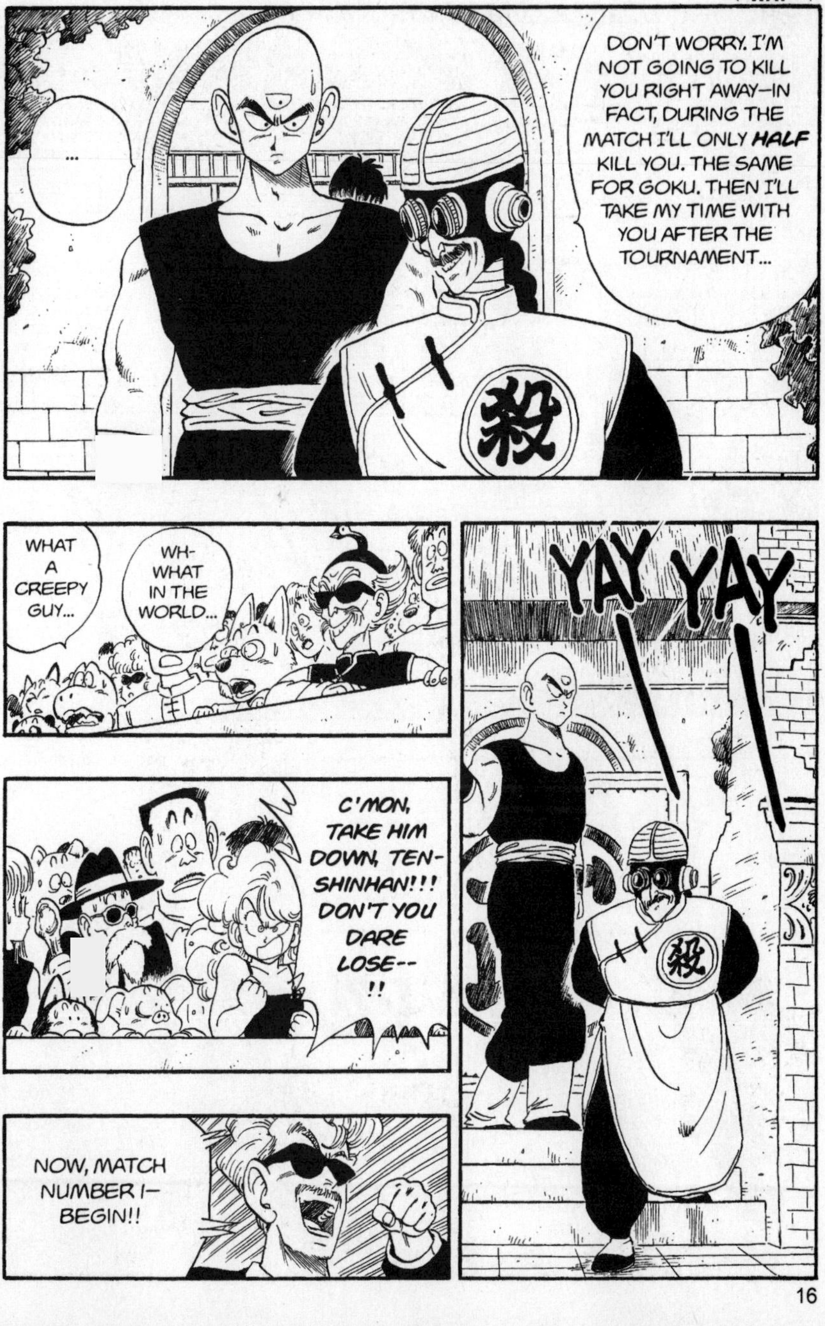

DON'T WORRY. I'M NOT GOING TO KILL YOU RIGHT AWAY—IN FACT, DURING THE MATCH I'LL ONLY **HALF** KILL YOU. THE SAME FOR GOKU. THEN I'LL TAKE MY TIME WITH YOU AFTER THE TOURNAMENT...
...
YAY YAY
WH-WHAT IN THE WORLD...
WHAT A CREEPY GUY...
C'MON, TAKE HIM DOWN, TEN-SHINHAN!!! DON'T YOU DARE LOSE--!!
NOW, MATCH NUMBER 1—BEGIN!!

READ THIS WAY

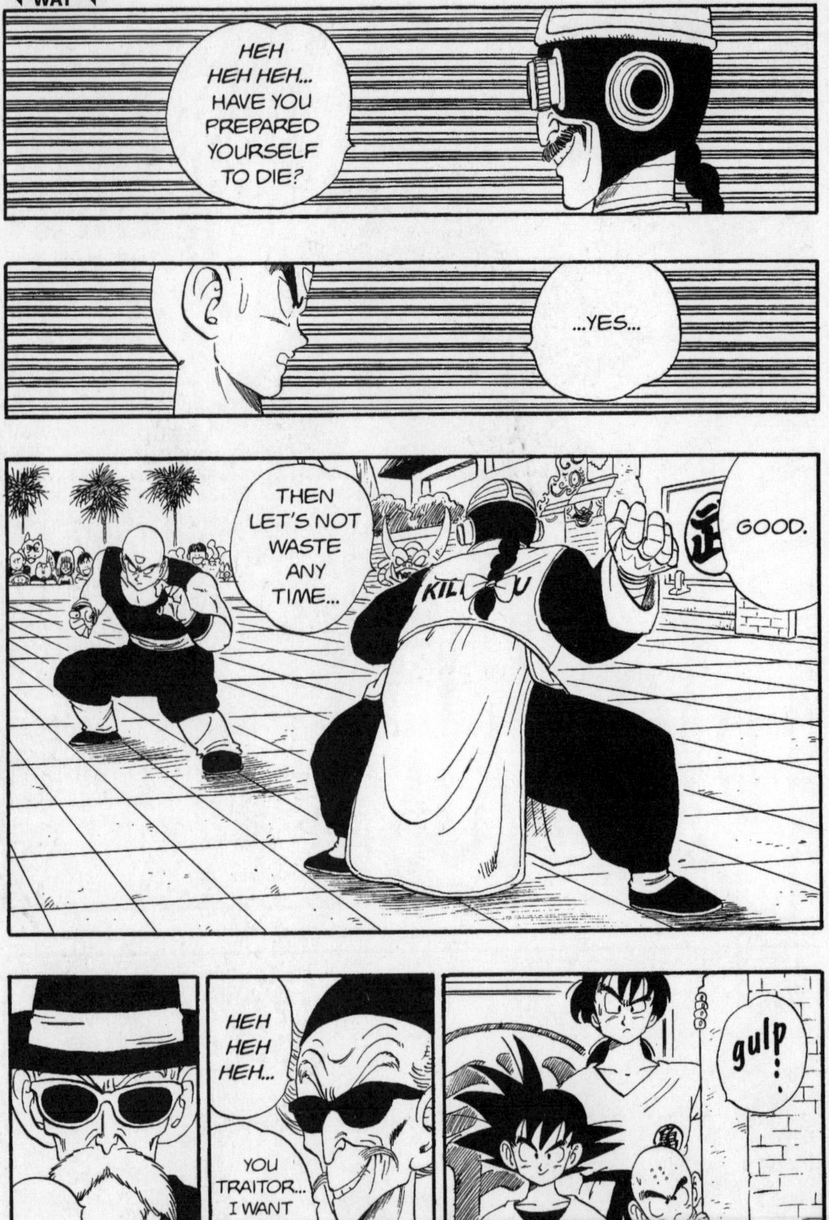
HEH HEH HEH... HAVE YOU PREPARED YOURSELF TO DIE?
...YES...
GOOD.
THEN LET'S NOT WASTE ANY TIME...
gulp...
HEH HEH HEH...
YOU TRAITOR... I WANT TO SEE YOU CRY!
NOW...

READ THIS WAY

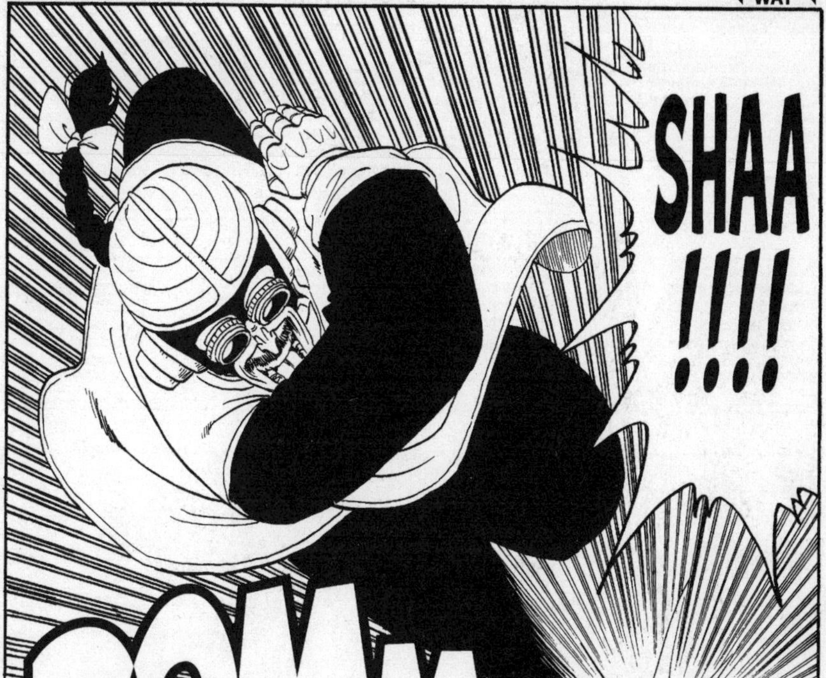
SHAA!!!!
DOMM

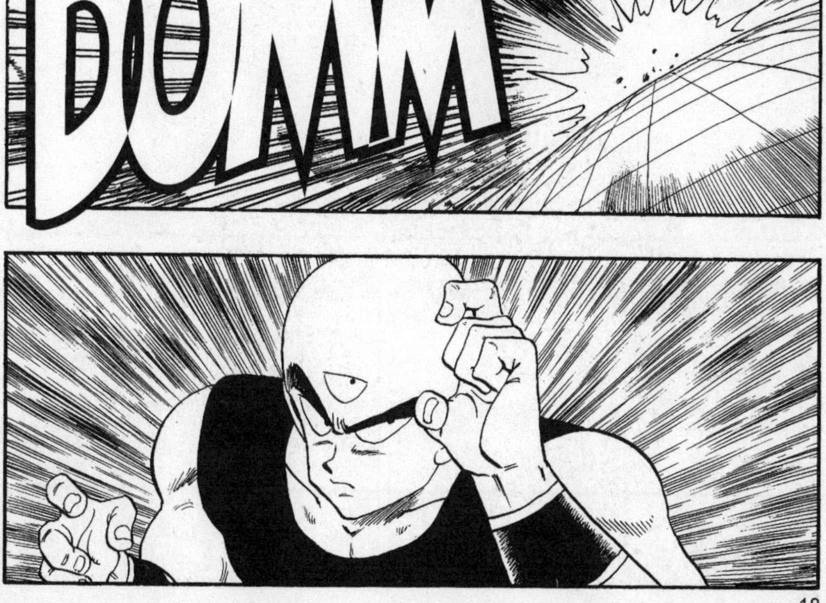

READ THIS WAY

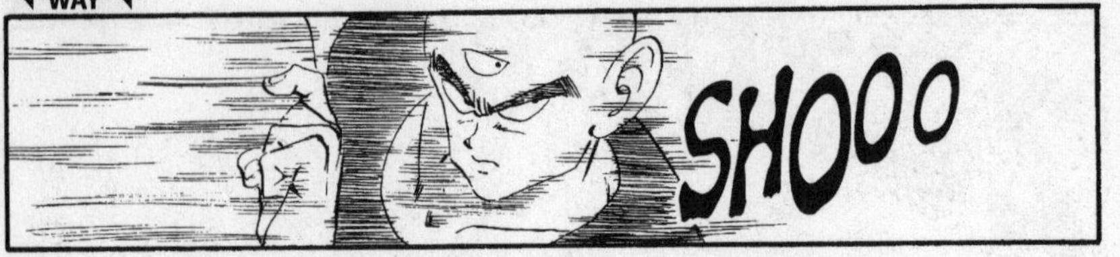
SHOOO

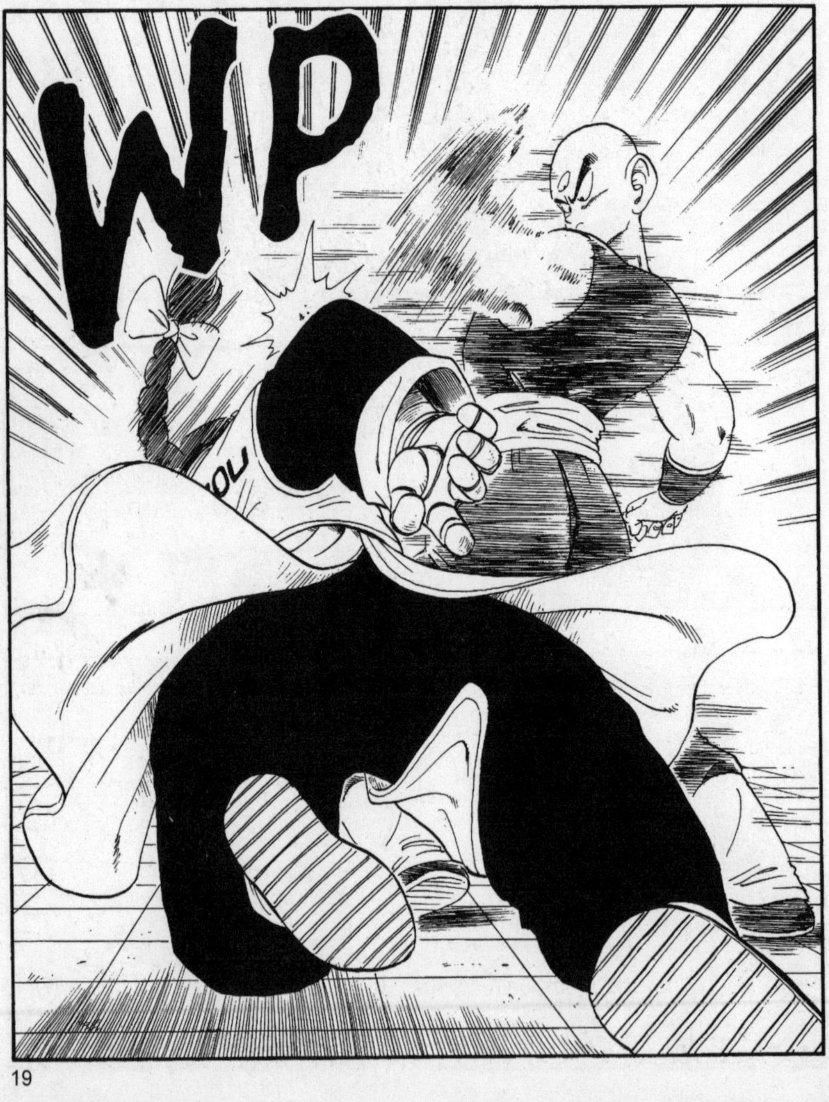
WIP

READ THIS WAY

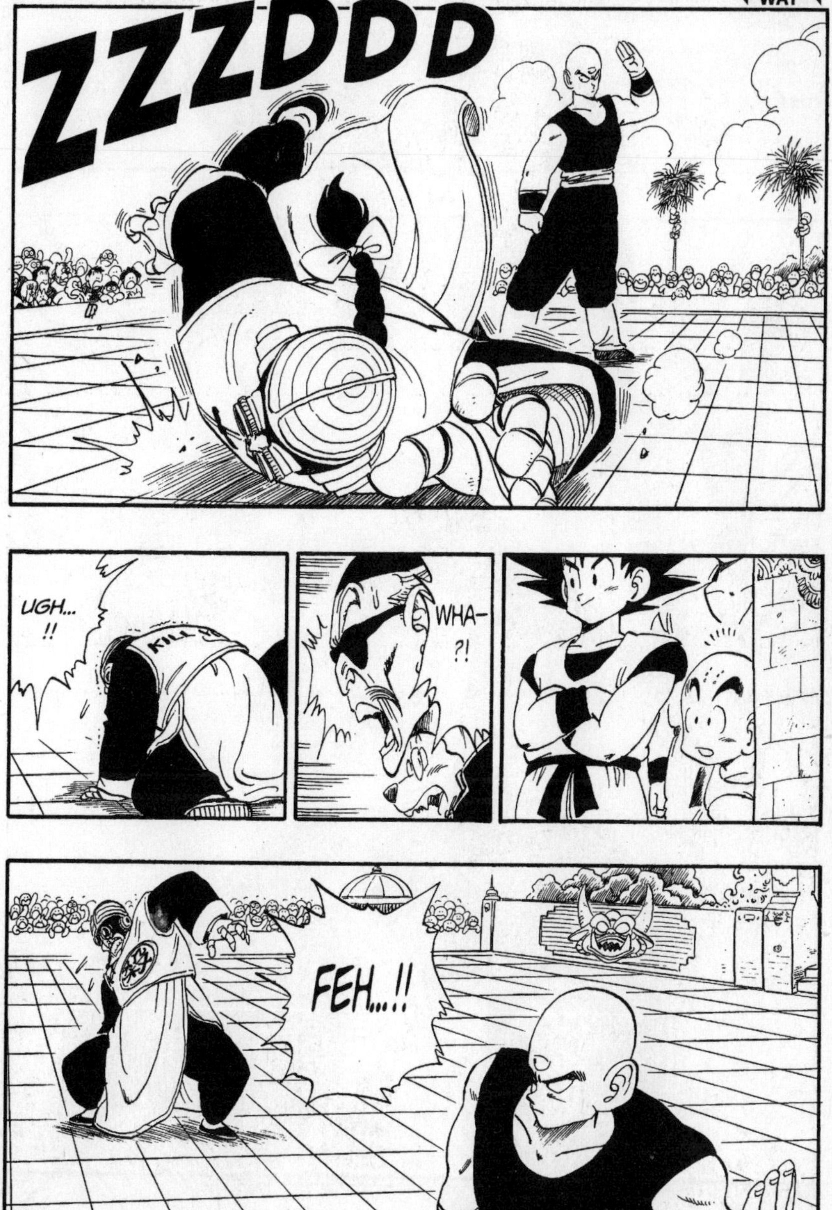

ZZZDDD
WHA-?!
UGH...!!
FEH...!!

READ THIS WAY

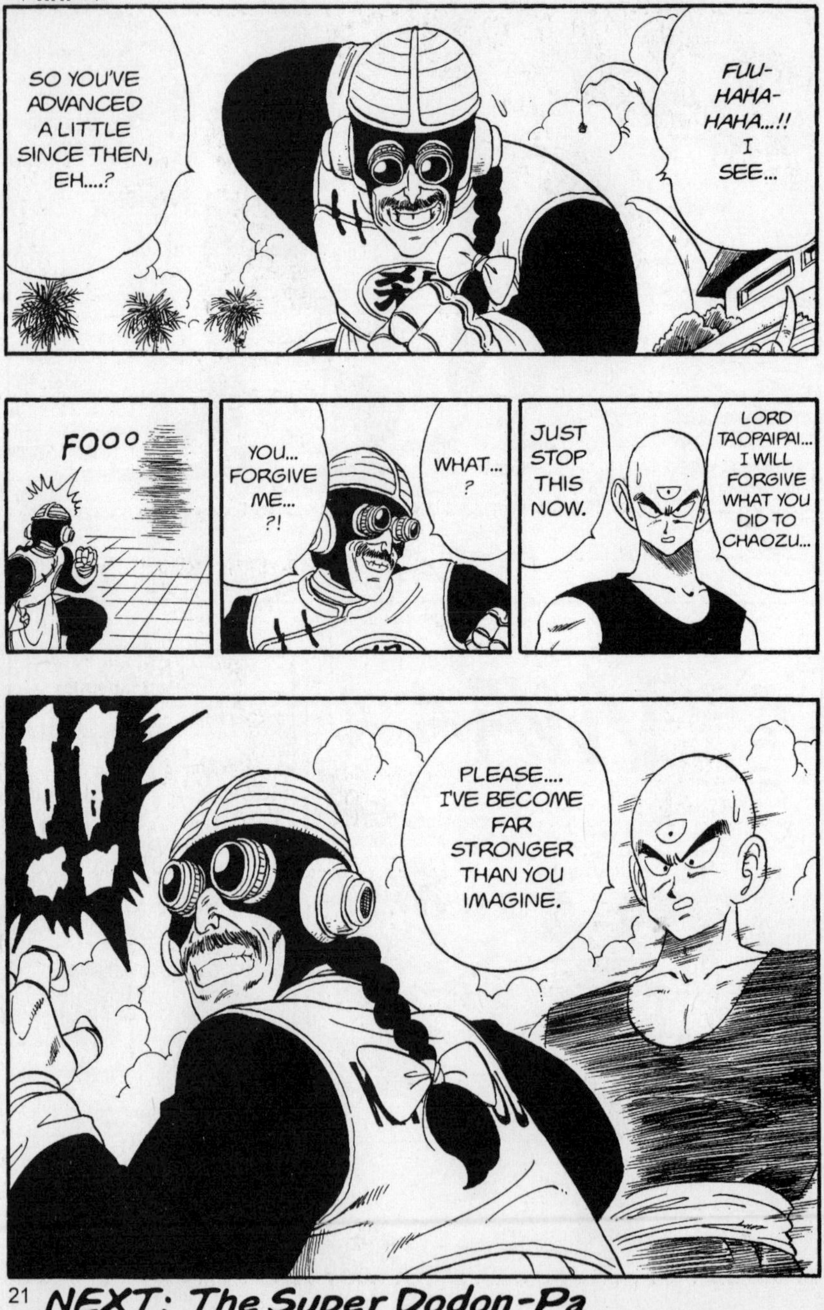
FUU-HAHA-HAHA...!! I SEE...
SO YOU'VE ADVANCED A LITTLE SINCE THEN, EH....?
LORD TAOPAIPAI... I WILL FORGIVE WHAT YOU DID TO CHAOZU...
JUST STOP THIS NOW.
WHAT... ?
YOU... FORGIVE ME... ?!
FOOO
PLEASE.... I'VE BECOME FAR STRONGER THAN YOU IMAGINE.

NEXT: The Super Dodon-Pa

Tale 170 • The Assassin's Struggles

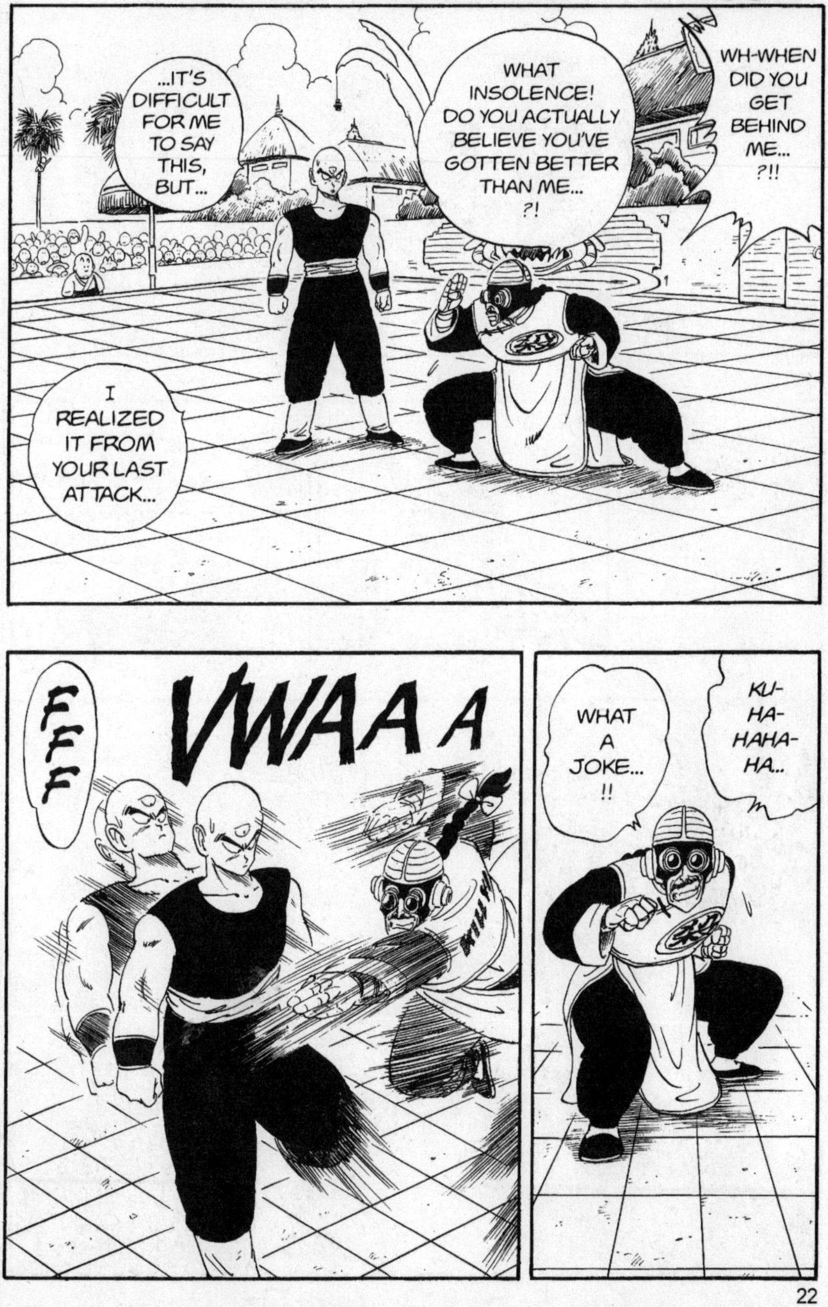
WH-WHEN DID YOU GET BEHIND ME... ?!!
WHAT INSOLENCE! DO YOU ACTUALLY BELIEVE YOU'VE GOTTEN BETTER THAN ME... ?!
...IT'S DIFFICULT FOR ME TO SAY THIS, BUT...
I REALIZED IT FROM YOUR LAST ATTACK...
KU-HA-HAHA-HA...
WHAT A JOKE... !!
VWAAA A
FFF

READ THIS WAY

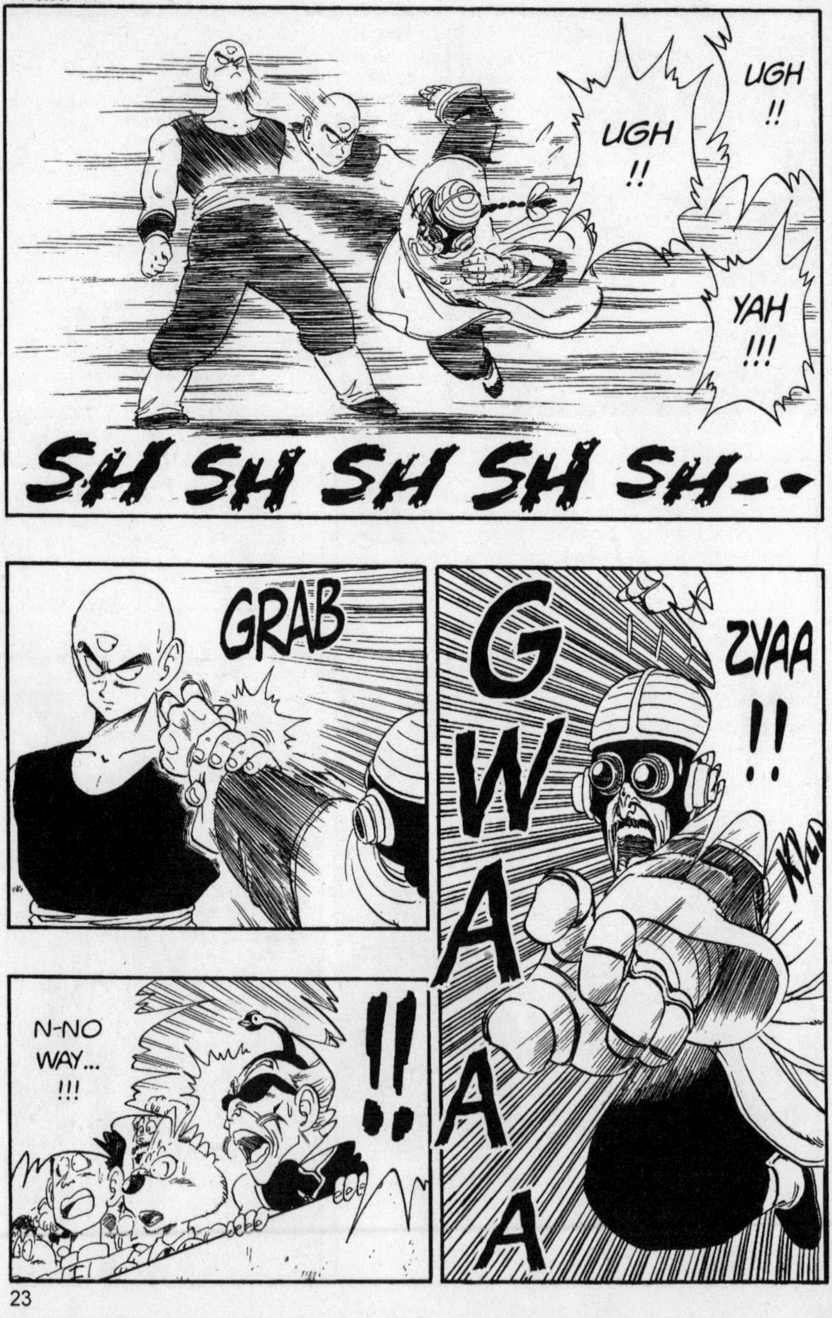
UGH !!
UGH !!
YAH !!!
SH SH SH SH SH--
ZYAA !!
GWAAAA
GRAB
!!
N-NO WAY... !!!

READ THIS WAY

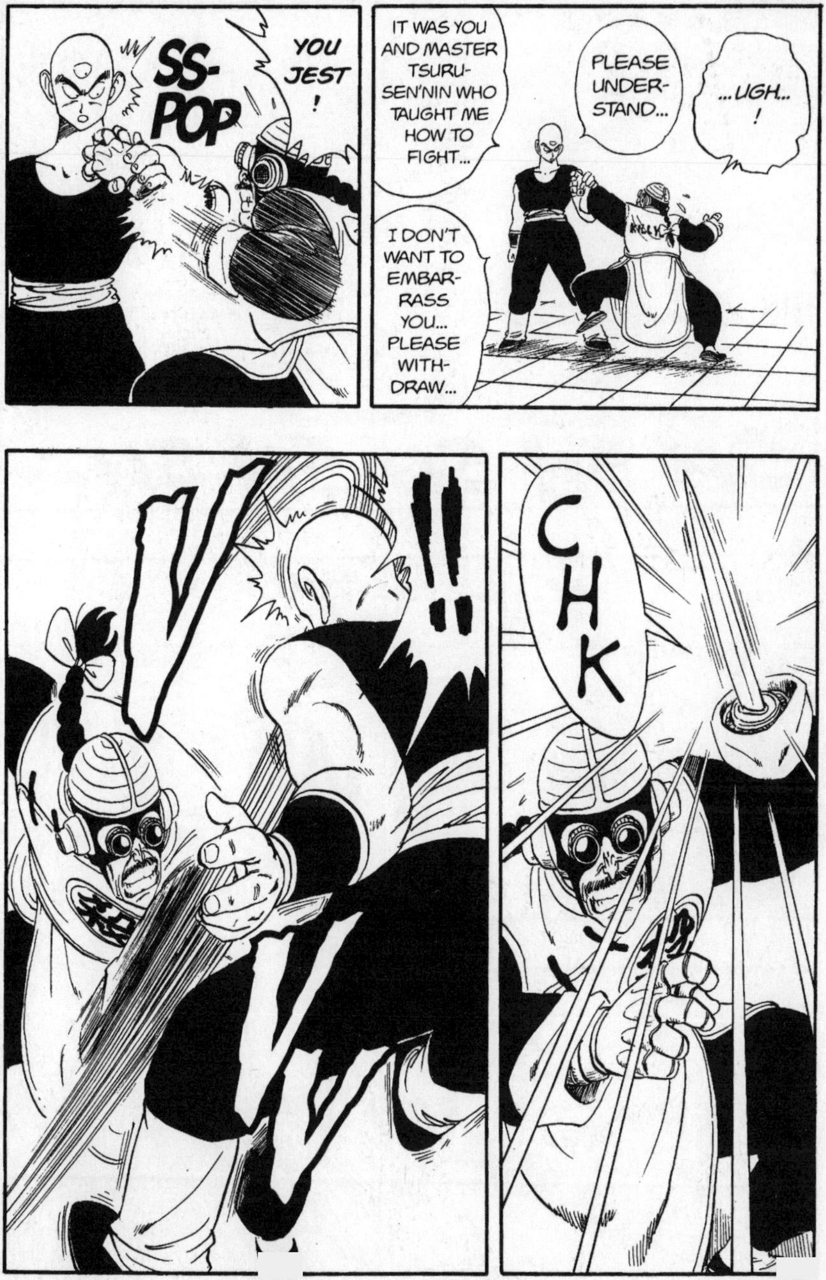

...UGH...!
PLEASE UNDERSTAND...
IT WAS YOU AND MASTER TSURU-SEN'NIN WHO TAUGHT ME HOW TO FIGHT...
I DON'T WANT TO EMBARRASS YOU... PLEASE WITHDRAW...
YOU JEST!
SS-POP
CHK
!!

READ THIS WAY

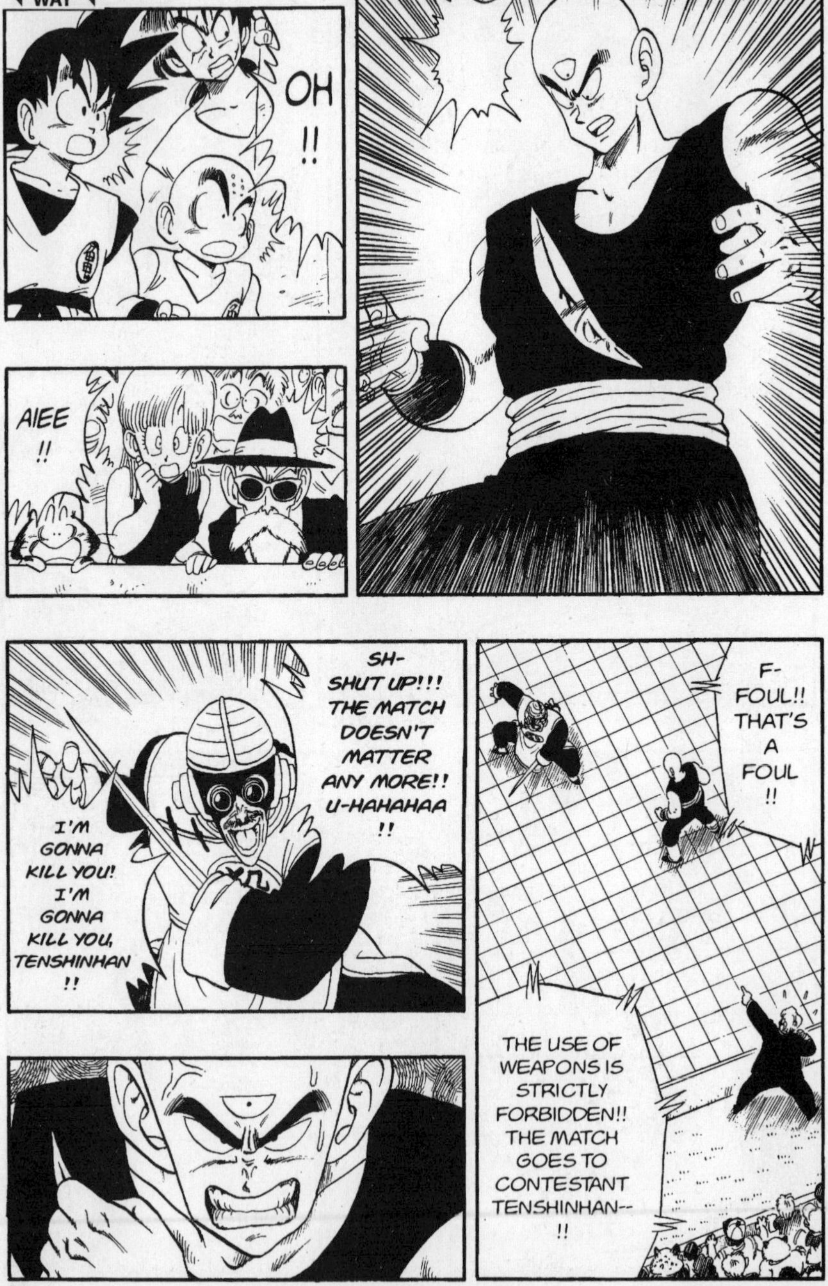

OH !!
AIEE !!
F- FOUL!! THAT'S A FOUL !!
THE USE OF WEAPONS IS STRICTLY FORBIDDEN!! THE MATCH GOES TO CONTESTANT TENSHINHAN-- !!
SH- SHUT UP!!! THE MATCH DOESN'T MATTER ANY MORE!! U-HAHAHAA !!
I'M GONNA KILL YOU! I'M GONNA KILL YOU, TENSHINHAN !!

READ THIS WAY

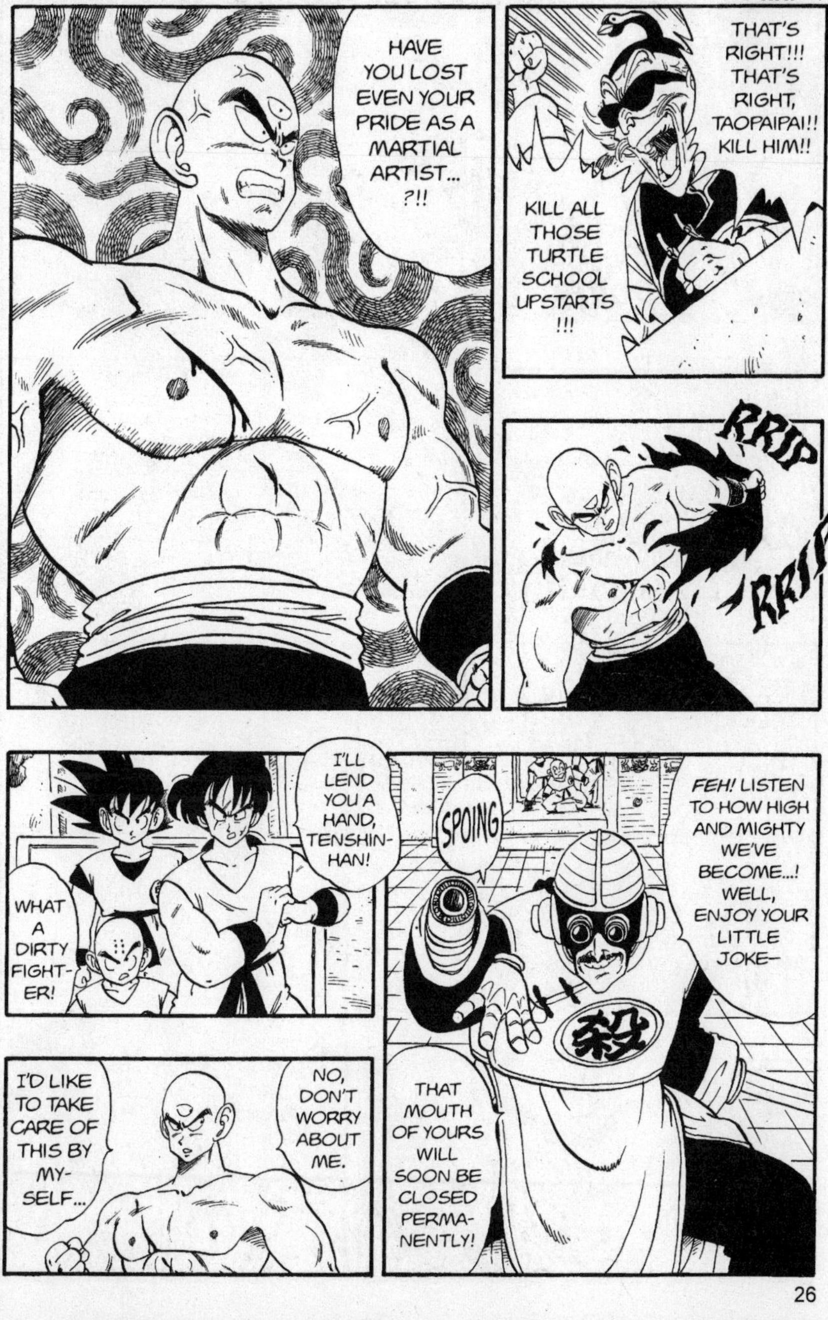
THAT'S RIGHT!!! THAT'S RIGHT, TAOPAIPAI!! KILL HIM!!
KILL ALL THOSE TURTLE SCHOOL UPSTARTS !!!
RRIP
RRIP
HAVE YOU LOST EVEN YOUR PRIDE AS A MARTIAL ARTIST... ?!!
FEH! LISTEN TO HOW HIGH AND MIGHTY WE'VE BECOME...! WELL, ENJOY YOUR LITTLE JOKE—
SPOING
THAT MOUTH OF YOURS WILL SOON BE CLOSED PERMA-NENTLY!
I'LL LEND YOU A HAND, TENSHIN-HAN!
WHAT A DIRTY FIGHT-ER!
NO, DON'T WORRY ABOUT ME.
I'D LIKE TO TAKE CARE OF THIS BY MY-SELF...

READ THIS WAY

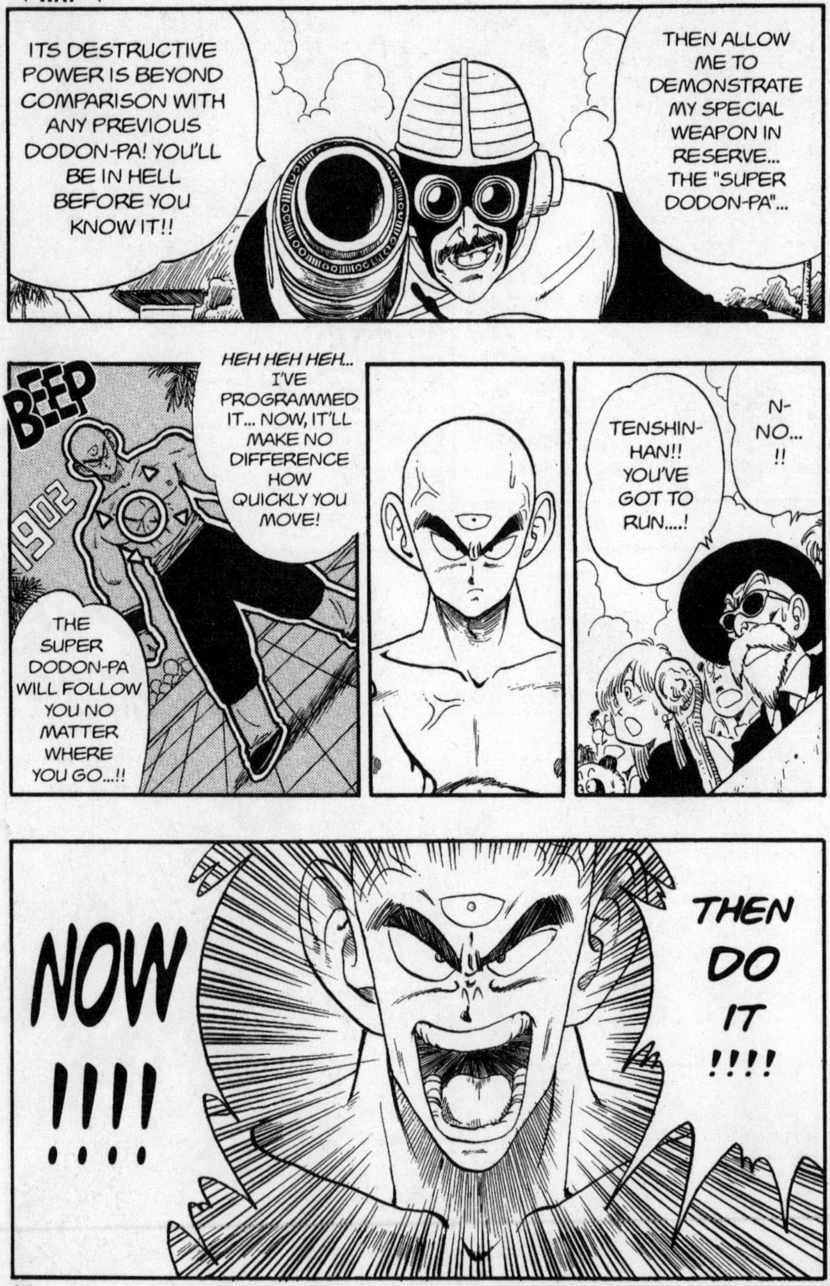

THEN ALLOW ME TO DEMONSTRATE MY SPECIAL WEAPON IN RESERVE... THE "SUPER DODON-PA"...
ITS DESTRUCTIVE POWER IS BEYOND COMPARISON WITH ANY PREVIOUS DODON-PA! YOU'LL BE IN HELL BEFORE YOU KNOW IT!!
N-NO...!!
TENSHINHAN!! YOU'VE GOT TO RUN....!
HEH HEH HEH... I'VE PROGRAMMED IT... NOW, IT'LL MAKE NO DIFFERENCE HOW QUICKLY YOU MOVE!
BEEP
1902
THE SUPER DODON-PA WILL FOLLOW YOU NO MATTER WHERE YOU GO...!!
THEN DO IT!!!!
NOW!!!!!

READ THIS WAY

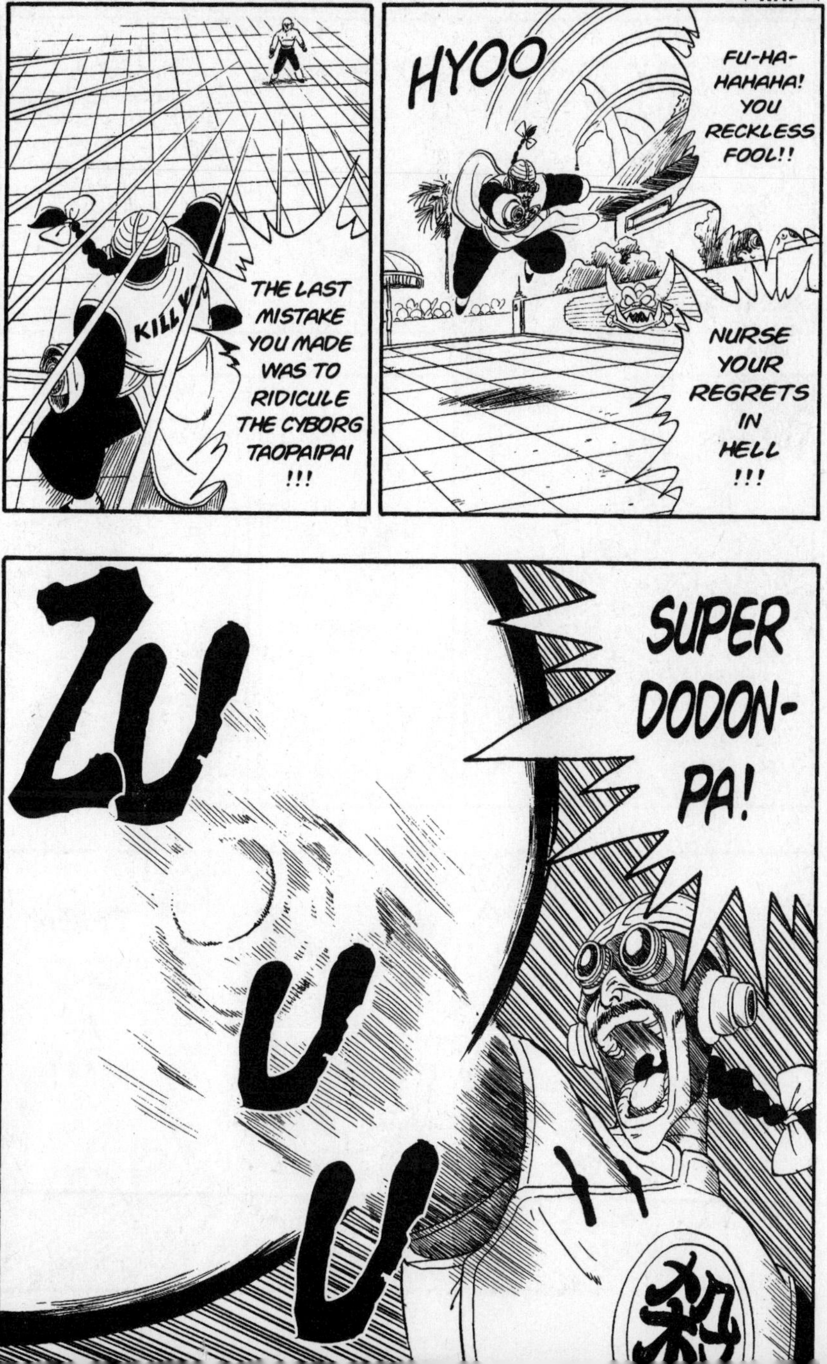
FU-HA-HAHAHA! YOU RECKLESS FOOL!!
HYOO
NURSE YOUR REGRETS IN HELL!!!
THE LAST MISTAKE YOU MADE WAS TO RIDICULE THE CYBORG TAOPAIPAI!!!
SUPER DODON-PA!
ZUUUU

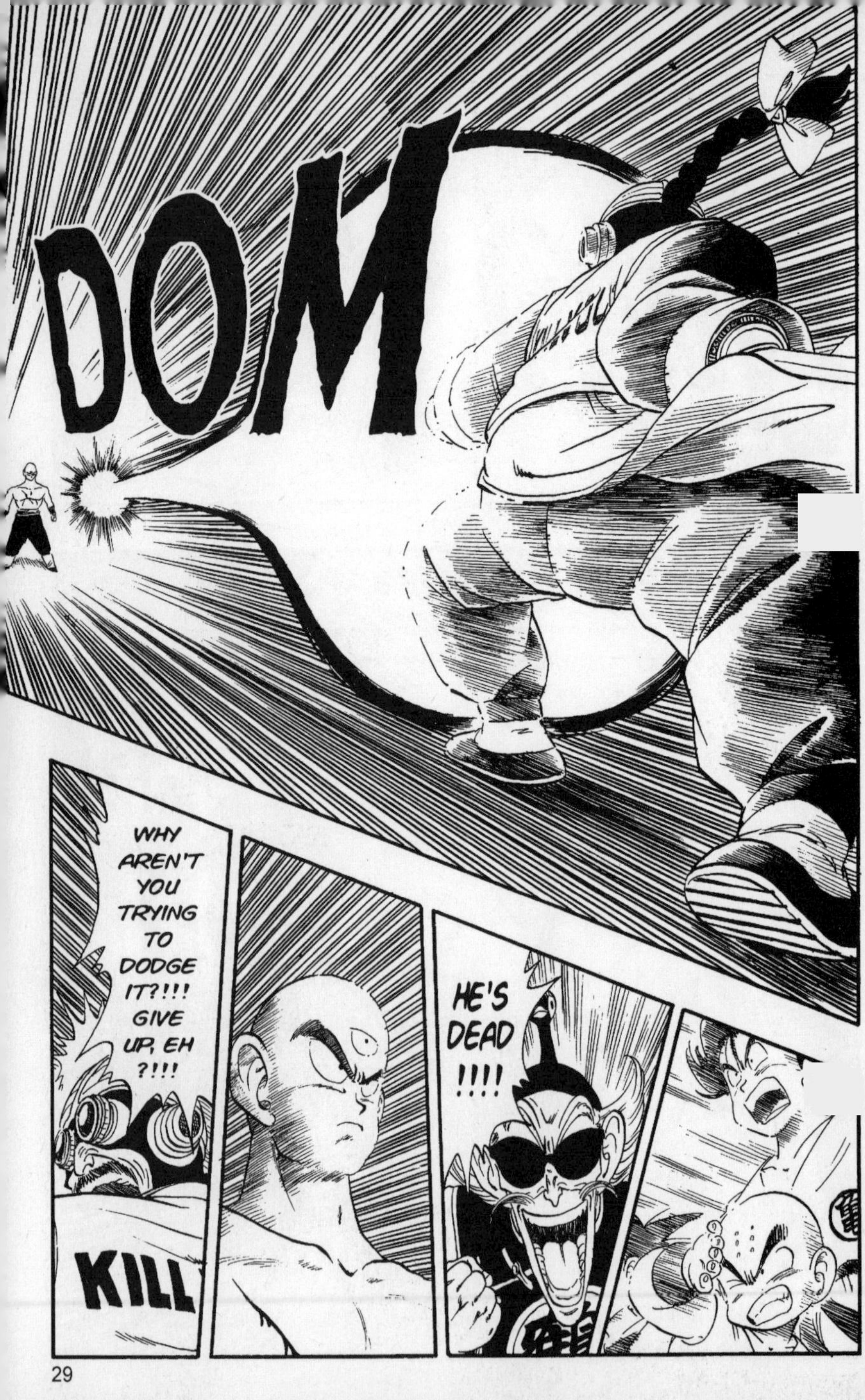
DOM
HE'S DEAD !!!!
WHY AREN'T YOU TRYING TO DODGE IT?!!! GIVE UP, EH ?!!!
KILL

READ THIS WAY

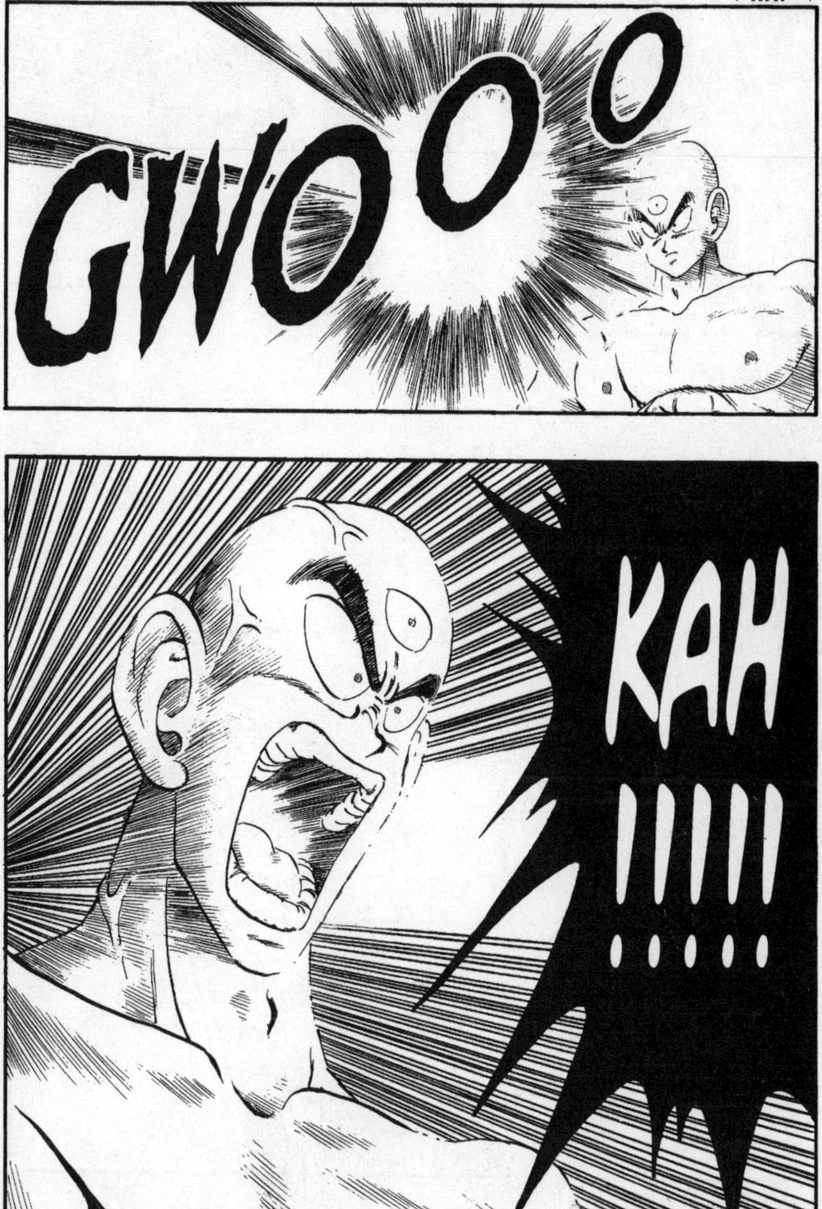
GWOOOO
KAH!!!!!!

READ THIS WAY

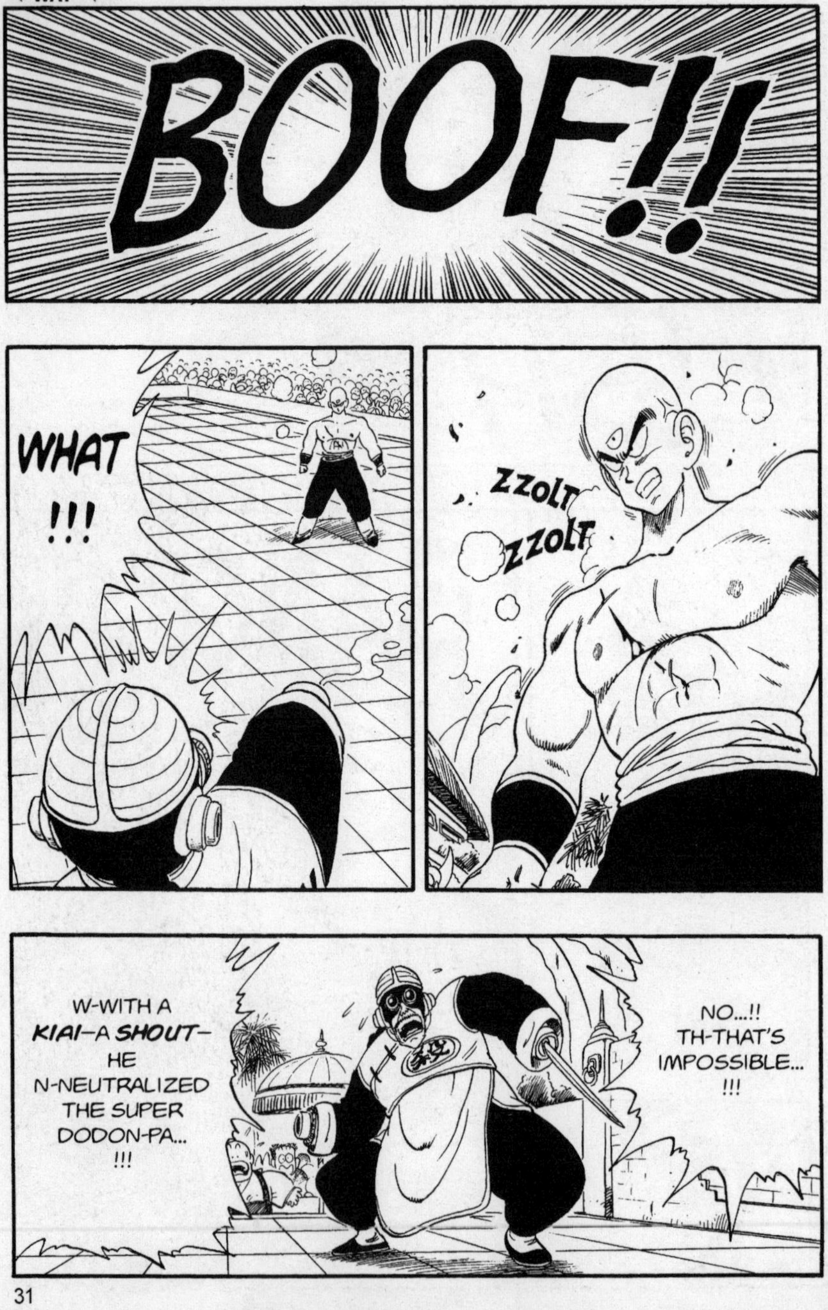
BOOF!!
ZZOLT
ZZOLT
WHAT !!!
NO...!! TH-THAT'S IMPOSSIBLE... !!!
W-WITH A *KIAI*—A *SHOUT*— HE N-NEUTRALIZED THE SUPER DODON-PA... !!!

READ THIS WAY

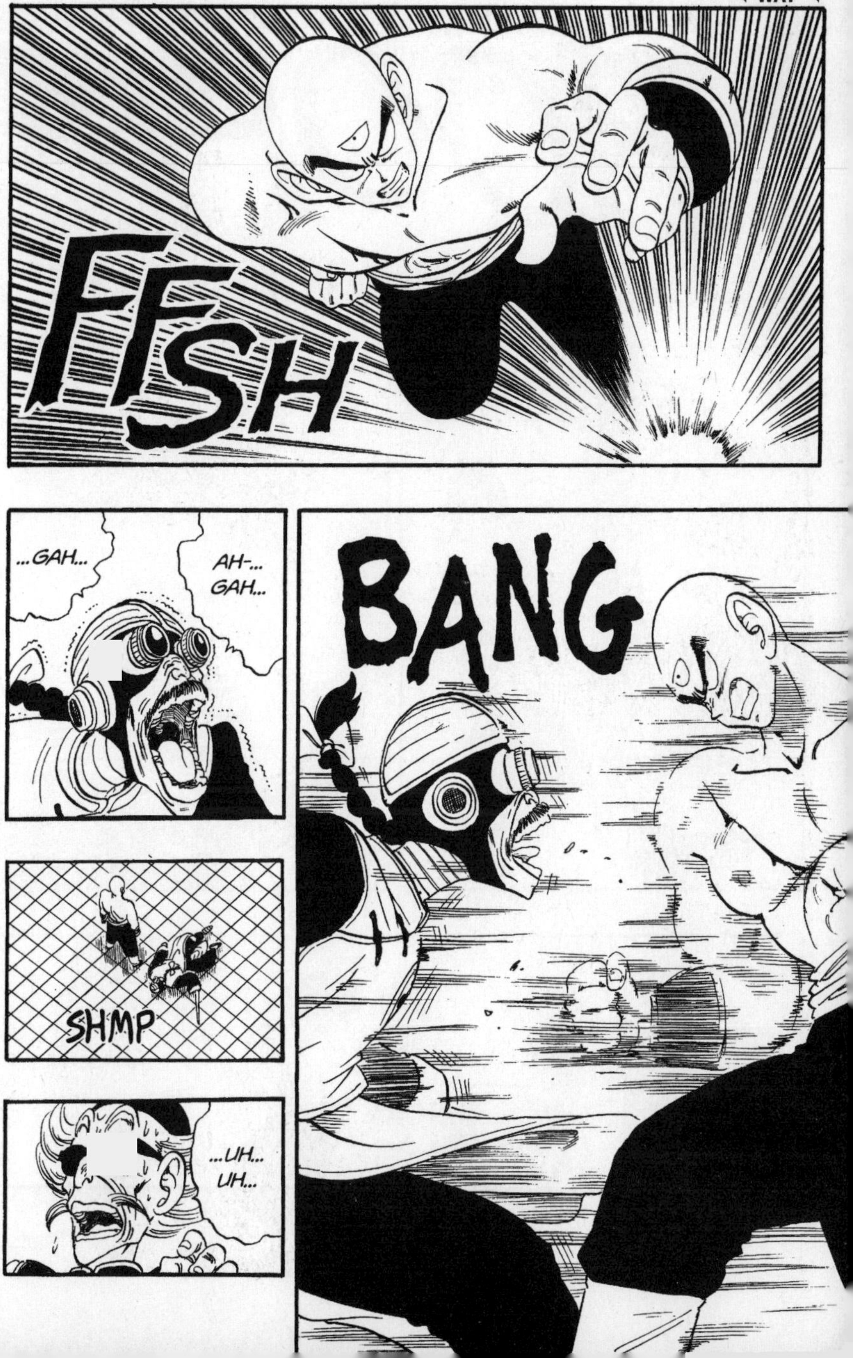
FFSH
BANG
AH-... GAH...
...GAH...
SHMP
...UH... UH...

READ THIS WAY

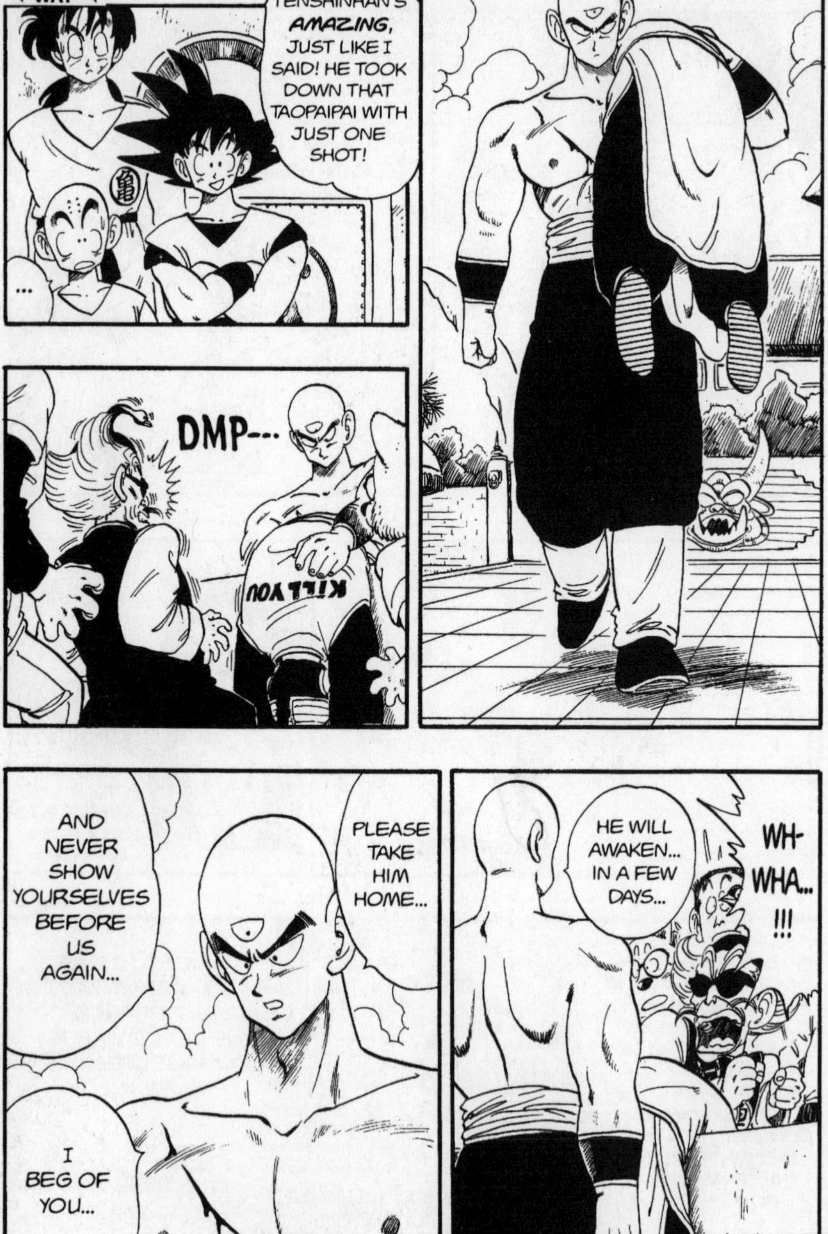
TENSHINHAN'S AMAZING, JUST LIKE I SAID! HE TOOK DOWN THAT TAOPAIPAI WITH JUST ONE SHOT!
...
DMP---
KILL YOU
HE WILL AWAKEN... IN A FEW DAYS...
WH-WHA...!!!
PLEASE TAKE HIM HOME...
AND NEVER SHOW YOURSELVES BEFORE US AGAIN...
I BEG OF YOU...

READ THIS WAY

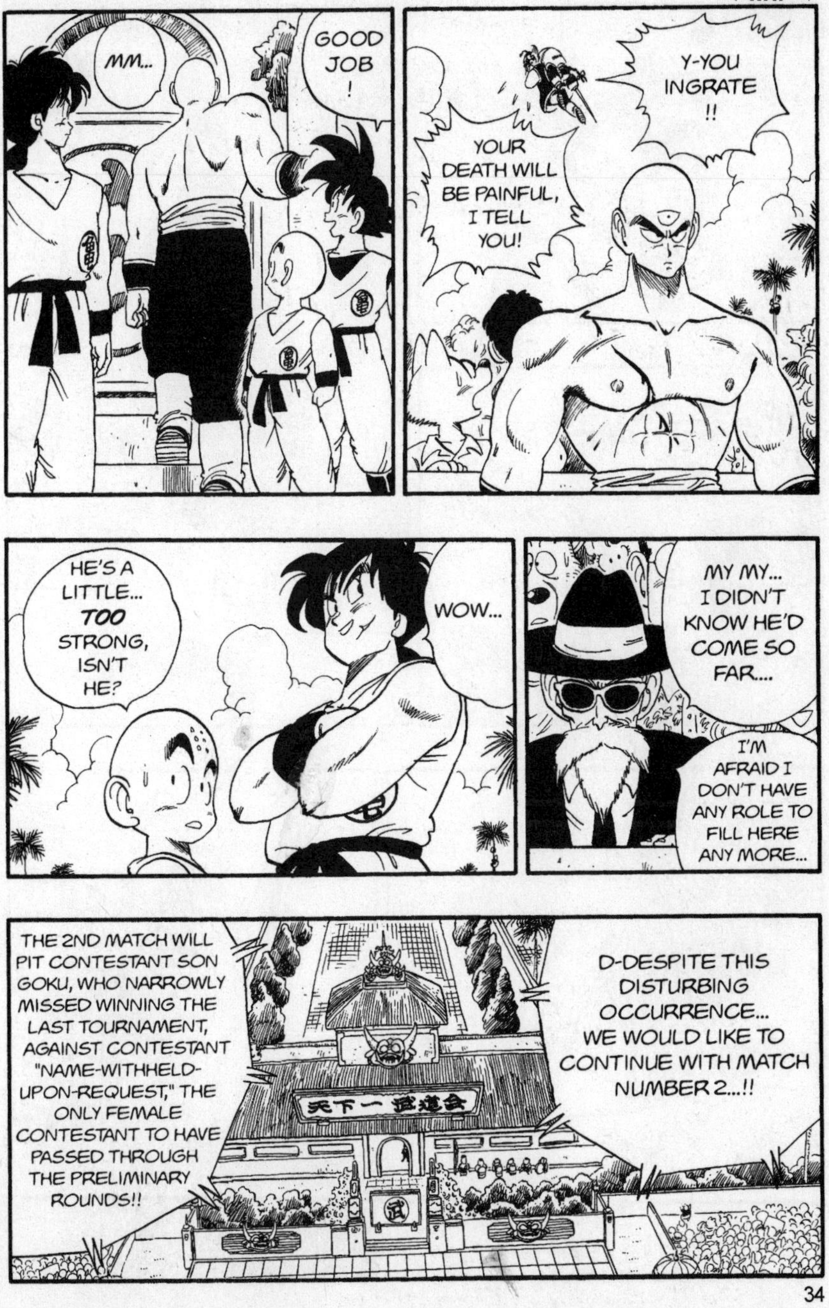

Y-YOU INGRATE !!
YOUR DEATH WILL BE PAINFUL, I TELL YOU!
GOOD JOB !
MM...
MY MY... I DIDN'T KNOW HE'D COME SO FAR....
I'M AFRAID I DON'T HAVE ANY ROLE TO FILL HERE ANY MORE...
WOW...
HE'S A LITTLE... ***TOO*** STRONG, ISN'T HE?
D-DESPITE THIS DISTURBING OCCURRENCE... WE WOULD LIKE TO CONTINUE WITH MATCH NUMBER 2...!!
天下一武道会
THE 2ND MATCH WILL PIT CONTESTANT SON GOKU, WHO NARROWLY MISSED WINNING THE LAST TOURNAMENT, AGAINST CONTESTANT "NAME-WITHHELD-UPON-REQUEST," THE ONLY FEMALE CONTESTANT TO HAVE PASSED THROUGH THE PRELIMINARY ROUNDS!!

READ THIS WAY

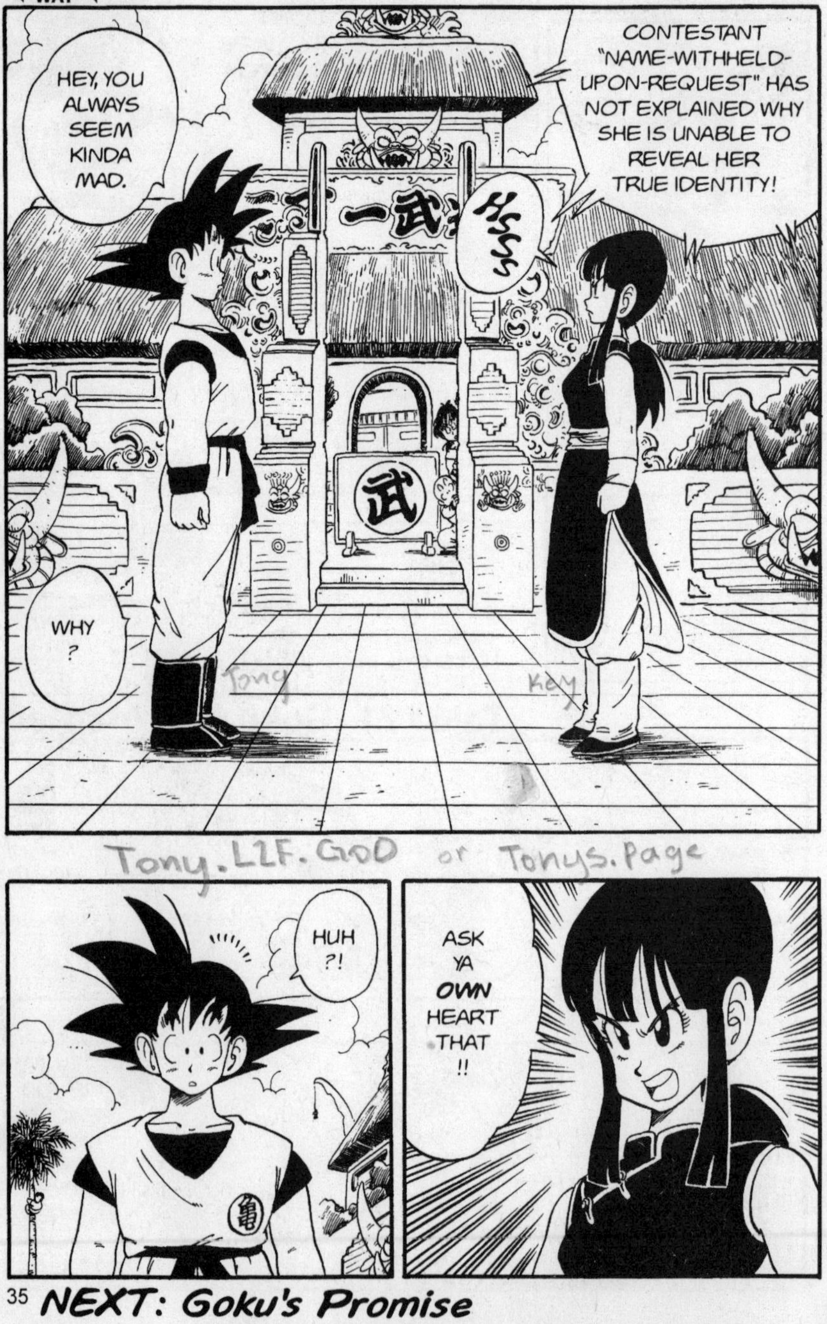

CONTESTANT "NAME-WITHHELD-UPON-REQUEST" HAS NOT EXPLAINED WHY SHE IS UNABLE TO REVEAL HER TRUE IDENTITY!
HSSS
HEY, YOU ALWAYS SEEM KINDA MAD.
WHY ?
Key
Tony
Tony.L2F.GOD or Tonys.page
ASK YA OWN HEART THAT !!
HUH ?!
...

 NEXT: Goku's Promise

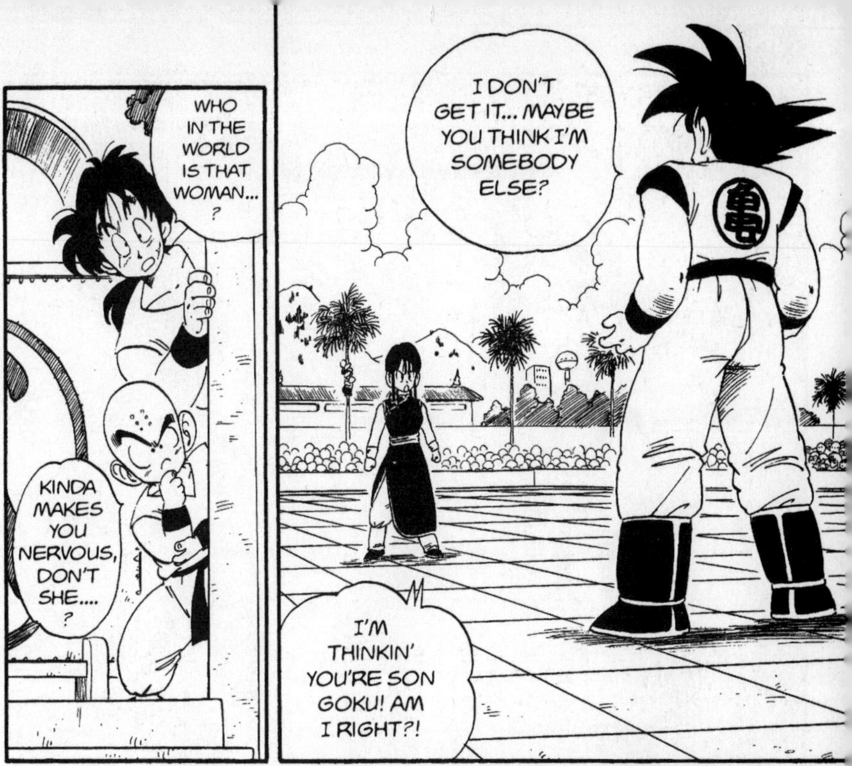
I DON'T GET IT... MAYBE YOU THINK I'M SOMEBODY ELSE?
I'M THINKIN' YOU'RE SON GOKU! AM I RIGHT?!
WHO IN THE WORLD IS THAT WOMAN... ?
KINDA MAKES YOU NERVOUS, DON'T SHE.... ?

Tale 171 • Goku Gets Married!

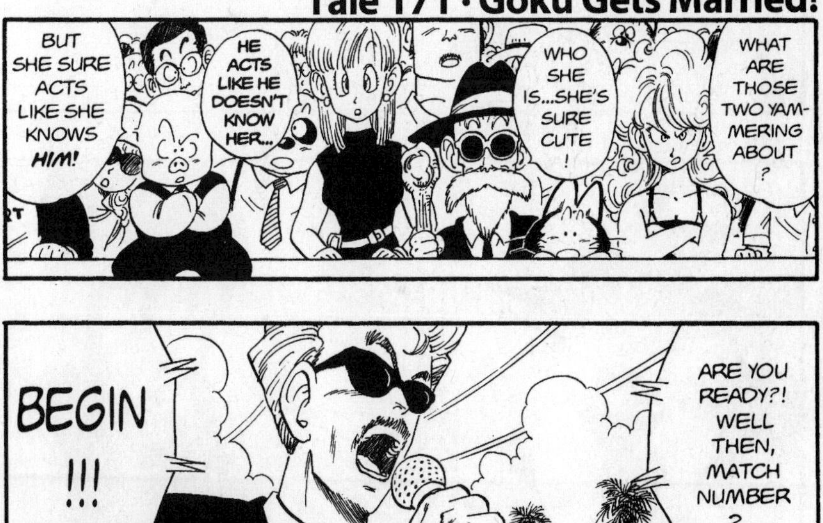
WHAT ARE THOSE TWO YAMMERING ABOUT ?
WHO SHE IS...SHE'S SURE CUTE !
HE ACTS LIKE HE DOESN'T KNOW HER...
BUT SHE SURE ACTS LIKE SHE KNOWS *HIM!*
ARE YOU READY?! WELL THEN, MATCH NUMBER 2...
BEGIN !!!

READ THIS WAY

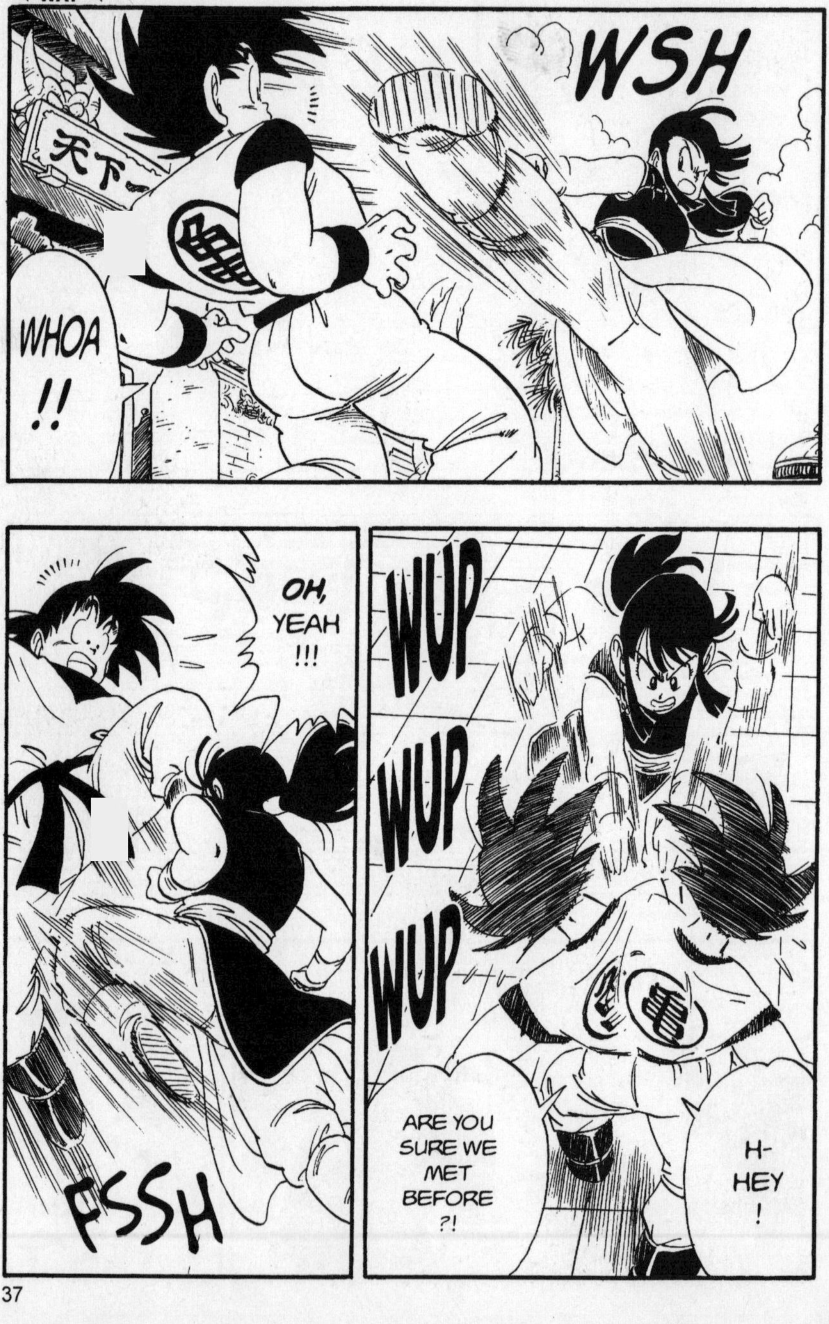
WSH
WHOA !!
WUP
WUP
WUP
H-HEY !
ARE YOU SURE WE MET BEFORE ?!
OH, YEAH !!!
FSSH

READ THIS WAY

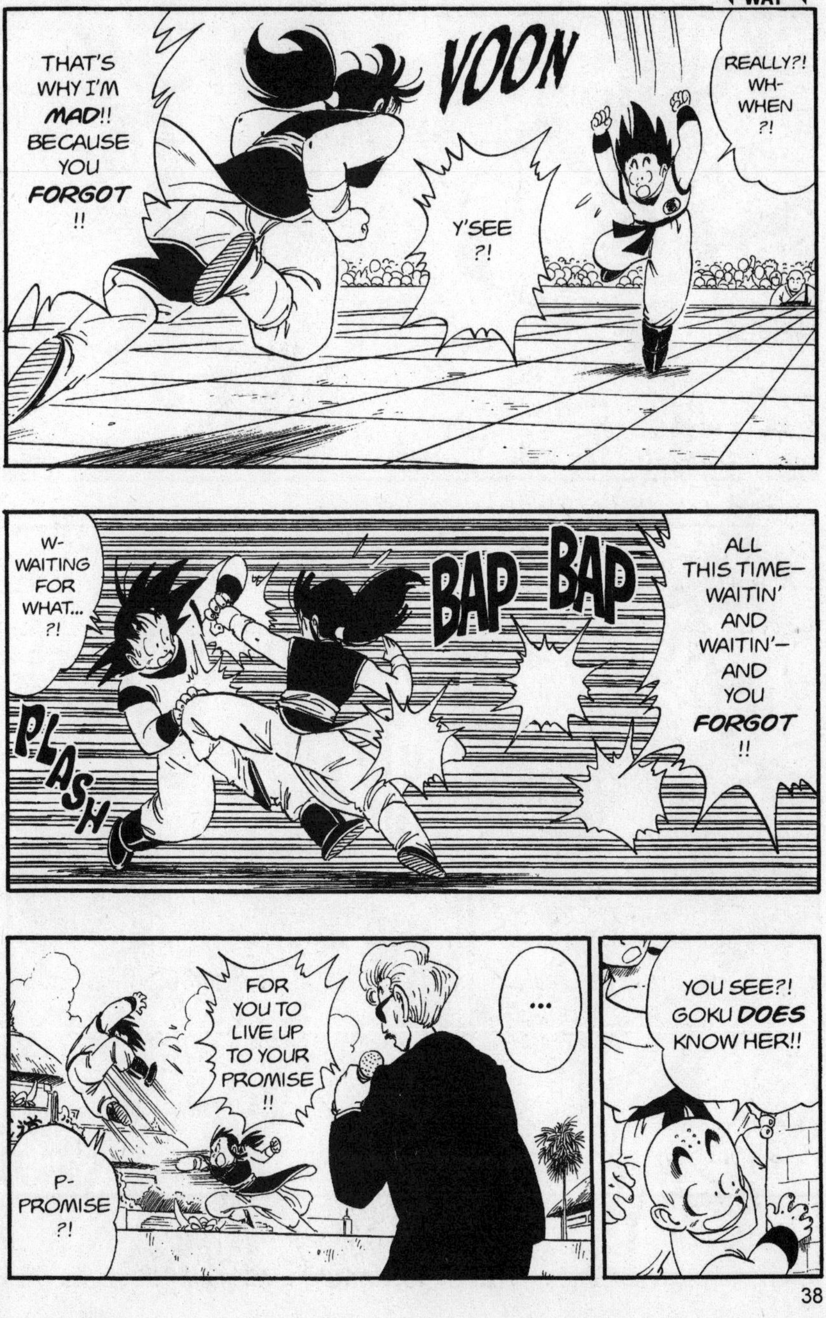
REALLY?! WH- WHEN ?!
VOON
Y'SEE ?!
THAT'S WHY I'M **MAD**!! BECAUSE YOU **FORGOT** !!
ALL THIS TIME— WAITIN' AND WAITIN'— AND YOU **FORGOT** !!
BAP BAP
W- WAITING FOR WHAT... ?!
PLASH
YOU SEE?! GOKU **DOES** KNOW HER!!
...
FOR YOU TO LIVE UP TO YOUR PROMISE !!
P- PROMISE ?!

READ THIS WAY

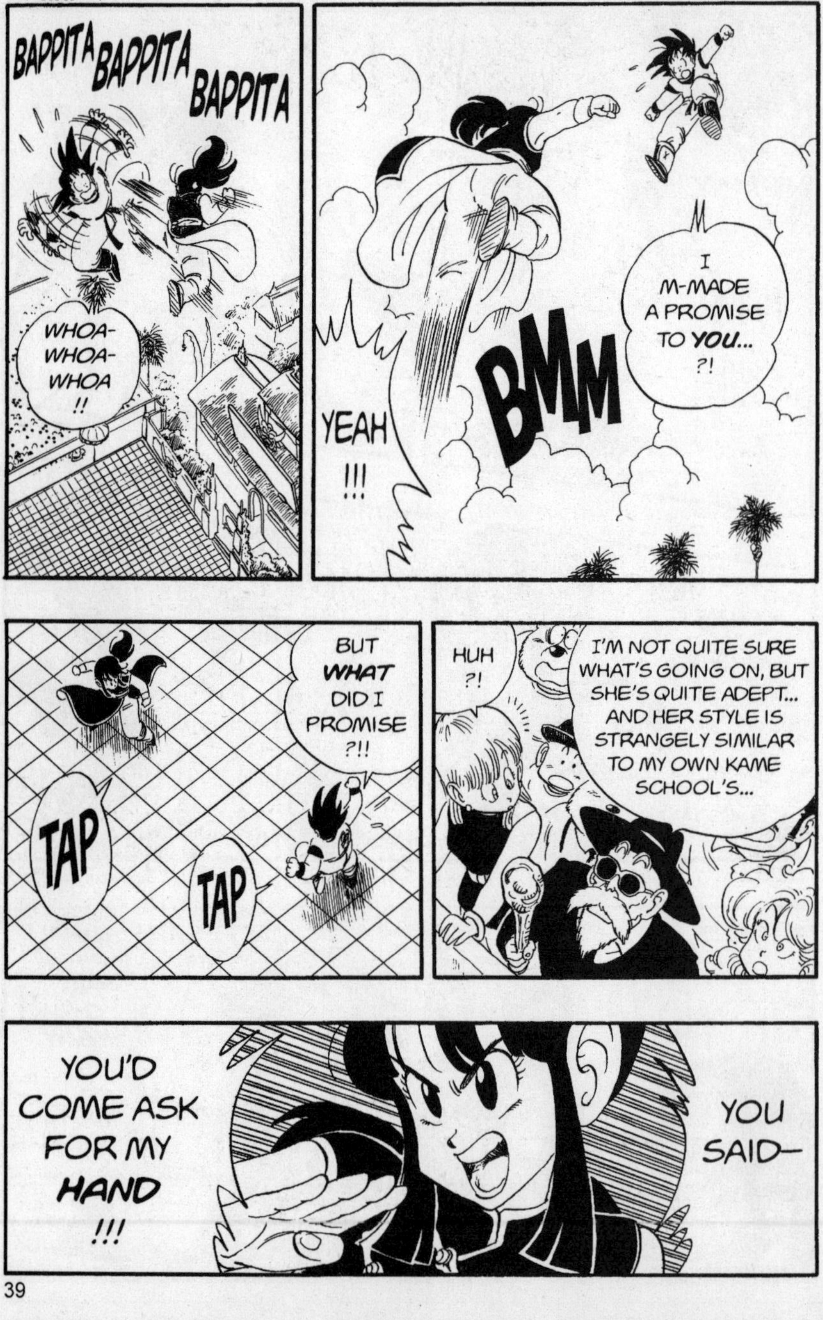
I M-MADE A PROMISE TO YOU...?!
BMM
YEAH!!!
BAPPITA BAPPITA BAPPITA
WHOA-WHOA-WHOA!!
I'M NOT QUITE SURE WHAT'S GOING ON, BUT SHE'S QUITE ADEPT... AND HER STYLE IS STRANGELY SIMILAR TO MY OWN KAME SCHOOL'S...
HUH?!
BUT WHAT DID I PROMISE?!!
TAP
TAP
YOU SAID—
YOU'D COME ASK FOR MY HAND!!!

READ THIS WAY

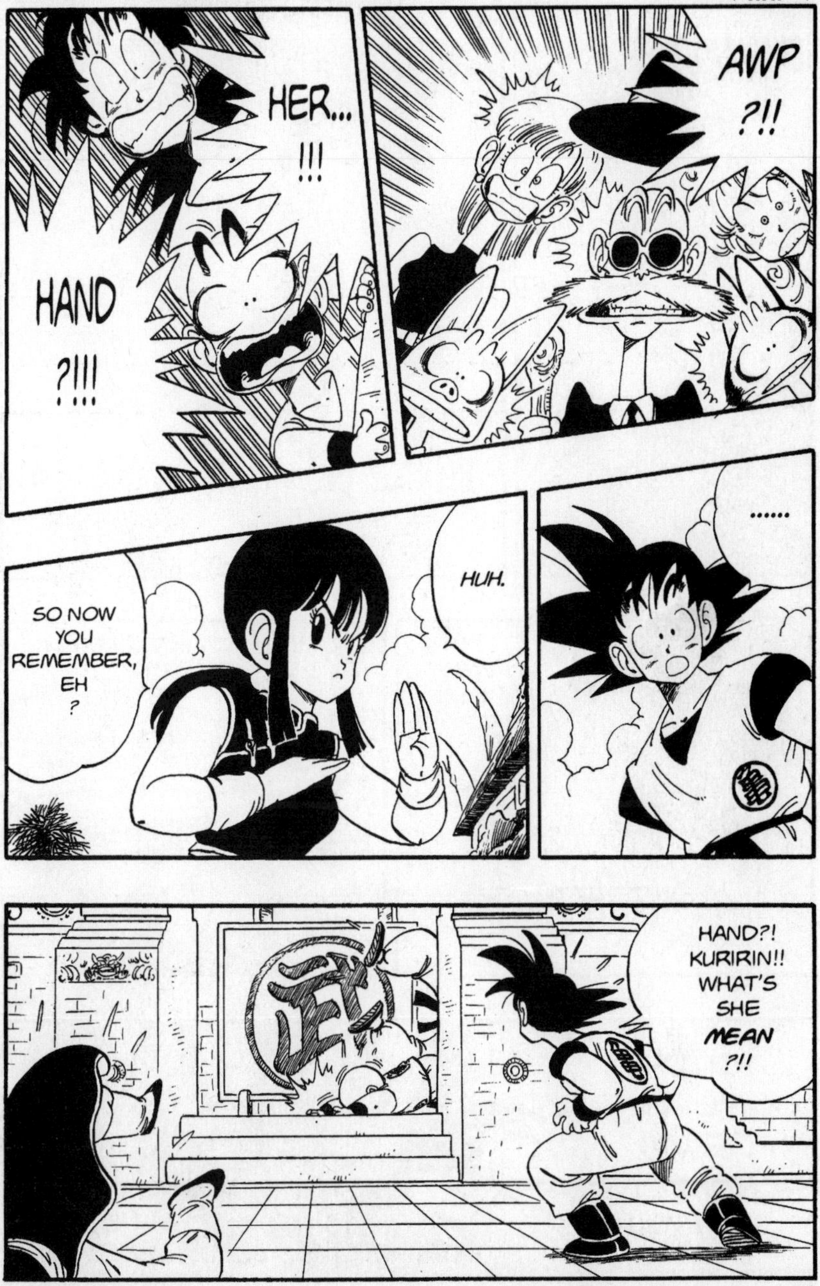

AWP ?!!
HER... !!!
HAND ?!!!
......
HUH.
SO NOW YOU REMEMBER, EH ?
HAND?! KURIRIN!! WHAT'S SHE *MEAN* ?!!

READ THIS WAY

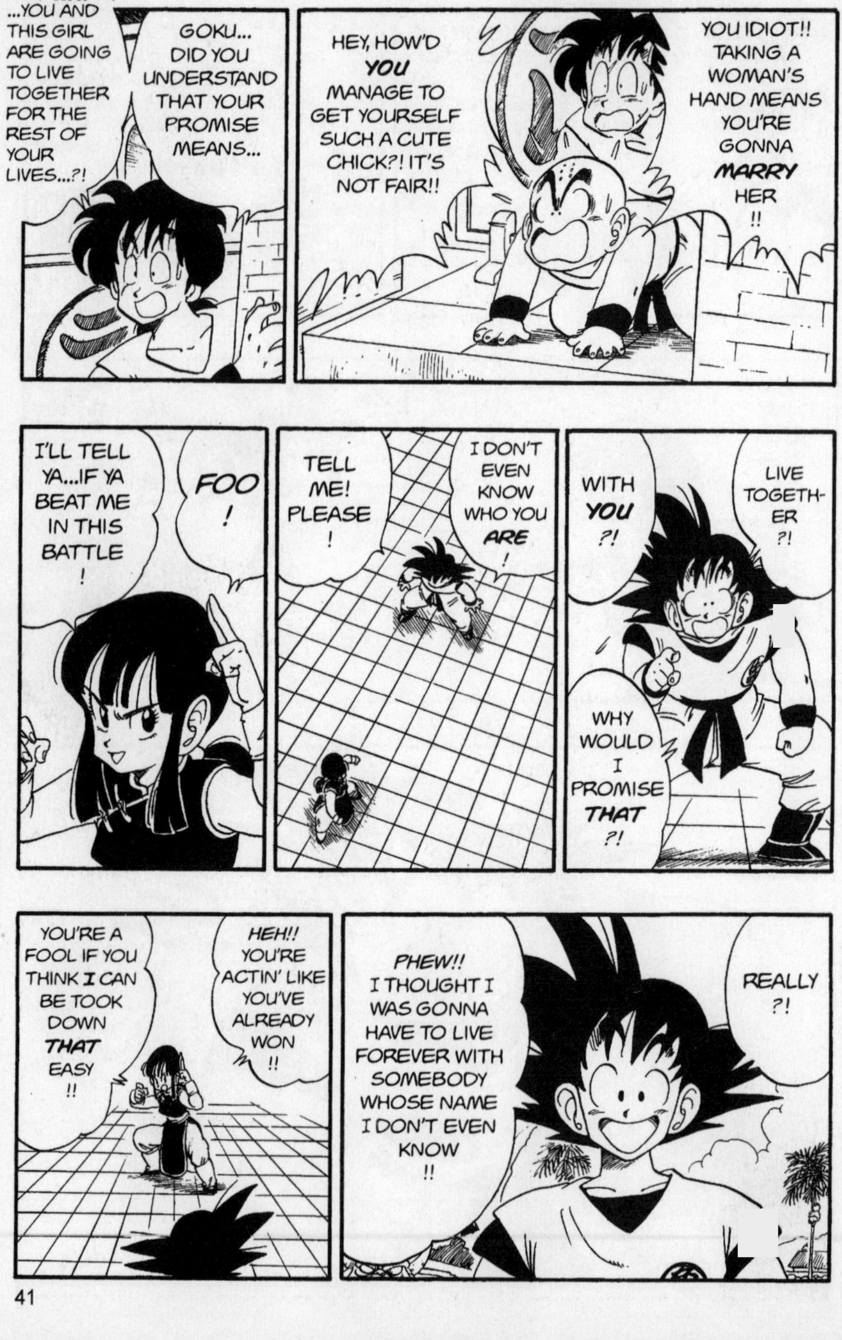
YOU IDIOT!! TAKING A WOMAN'S HAND MEANS YOU'RE GONNA MARRY HER!!
HEY, HOW'D YOU MANAGE TO GET YOURSELF SUCH A CUTE CHICK?! IT'S NOT FAIR!!
GOKU... DID YOU UNDERSTAND THAT YOUR PROMISE MEANS...
...YOU AND THIS GIRL ARE GOING TO LIVE TOGETHER FOR THE REST OF YOUR LIVES...?!
LIVE TOGETH-ER?!
WITH YOU?!
WHY WOULD I PROMISE THAT?!
I DON'T EVEN KNOW WHO YOU ARE!
TELL ME! PLEASE!
FOO!
I'LL TELL YA...IF YA BEAT ME IN THIS BATTLE!
REALLY?!
PHEW!! I THOUGHT I WAS GONNA HAVE TO LIVE FOREVER WITH SOMEBODY WHOSE NAME I DON'T EVEN KNOW!!
HEH!! YOU'RE ACTIN' LIKE YOU'VE ALREADY WON!!
YOU'RE A FOOL IF YOU THINK I CAN BE TOOK DOWN THAT EASY!!

READ THIS WAY

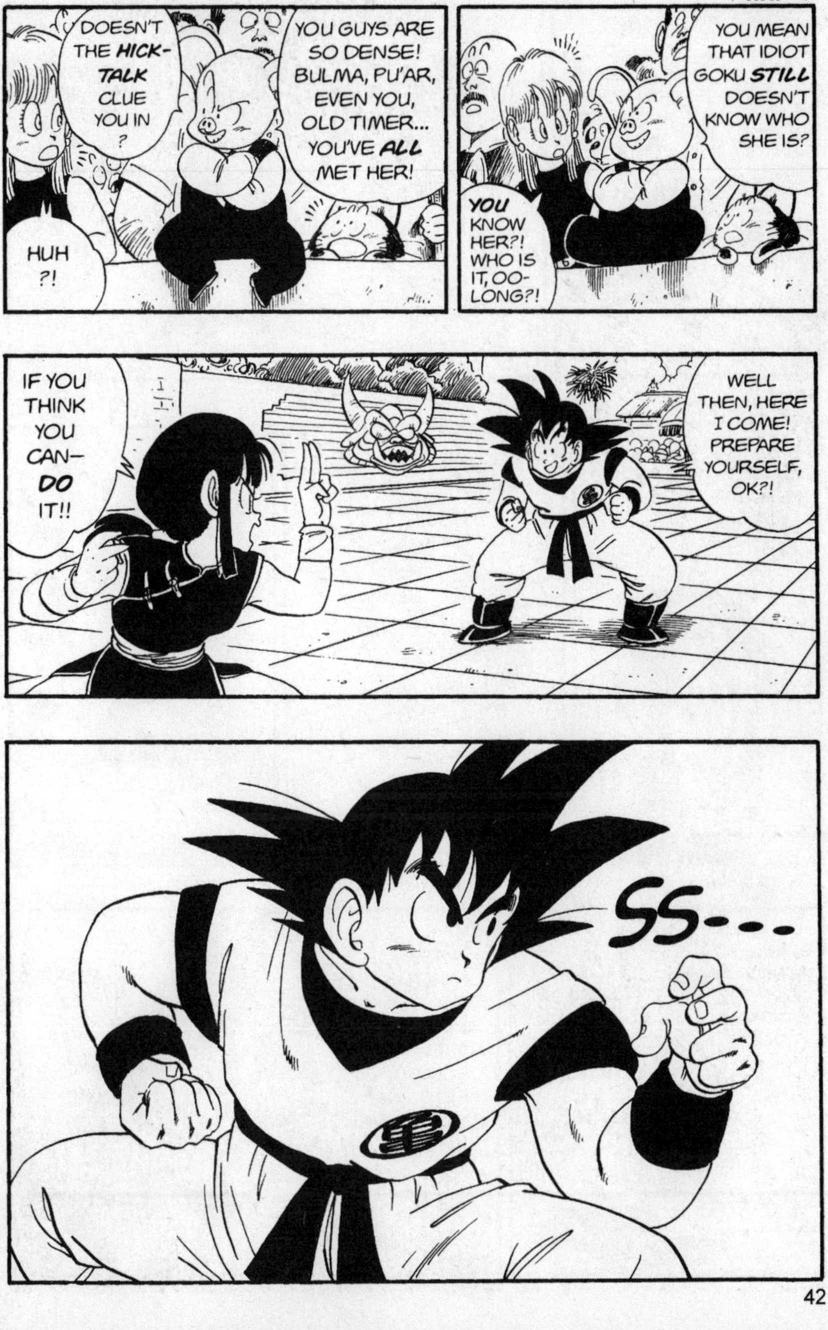
YOU MEAN THAT IDIOT GOKU **STILL** DOESN'T KNOW WHO SHE IS?
YOU KNOW HER?! WHO IS IT, OO-LONG?!
YOU GUYS ARE SO DENSE! BULMA, PU'AR, EVEN YOU, OLD TIMER... YOU'VE **ALL** MET HER!
DOESN'T THE **HICK-TALK** CLUE YOU IN ?
HUH ?!
WELL THEN, HERE I COME! PREPARE YOURSELF, OK?!
IF YOU THINK YOU CAN—**DO** IT!!
SS-...

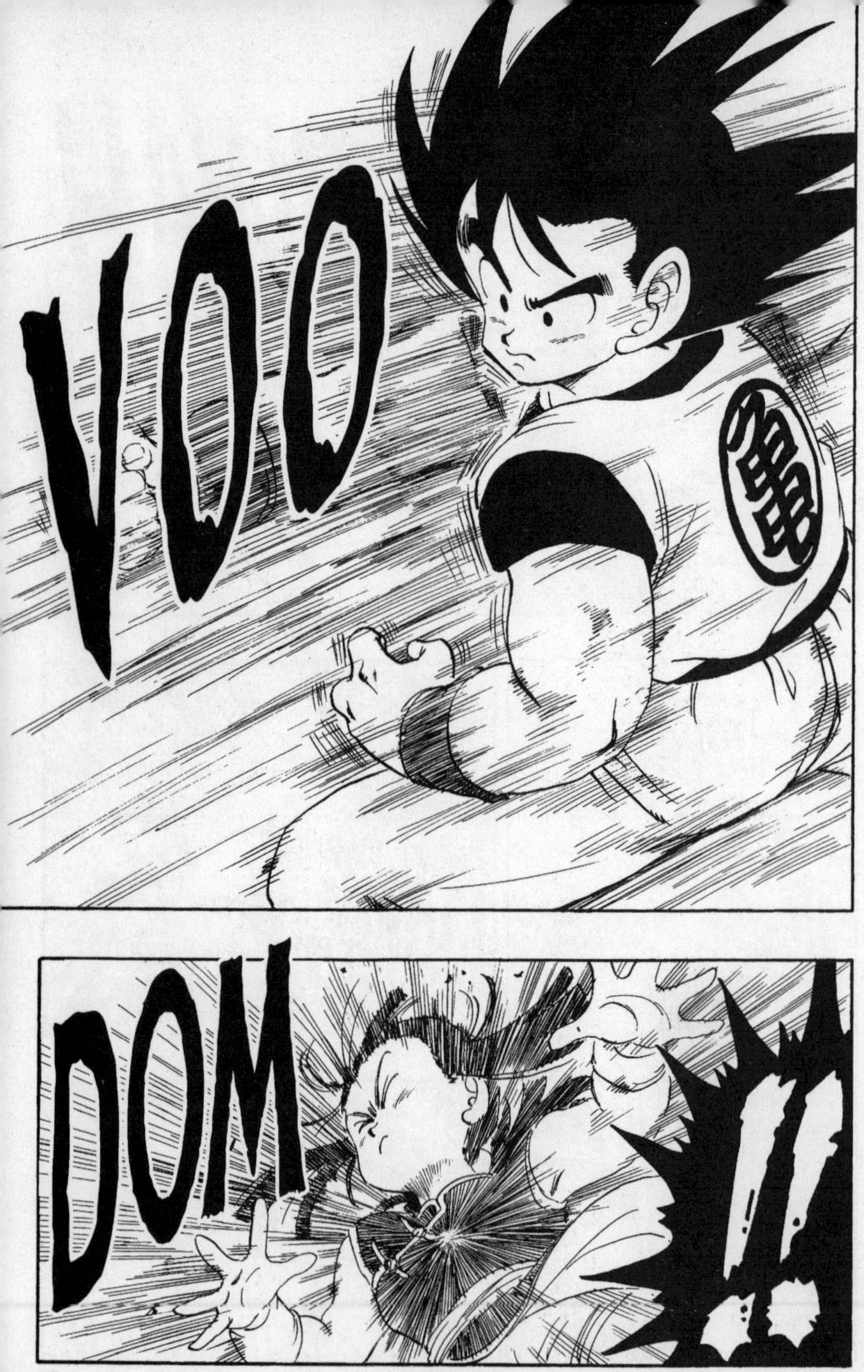
VOOO
DOM
!!

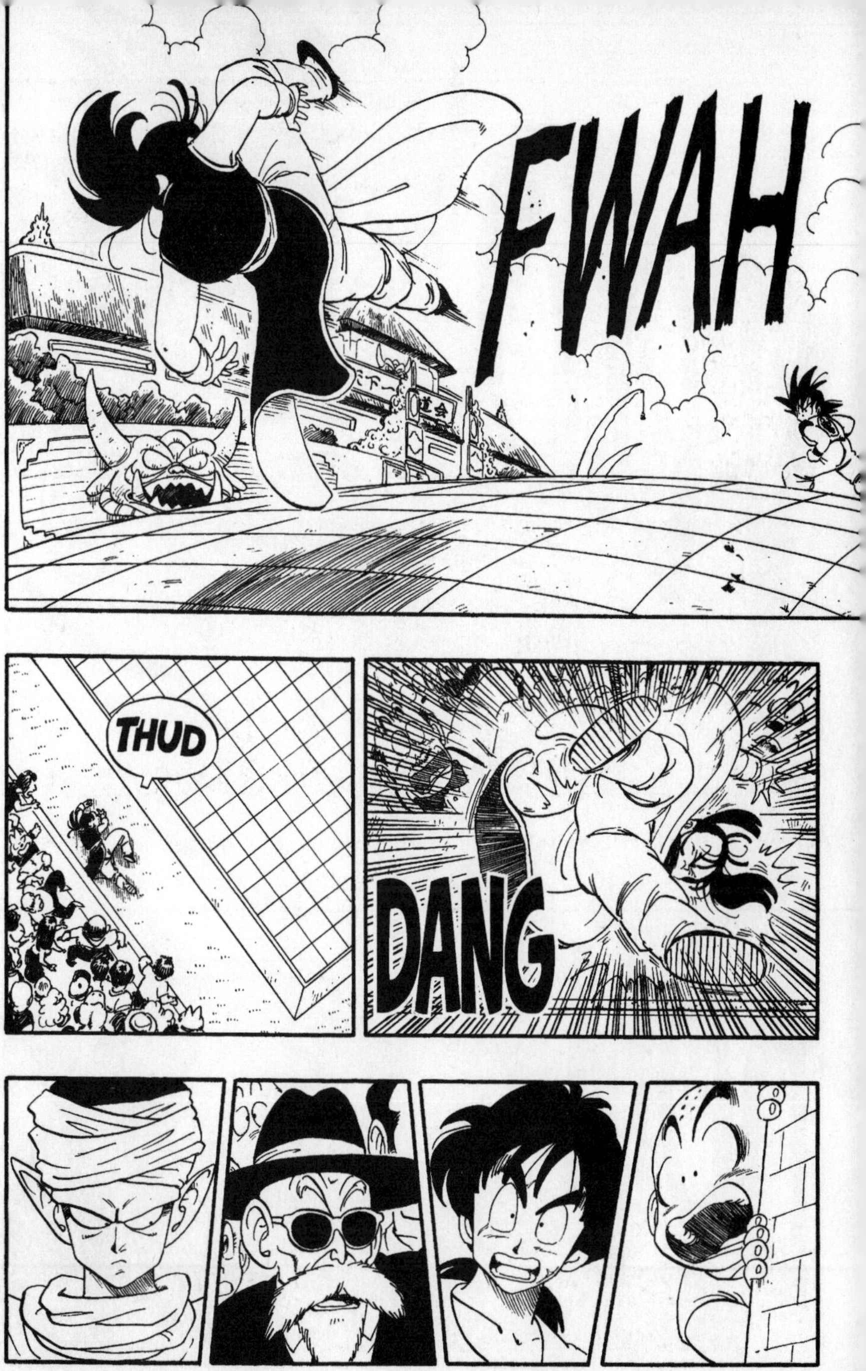
FWAH
DANG
THUD

READ THIS WAY

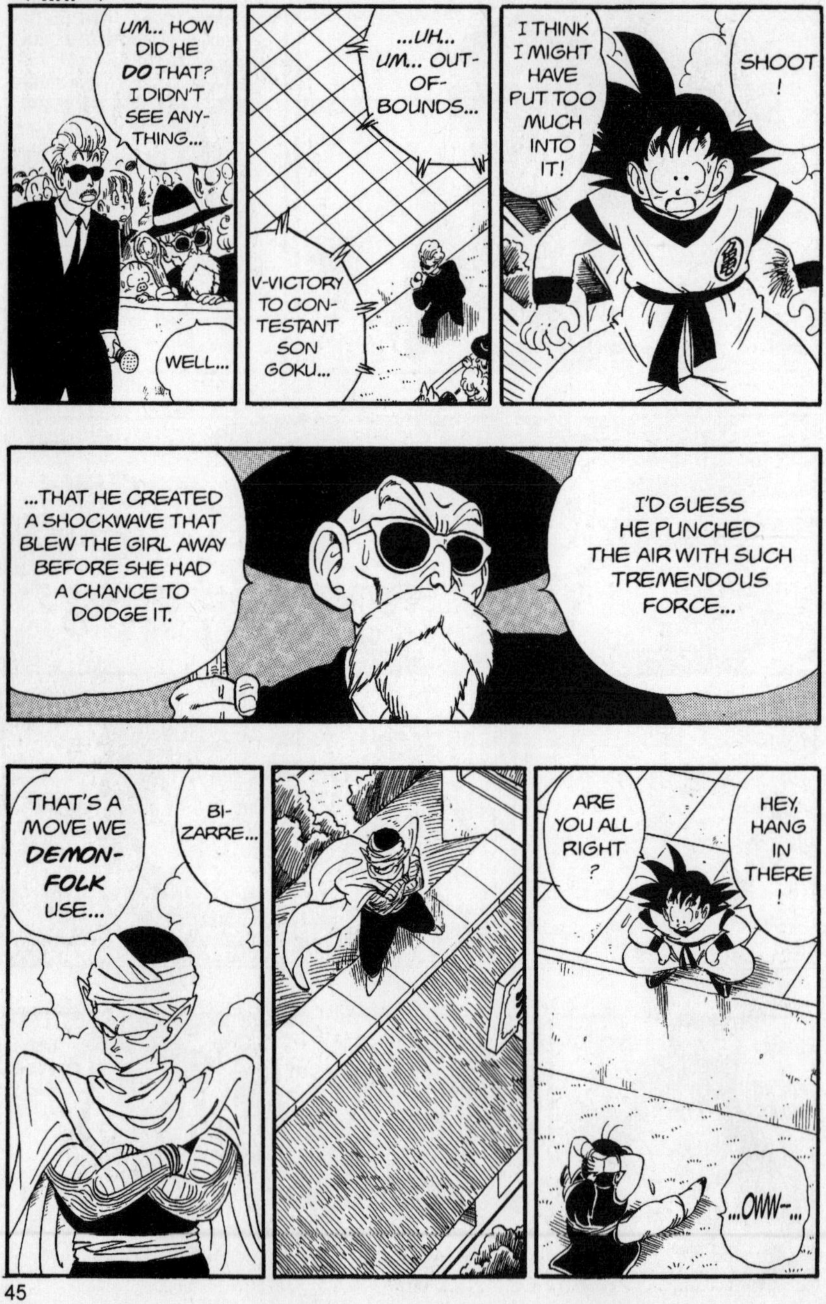
SHOOT!
I THINK I MIGHT HAVE PUT TOO MUCH INTO IT!
...UH... UM... OUT-OF-BOUNDS...
V-VICTORY TO CONTESTANT SON GOKU...
UM... HOW DID HE **DO** THAT? I DIDN'T SEE ANYTHING...
WELL...
I'D GUESS HE PUNCHED THE AIR WITH SUCH TREMENDOUS FORCE...
...THAT HE CREATED A SHOCKWAVE THAT BLEW THE GIRL AWAY BEFORE SHE HAD A CHANCE TO DODGE IT.
HEY, HANG IN THERE!
ARE YOU ALL RIGHT?
...OWW-...
BIZARRE...
THAT'S A MOVE WE **DEMON-FOLK** USE...

READ THIS WAY

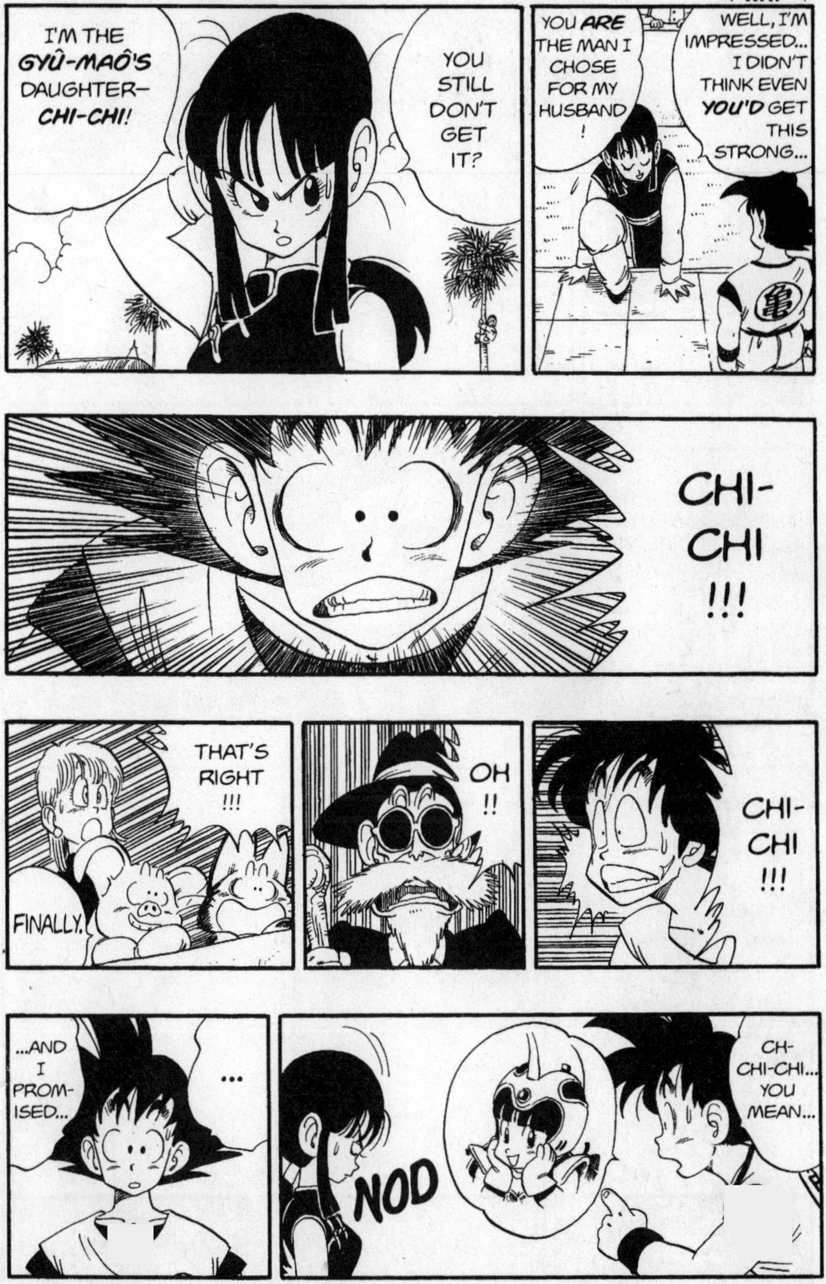
WELL, I'M IMPRESSED... I DIDN'T THINK EVEN YOU'D GET THIS STRONG...
YOU ARE THE MAN I CHOSE FOR MY HUSBAND!
YOU STILL DON'T GET IT?
I'M THE GYÛ-MAÔ'S DAUGHTER— CHI-CHI!
CHI-CHI!!!
CHI-CHI!!!
OH!!
THAT'S RIGHT!!!
FINALLY.
CH-CHI-CHI... YOU MEAN...
NOD
...
...AND I PROMISED...

READ THIS WAY

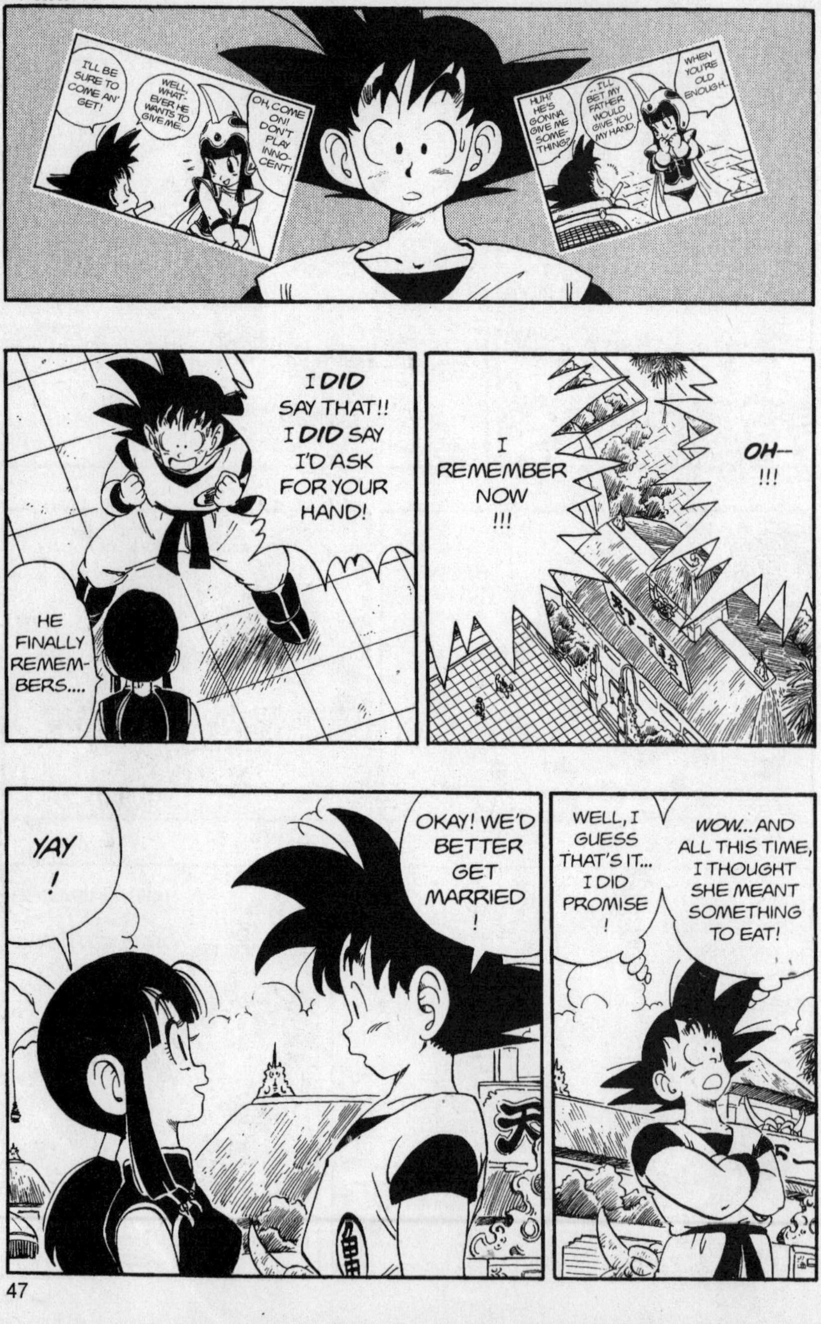
WHEN YOU'RE OLD ENOUGH..
...I'LL BET MY FATHER WOULD GIVE YOU MY HAND.
HUH? HE'S GONNA GIVE ME SOME-THING?
OH, COME ON! DON'T PLAY INNO-CENT!
WELL, WHAT-EVER HE WANTS TO GIVE ME...
I'LL BE SURE TO COME AN' GET!
OH-- !!!
I REMEMBER NOW !!!
I DID SAY THAT!! I DID SAY I'D ASK FOR YOUR HAND!
HE FINALLY REMEM-BERS....
WOW... AND ALL THIS TIME, I THOUGHT SHE MEANT SOMETHING TO EAT!
WELL, I GUESS THAT'S IT... I DID PROMISE!
OKAY! WE'D BETTER GET MARRIED!
YAY!

READ THIS WAY

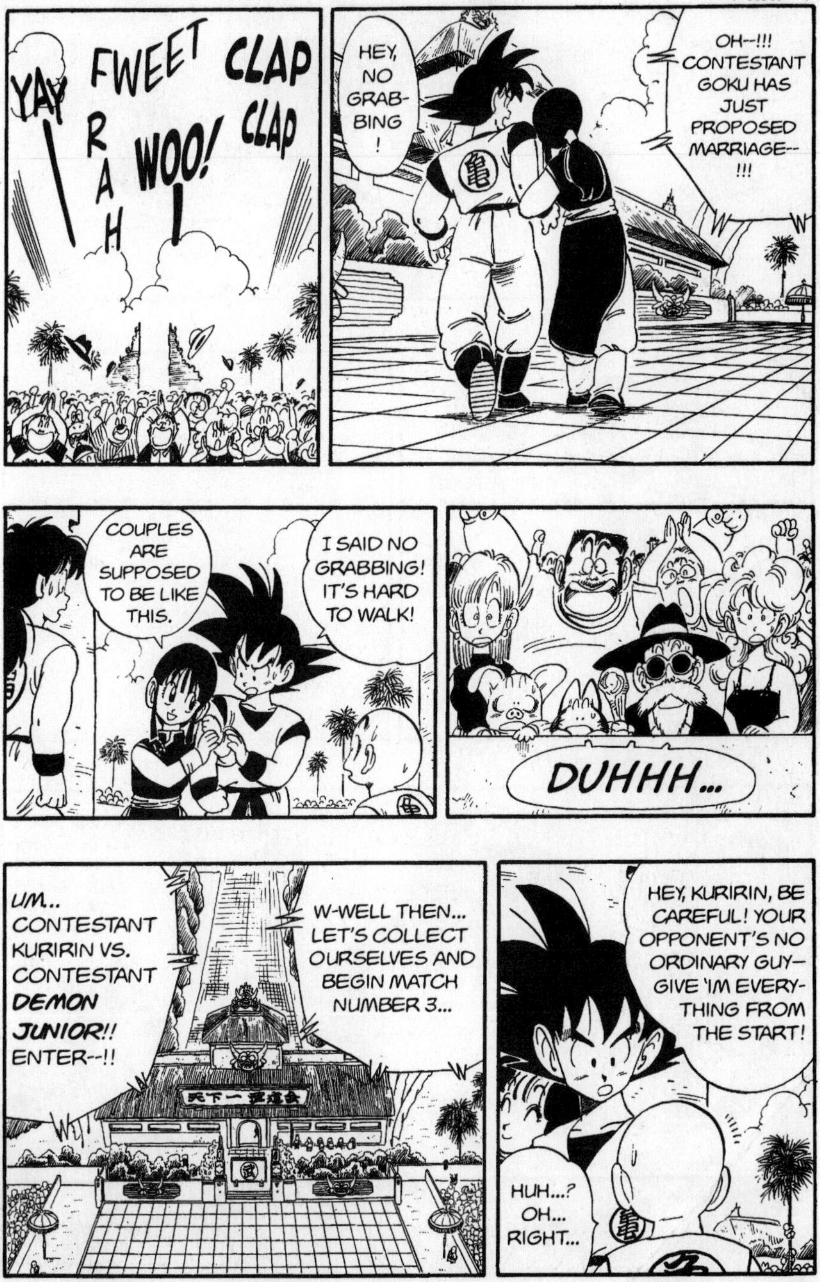

OH--!!! CONTESTANT GOKU HAS JUST PROPOSED MARRIAGE--!!!
HEY, NO GRABBING!
CLAP CLAP
WOO!
FWEET
RAH
YAY
DUHHH...
I SAID NO GRABBING! IT'S HARD TO WALK!
COUPLES ARE SUPPOSED TO BE LIKE THIS.
HEY, KURIRIN, BE CAREFUL! YOUR OPPONENT'S NO ORDINARY GUY-- GIVE 'IM EVERYTHING FROM THE START!
HUH...? OH... RIGHT...
W-WELL THEN... LET'S COLLECT OURSELVES AND BEGIN MATCH NUMBER 3...
UM... CONTESTANT KURIRIN VS. CONTESTANT DEMON JUNIOR!! ENTER--!!

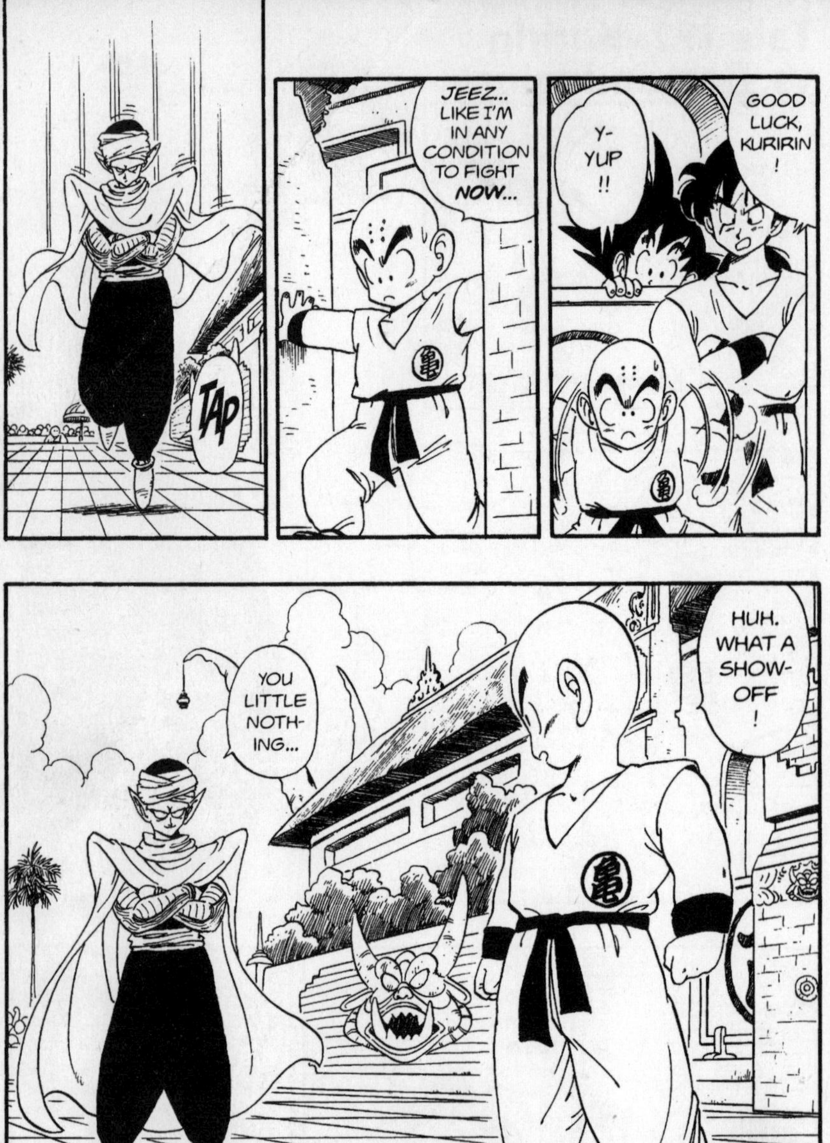
GOOD LUCK, KURIRIN!
Y-YUP!!
JEEZ... LIKE I'M IN ANY CONDITION TO FIGHT NOW...
TAP
HUH. WHAT A SHOW-OFF!
YOU LITTLE NOTHING...

***NEXT*: Kuririn's Chance For Revenge!**

Tale 172 • Kuririn vs. Demon Junior

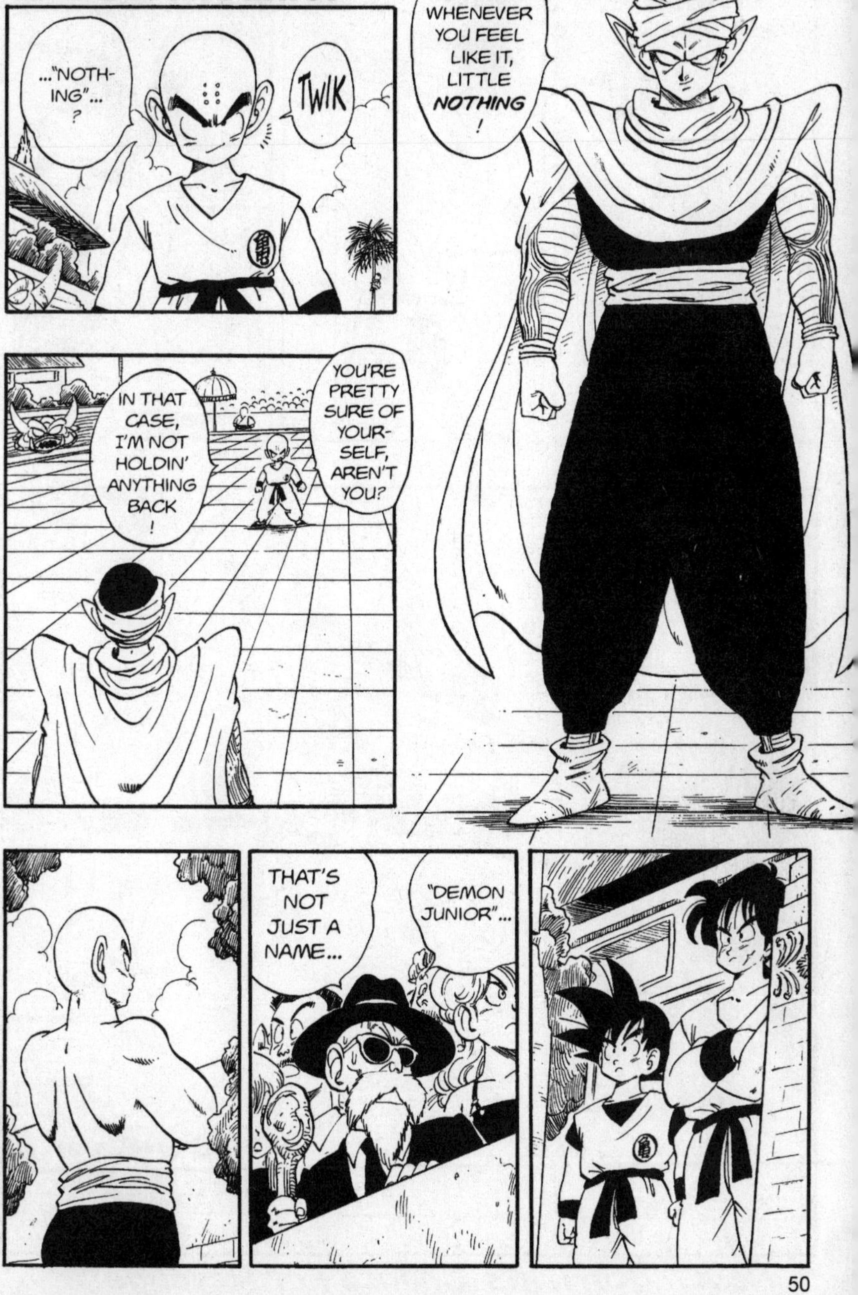
COME AT ME WHENEVER YOU FEEL LIKE IT, LITTLE ***NOTHING*** !
TWIK
..."NOTHING"... ?
YOU'RE PRETTY SURE OF YOURSELF, AREN'T YOU?
IN THAT CASE, I'M NOT HOLDIN' ANYTHING BACK !
"DEMON JUNIOR"...
THAT'S NOT JUST A NAME...

READ THIS WAY

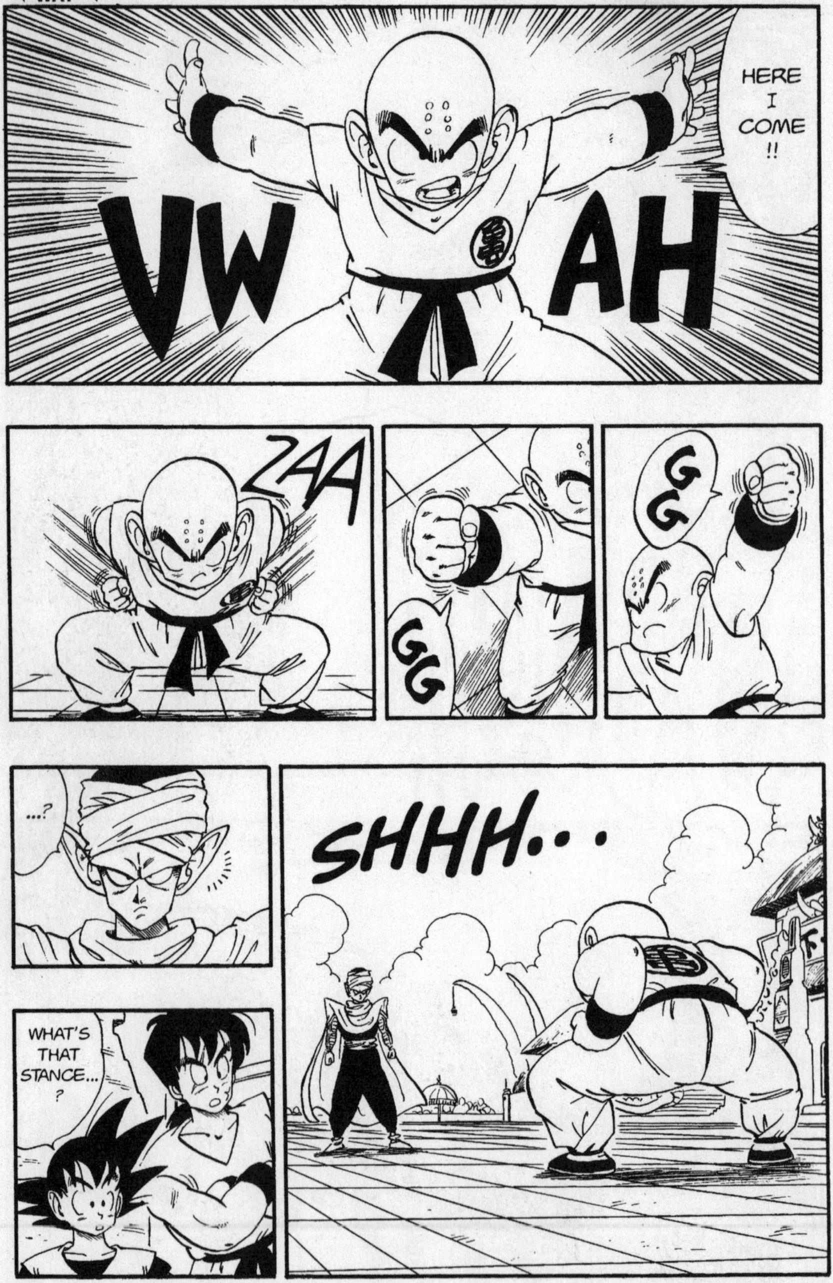

HERE I COME!!
VW AH
GG
GG
ZAA
SHHH...
...?
WHAT'S THAT STANCE...?

READ THIS WAY

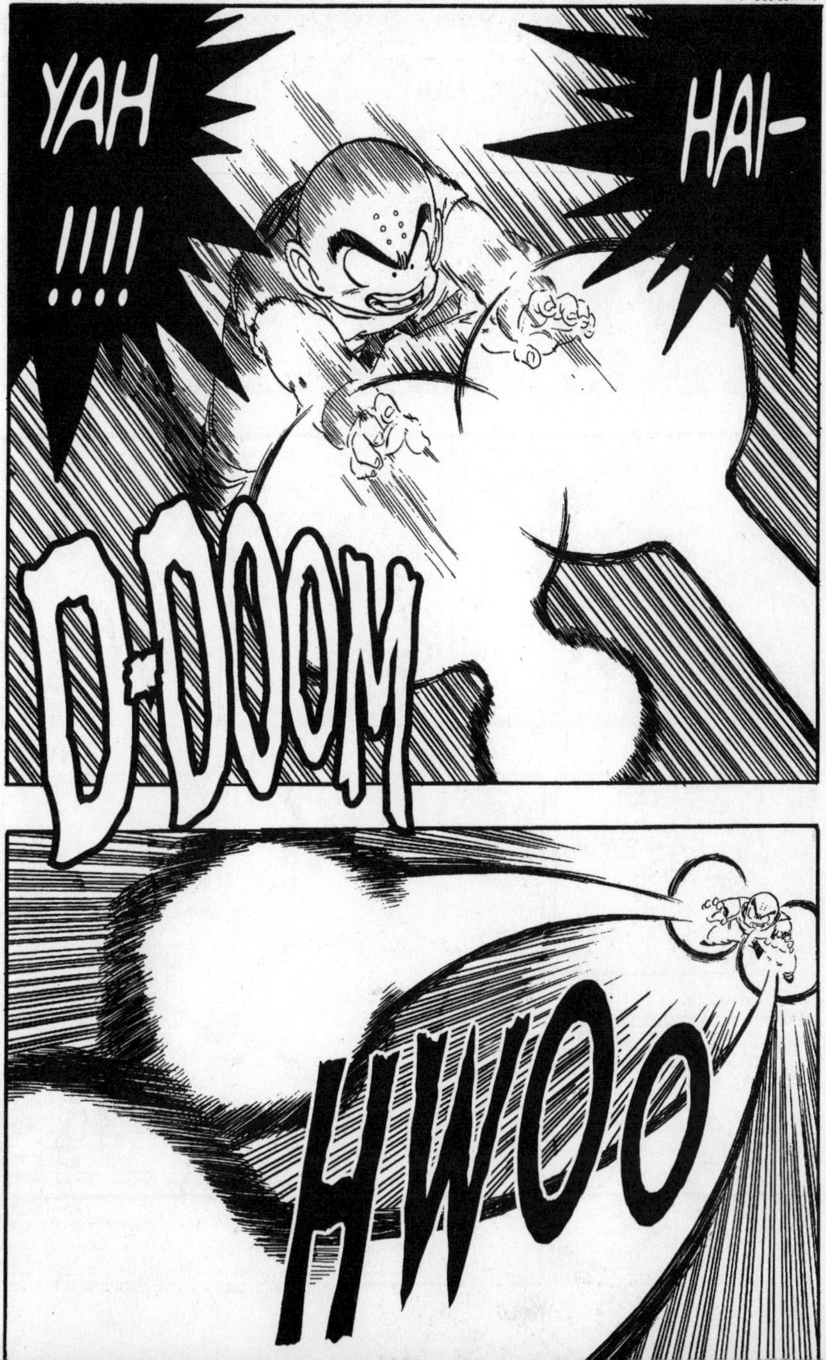
HAI-
YAH !!!!
D-DOOM
HWOO

READ THIS WAY

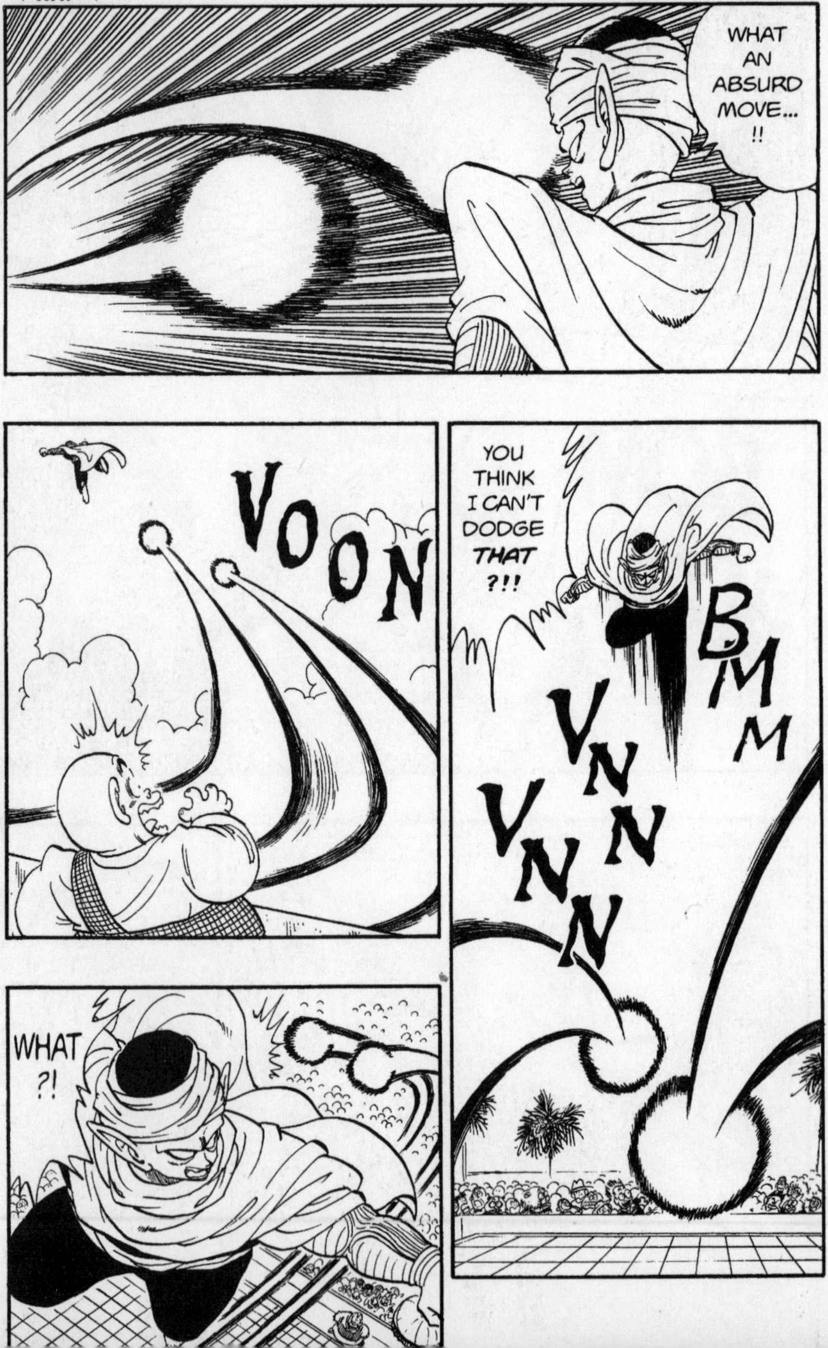
WHAT AN ABSURD MOVE...!!
YOU THINK I CAN'T DODGE *THAT*?!!
BMM
VNNN
VNNN
VOON
WHAT?!

READ THIS WAY

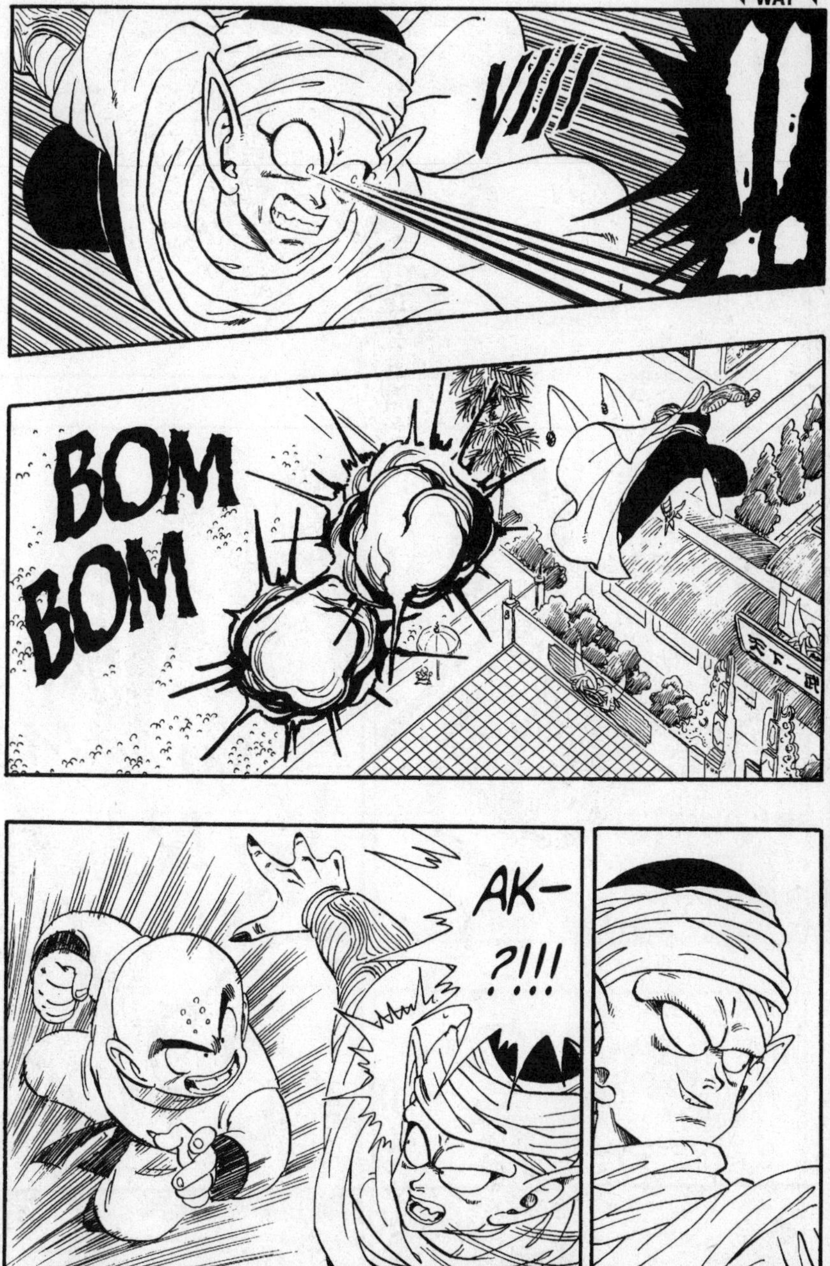

VIIII
!!
BOM
BOM
AK-
?!!!

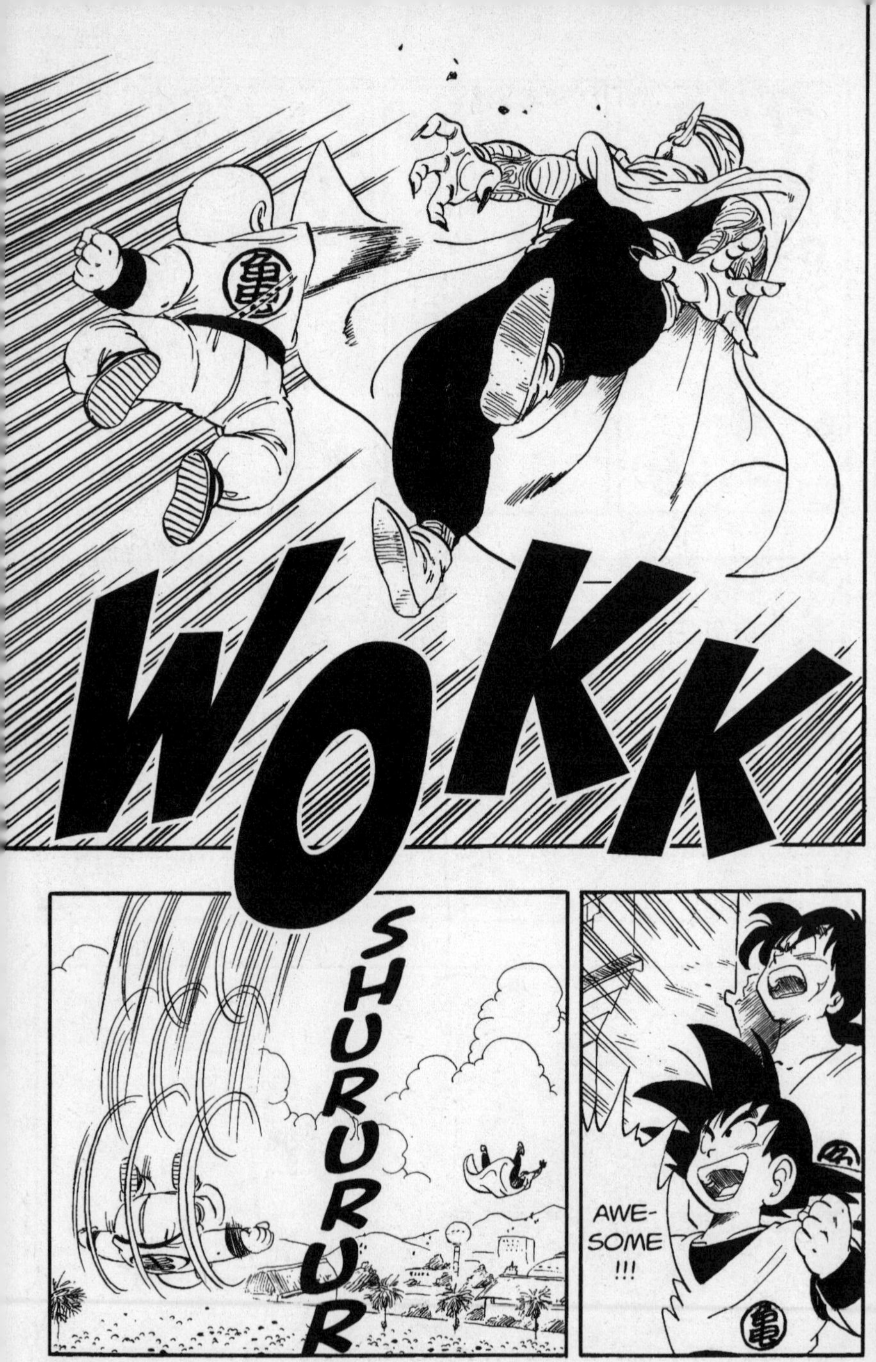
WOKK
AWE-SOME !!!
SHURURUR

READ THIS WAY

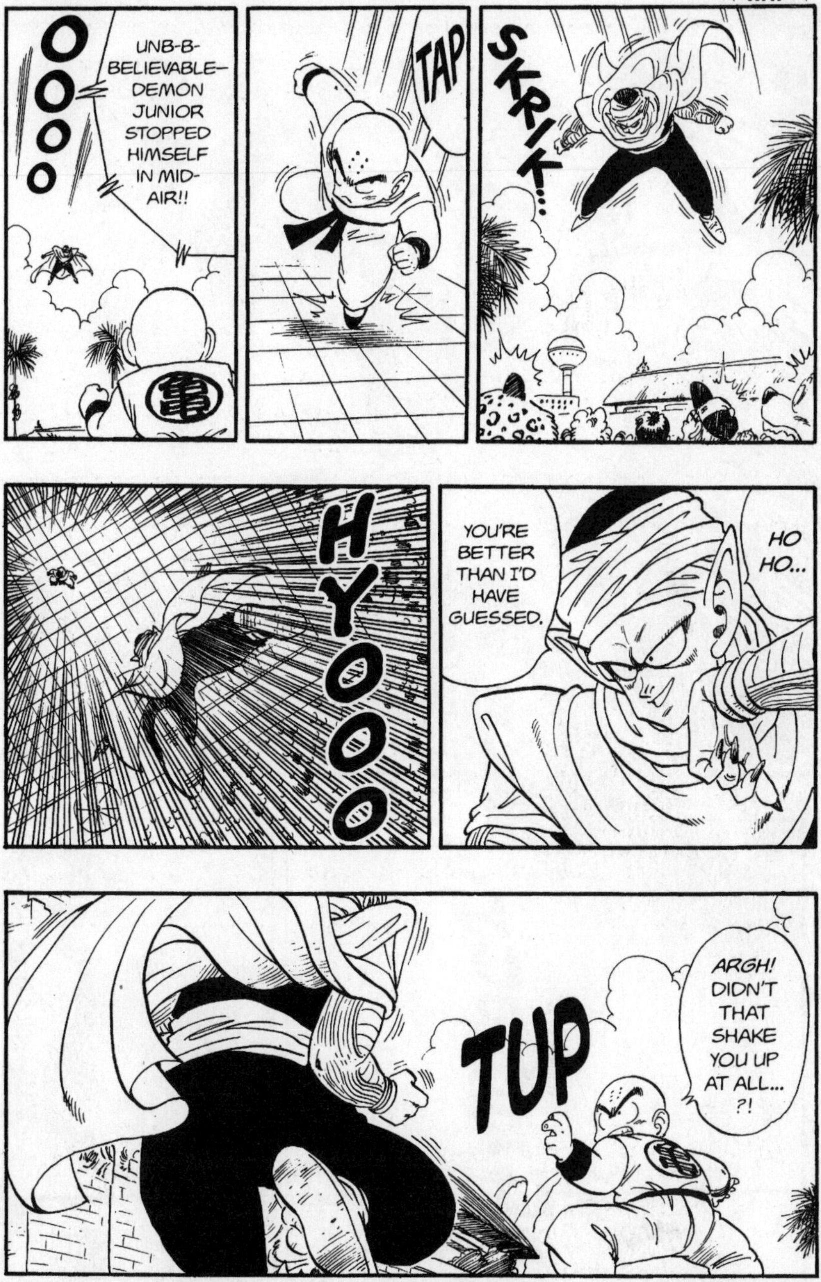
SKRIK...
TAP
OOOO
UNB-B-BELIEVABLE—DEMON JUNIOR STOPPED HIMSELF IN MID-AIR!!
HO HO...
YOU'RE BETTER THAN I'D HAVE GUESSED.
HYOOOO
ARGH! DIDN'T THAT SHAKE YOU UP AT ALL...?!
TUP

READ THIS WAY

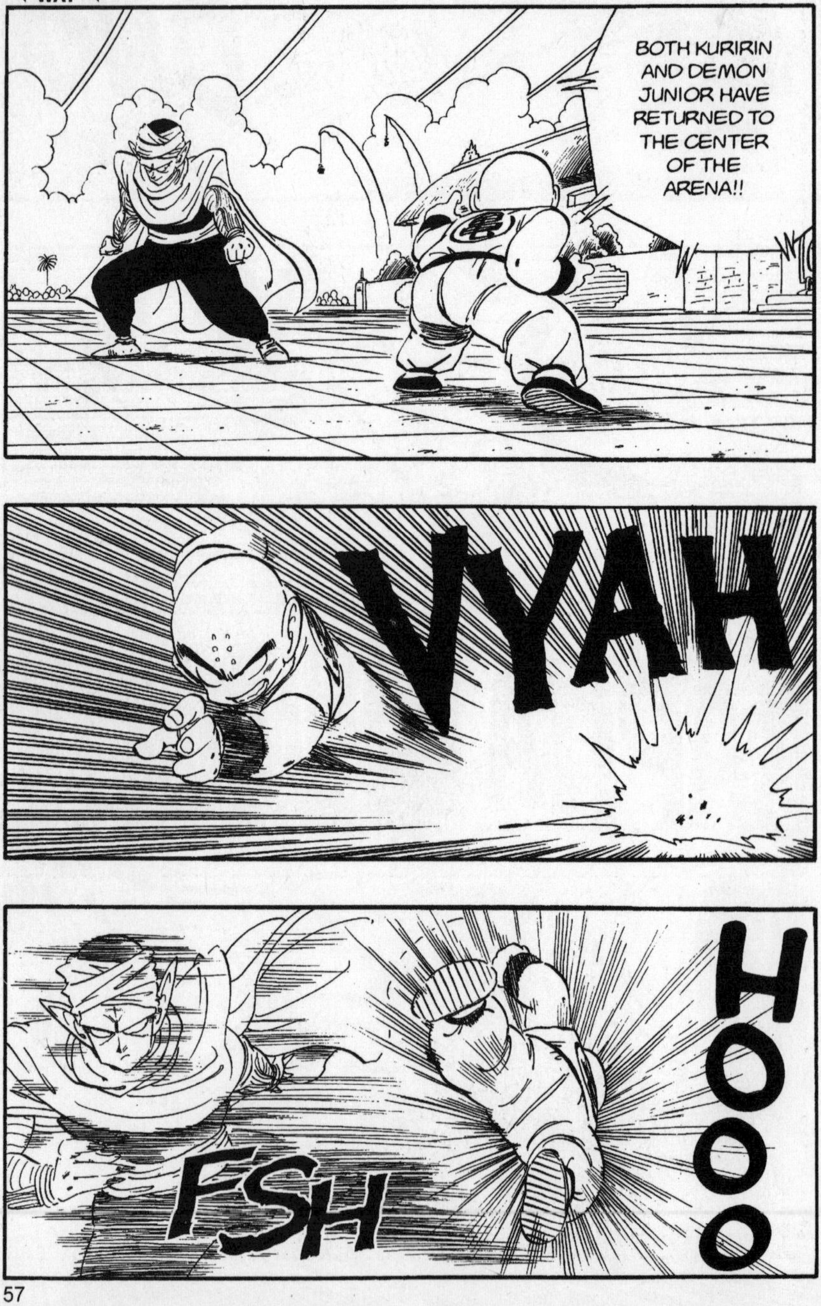
BOTH KURIRIN AND DEMON JUNIOR HAVE RETURNED TO THE CENTER OF THE ARENA!!
VYAH
HOOOO
FSH

READ THIS WAY

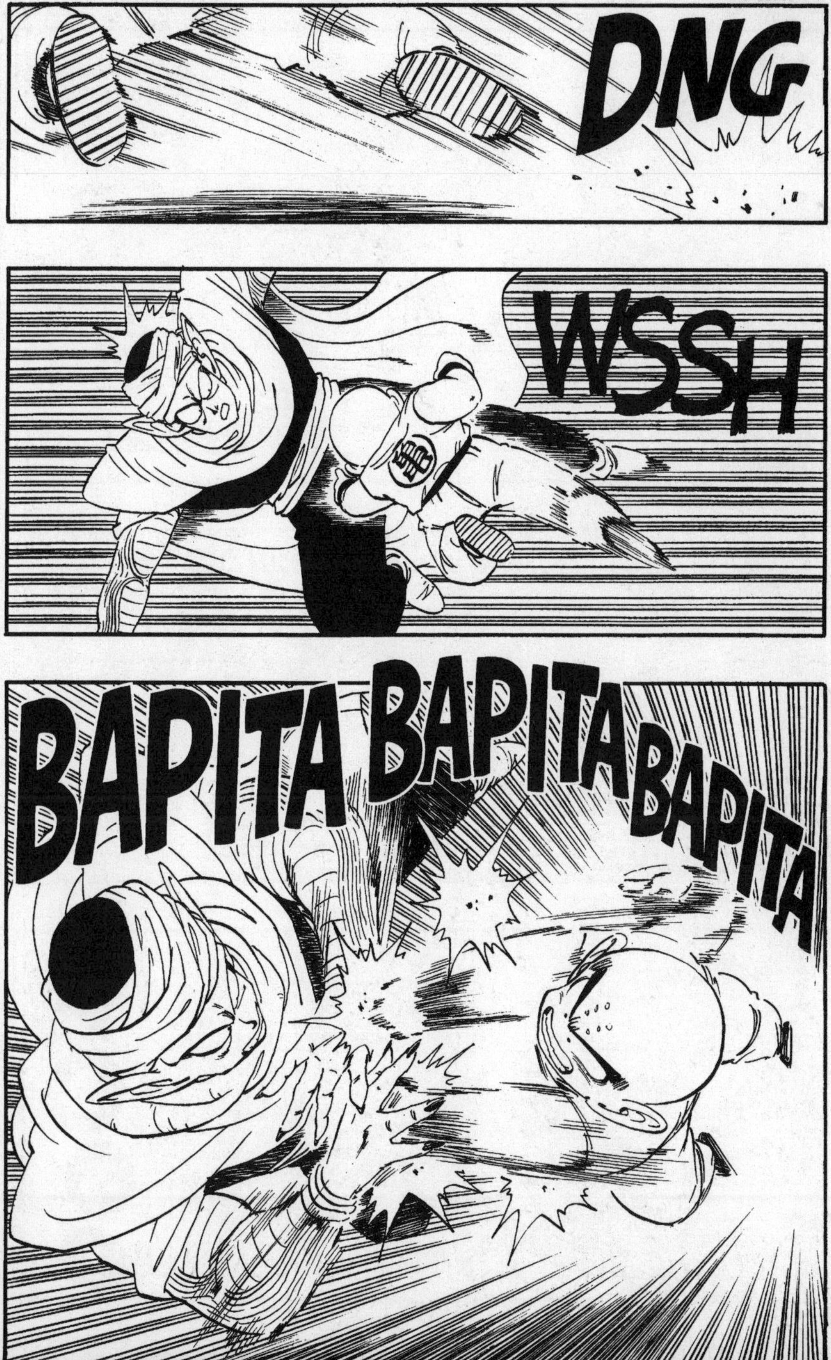
DNG
WSSH
BAPITA BAPITA BAPITA BAPITA

READ THIS WAY

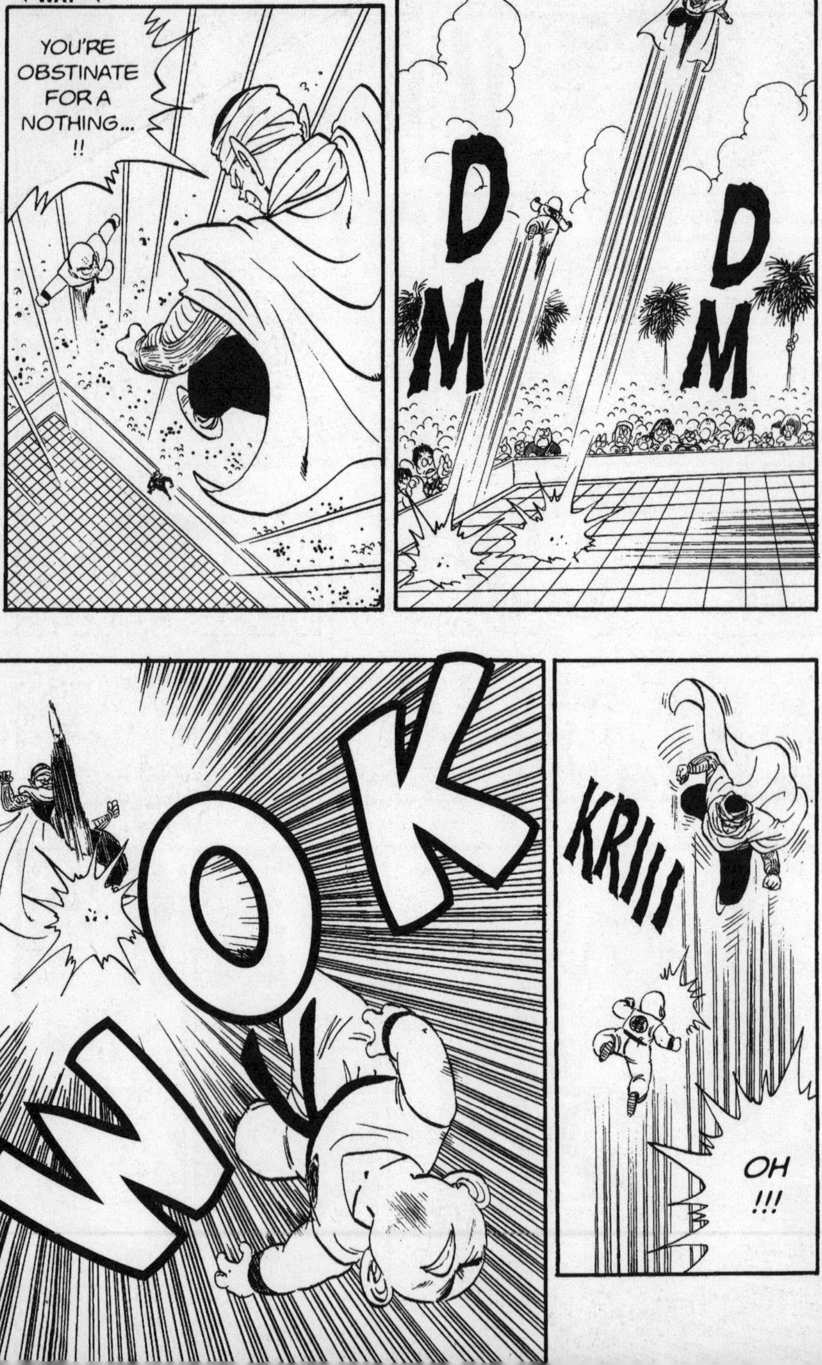
DM
DM
YOU'RE OBSTINATE FOR A NOTHING... !!
KRIII
OH !!!
WOK

READ THIS WAY

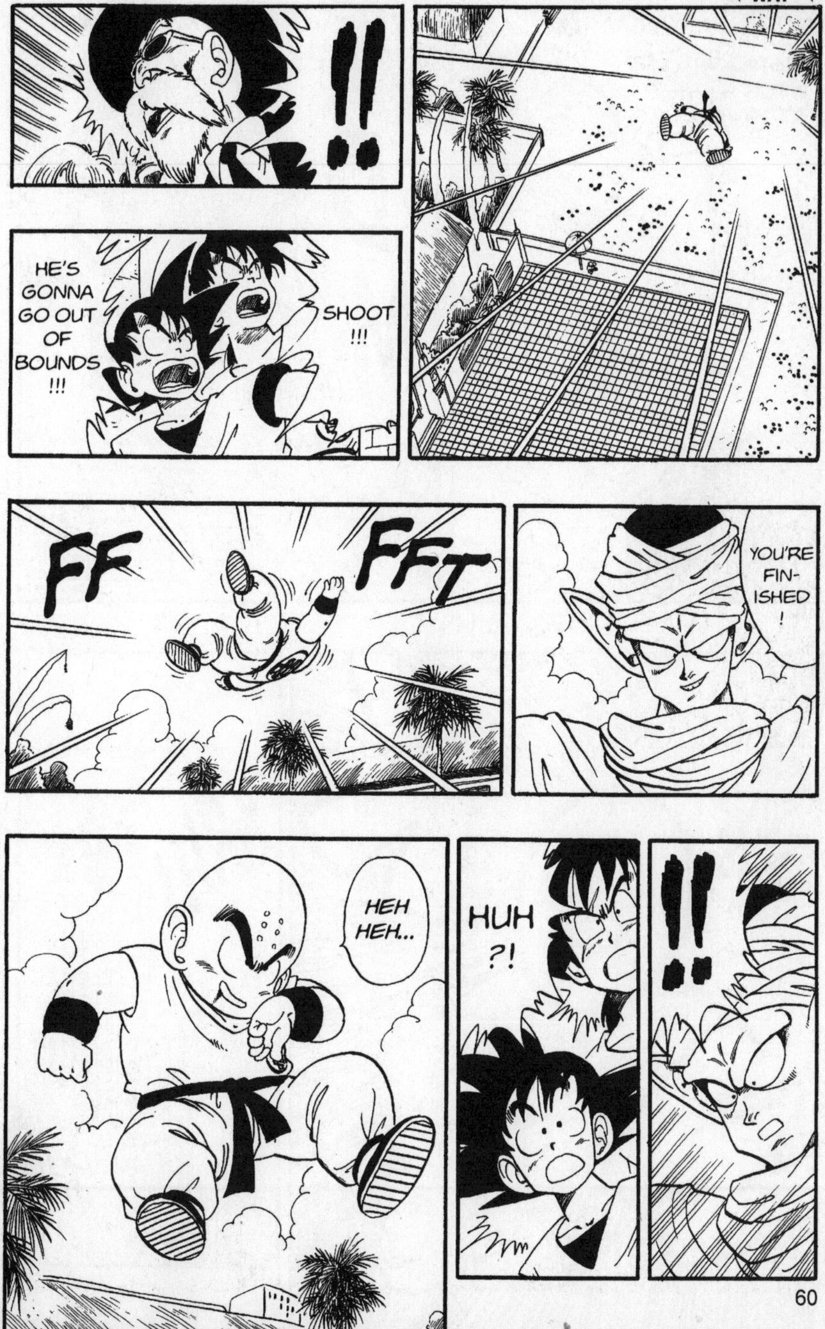

!!
SHOOT!!!
HE'S GONNA GO OUT OF BOUNDS!!!
YOU'RE FIN-ISHED!
FF
FFT
!!
HUH?!
HEH HEH...

READ THIS WAY

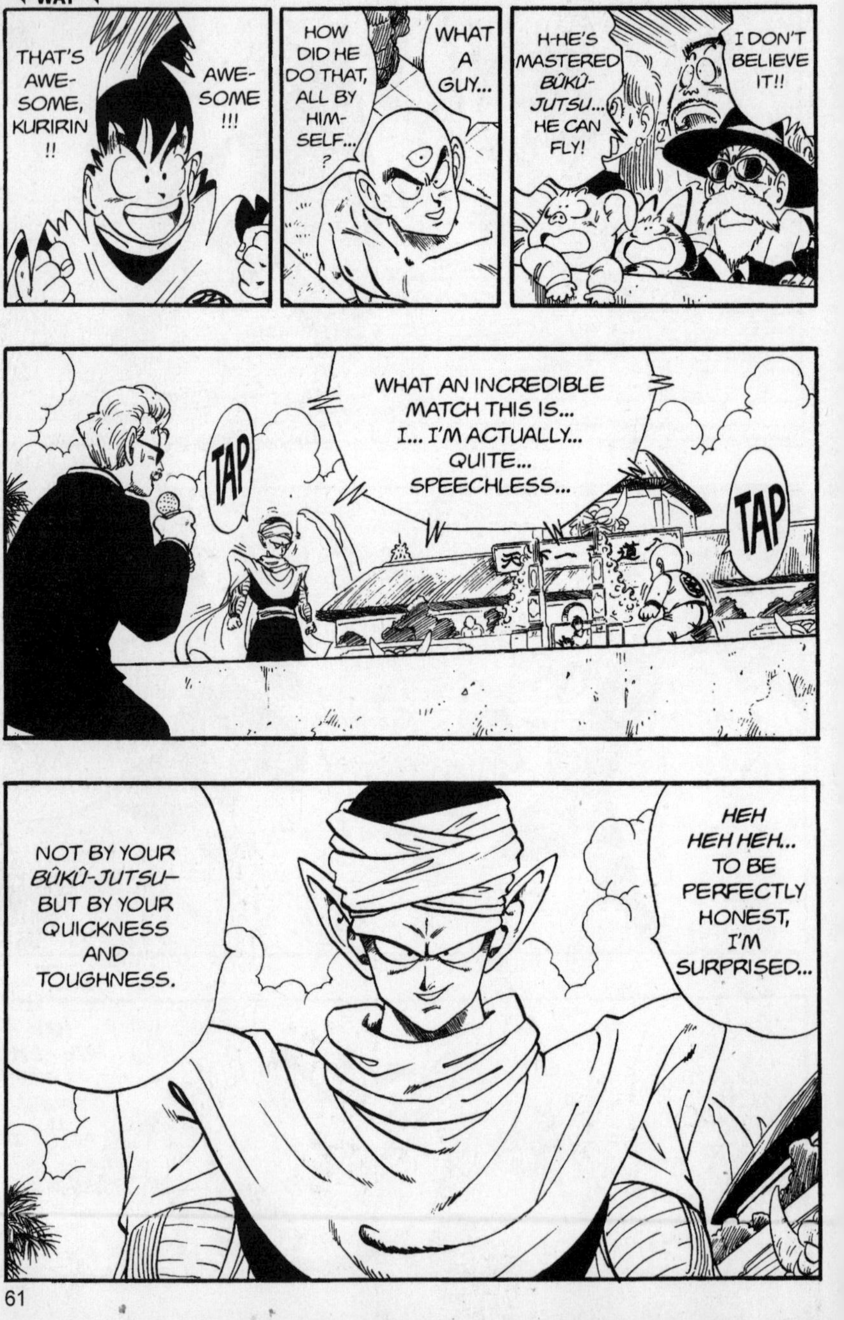
I DON'T BELIEVE IT!!
H-HE'S MASTERED *BÛKÛ-JUTSU*... HE CAN FLY!
WHAT A GUY...
HOW DID HE DO THAT, ALL BY HIMSELF...?
AWESOME!!!
THAT'S AWESOME, KURIRIN!!
WHAT AN INCREDIBLE MATCH THIS IS... I... I'M ACTUALLY... QUITE... SPEECHLESS...
TAP
TAP
HEH HEH HEH... TO BE PERFECTLY HONEST, I'M SURPRISED...
NOT BY YOUR *BÛKÛ-JUTSU*– BUT BY YOUR QUICKNESS AND TOUGHNESS.

READ THIS WAY

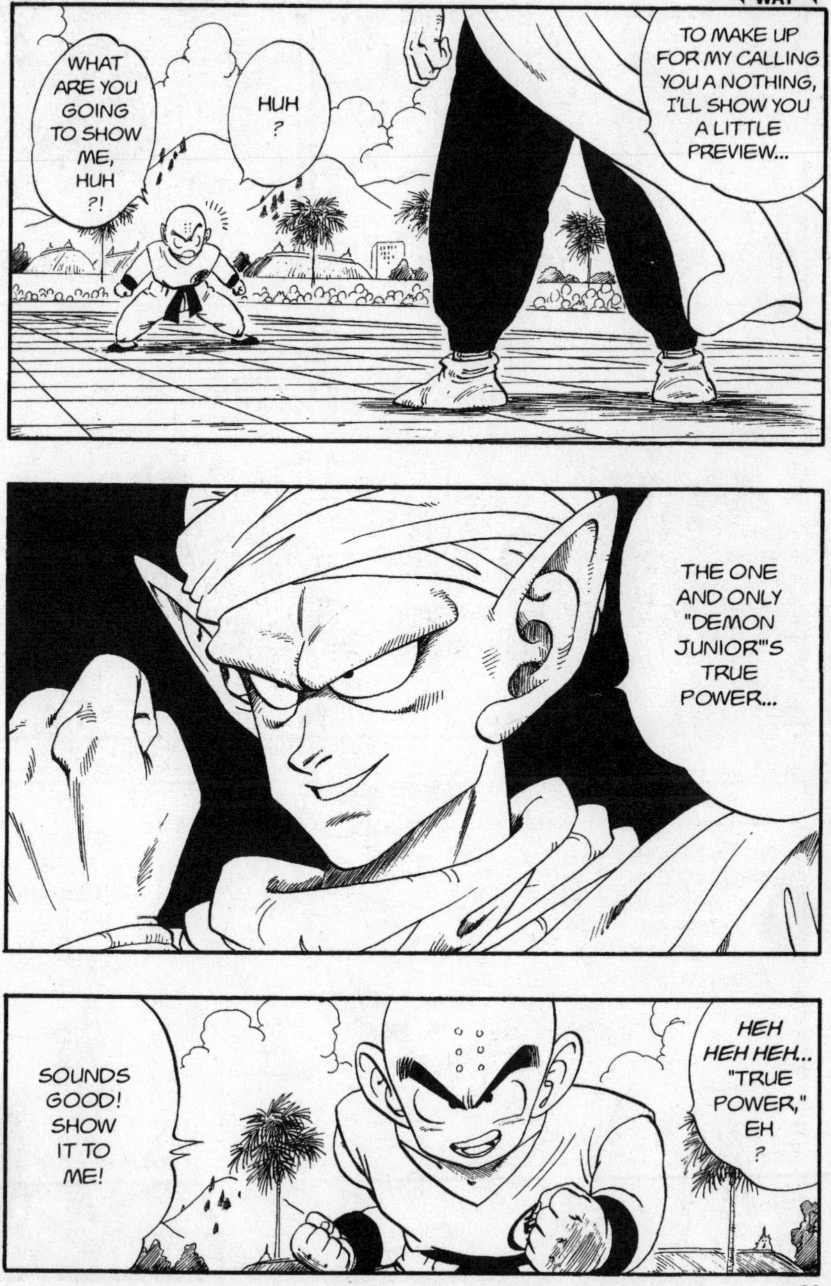
TO MAKE UP FOR MY CALLING YOU A NOTHING, I'LL SHOW YOU A LITTLE PREVIEW...
HUH ?
WHAT ARE YOU GOING TO SHOW ME, HUH ?!
THE ONE AND ONLY "DEMON JUNIOR"'S TRUE POWER...
HEH HEH HEH... "TRUE POWER," EH ?
SOUNDS GOOD! SHOW IT TO ME!

READ THIS WAY

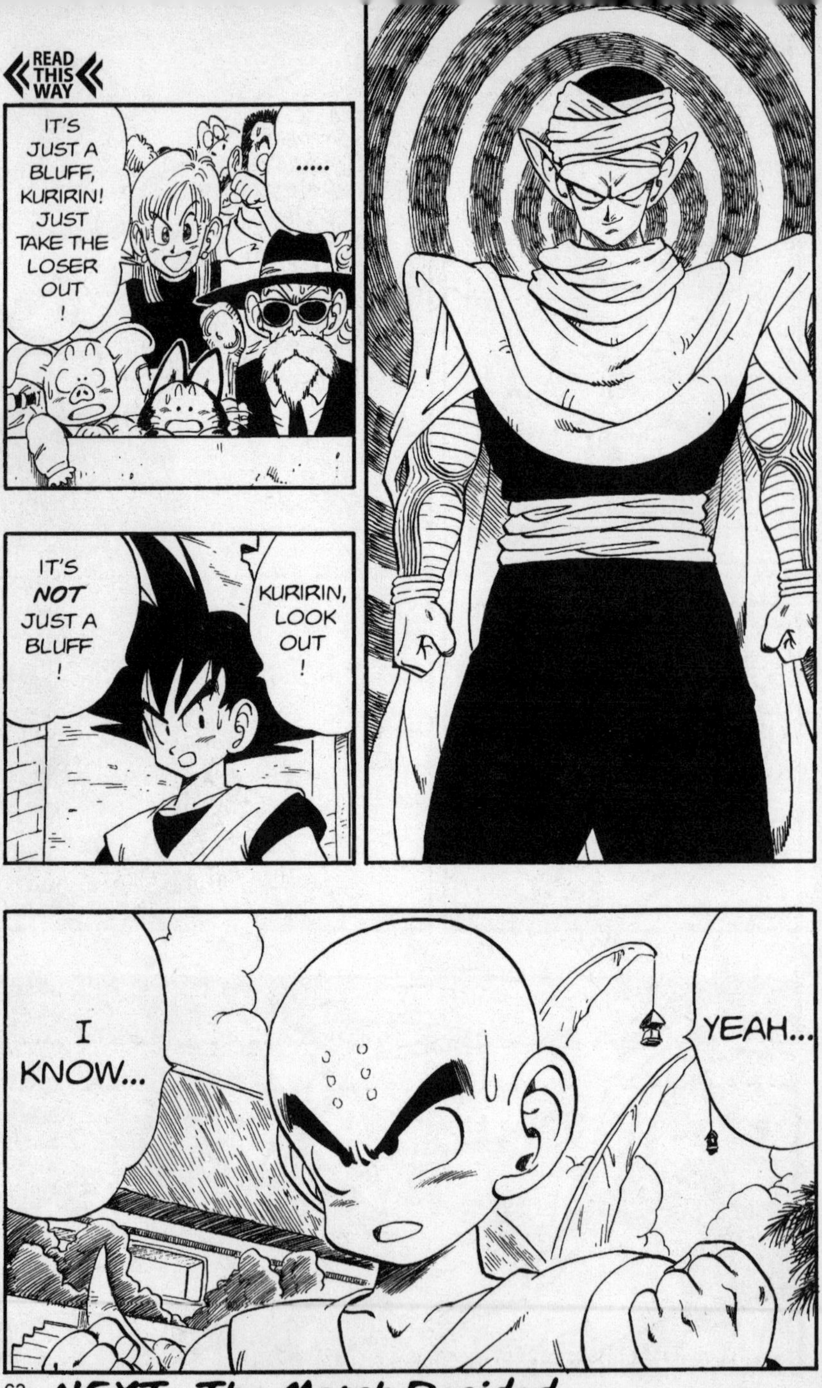
.....
IT'S JUST A BLUFF, KURIRIN! JUST TAKE THE LOSER OUT!
KURIRIN, LOOK OUT!
IT'S NOT JUST A BLUFF!
YEAH...
I KNOW...

NEXT: The Match Decided

Tale 173·Kuririn vs. Demon Junior, Part 2

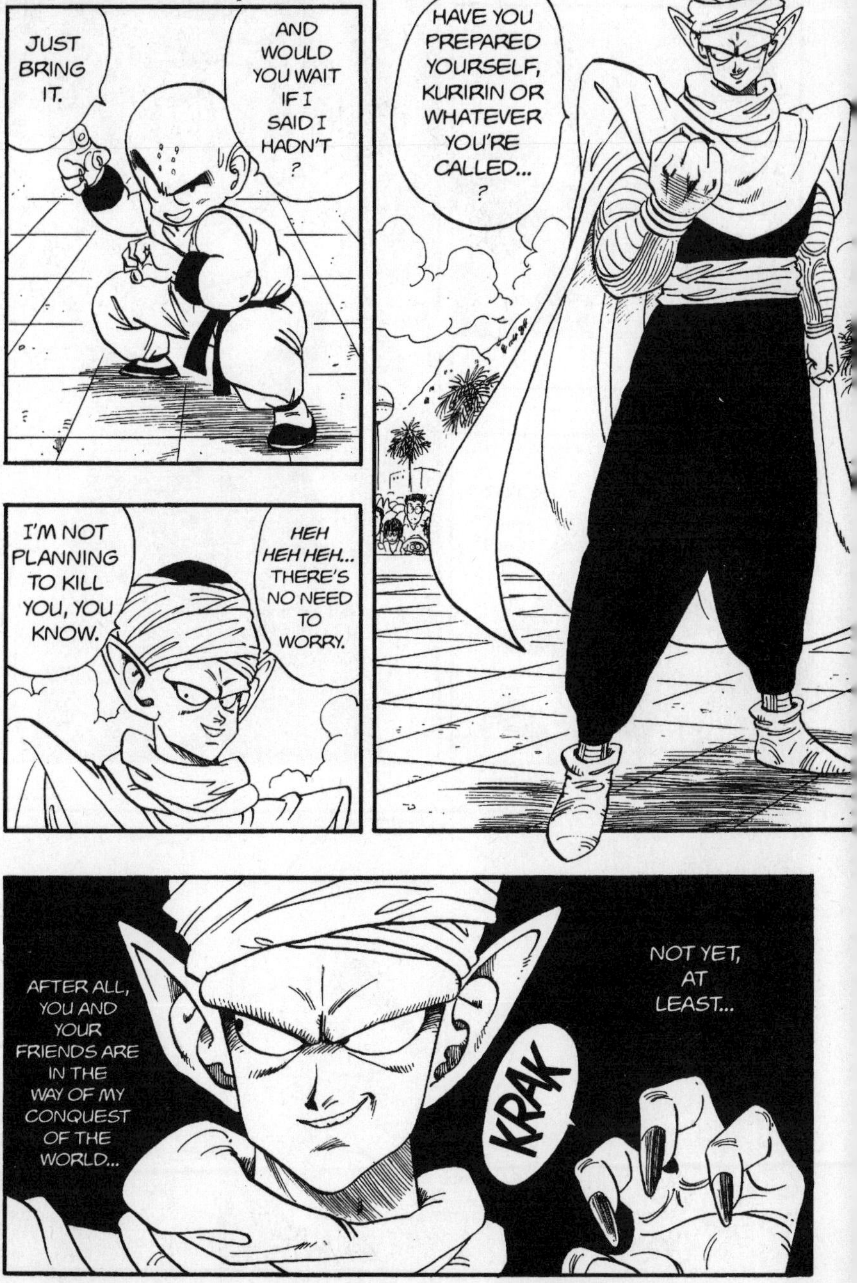
HAVE YOU PREPARED YOURSELF, KURIRIN OR WHATEVER YOU'RE CALLED...?
AND WOULD YOU WAIT IF I SAID I HADN'T?
JUST BRING IT.
HEH HEH HEH... THERE'S NO NEED TO WORRY.
I'M NOT PLANNING TO KILL YOU, YOU KNOW.
NOT YET, AT LEAST...
KRAK
AFTER ALL, YOU AND YOUR FRIENDS ARE IN THE WAY OF MY CONQUEST OF THE WORLD...

READ THIS WAY

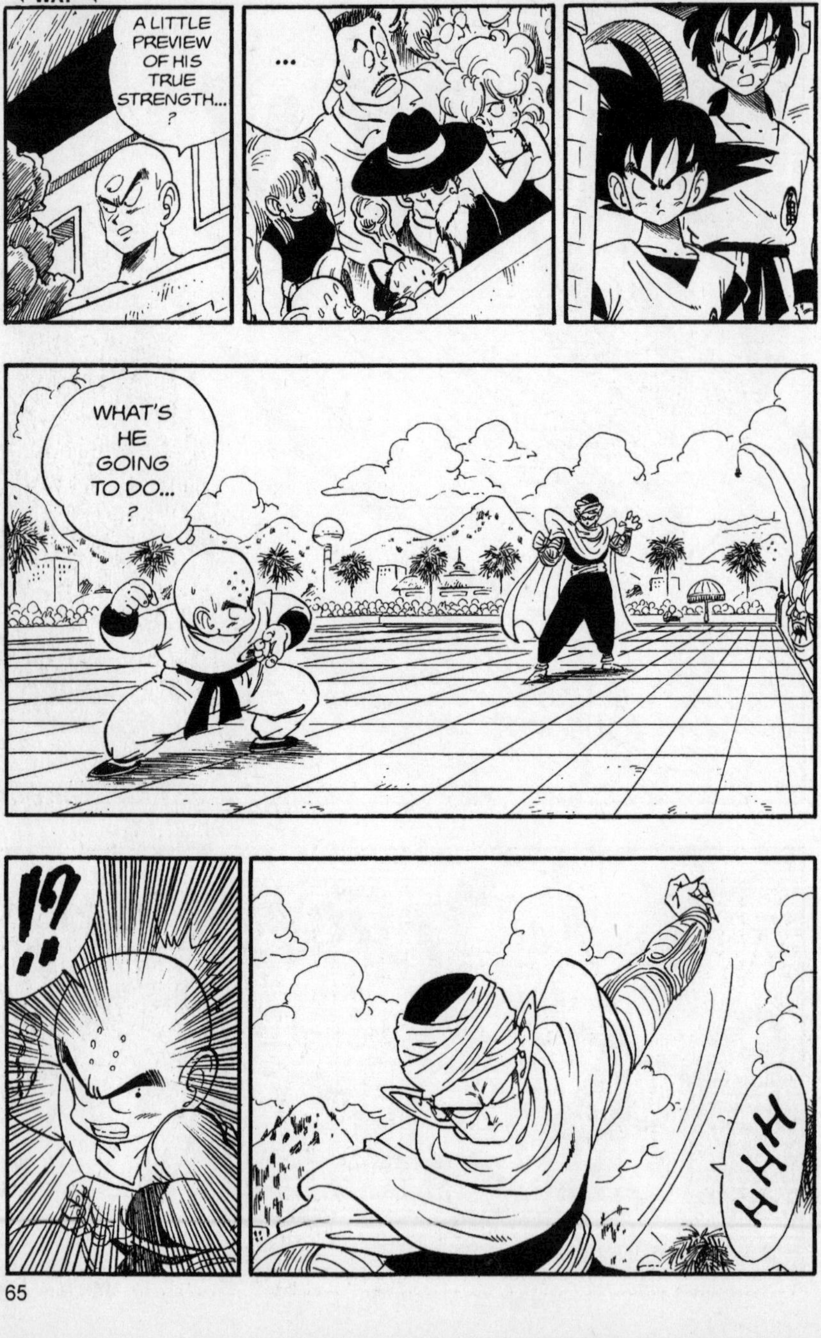
...
A LITTLE PREVIEW OF HIS TRUE STRENGTH...?
WHAT'S HE GOING TO DO...?
HHH
!?

READ THIS WAY

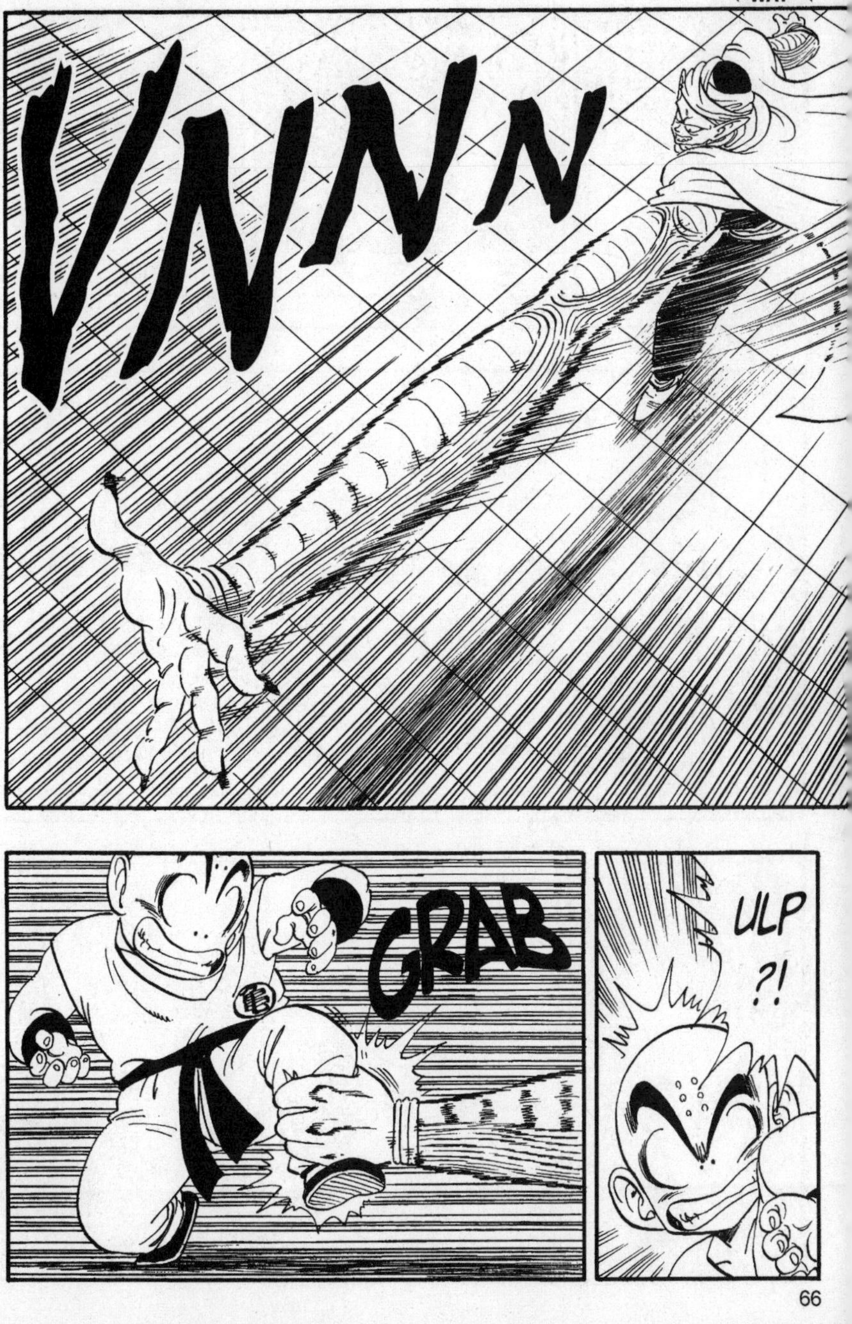

VNNN
ULP
?!
GRAB

READ THIS WAY

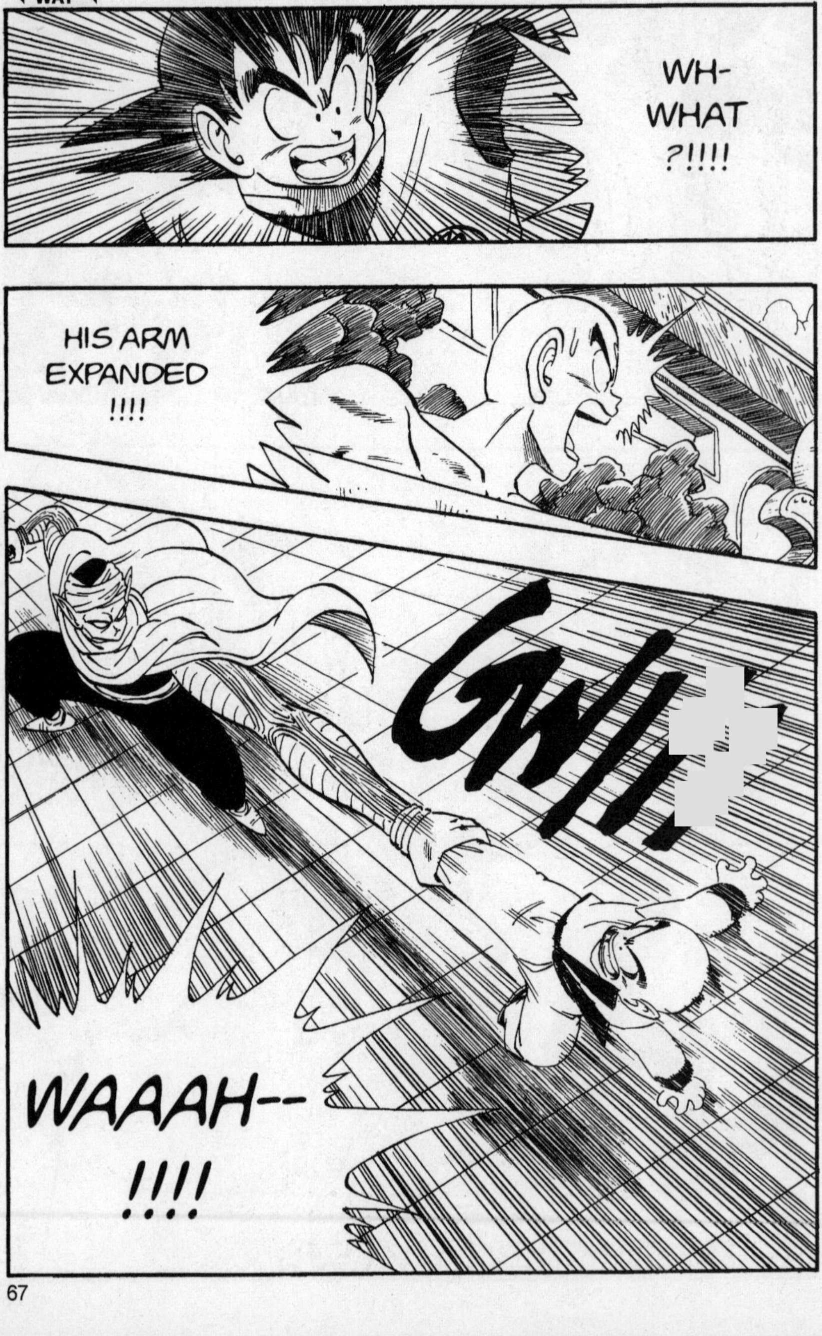
WH- WHAT ?!!!!
HIS ARM EXPANDED !!!!
GWII
WAAAH-- !!!!

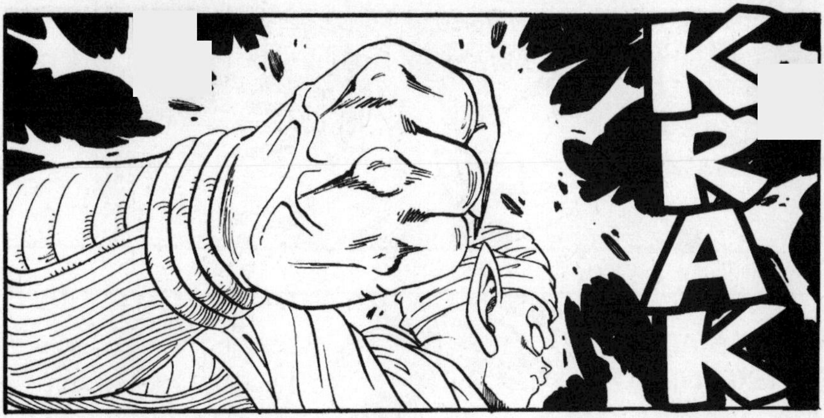
KRAK
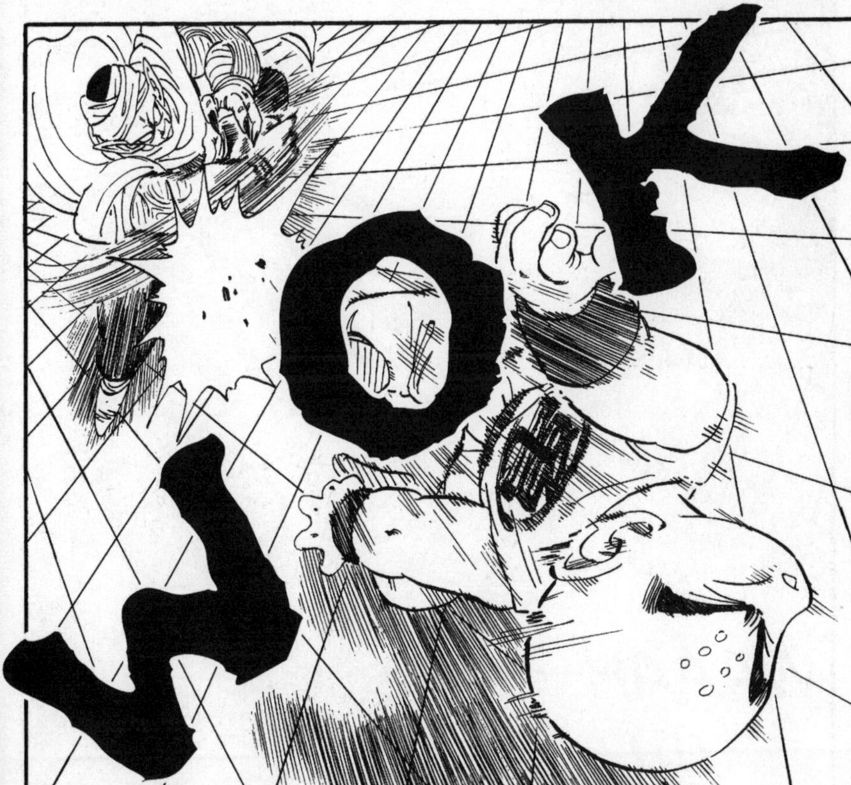

READ THIS WAY

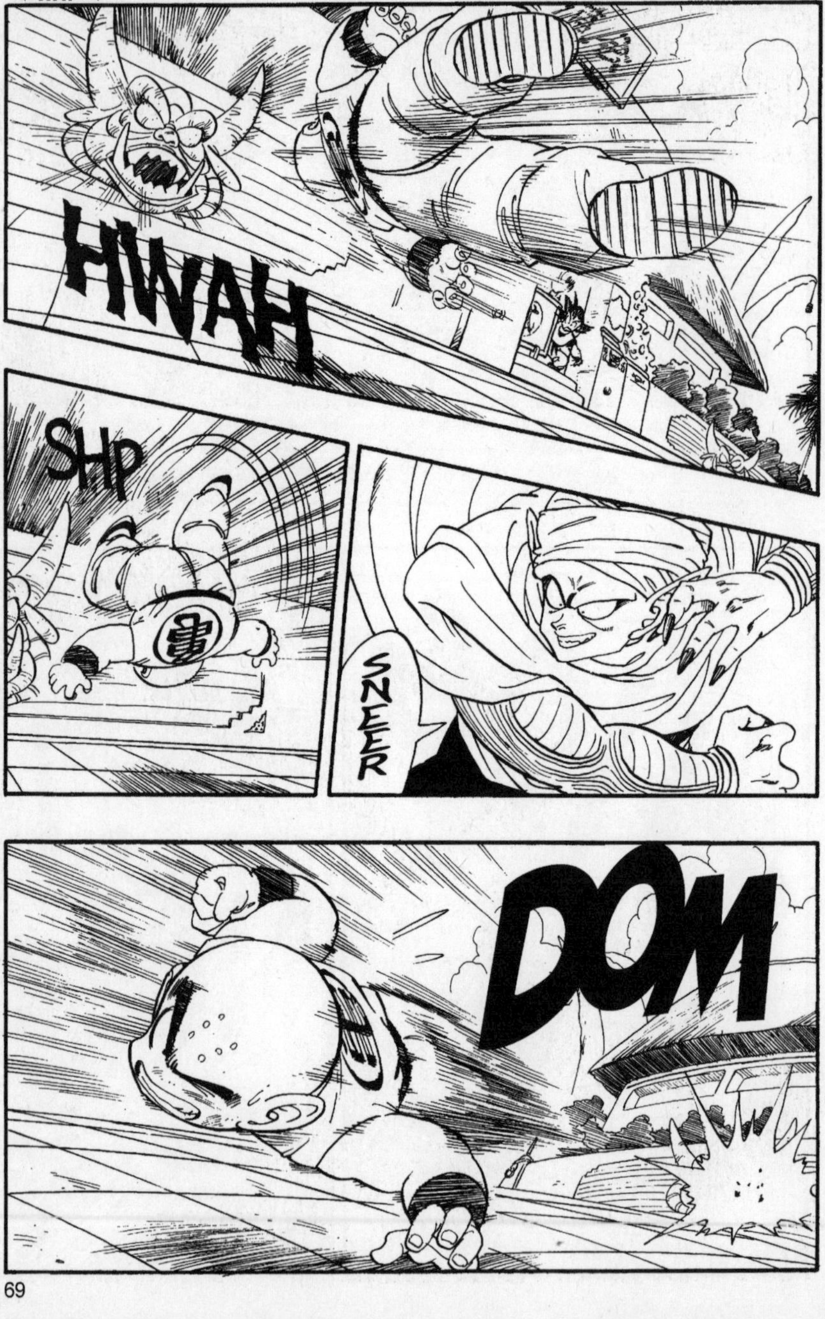
HWAH
SNEER
SHP
DOM

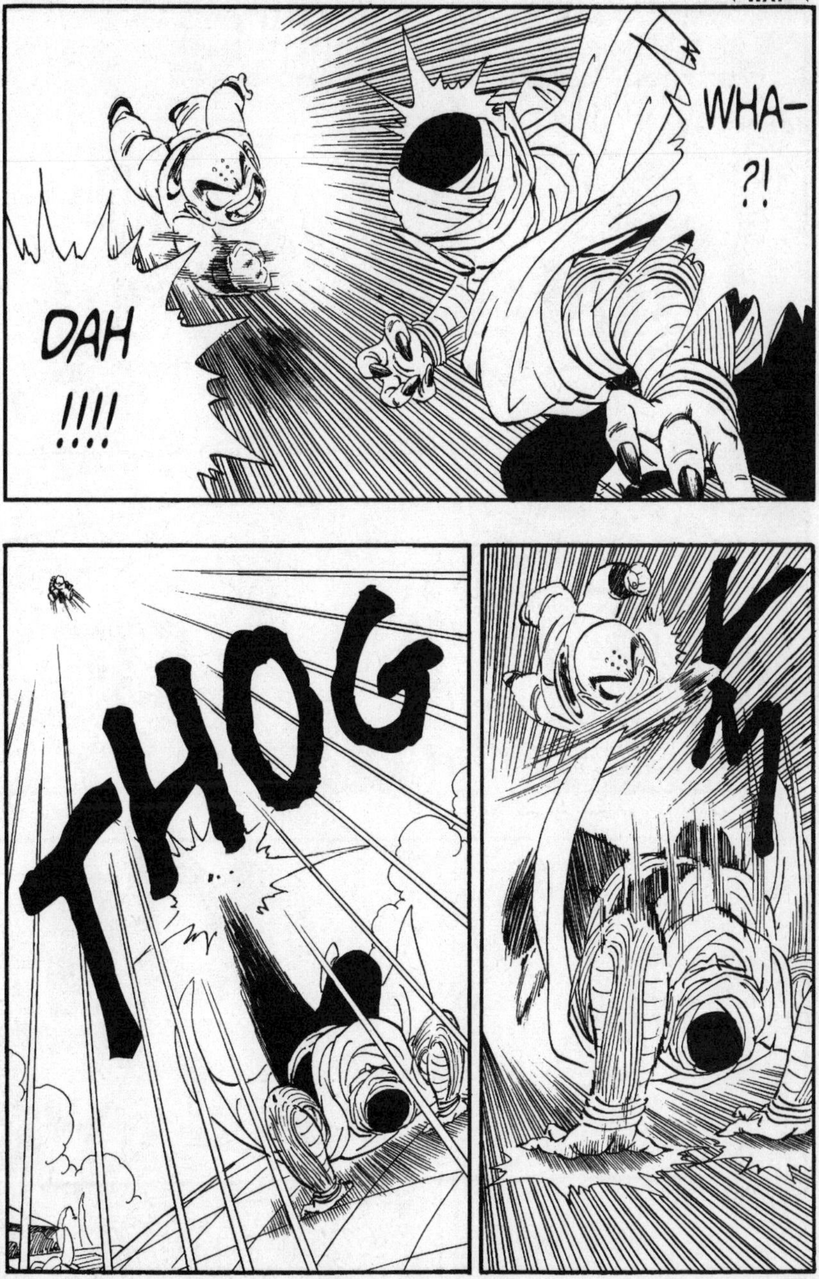
WHA-?!
DAH!!!!
KM!
THOG

READ THIS WAY

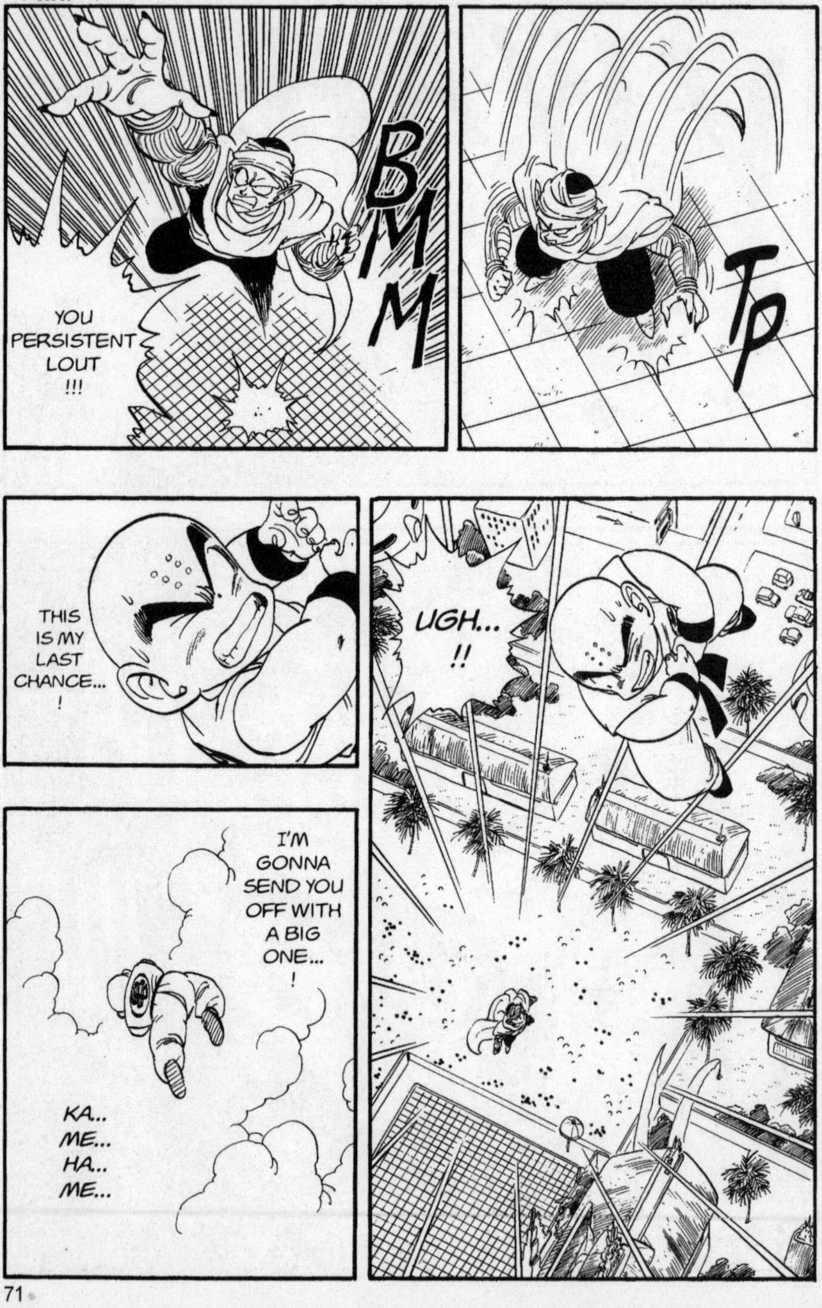

TP
BMM
YOU PERSISTENT LOUT !!!
UGH... !!
THIS IS MY LAST CHANCE... !
I'M GONNA SEND YOU OFF WITH A BIG ONE... !
KA... ME... HA... ME...

READ THIS WAY

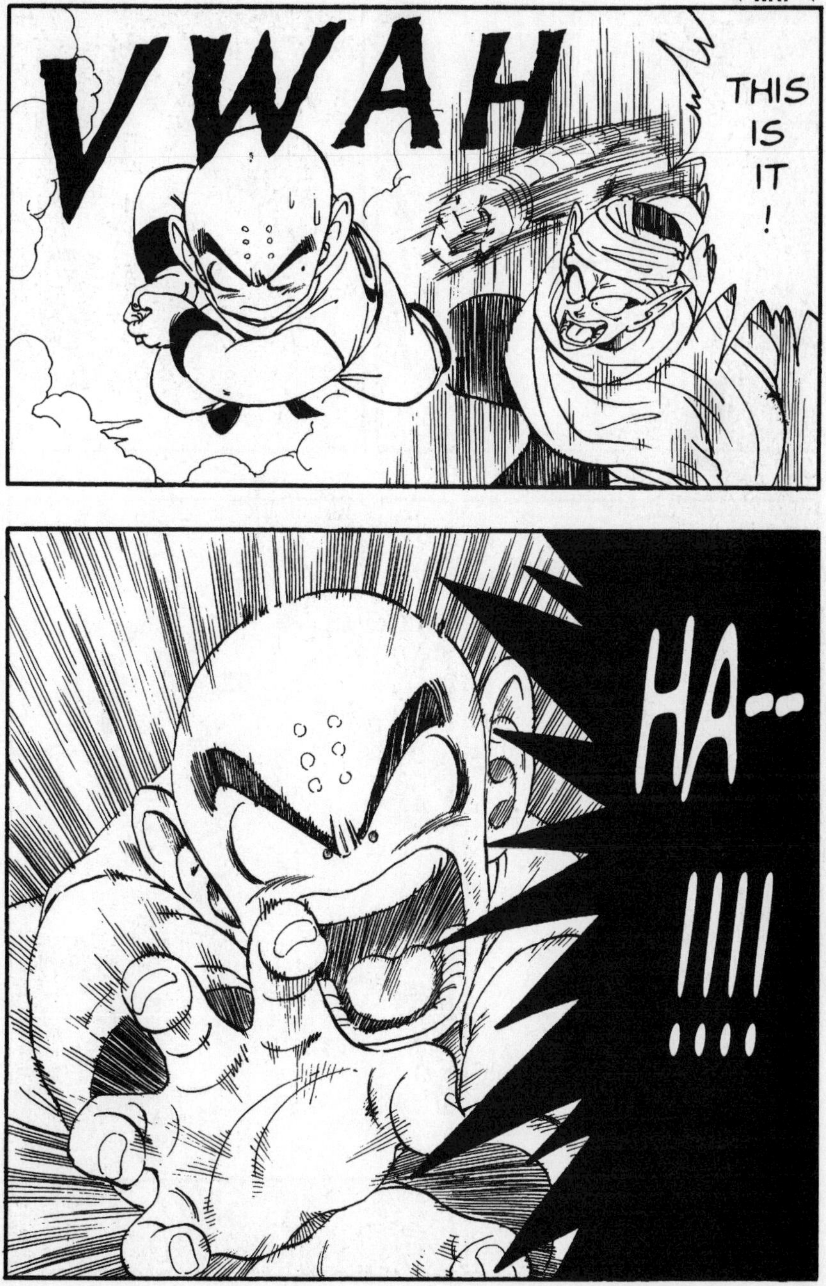
THIS IS IT!
VWAH
HA--!!!!!....

READ THIS WAY

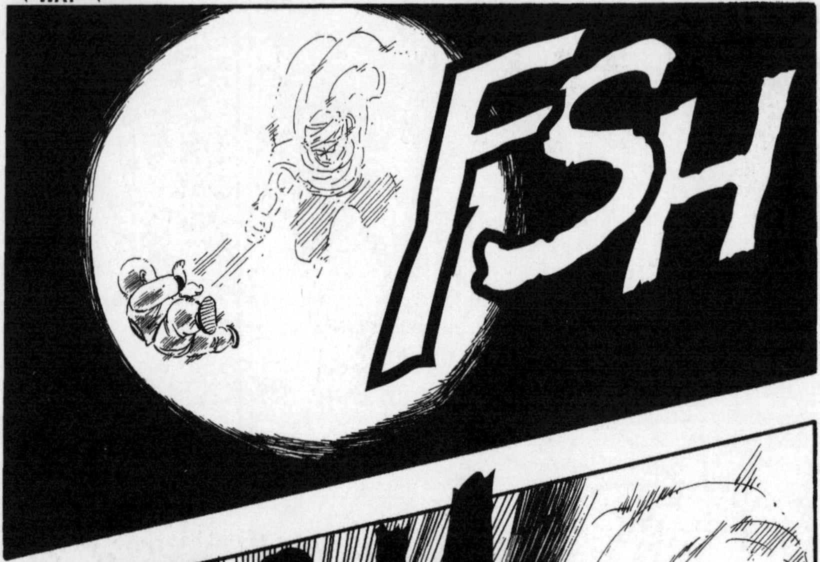
FSH

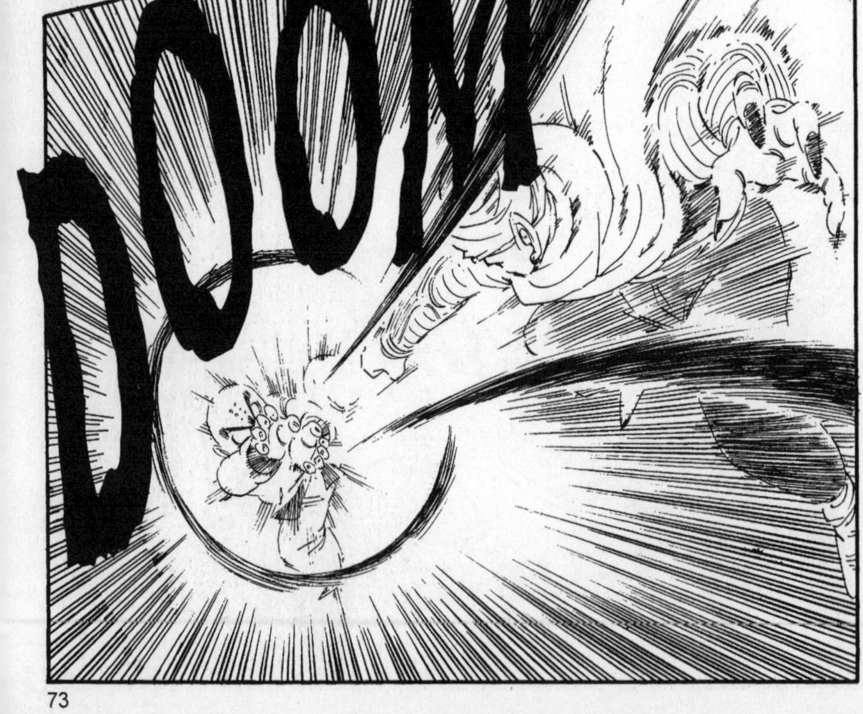
DOOM

READ THIS WAY

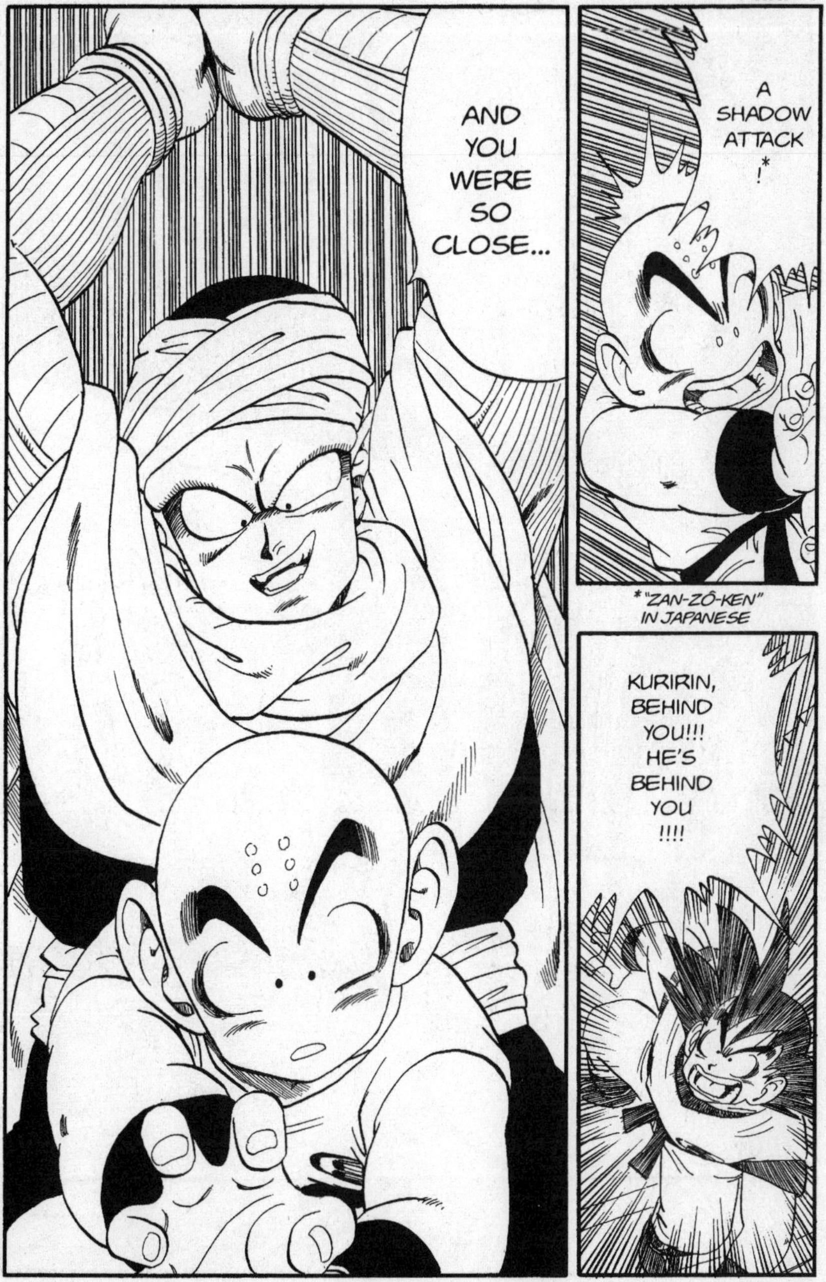
A SHADOW ATTACK !*
*"ZAN-ZÔ-KEN" IN JAPANESE
KURIRIN, BEHIND YOU!!! HE'S BEHIND YOU !!!!
AND YOU WERE SO CLOSE...

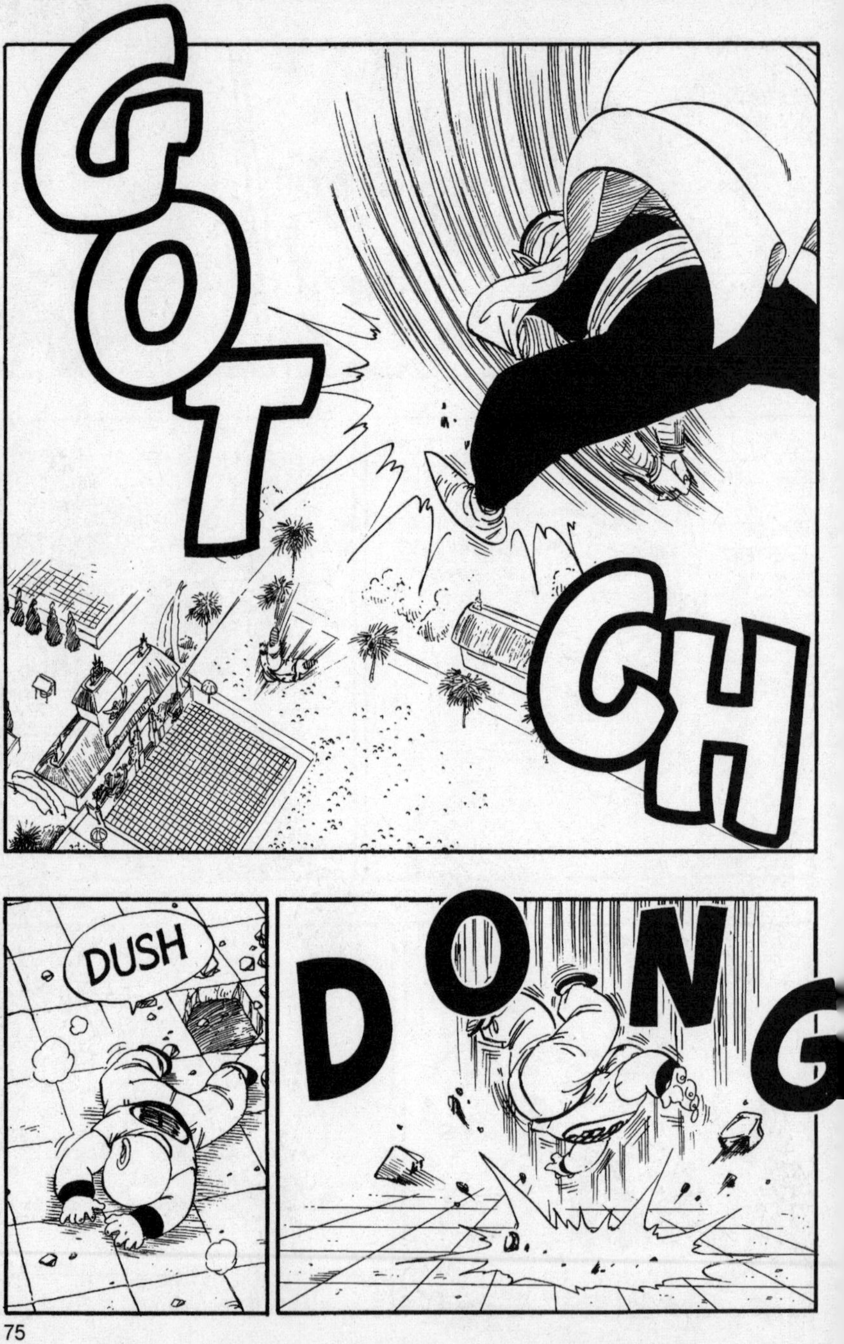
GOT
CH
DONG
DUSH

READ THIS WAY

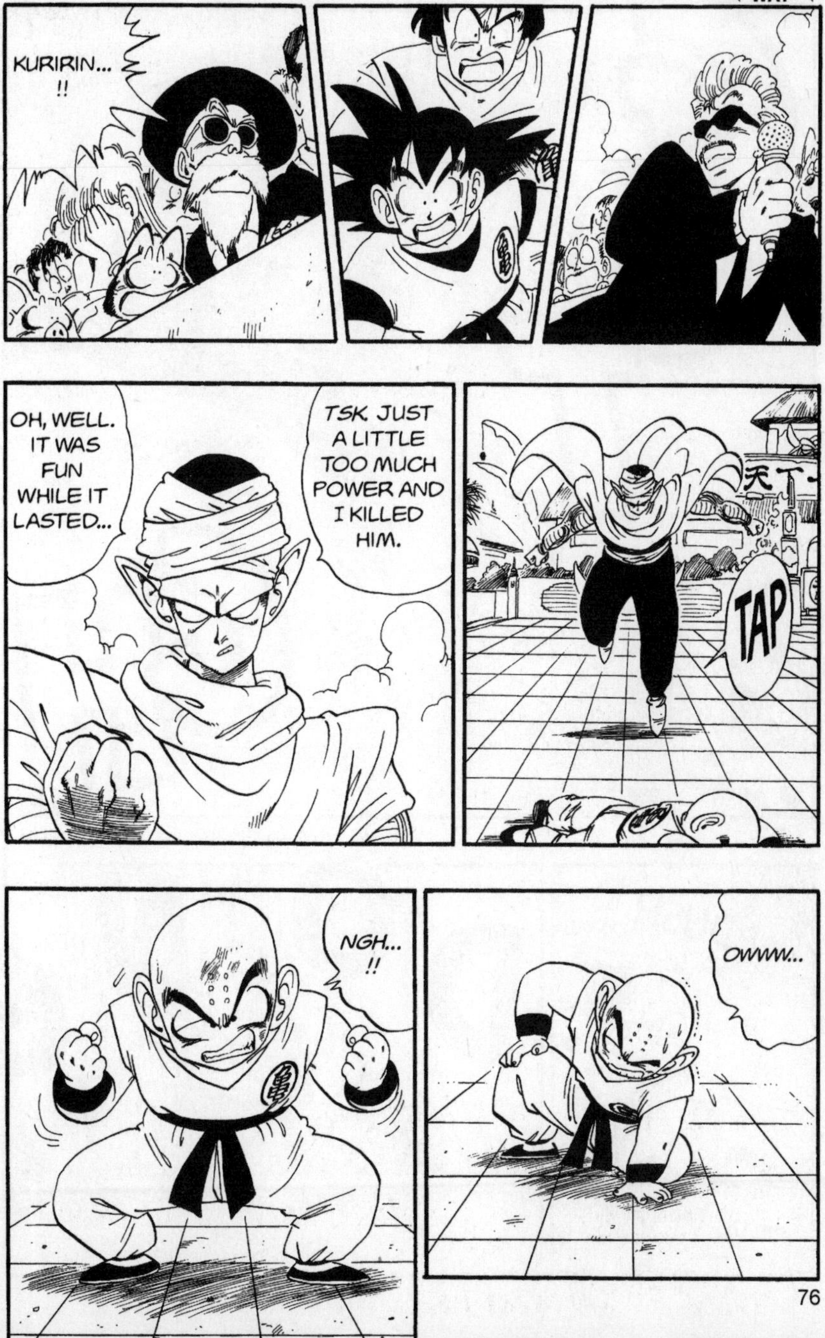
KURIRIN... !!
TAP
TSK. JUST A LITTLE TOO MUCH POWER AND I KILLED HIM.
OH, WELL. IT WAS FUN WHILE IT LASTED...
OWWW...
NGH... !!

READ THIS WAY

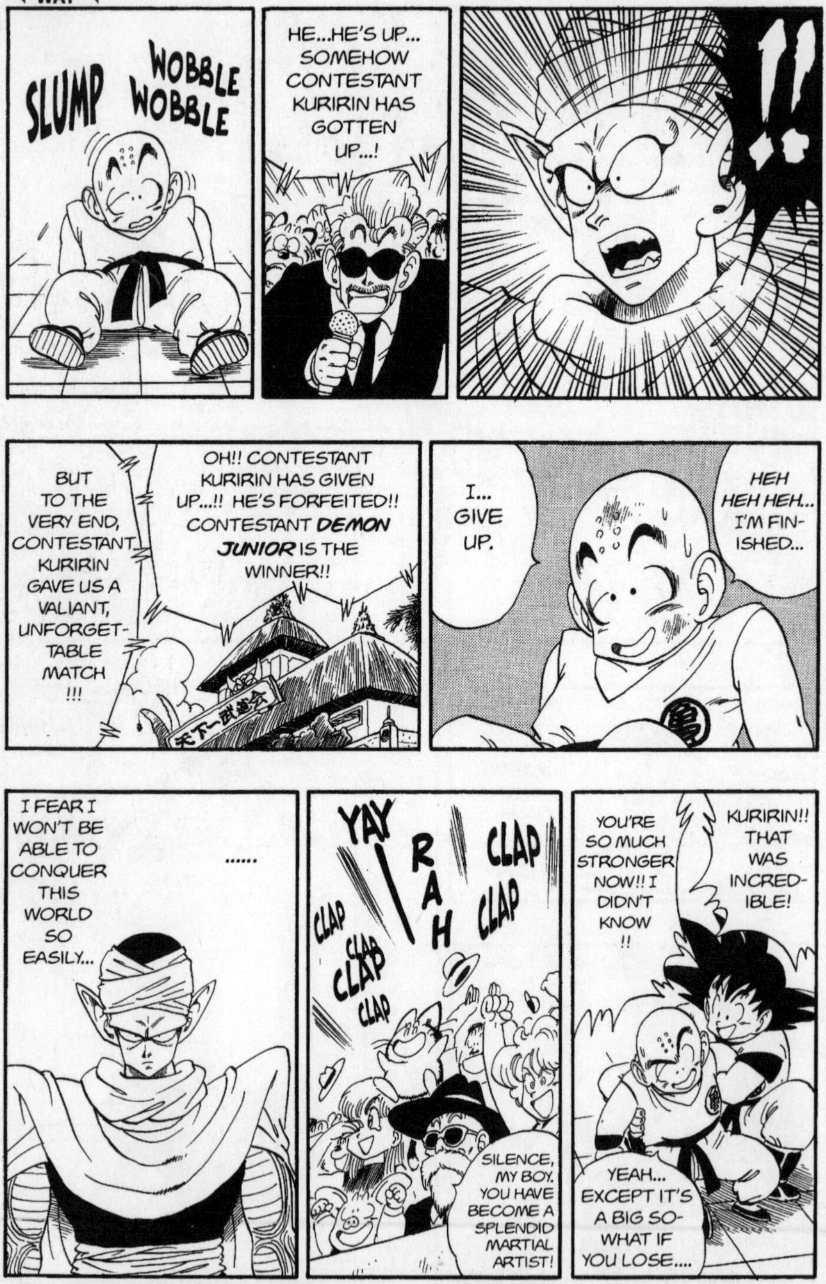
!!
HE...HE'S UP... SOMEHOW CONTESTANT KURIRIN HAS GOTTEN UP...!
WOBBLE WOBBLE
SLUMP
HEH HEH HEH... I'M FIN-ISHED...
I... GIVE UP.
OH!! CONTESTANT KURIRIN HAS GIVEN UP...!! HE'S FORFEITED!! CONTESTANT **DEMON JUNIOR** IS THE WINNER!!
BUT TO THE VERY END, CONTESTANT KURIRIN GAVE US A VALIANT, UNFORGET-TABLE MATCH !!!
KURIRIN!! THAT WAS INCRED-IBLE!
YOU'RE SO MUCH STRONGER NOW!! I DIDN'T KNOW !!
YEAH... EXCEPT IT'S A BIG SO-WHAT IF YOU LOSE....
CLAP
CLAP
RAH
YAY
CLAP
CLAP
CLAP
CLAP
SILENCE, MY BOY. YOU HAVE BECOME A SPLENDID MARTIAL ARTIST!
......
I FEAR I WON'T BE ABLE TO CONQUER THIS WORLD SO EASILY...

NEXT: Yamcha vs....Who?

Tale 174 · Yamcha vs. Shen

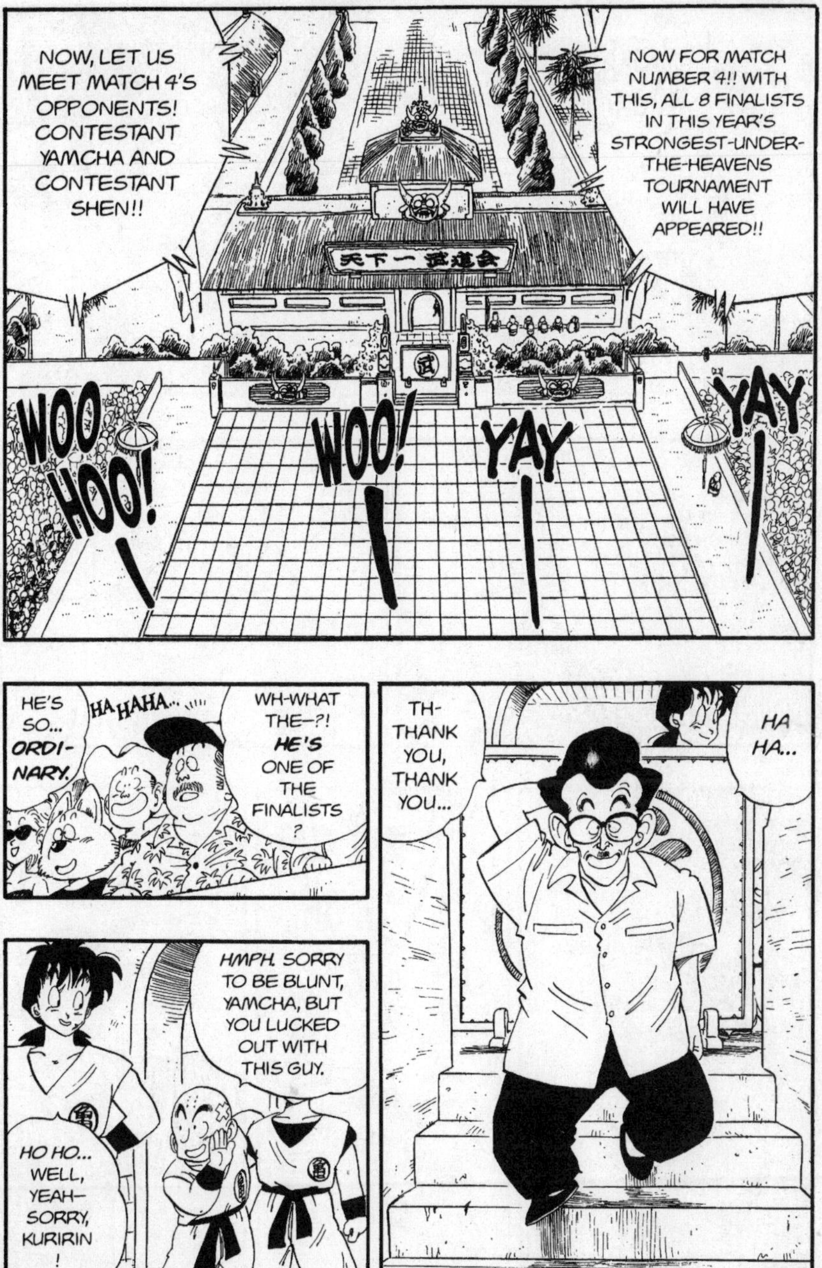

NOW FOR MATCH NUMBER 4!! WITH THIS, ALL 8 FINALISTS IN THIS YEAR'S STRONGEST-UNDER-THE-HEAVENS TOURNAMENT WILL HAVE APPEARED!!
NOW, LET US MEET MATCH 4'S OPPONENTS! CONTESTANT YAMCHA AND CONTESTANT SHEN!!
天下一武道会
YAY!
YAY!
WOO!
WOO HOO!
HA HA...
TH-THANK YOU, THANK YOU...
WH-WHAT THE–?! HE'S ONE OF THE FINALISTS?
HA HAHA...
HE'S SO... ORDINARY.
HMPH. SORRY TO BE BLUNT, YAMCHA, BUT YOU LUCKED OUT WITH THIS GUY.
HO HO... WELL, YEAH–SORRY, KURIRIN!

READ THIS WAY

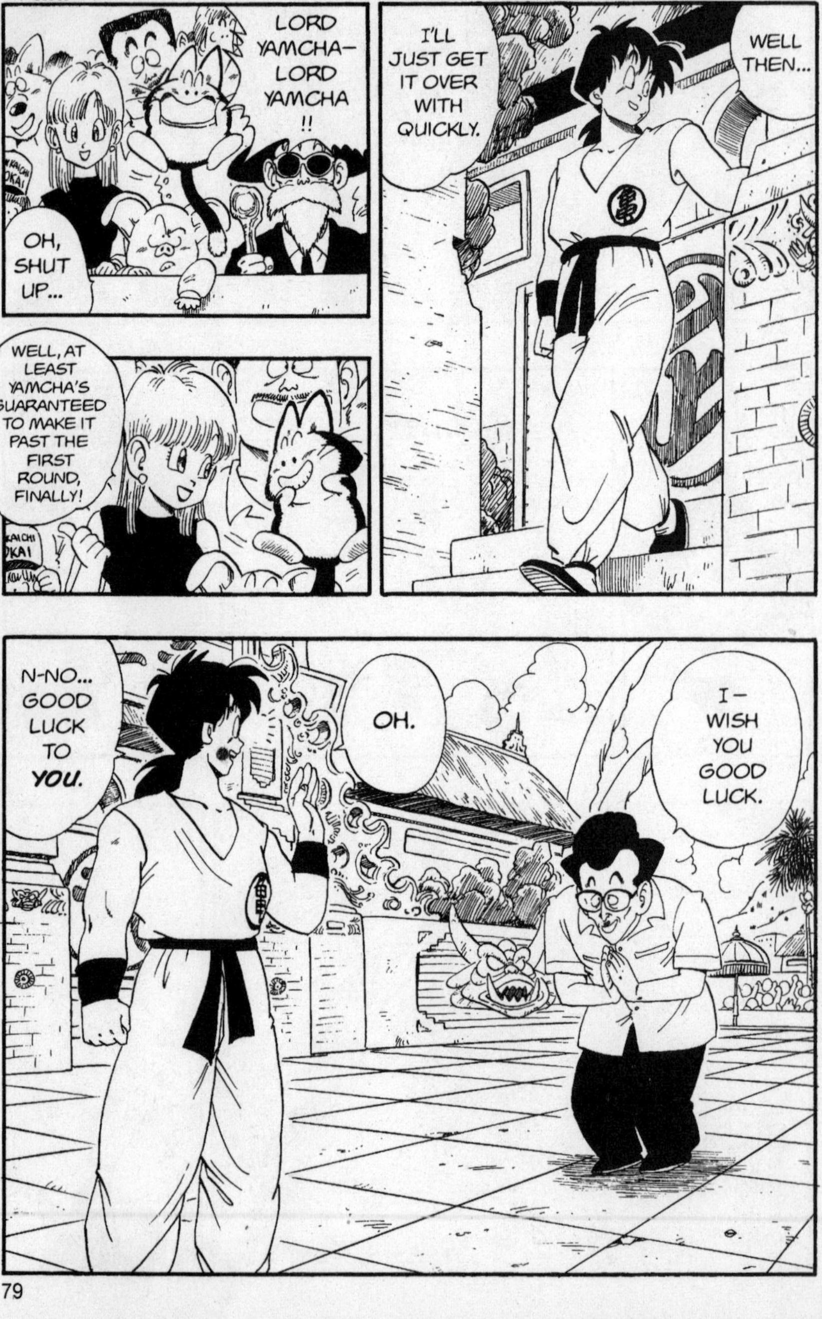
WELL THEN...
I'LL JUST GET IT OVER WITH QUICKLY.
LORD YAMCHA— LORD YAMCHA !!
OH, SHUT UP...
WELL, AT LEAST YAMCHA'S GUARANTEED TO MAKE IT PAST THE FIRST ROUND, FINALLY!
I— WISH YOU GOOD LUCK.
OH.
N-NO... GOOD LUCK TO ***YOU.***

READ THIS WAY

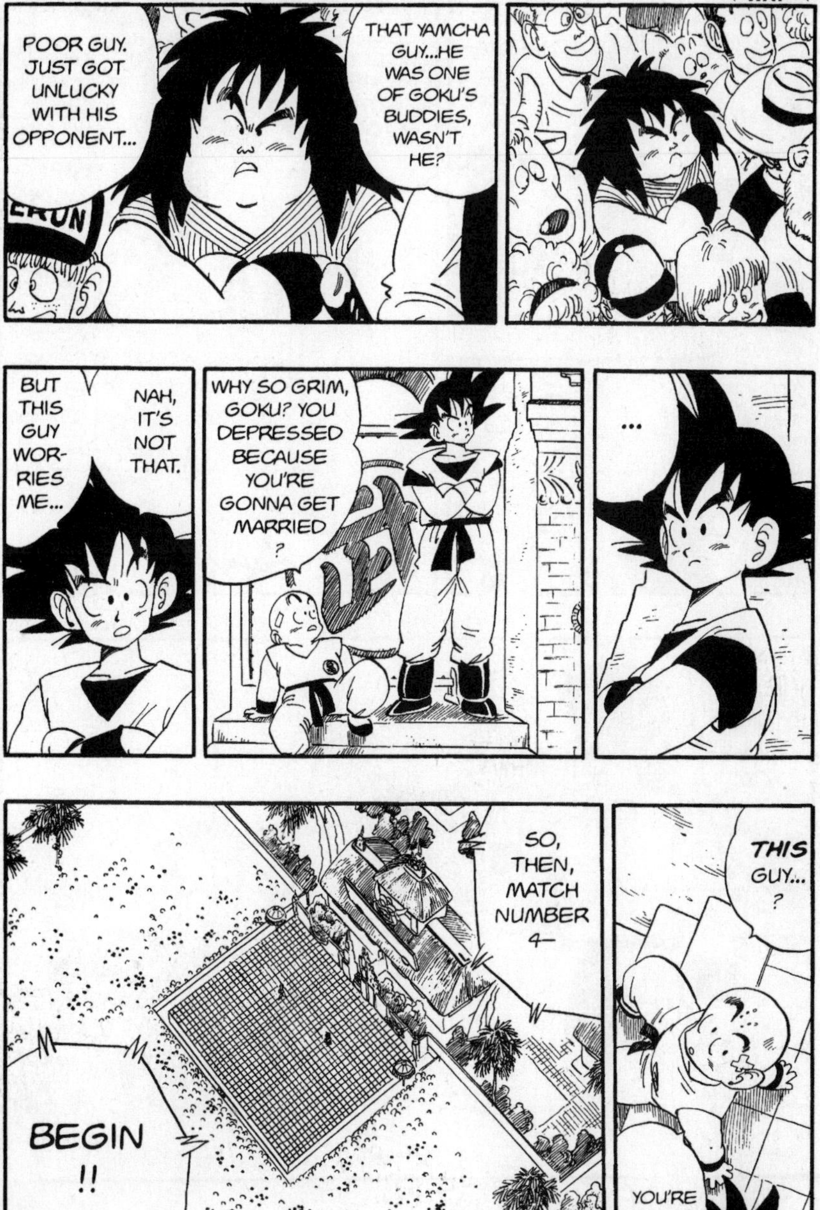
THAT YAMCHA GUY...HE WAS ONE OF GOKU'S BUDDIES, WASN'T HE?
POOR GUY. JUST GOT UNLUCKY WITH HIS OPPONENT...
...
WHY SO GRIM, GOKU? YOU DEPRESSED BECAUSE YOU'RE GONNA GET MARRIED?
NAH, IT'S NOT THAT.
BUT THIS GUY WORRIES ME...
THIS GUY...?
YOU'RE KIDDING...
SO, THEN, MATCH NUMBER 4—
BEGIN!!

READ THIS WAY

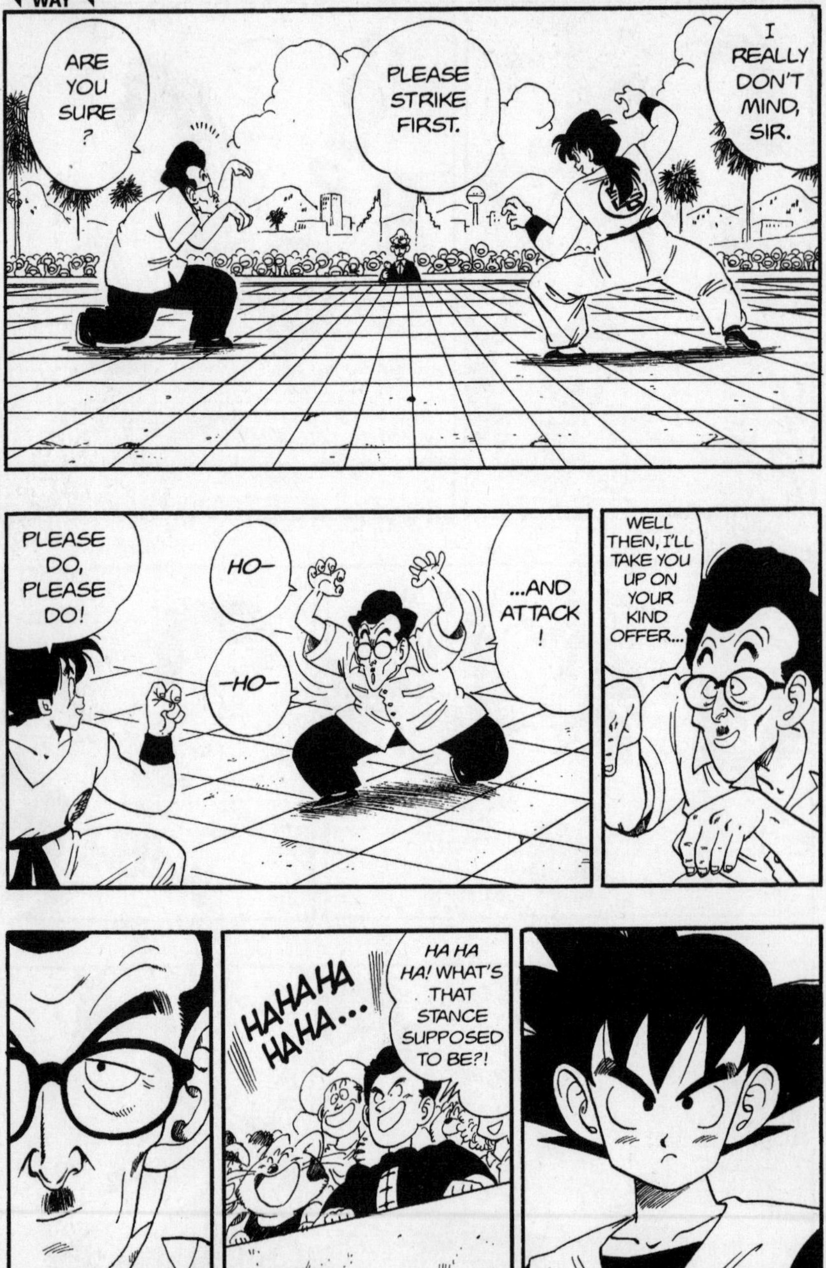
I REALLY DON'T MIND, SIR.
PLEASE STRIKE FIRST.
ARE YOU SURE?
WELL THEN, I'LL TAKE YOU UP ON YOUR KIND OFFER...
...AND ATTACK!
HO-
-HO-
PLEASE DO, PLEASE DO!
HA HA HA! WHAT'S THAT STANCE SUPPOSED TO BE?!
HAHAHA HAHA...

READ THIS WAY

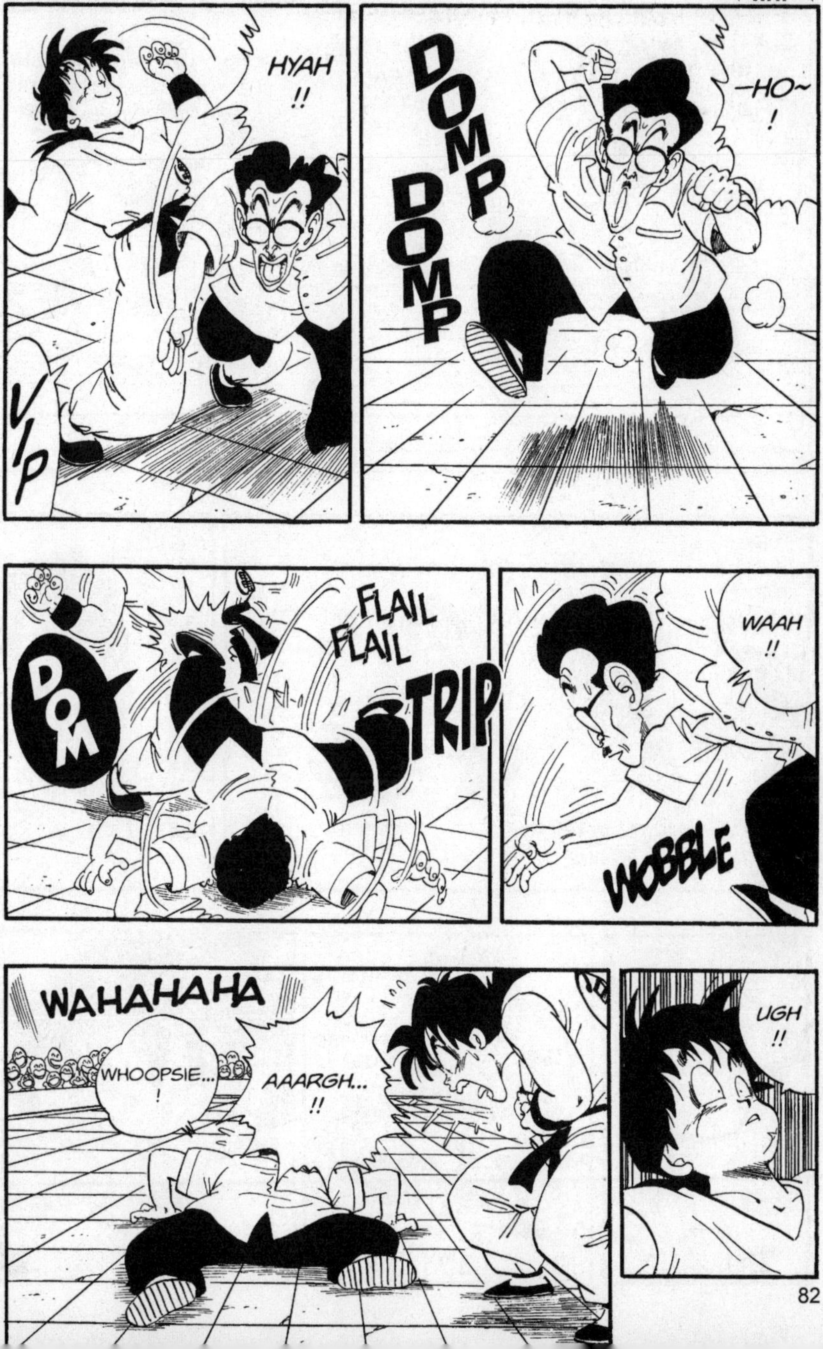
-HO~ !
DOMP DOMP
DOMP DOMP
HYAH !!
VIP
WAAH !!
WOBBLE
FLAIL FLAIL
TRIP
DOM
UGH !!
WAHAHAHA
AAARGH... !!
WHOOPSIE... !

READ THIS WAY

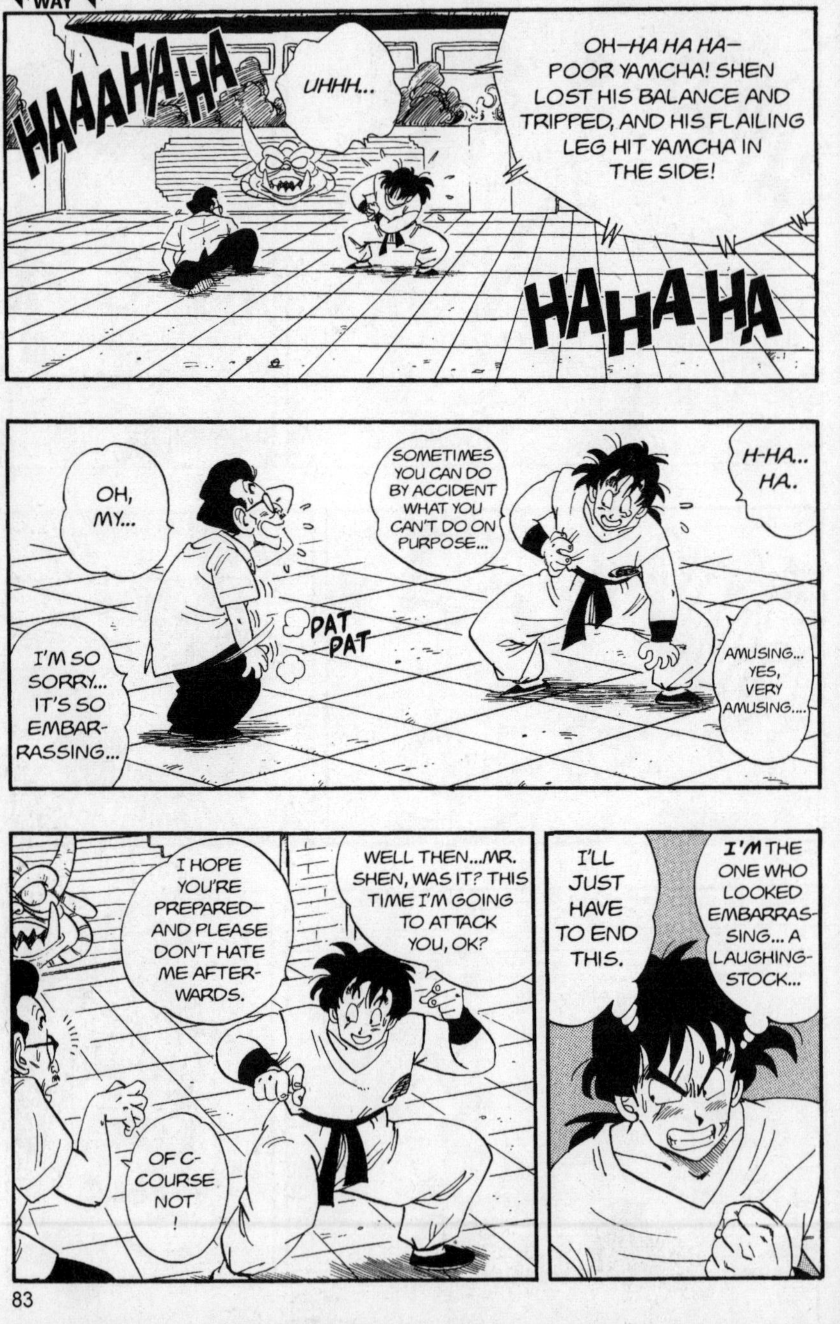
OH—HA HA HA— POOR YAMCHA! SHEN LOST HIS BALANCE AND TRIPPED, AND HIS FLAILING LEG HIT YAMCHA IN THE SIDE!
UHHH...
HAAAHAHA
HAHA HA
H-HA.. HA..
SOMETIMES YOU CAN DO BY ACCIDENT WHAT YOU CAN'T DO ON PURPOSE...
OH, MY...
AMUSING... YES, VERY AMUSING....
PAT PAT
I'M SO SORRY... IT'S SO EMBAR-RASSING...
I'M THE ONE WHO LOOKED EMBARRAS-SING... A LAUGHING-STOCK...
I'LL JUST HAVE TO END THIS.
WELL THEN...MR. SHEN, WAS IT? THIS TIME I'M GOING TO ATTACK YOU, OK?
I HOPE YOU'RE PREPARED-AND PLEASE DON'T HATE ME AFTER-WARDS.
OF C-COURSE NOT !

READ THIS WAY

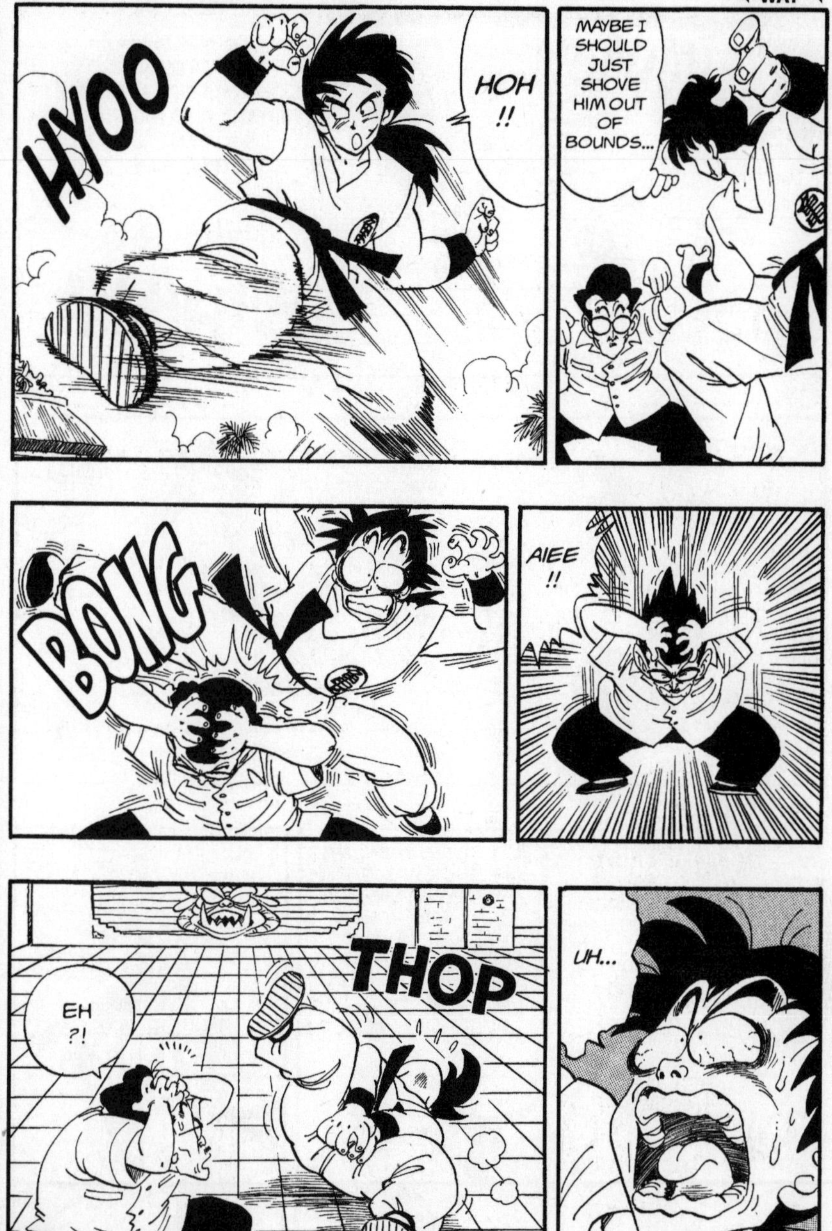
MAYBE I SHOULD JUST SHOVE HIM OUT OF BOUNDS...
HOH !!
HYOO
AIEE !!
BONG
UH...
THOP
EH ?!

READ THIS WAY

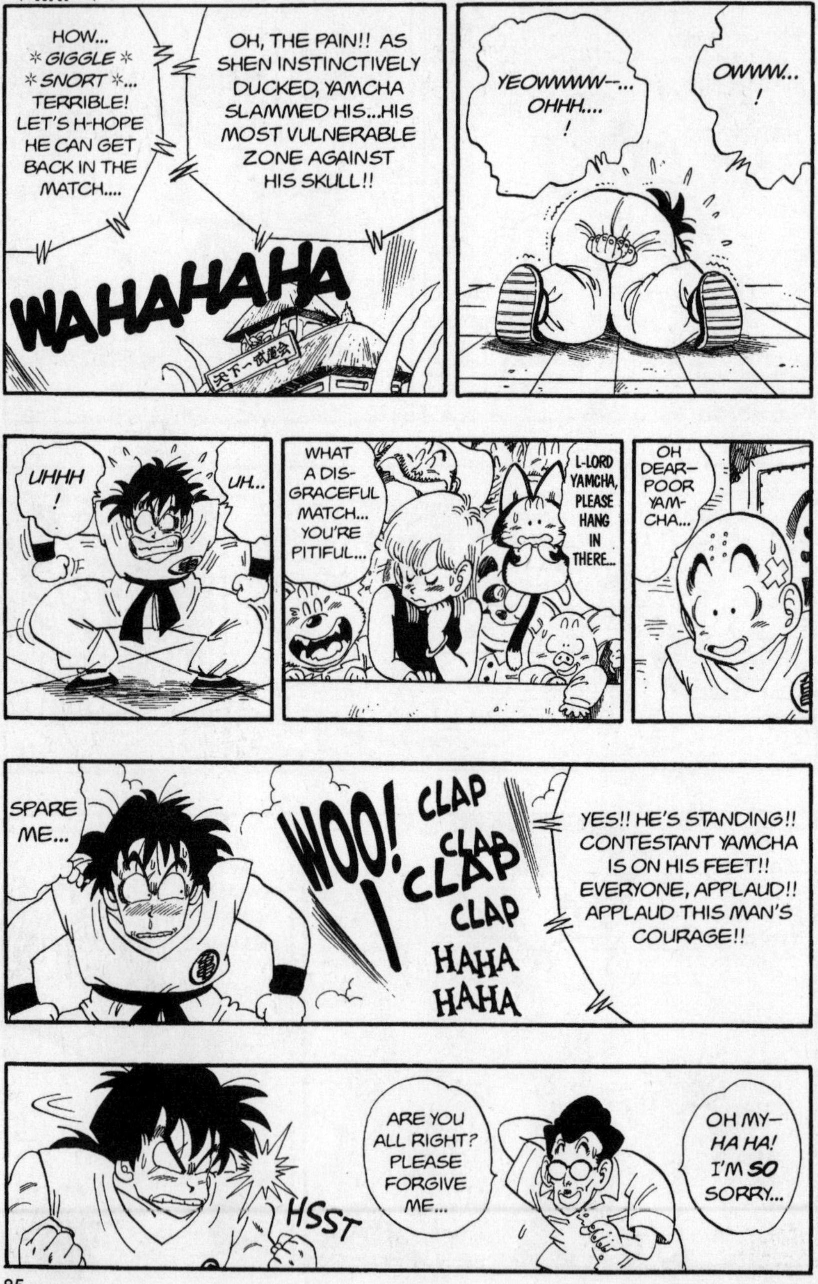
OWWW... !
YEOWWWW--... OHHH.... !
OH, THE PAIN!! AS SHEN INSTINCTIVELY DUCKED, YAMCHA SLAMMED HIS...HIS MOST VULNERABLE ZONE AGAINST HIS SKULL!!
HOW... *GIGGLE* *SNORT*... TERRIBLE! LET'S H-HOPE HE CAN GET BACK IN THE MATCH....
WAHAHAHA
天下一武道会
OH DEAR— POOR YAMCHA...
L-LORD YAMCHA, PLEASE HANG IN THERE...
WHAT A DISGRACEFUL MATCH... YOU'RE PITIFUL...
UH...
UHHH !
YES!! HE'S STANDING!! CONTESTANT YAMCHA IS ON HIS FEET!! EVERYONE, APPLAUD!! APPLAUD THIS MAN'S COURAGE!!
CLAP CLAP CLAP CLAP
WOO!!
HAHA HAHA
SPARE ME...
OH MY— HA HA! I'M SO SORRY...
ARE YOU ALL RIGHT? PLEASE FORGIVE ME...
HSST

READ THIS WAY

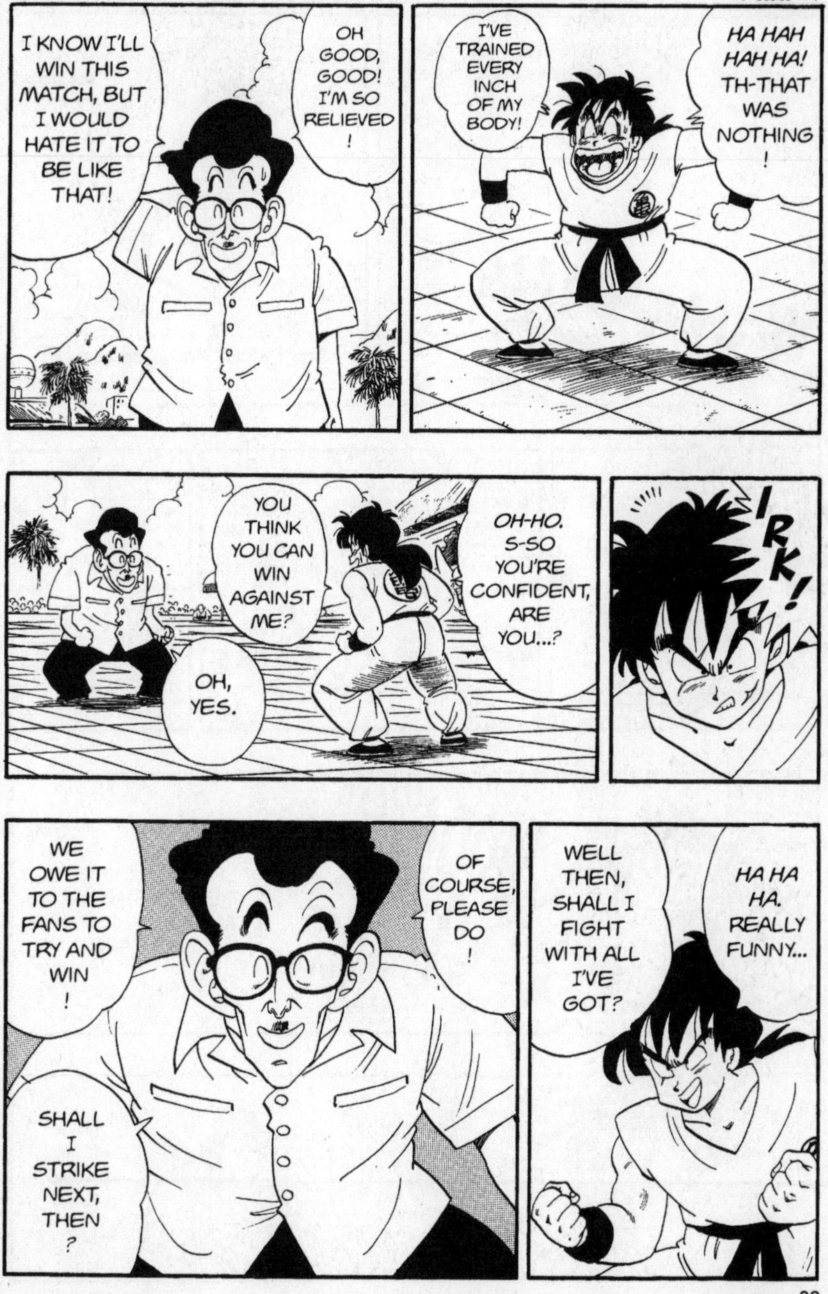
HA HAH HAH HA! TH-THAT WAS NOTHING!
I'VE TRAINED EVERY INCH OF MY BODY!
OH GOOD, GOOD! I'M SO RELIEVED!
I KNOW I'LL WIN THIS MATCH, BUT I WOULD HATE IT TO BE LIKE THAT!
IRK!
OH-HO. S-SO YOU'RE CONFIDENT, ARE YOU...?
YOU THINK YOU CAN WIN AGAINST ME?
OH, YES.
HA HA HA. REALLY FUNNY...
WELL THEN, SHALL I FIGHT WITH ALL I'VE GOT?
OF COURSE, PLEASE DO!
WE OWE IT TO THE FANS TO TRY AND WIN!
SHALL I STRIKE NEXT, THEN?

READ THIS WAY

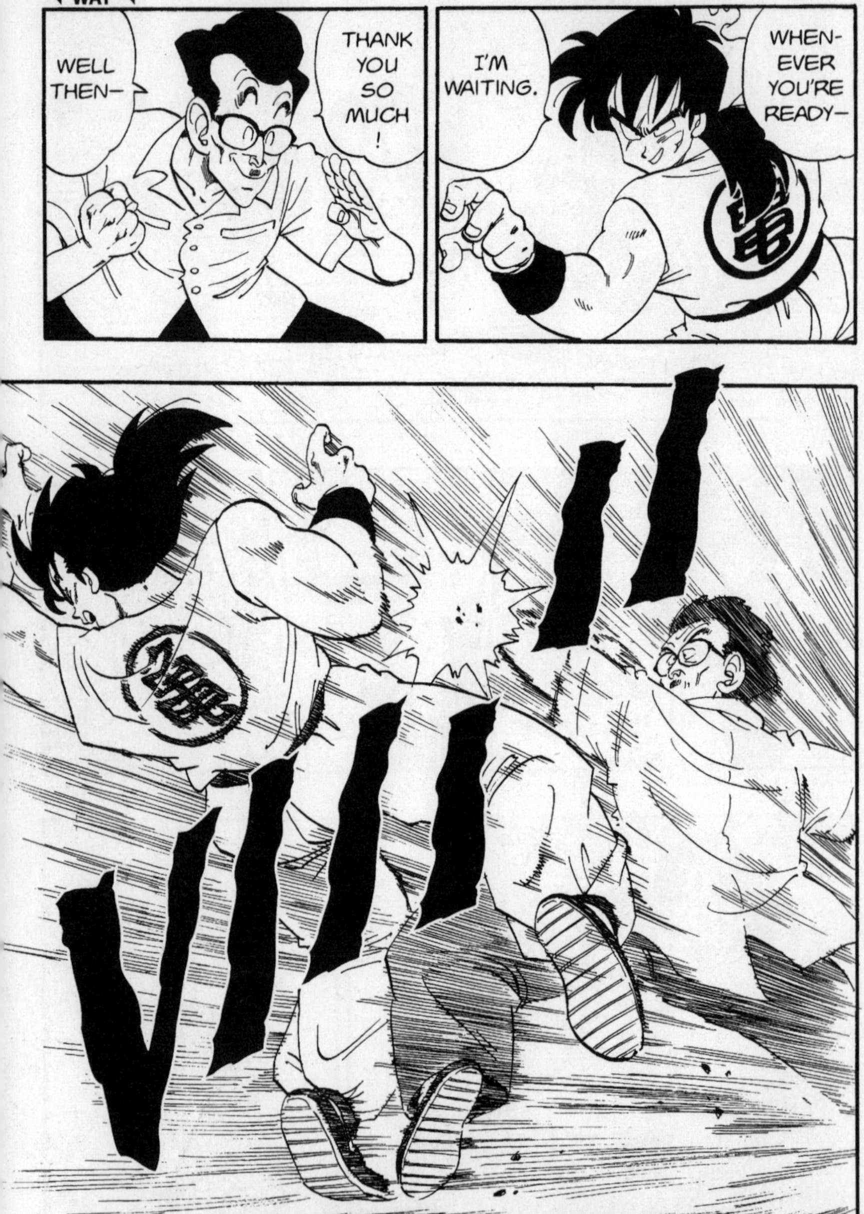

WHEN-EVER YOU'RE READY-
I'M WAITING.
THANK YOU SO MUCH!
WELL THEN-

READ THIS WAY

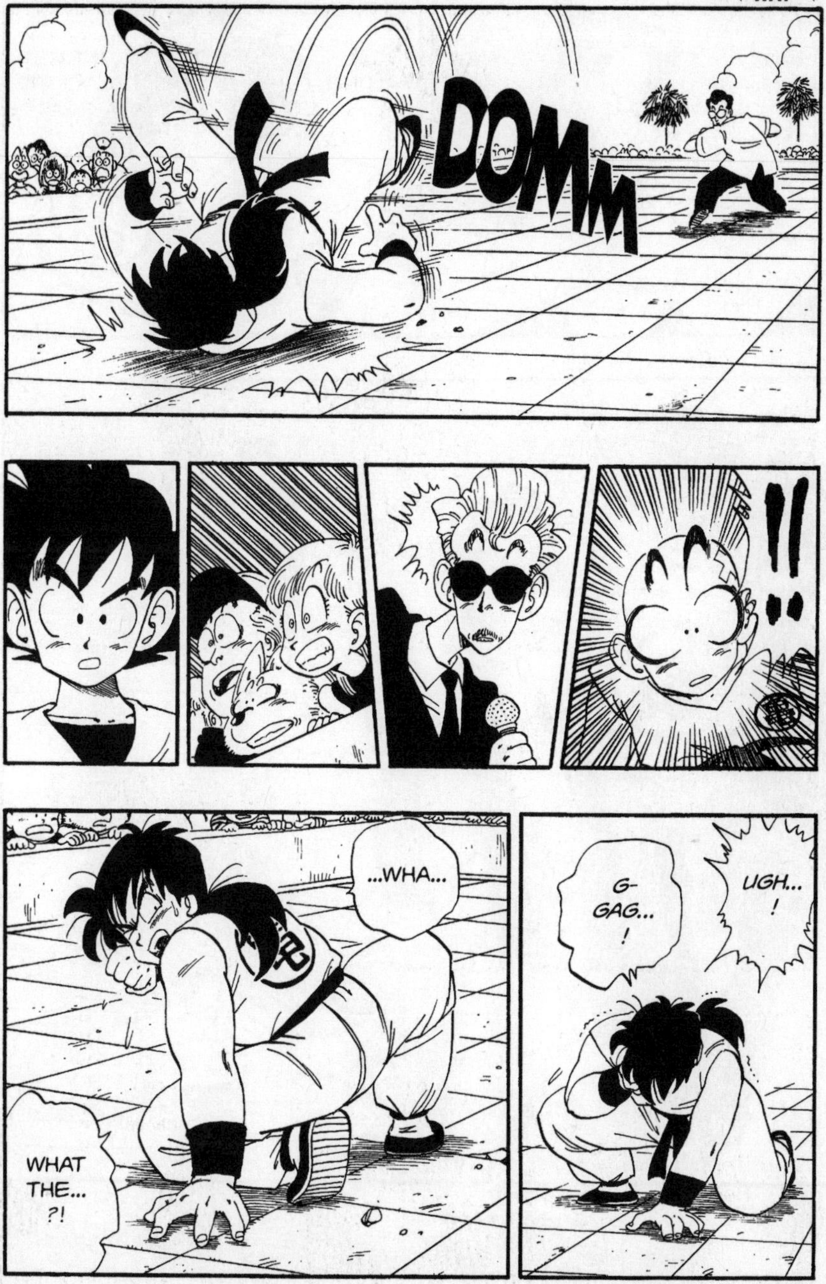
DOMM
!!
UGH... !
G- GAG... !
...WHA...
WHAT THE... ?!

READ THIS WAY

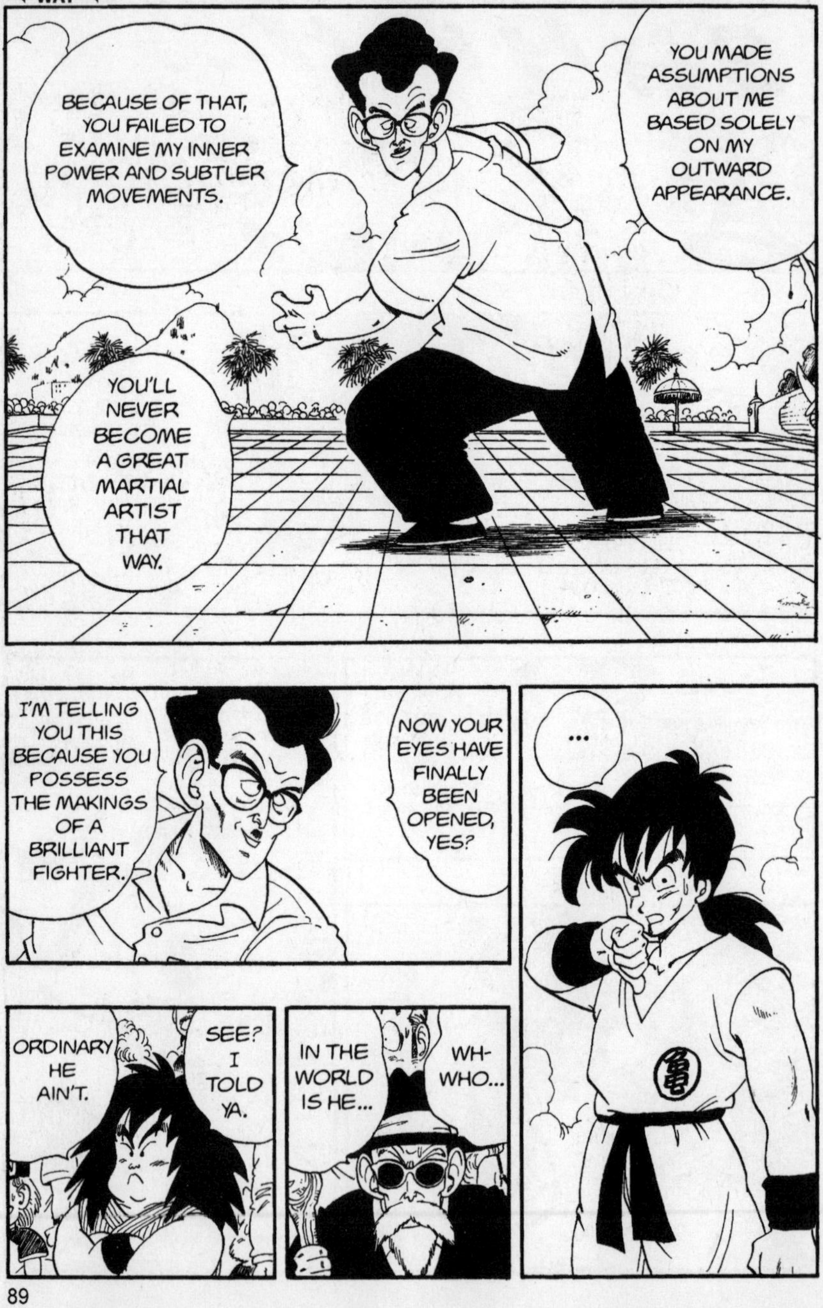
YOU MADE ASSUMPTIONS ABOUT ME BASED SOLELY ON MY OUTWARD APPEARANCE.
BECAUSE OF THAT, YOU FAILED TO EXAMINE MY INNER POWER AND SUBTLER MOVEMENTS.
YOU'LL NEVER BECOME A GREAT MARTIAL ARTIST THAT WAY.
...
NOW YOUR EYES HAVE FINALLY BEEN OPENED, YES?
I'M TELLING YOU THIS BECAUSE YOU POSSESS THE MAKINGS OF A BRILLIANT FIGHTER.
WH- WHO...
IN THE WORLD IS HE...
SEE? I TOLD YA.
ORDINARY HE AIN'T.

READ THIS WAY

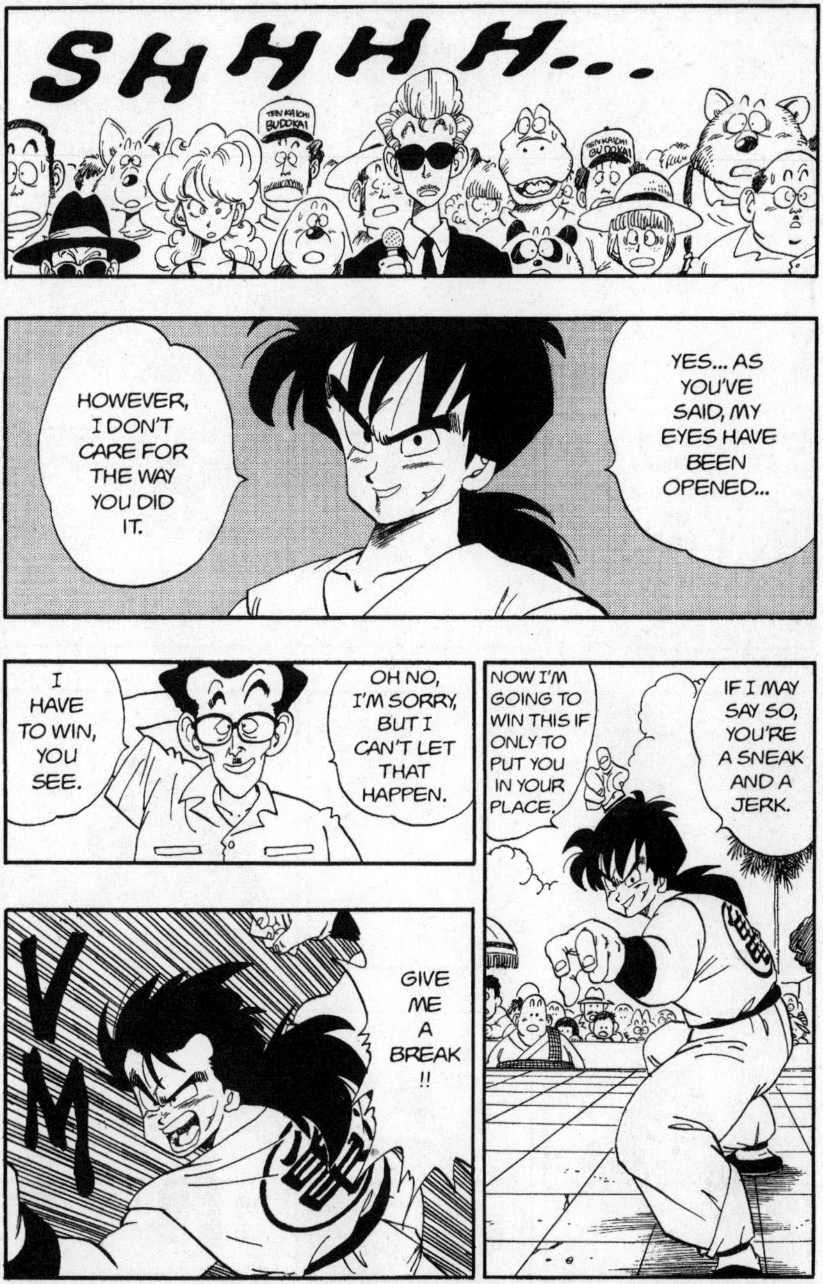
SHHHH...
TEN KAICHI BUDOKAI
TEN KAICHI BUDOKAI
YES... AS YOU'VE SAID, MY EYES HAVE BEEN OPENED...
HOWEVER, I DON'T CARE FOR THE WAY YOU DID IT.
IF I MAY SAY SO, YOU'RE A SNEAK AND A JERK.
NOW I'M GOING TO WIN THIS IF ONLY TO PUT YOU IN YOUR PLACE.
OH NO, I'M SORRY, BUT I CAN'T LET THAT HAPPEN.
I HAVE TO WIN, YOU SEE.
GIVE ME A BREAK !!
VM

READ THIS WAY

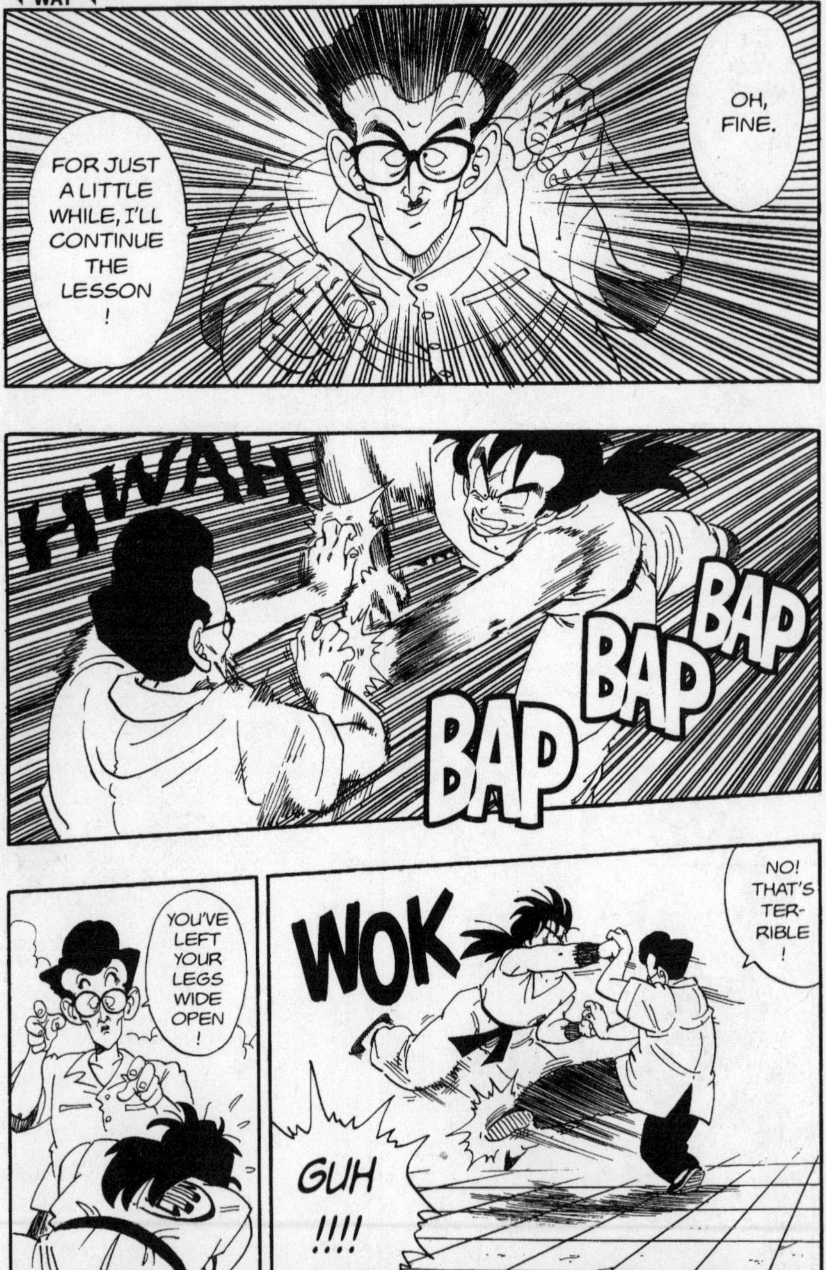

OH, FINE.
FOR JUST A LITTLE WHILE, I'LL CONTINUE THE LESSON!
HWAH
BAP
BAP
BAP
NO! THAT'S TER-RIBLE!
WOK
GUH !!!!
YOU'VE LEFT YOUR LEGS WIDE OPEN!

NEXT: Who Is Shen?

Tale 175 • "Shen"

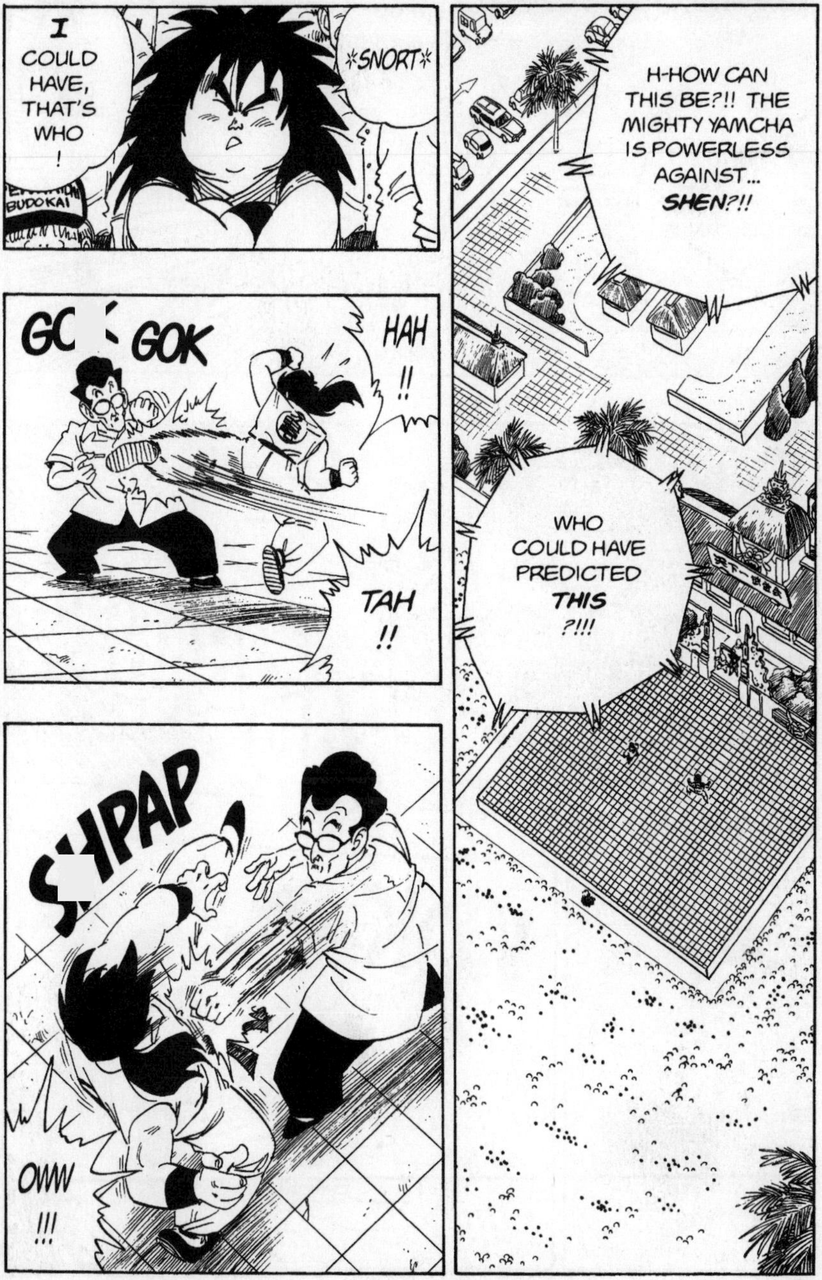

H-HOW CAN THIS BE?!! THE MIGHTY YAMCHA IS POWERLESS AGAINST... **SHEN**?!!
WHO COULD HAVE PREDICTED **THIS** ?!!!
SNORT
I COULD HAVE, THAT'S WHO !
BUDOKAI
HAH !!
GOK
TAH !!
OWW !!!

READ THIS WAY

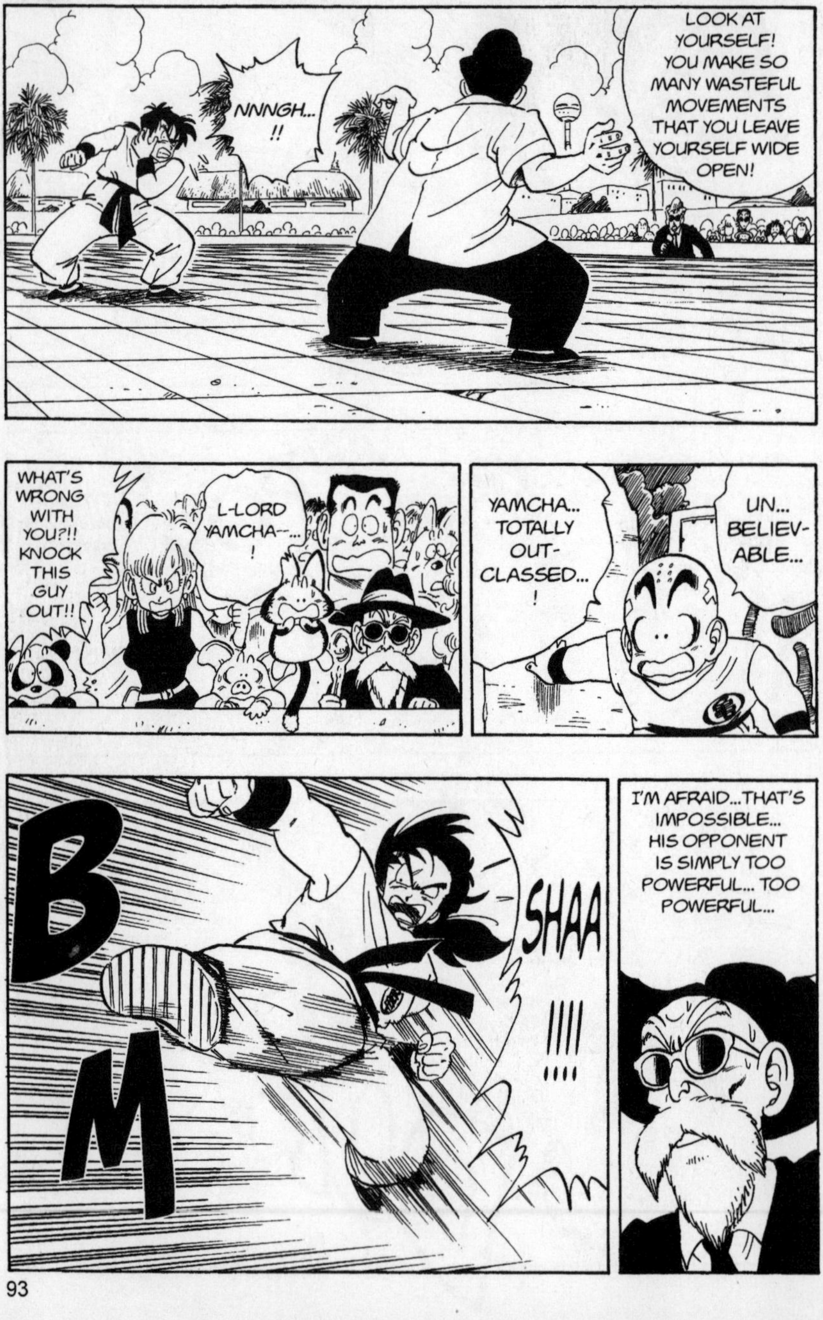

LOOK AT YOURSELF! YOU MAKE SO MANY WASTEFUL MOVEMENTS THAT YOU LEAVE YOURSELF WIDE OPEN!
NNNGH... !!
UN... BELIEV-ABLE...
YAMCHA... TOTALLY OUT-CLASSED... !
L-LORD YAMCHA--... !
WHAT'S WRONG WITH YOU?!! KNOCK THIS GUY OUT!!
I'M AFRAID...THAT'S IMPOSSIBLE... HIS OPPONENT IS SIMPLY TOO POWERFUL... TOO POWERFUL...
SHAA !!!!
BM

READ THIS WAY

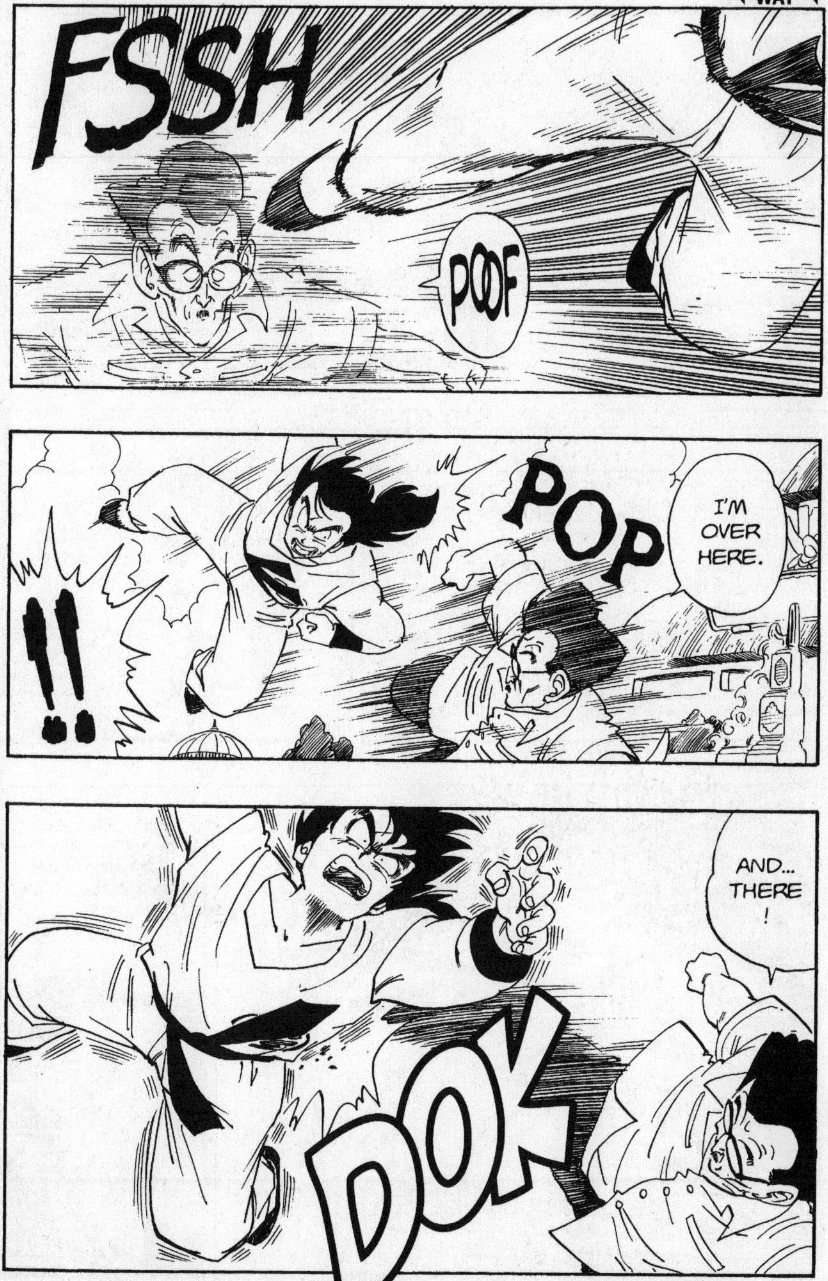

FSSH
POOF
I'M OVER HERE.
POP
!!
AND... THERE!
DOK

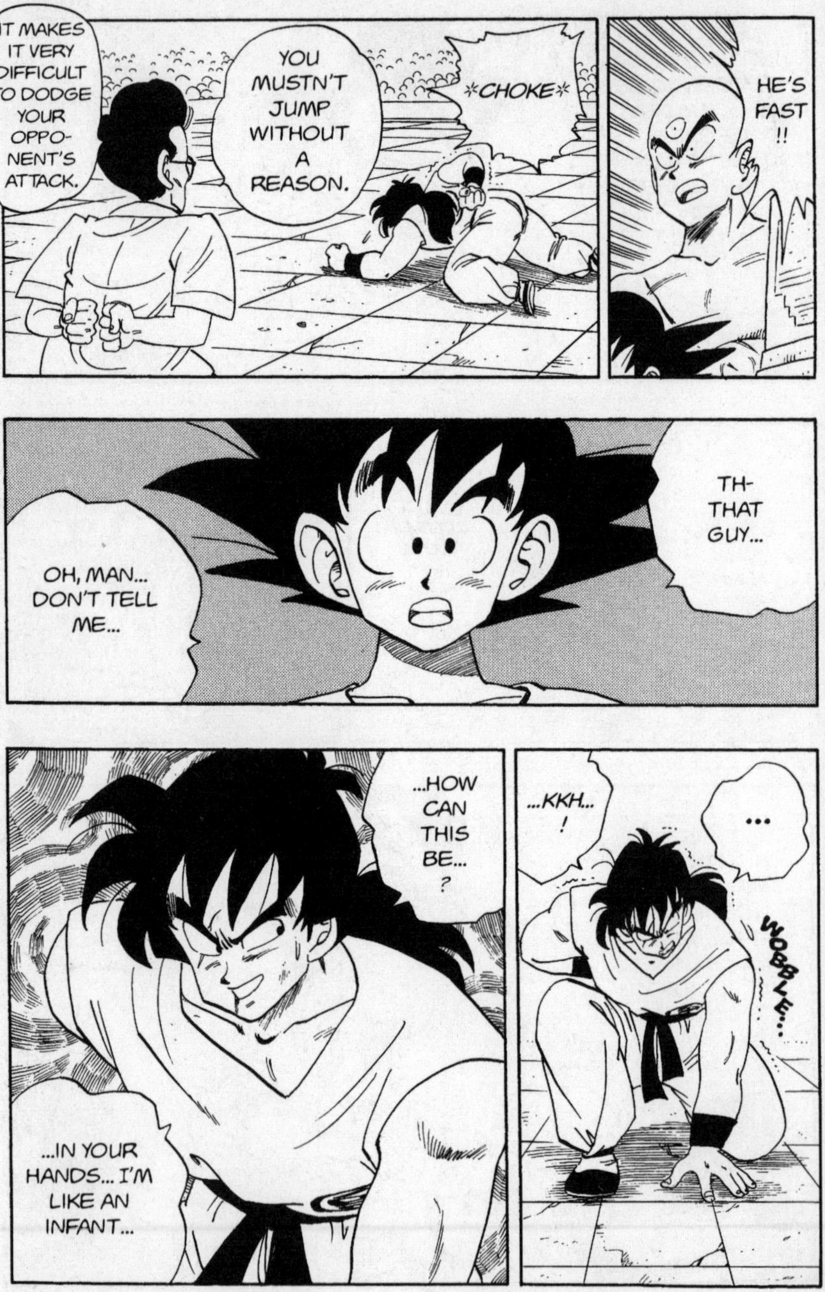
HE'S FAST !!
CHOKE
YOU MUSTN'T JUMP WITHOUT A REASON.
IT MAKES IT VERY DIFFICULT TO DODGE YOUR OPPO-NENT'S ATTACK.
TH- THAT GUY...
OH, MAN... DON'T TELL ME...
...
...KKH... !
WOBBLE...
...HOW CAN THIS BE... ?
...IN YOUR HANDS... I'M LIKE AN INFANT...

READ THIS WAY

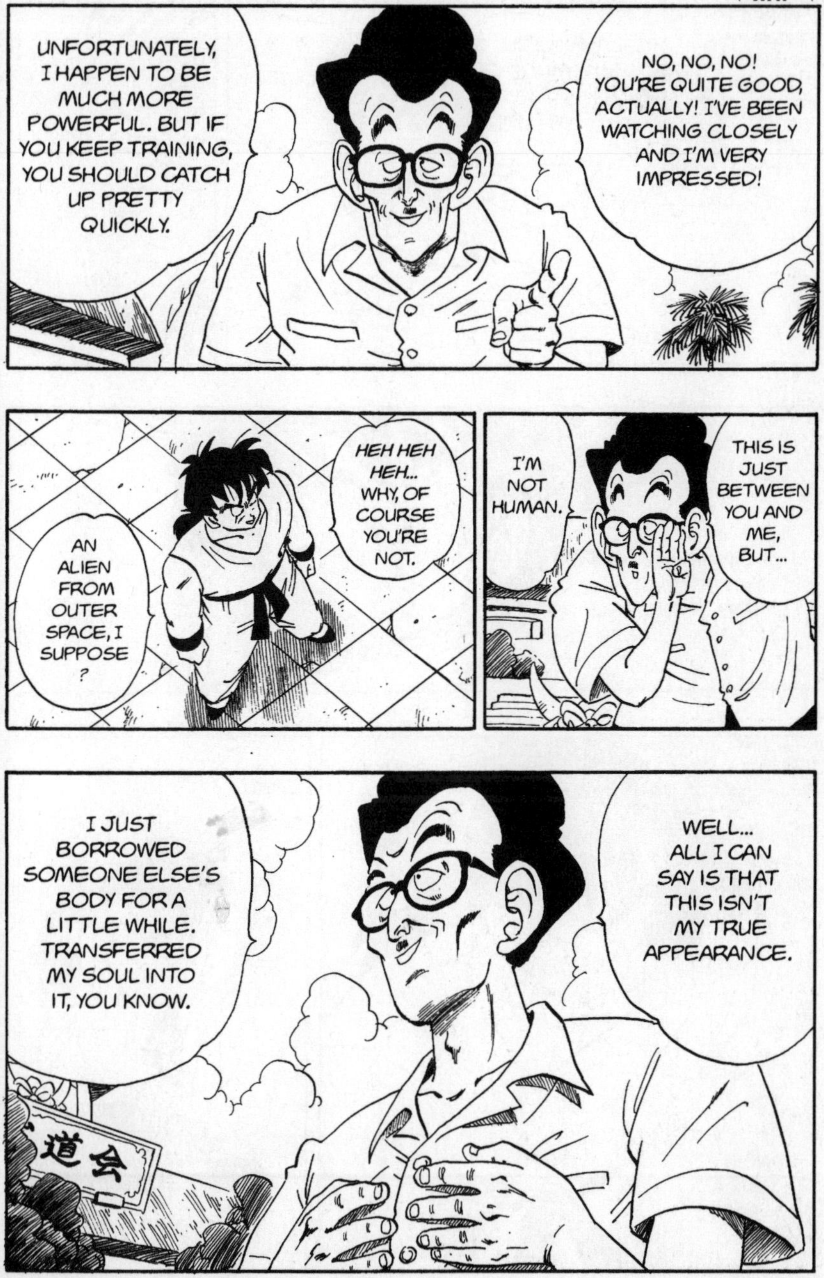

NO, NO, NO! YOU'RE QUITE GOOD, ACTUALLY! I'VE BEEN WATCHING CLOSELY AND I'M VERY IMPRESSED!
UNFORTUNATELY, I HAPPEN TO BE MUCH MORE POWERFUL. BUT IF YOU KEEP TRAINING, YOU SHOULD CATCH UP PRETTY QUICKLY.
THIS IS JUST BETWEEN YOU AND ME, BUT...
I'M NOT HUMAN.
HEH HEH HEH... WHY, OF COURSE YOU'RE NOT.
AN ALIEN FROM OUTER SPACE, I SUPPOSE?
WELL... ALL I CAN SAY IS THAT THIS ISN'T MY TRUE APPEARANCE.
I JUST BORROWED SOMEONE ELSE'S BODY FOR A LITTLE WHILE. TRANSFERRED MY SOUL INTO IT, YOU KNOW.
道会

READ THIS WAY

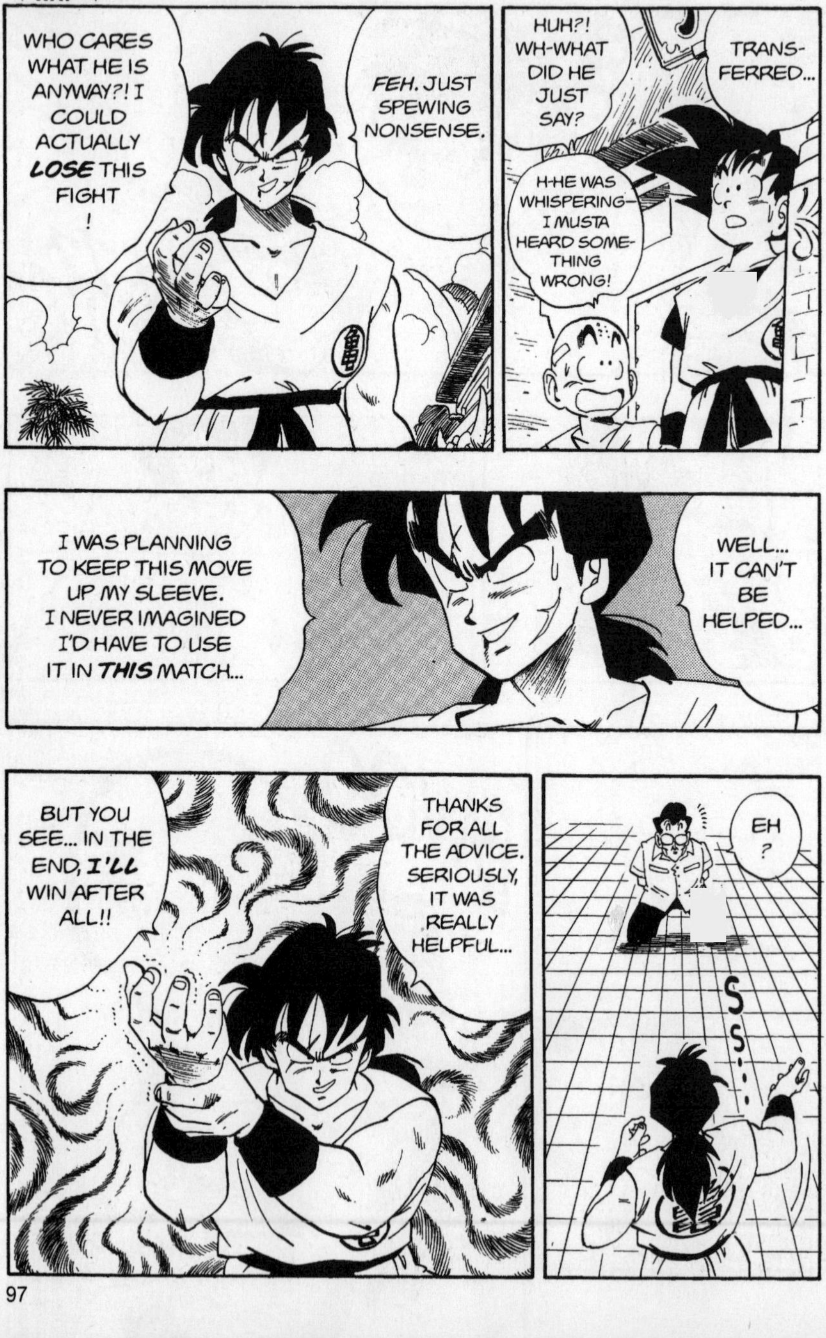
TRANS-FERRED...
HUH?! WH-WHAT DID HE JUST SAY?
H-HE WAS WHISPERING—I MUSTA HEARD SOME-THING WRONG!
FEH. JUST SPEWING NONSENSE.
WHO CARES WHAT HE IS ANYWAY?! I COULD ACTUALLY LOSE THIS FIGHT!
WELL... IT CAN'T BE HELPED...
I WAS PLANNING TO KEEP THIS MOVE UP MY SLEEVE. I NEVER IMAGINED I'D HAVE TO USE IT IN THIS MATCH...
EH?
SS...
THANKS FOR ALL THE ADVICE. SERIOUSLY, IT WAS REALLY HELPFUL...
BUT YOU SEE... IN THE END, I'LL WIN AFTER ALL!!

READ THIS WAY

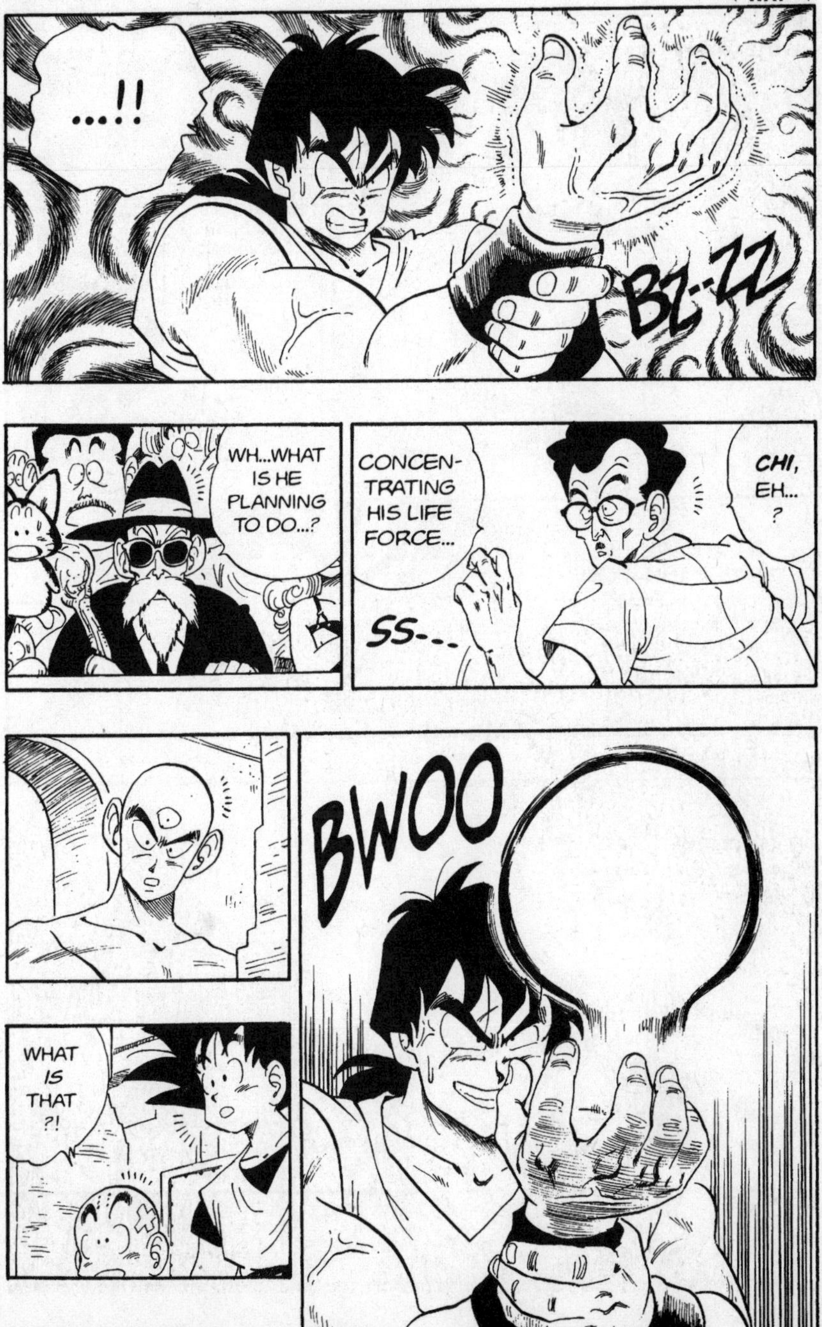
...!!
BZ-ZZ
CHI, EH...?
CONCEN-TRATING HIS LIFE FORCE...
SS---
WH...WHAT IS HE PLANNING TO DO...?
BWOO
WHAT IS THAT?!

READ THIS WAY

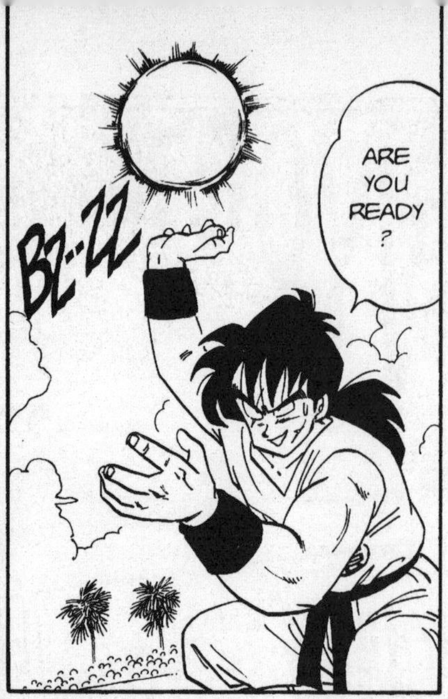
ARE YOU READY ?
BZ-ZZ

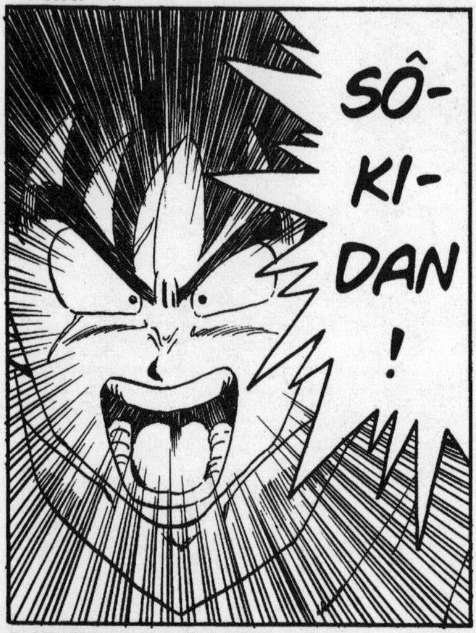
SÔ-KI-DAN !

• SPINNING CHI BULLET

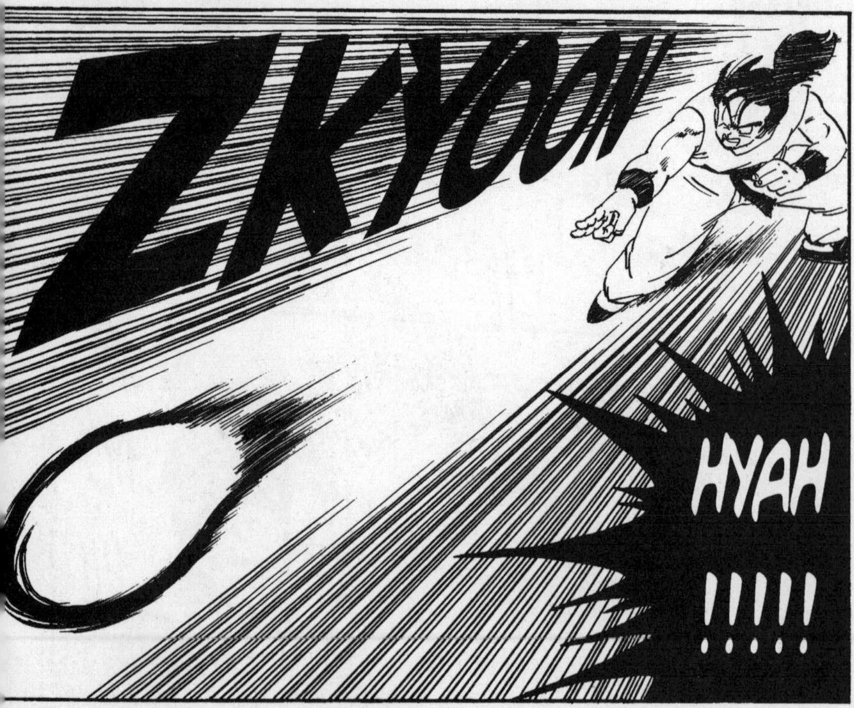
ZKYOON
HYAH !!!!!

READ THIS WAY

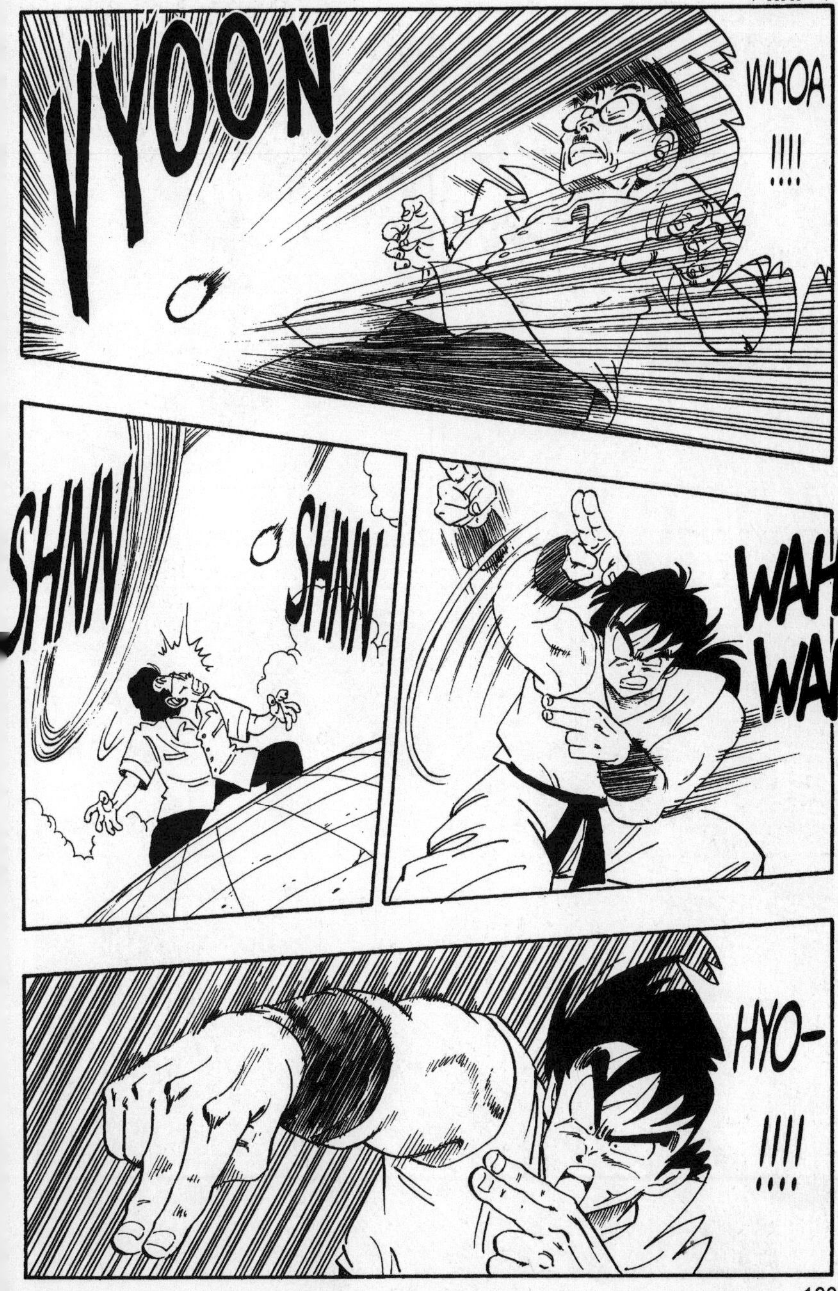
WHOA!!!!
VYOON
WAH WAH
SHNN
SHNN
HYO-!!!!

READ THIS WAY

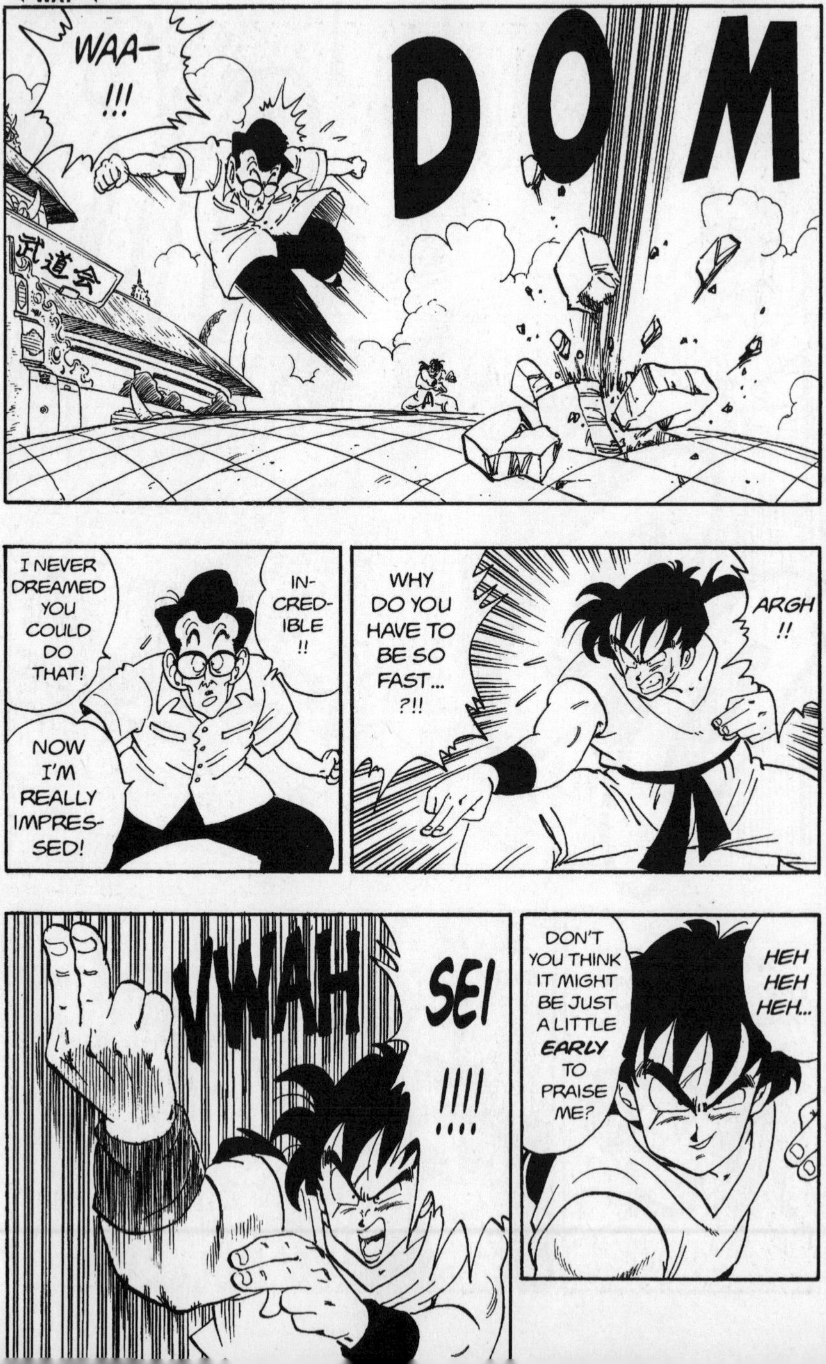
DOM
WAA- !!!
ARGH !!
WHY DO YOU HAVE TO BE SO FAST... ?!!
INCREDIBLE !!
I NEVER DREAMED YOU COULD DO THAT!
NOW I'M REALLY IMPRESSED!
HEH HEH HEH...
DON'T YOU THINK IT MIGHT BE JUST A LITTLE EARLY TO PRAISE ME?
SEI !!!!
VWAH

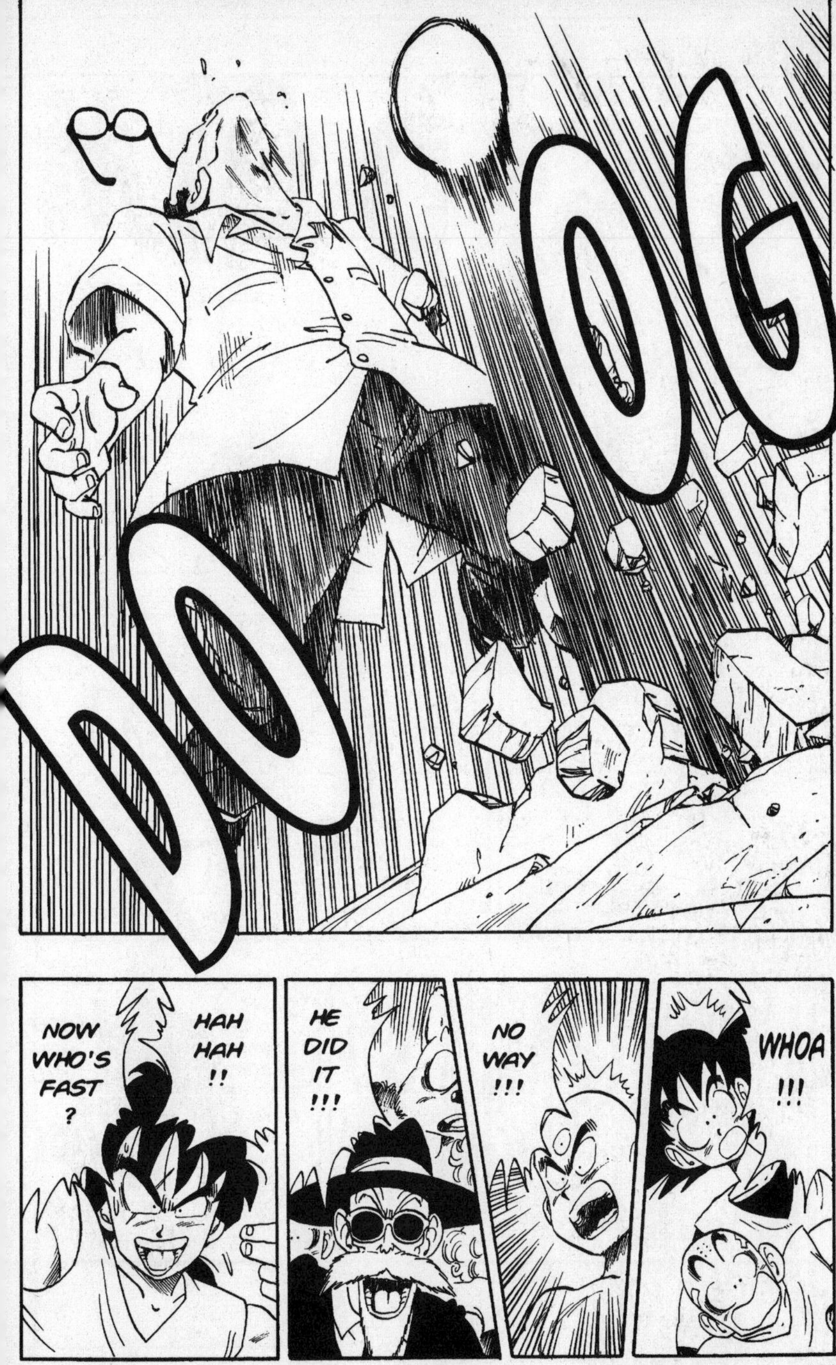
DOOOG
WHOA !!!
NO WAY !!!
HE DID IT !!!
HAH HAH !!
NOW WHO'S FAST ?

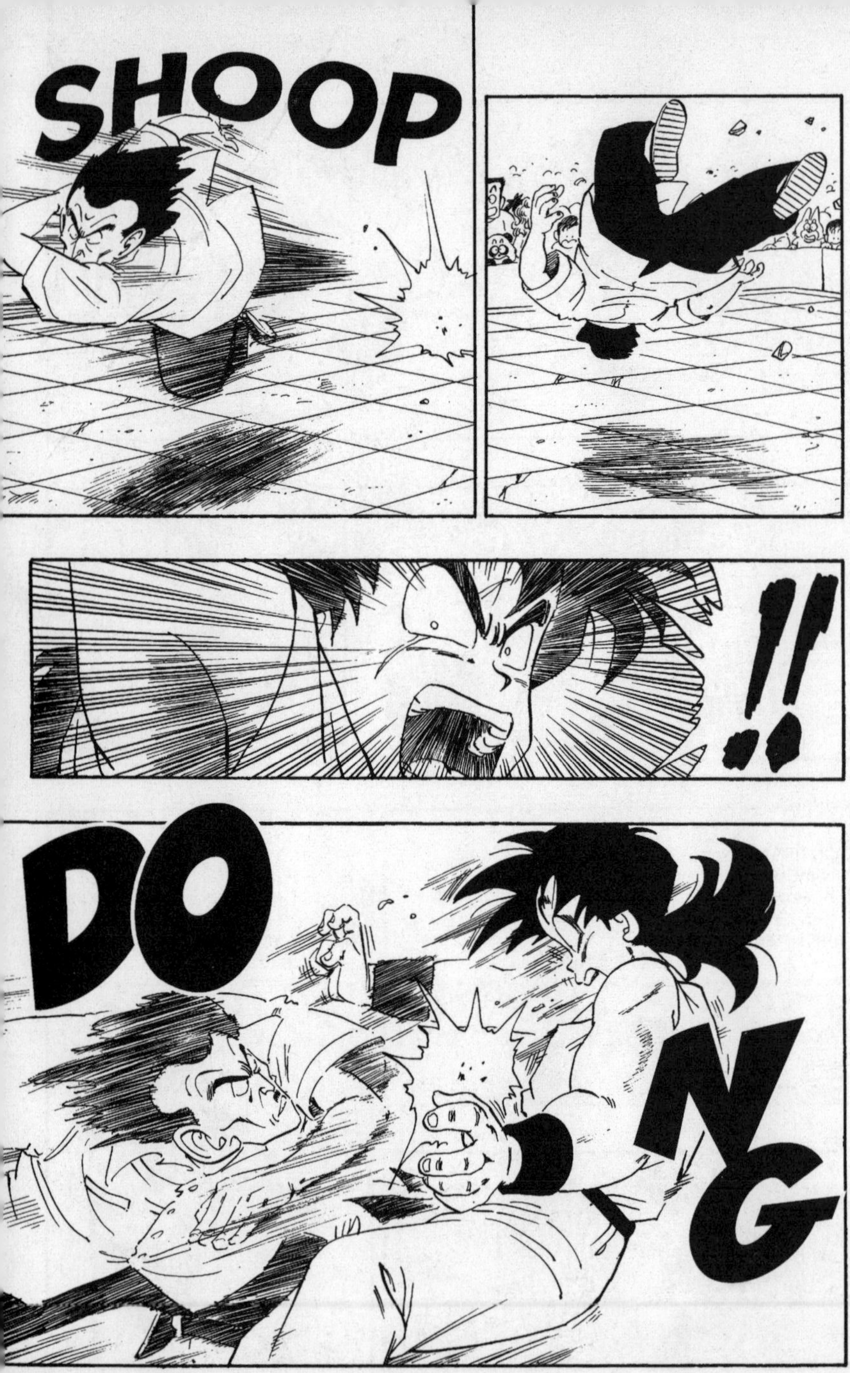
SHOOP
!!
DONG

READ THIS WAY

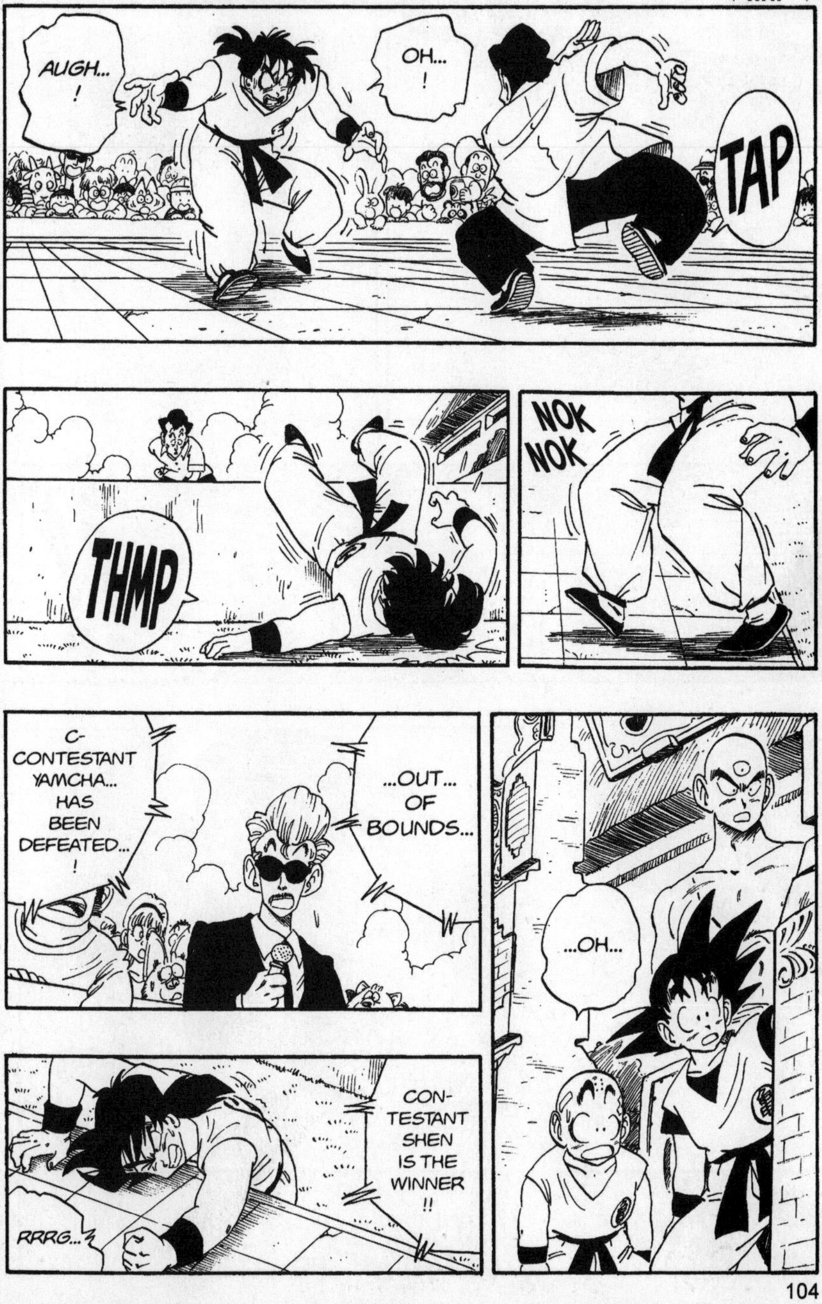
TAP
OH... !
AUGH... !
NOK NOK
THMP
...OH...
...OUT... OF BOUNDS...
C-CONTESTANT YAMCHA... HAS BEEN DEFEATED... !
CON-TESTANT SHEN IS THE WINNER !!
RRRG...

READ THIS WAY

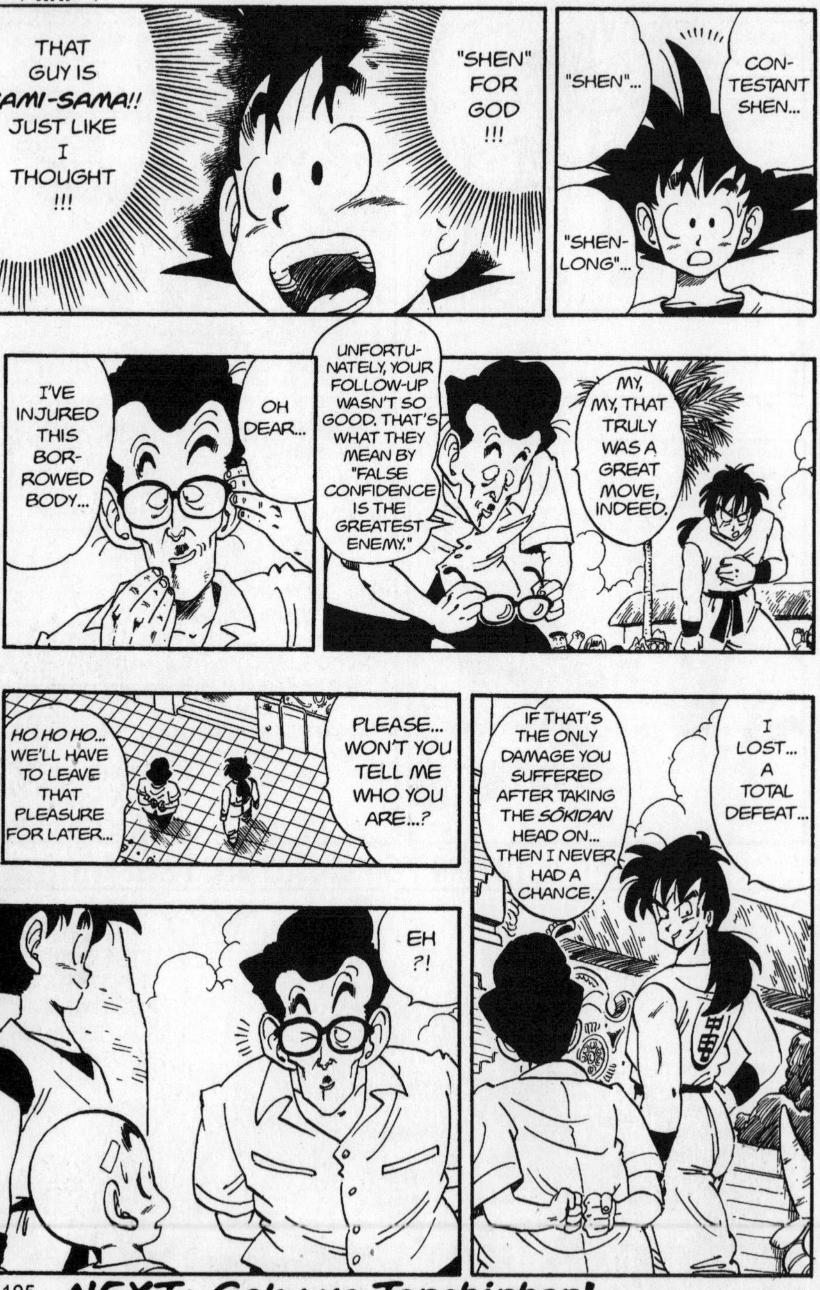
CON-TESTANT SHEN...
"SHEN"...
"SHEN-LONG"...
"SHEN" FOR GOD !!!
THAT GUY IS *KAMI-SAMA!!* JUST LIKE I THOUGHT !!!
MY, MY, THAT TRULY WAS A GREAT MOVE, INDEED.
UNFORTU-NATELY, YOUR FOLLOW-UP WASN'T SO GOOD. THAT'S WHAT THEY MEAN BY "FALSE CONFIDENCE IS THE GREATEST ENEMY."
OH DEAR...
I'VE INJURED THIS BOR-ROWED BODY...
I LOST... A TOTAL DEFEAT...
IF THAT'S THE ONLY DAMAGE YOU SUFFERED AFTER TAKING THE *SÔKIDAN* HEAD ON... THEN I NEVER HAD A CHANCE.
PLEASE... WON'T YOU TELL ME WHO YOU ARE...?
HO HO HO... WE'LL HAVE TO LEAVE THAT PLEASURE FOR LATER...
EH ?!

NEXT: Goku vs. Tenshinhan!

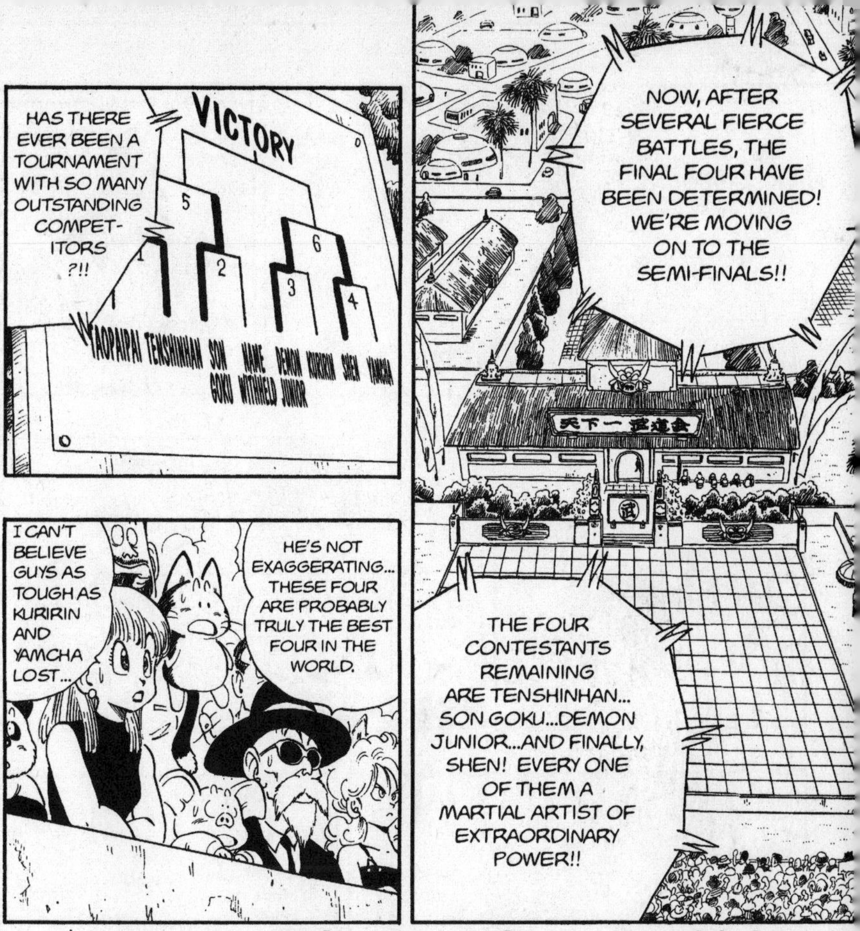
NOW, AFTER SEVERAL FIERCE BATTLES, THE FINAL FOUR HAVE BEEN DETERMINED! WE'RE MOVING ON TO THE SEMI-FINALS!!
天下一武道会
THE FOUR CONTESTANTS REMAINING ARE TENSHINHAN... SON GOKU...DEMON JUNIOR...AND FINALLY, SHEN! EVERY ONE OF THEM A MARTIAL ARTIST OF EXTRAORDINARY POWER!!
HAS THERE EVER BEEN A TOURNAMENT WITH SO MANY OUTSTANDING COMPET-ITORS ?!!
VICTORY
5
6
1
2
3
4
TAOPAIPAI TENSHINHAN SON GOKU NAME WITHHELD DEMON JUNIOR KURIRIN SHEN YAMCHA
HE'S NOT EXAGGERATING... THESE FOUR ARE PROBABLY TRULY THE BEST FOUR IN THE WORLD.
I CAN'T BELIEVE GUYS AS TOUGH AS KURIRIN AND YAMCHA LOST...

Tale 176 • Goku vs. Tenshinhan

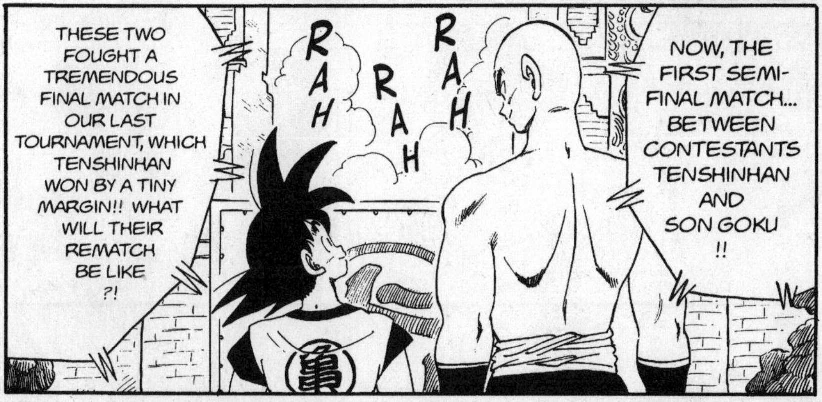
NOW, THE FIRST SEMI-FINAL MATCH... BETWEEN CONTESTANTS TENSHINHAN AND SON GOKU !!
RAH RAH RAH
THESE TWO FOUGHT A TREMENDOUS FINAL MATCH IN OUR LAST TOURNAMENT, WHICH TENSHINHAN WON BY A TINY MARGIN!! WHAT WILL THEIR REMATCH BE LIKE ?!

READ THIS WAY

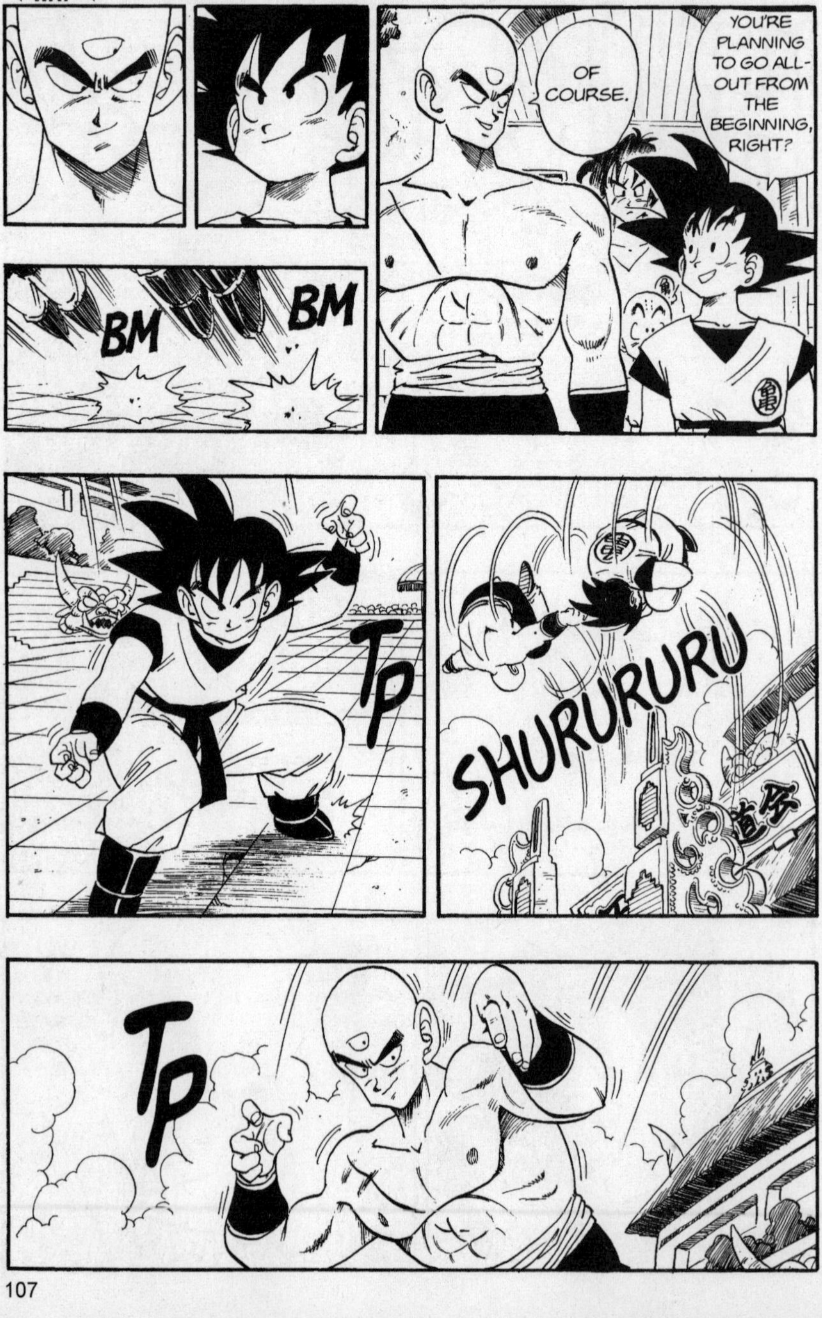
YOU'RE PLANNING TO GO ALL-OUT FROM THE BEGINNING, RIGHT?
OF COURSE.
BM
BM
SHURURURU
TP
TP

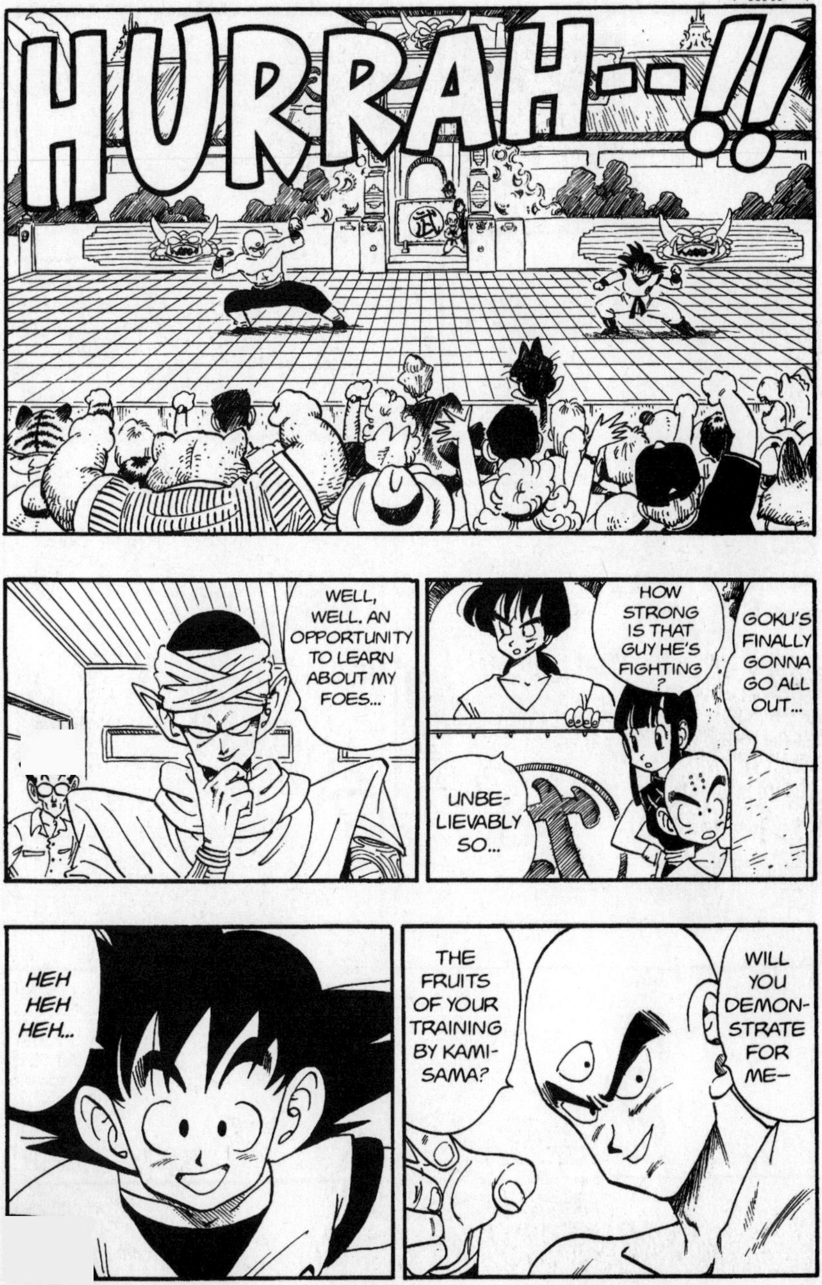
HURRAH--!!
GOKU'S FINALLY GONNA GO ALL OUT...
HOW STRONG IS THAT GUY HE'S FIGHTING?
UNBE-LIEVABLY SO...
WELL, WELL. AN OPPORTUNITY TO LEARN ABOUT MY FOES...
WILL YOU DEMON-STRATE FOR ME--
THE FRUITS OF YOUR TRAINING BY KAMI-SAMA?
HEH HEH HEH...

READ THIS WAY

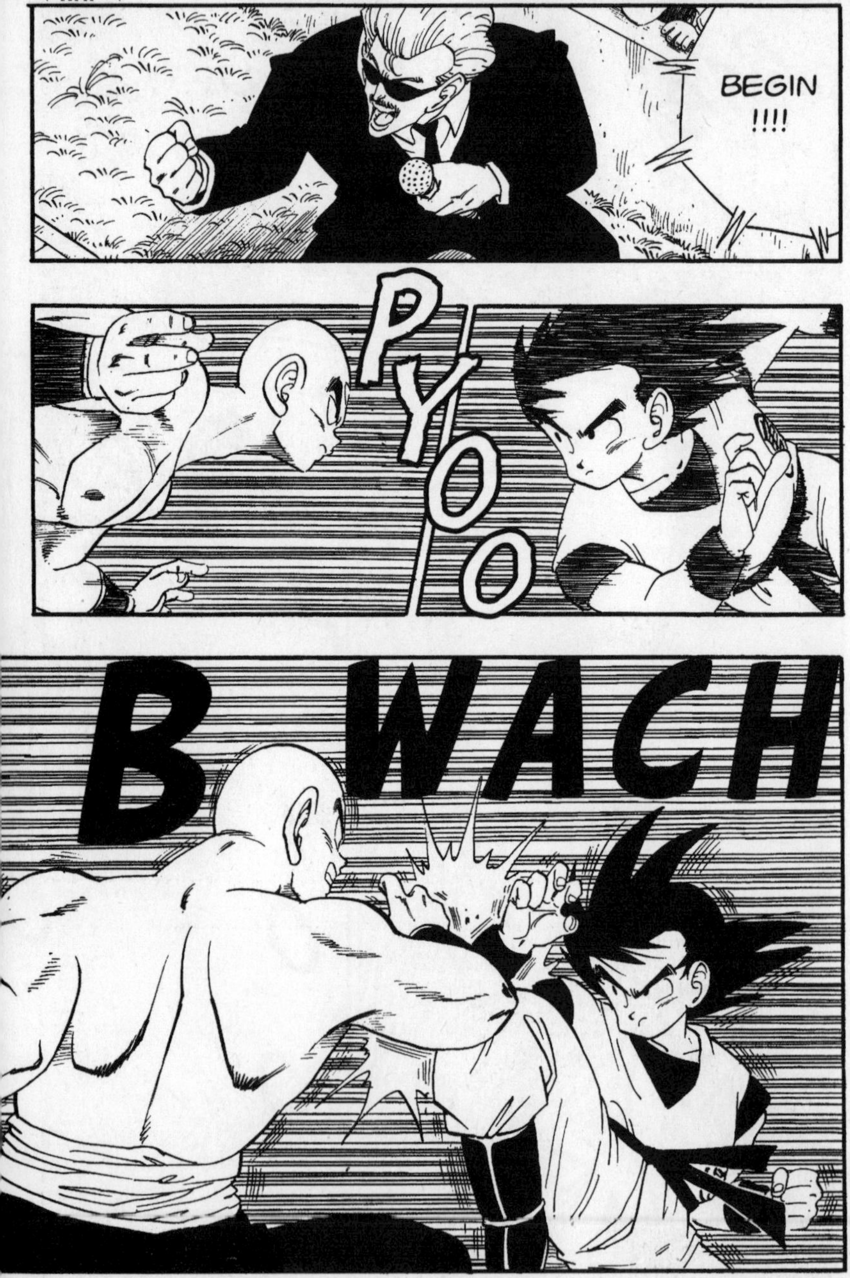
BEGIN !!!!
PYOO
BWACH

READ THIS WAY

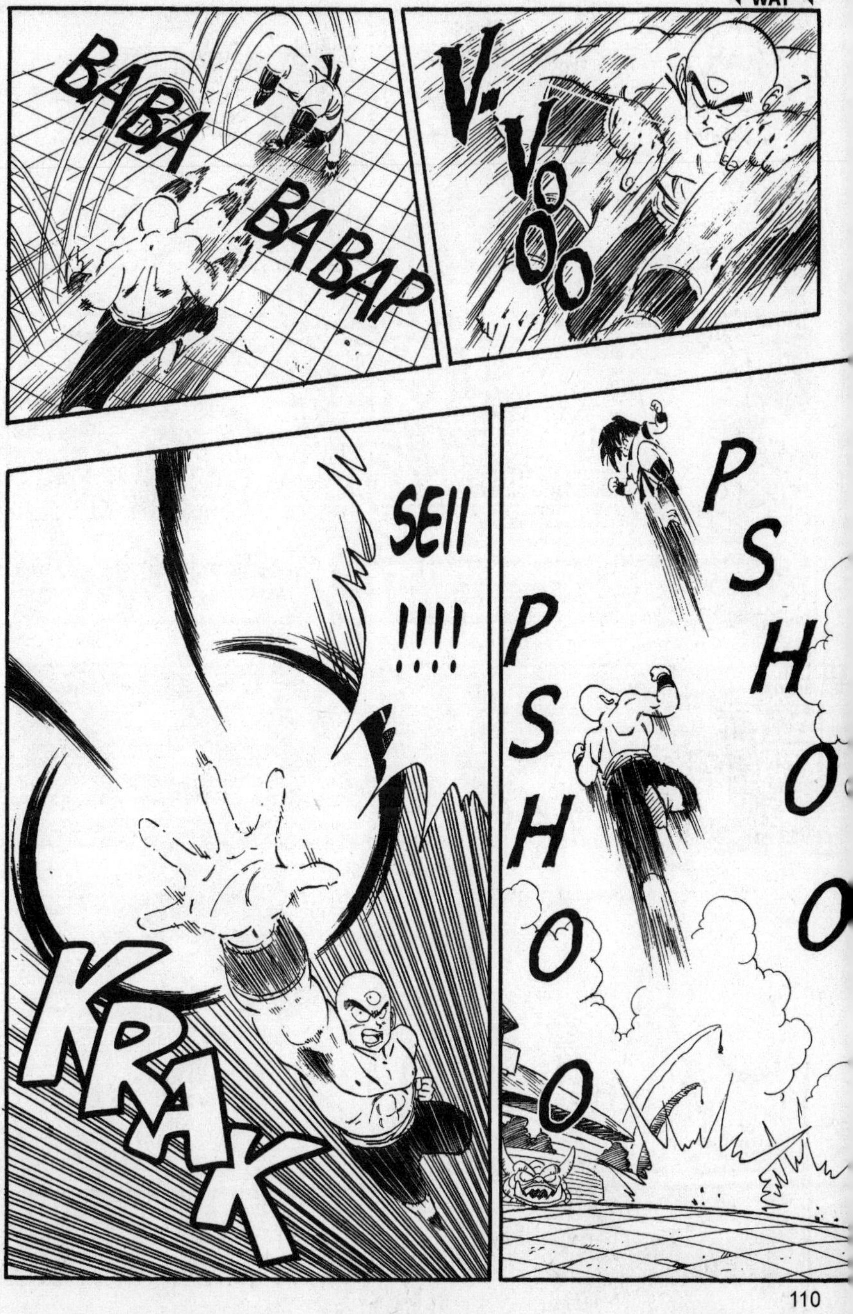
V-VOOO
BABA BABABAP
PSHOO
PSHOO
SEII!!!!
KRAK

READ THIS WAY

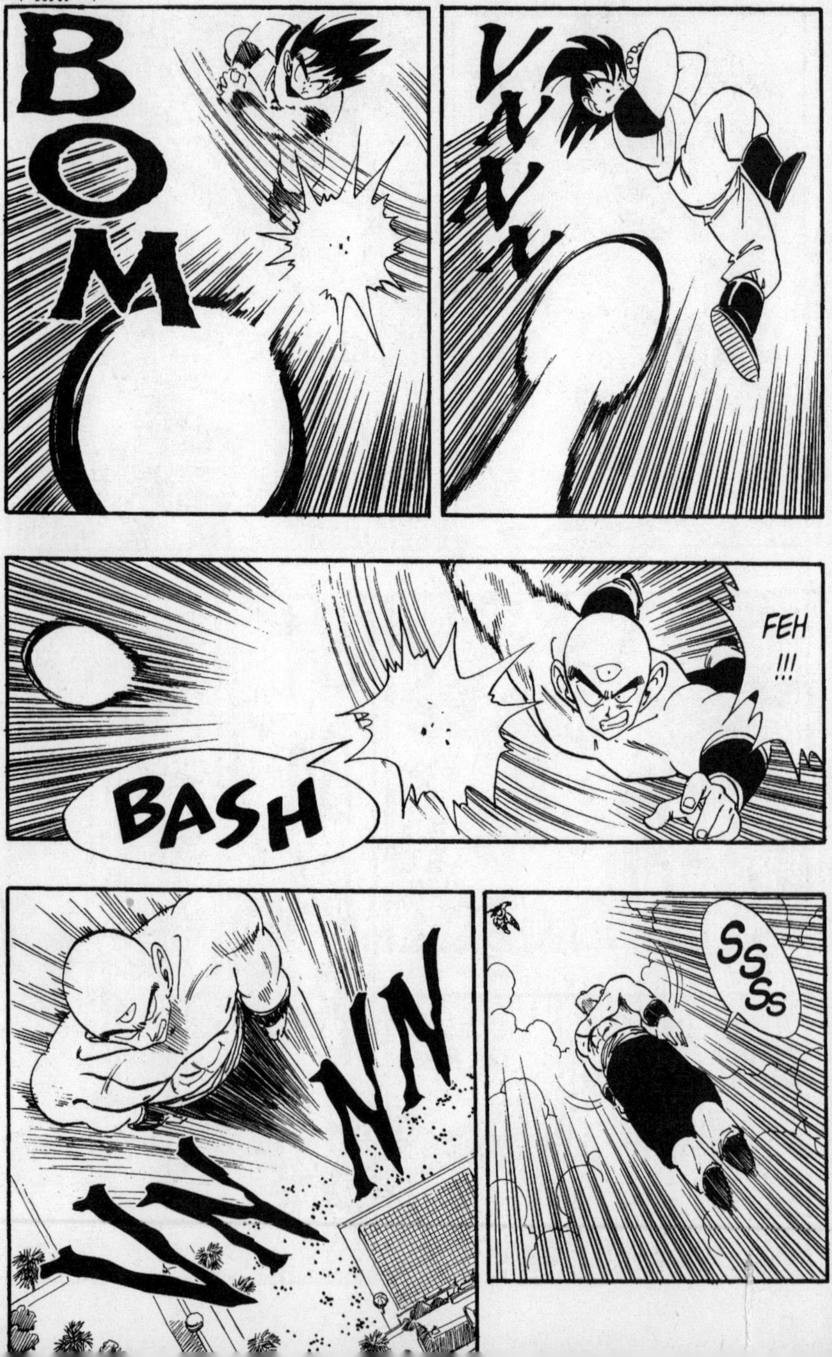
VNNN
BOM
FEH !!!
BASH
SSSS
NNNN

READ THIS WAY

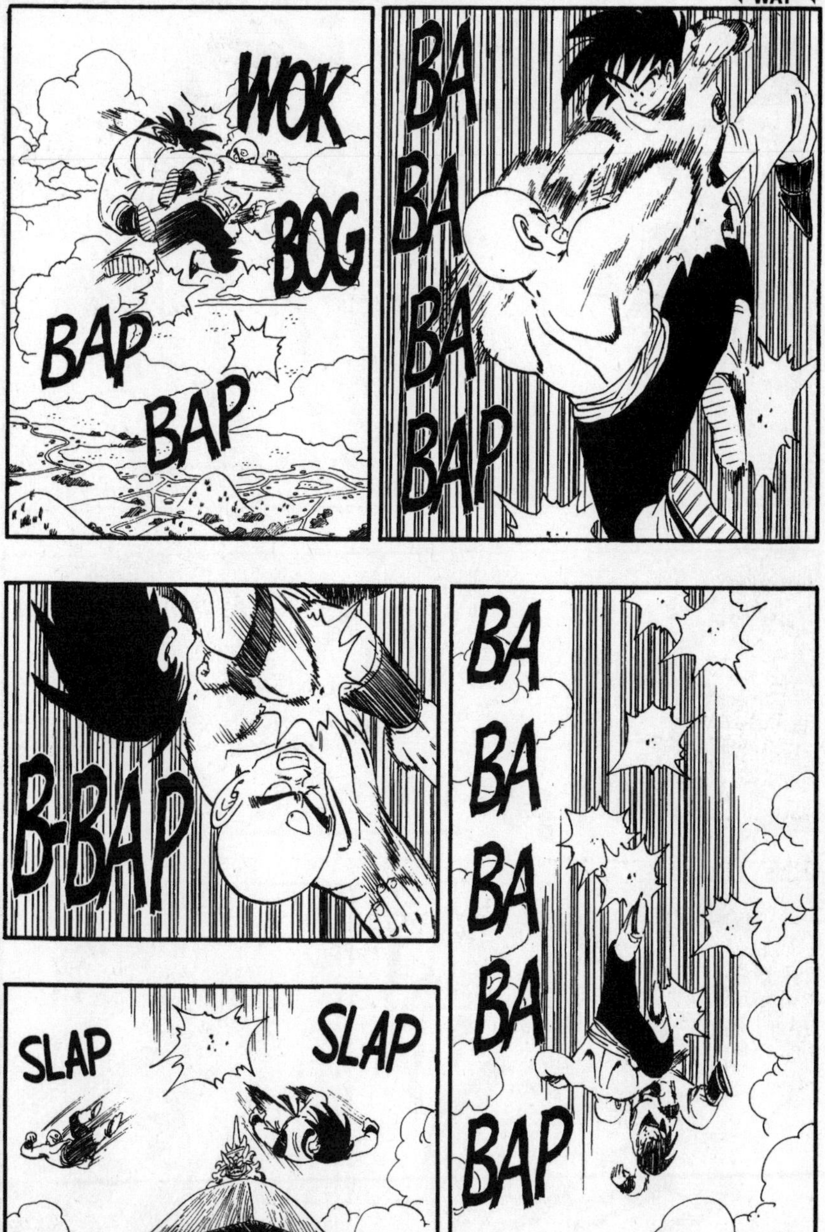
BA
BA
BA
BAP
WOK
BOG
BAP
BAP
BA
BA
BA
BA
BAP
B-BAP
SLAP
SLAP

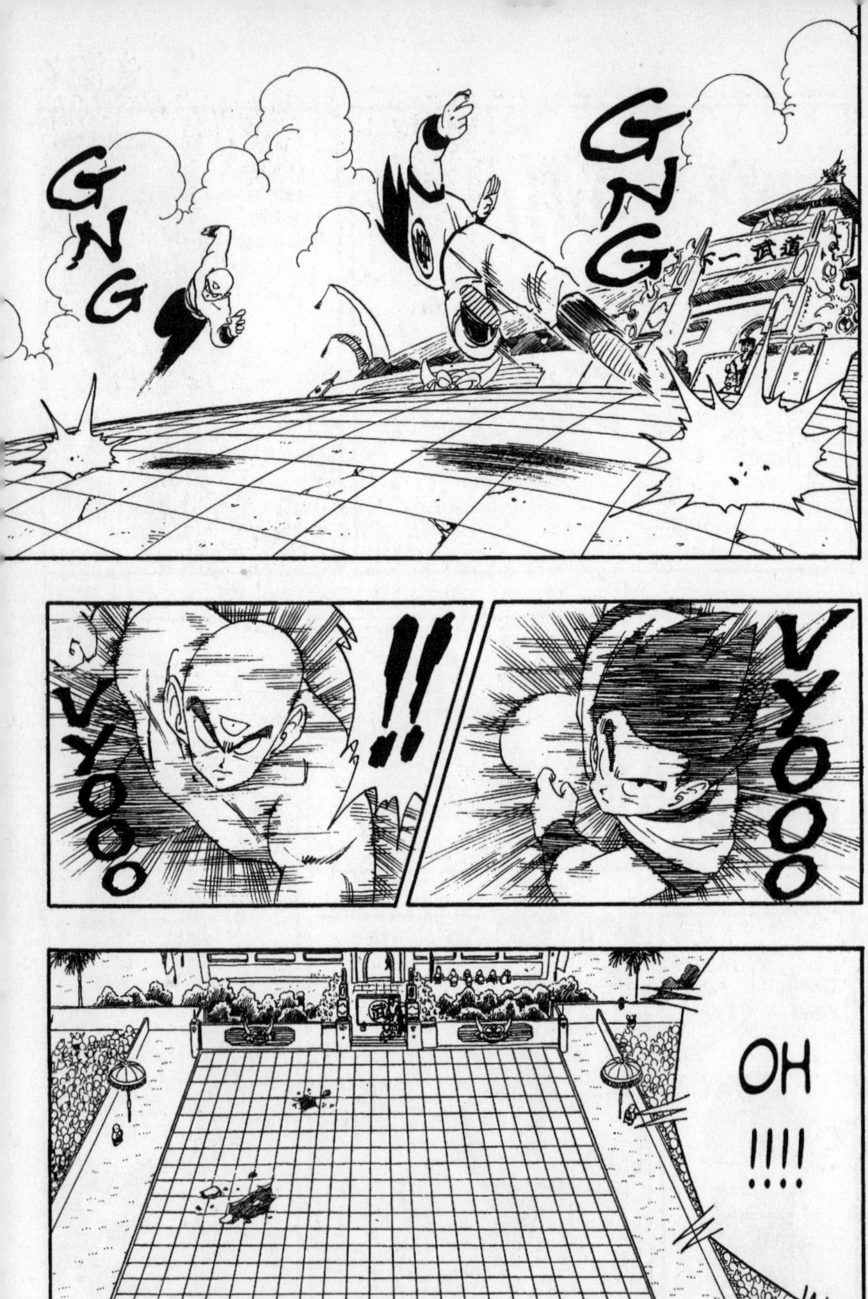
GNG
GNG
VYOOO
!!
VYOOO
OH
!!!!

READ THIS WAY

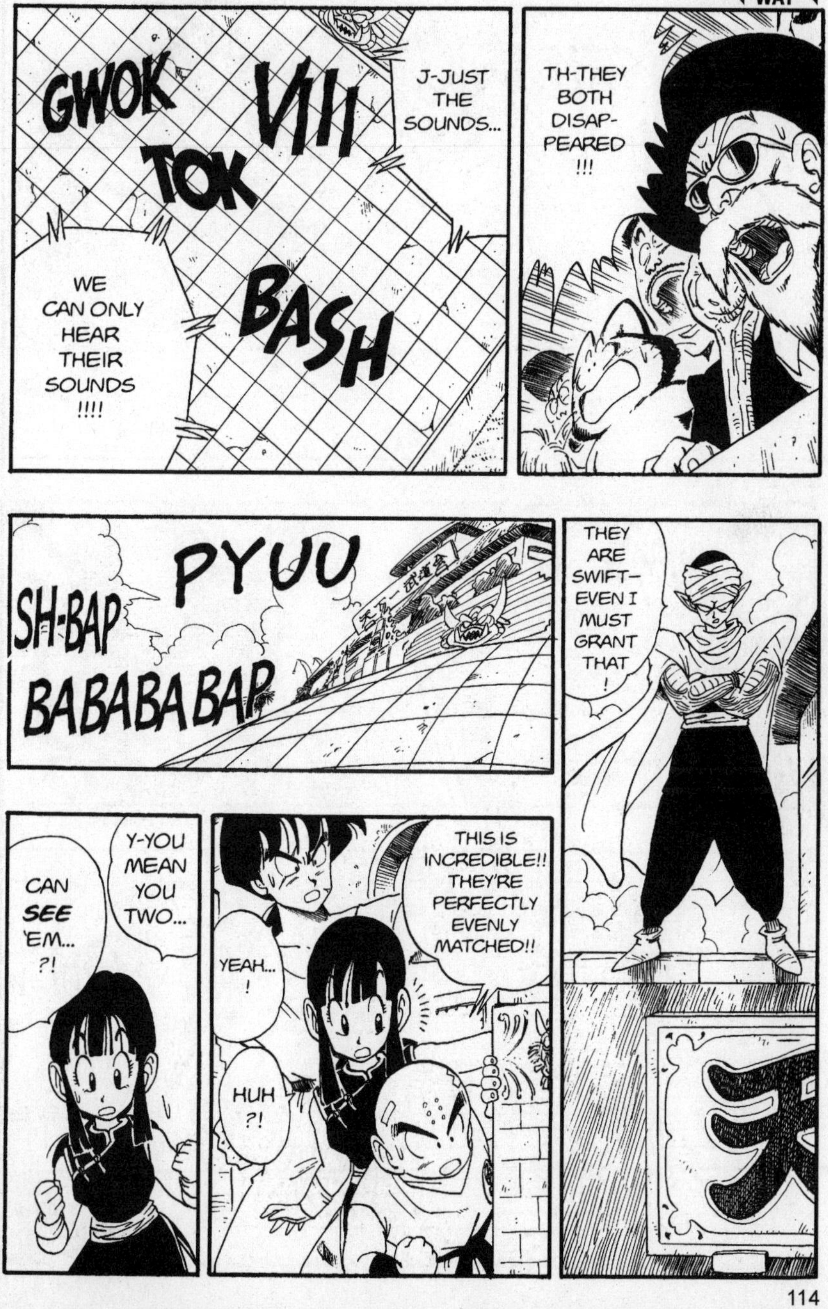
TH-THEY BOTH DISAP-PEARED!!!
J-JUST THE SOUNDS...
VIII
GWOK
TOK
BASH
WE CAN ONLY HEAR THEIR SOUNDS!!!!
THEY ARE SWIFT—EVEN I MUST GRANT THAT!
PYUU
SH-BAP
BABABABAP
THIS IS INCREDIBLE!! THEY'RE PERFECTLY EVENLY MATCHED!!
YEAH...!
HUH?!
Y-YOU MEAN YOU TWO...
CAN **SEE** 'EM...?!

READ THIS WAY

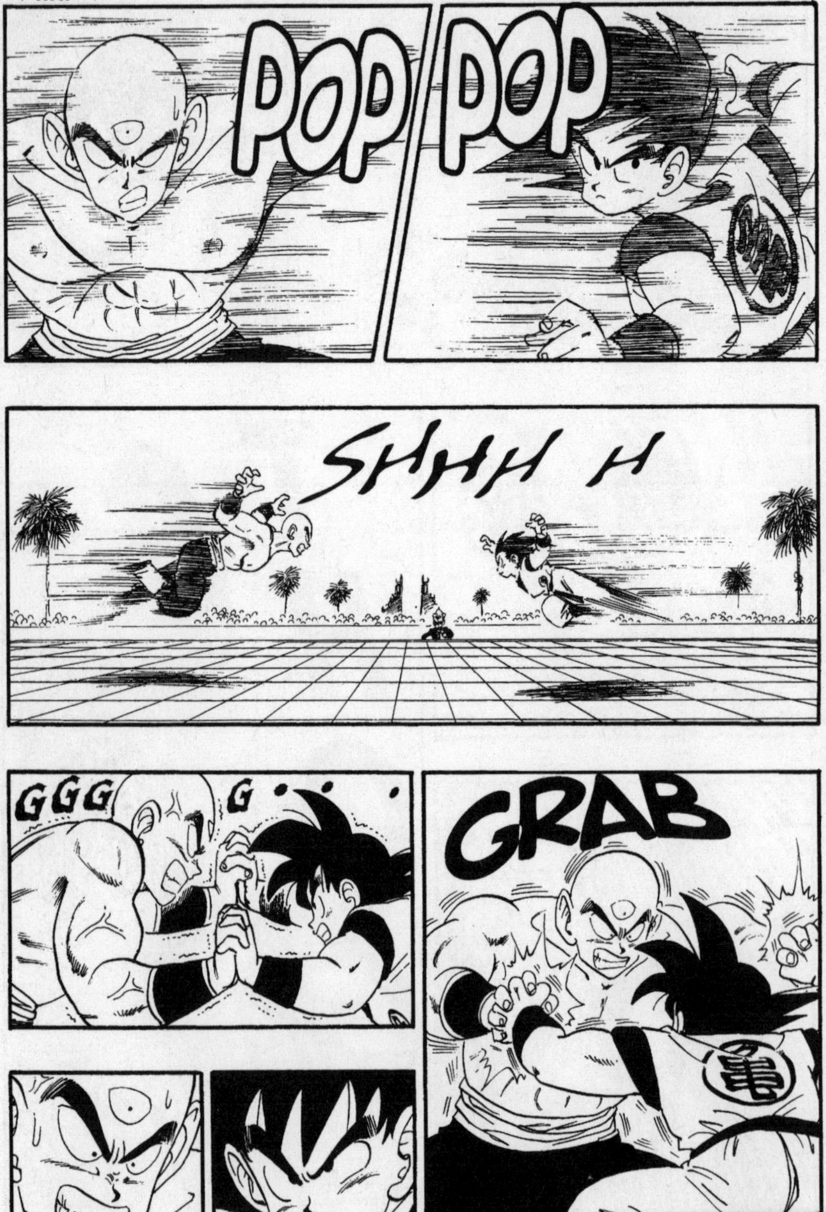
POP
POP
SHHH H
GRAB
亀
GGG
G

READ THIS WAY

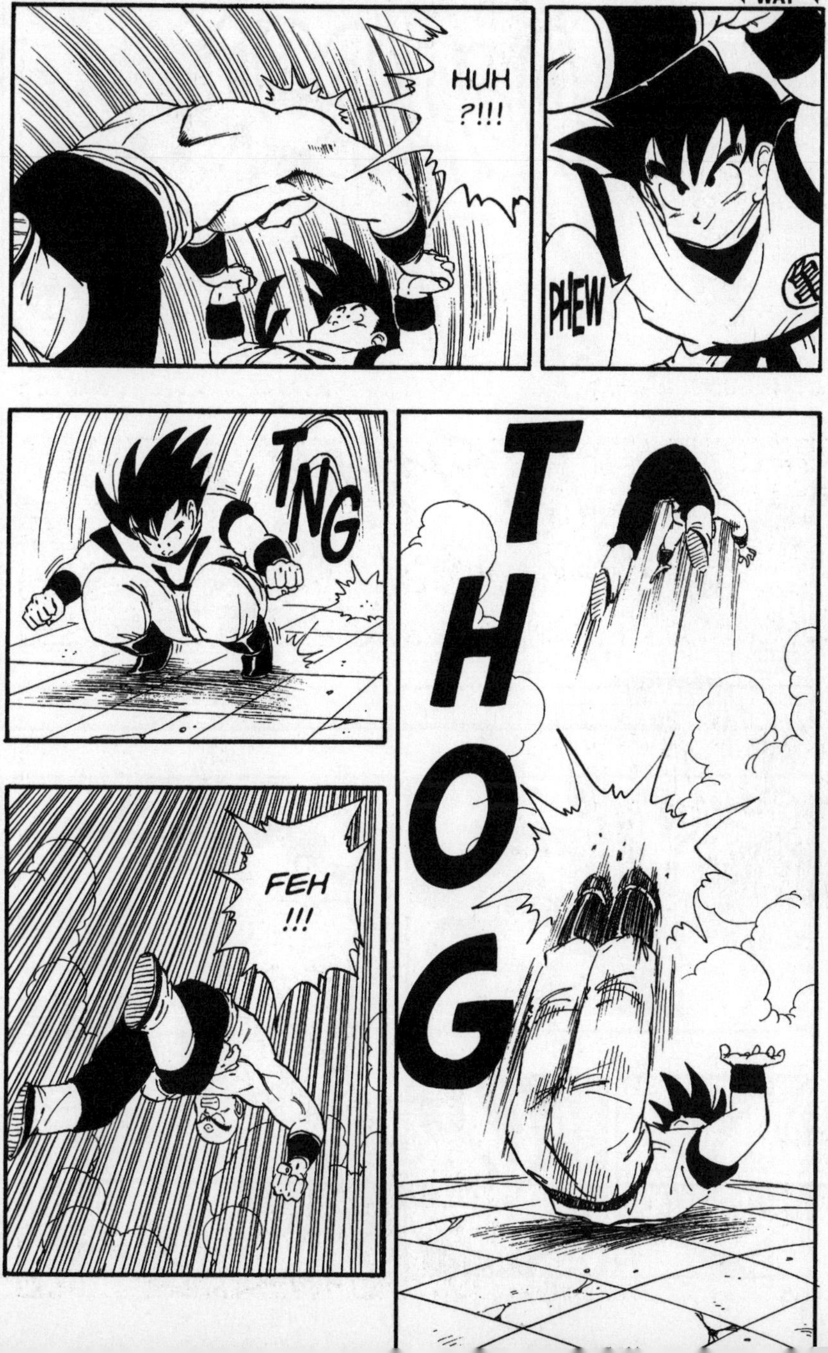
PHEW
HUH ?!!!
THOG
TNG
FEH !!!

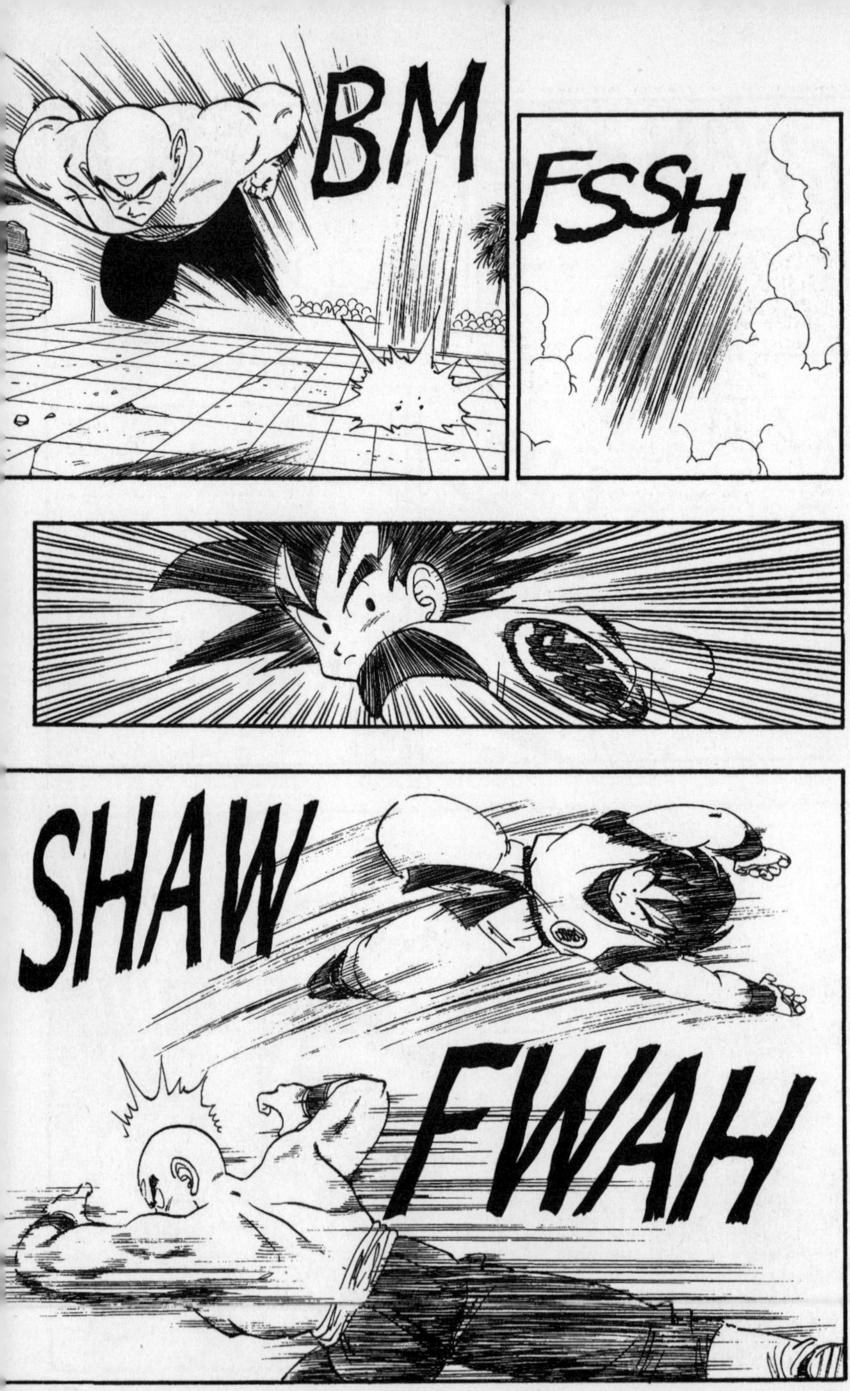
FSSH
BM
SHAW
FWAH

READ THIS WAY

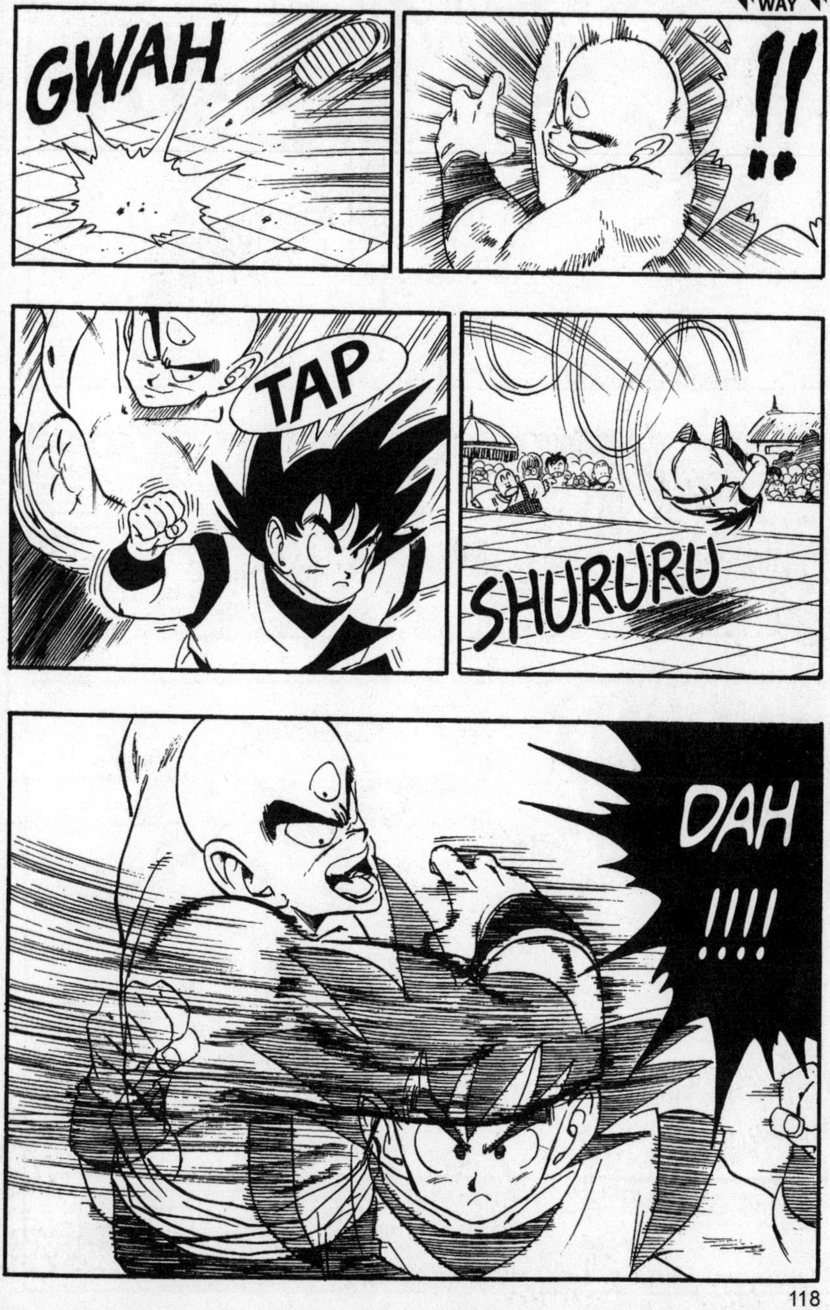
!!
GWAH
SHURURU
TAP
DAH!!!!

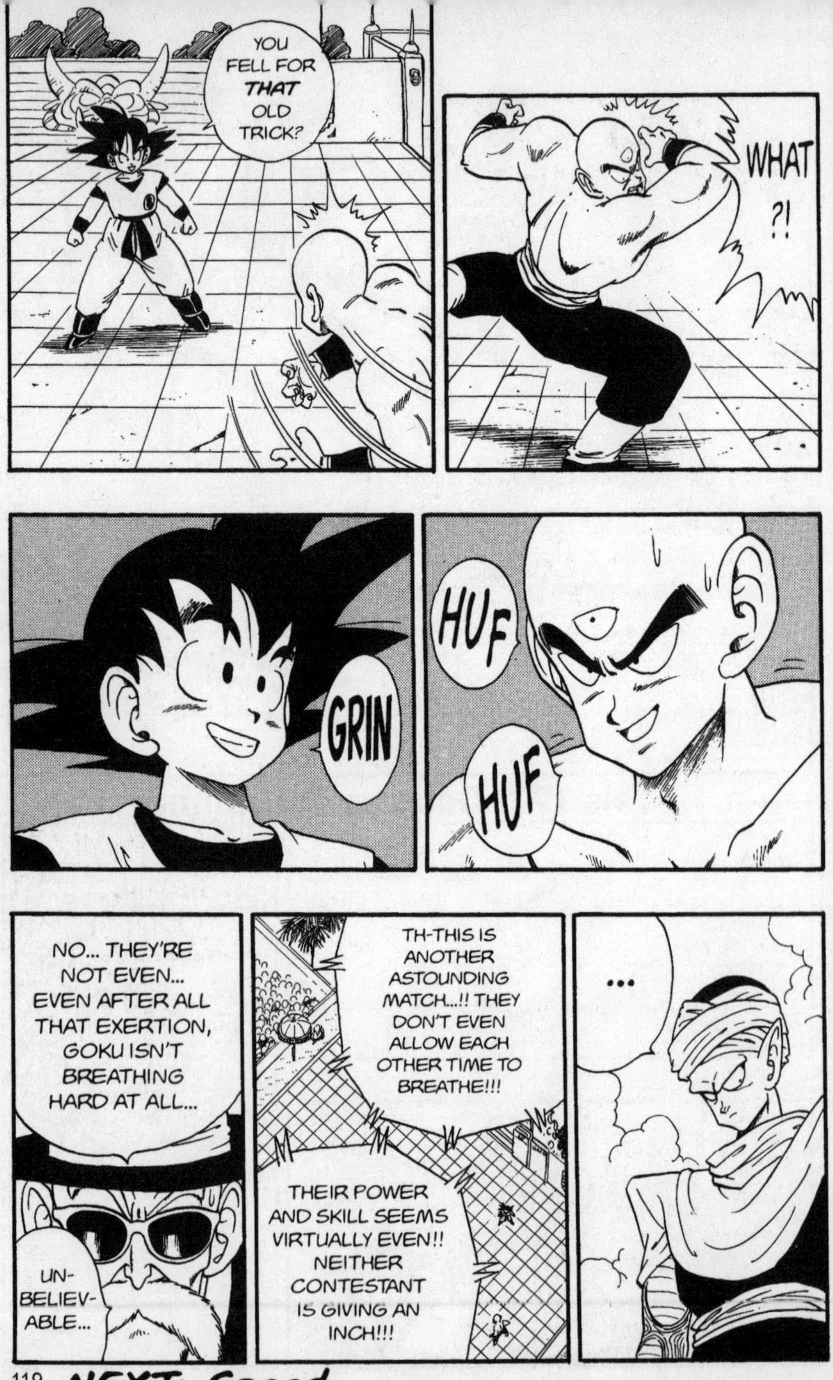
WHAT ?!
YOU FELL FOR THAT OLD TRICK?
HUF
HUF
GRIN
...
TH-THIS IS ANOTHER ASTOUNDING MATCH...!! THEY DON'T EVEN ALLOW EACH OTHER TIME TO BREATHE!!!
THEIR POWER AND SKILL SEEMS VIRTUALLY EVEN!! NEITHER CONTESTANT IS GIVING AN INCH!!!
NO... THEY'RE NOT EVEN... EVEN AFTER ALL THAT EXERTION, GOKU ISN'T BREATHING HARD AT ALL...
UN-BELIEV-ABLE...

 ***NEXT:* Speed**

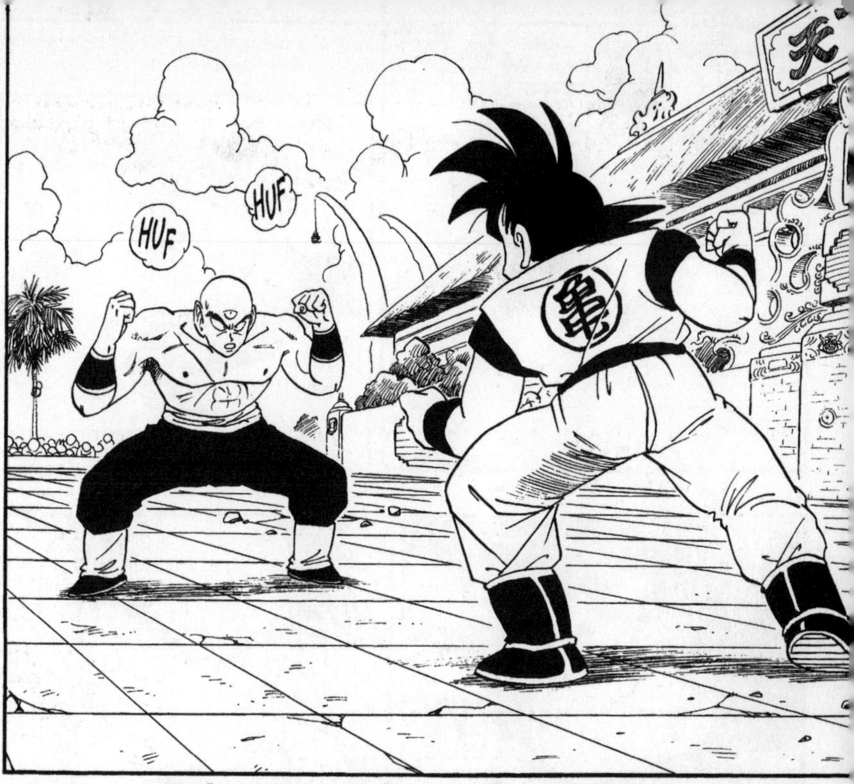
HUF
HUF

Tale 177 · Goku vs. Tenshinhan, Part 2

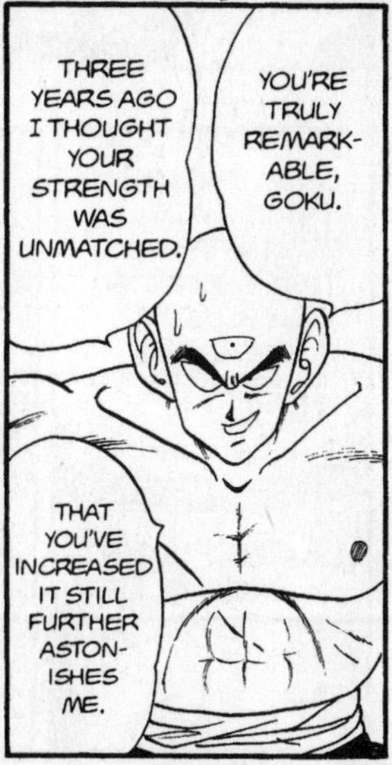
YOU'RE TRULY REMARKABLE, GOKU.
THREE YEARS AGO I THOUGHT YOUR STRENGTH WAS UNMATCHED.
THAT YOU'VE INCREASED IT STILL FURTHER ASTONISHES ME.

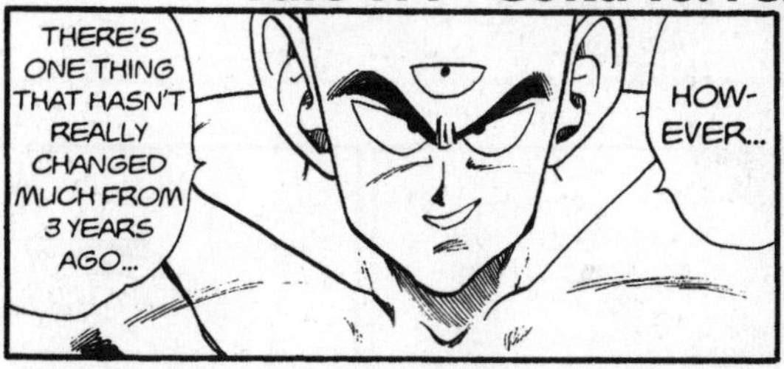
HOW-EVER...
THERE'S ONE THING THAT HASN'T REALLY CHANGED MUCH FROM 3 YEARS AGO...

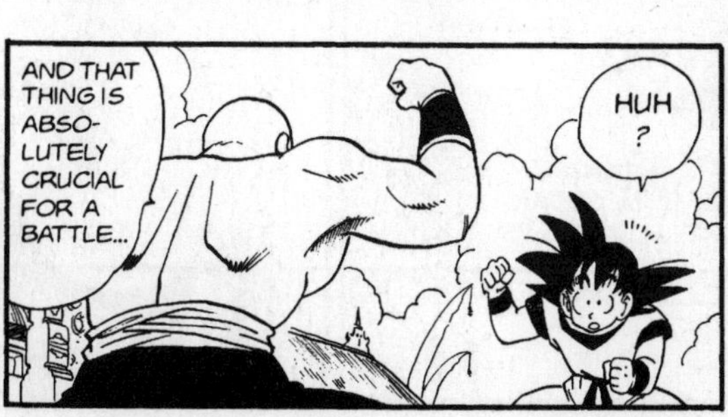
AND THAT THING IS ABSO-LUTELY CRUCIAL FOR A BATTLE...
HUH ?

READ THIS WAY

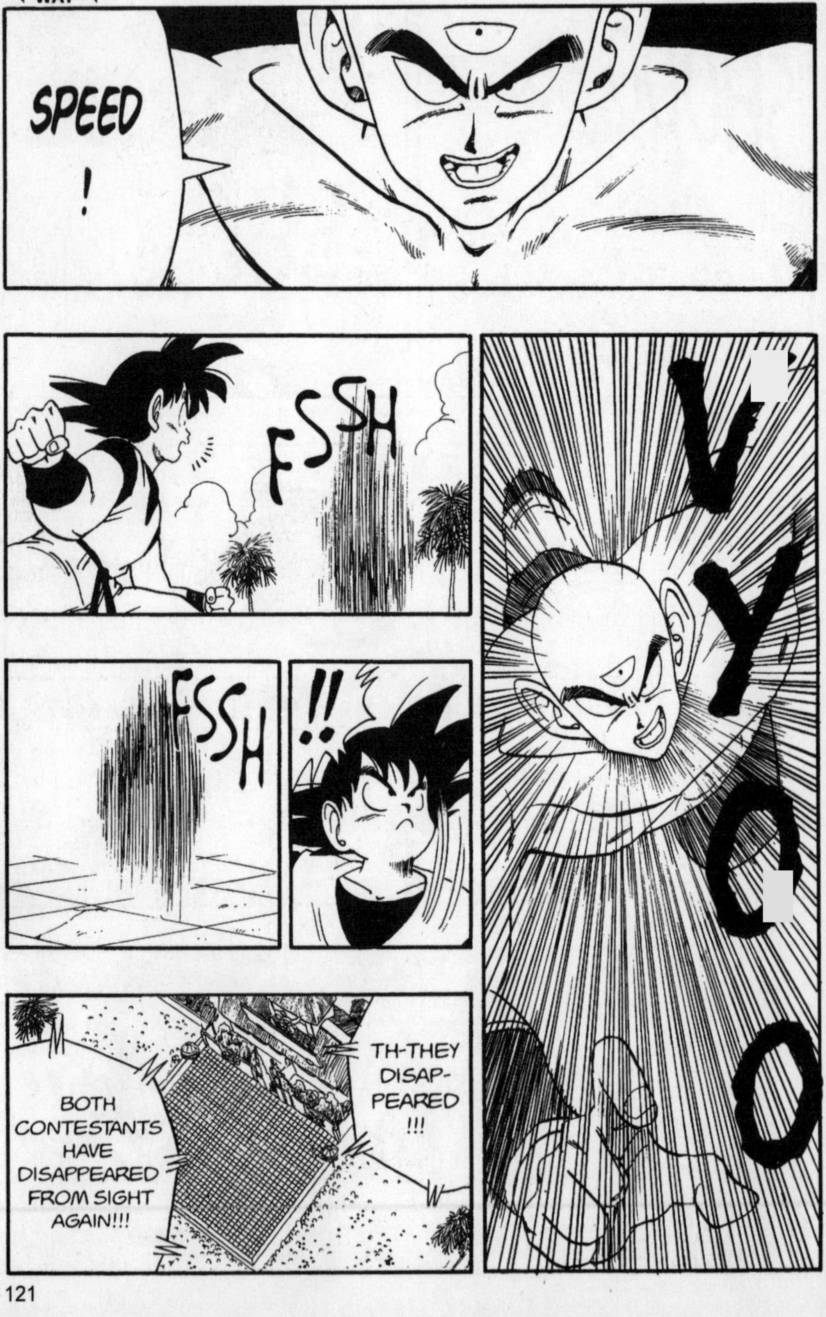

SPEED!
VYOO
FSSH
!!
FSSH
TH-THEY DISAPPEARED!!!
BOTH CONTESTANTS HAVE DISAPPEARED FROM SIGHT AGAIN!!!

READ THIS WAY

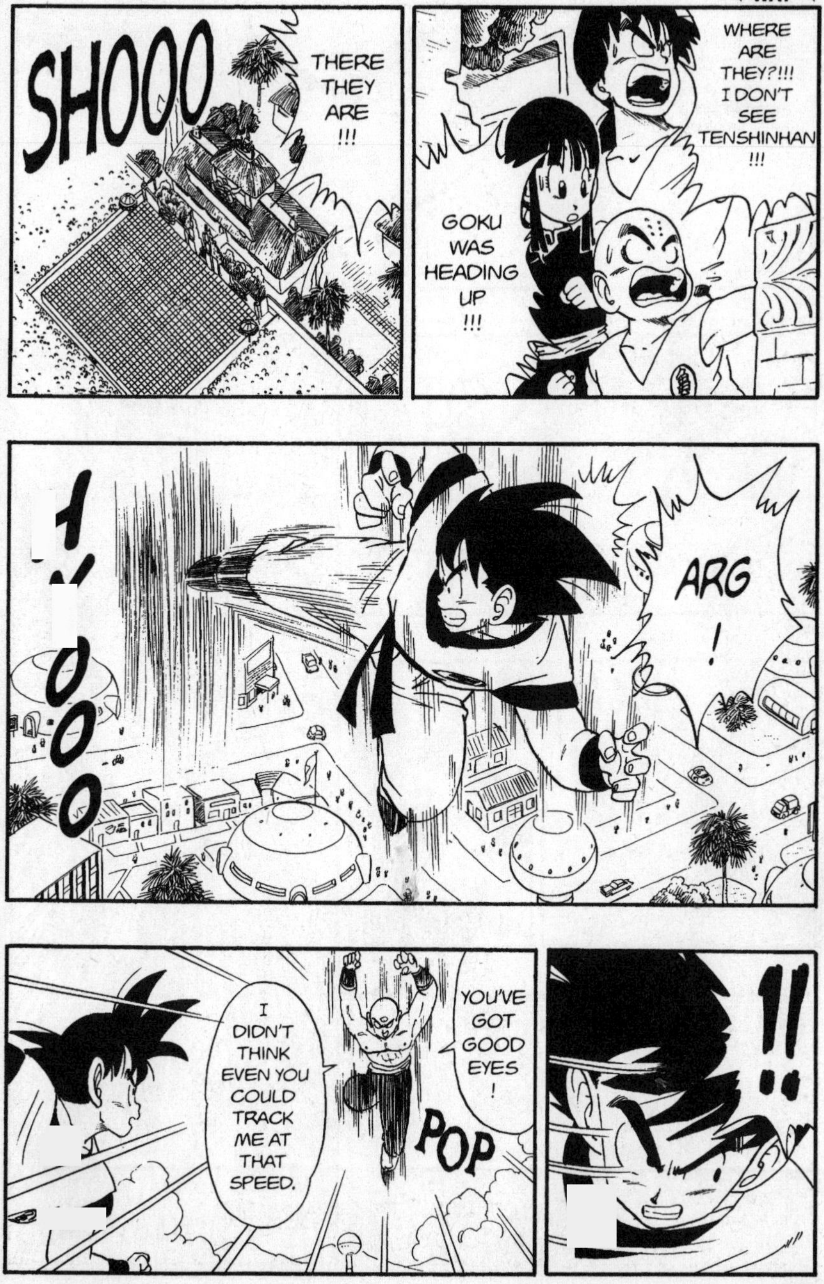
WHERE ARE THEY?!!! I DON'T SEE TENSHINHAN!!!
GOKU WAS HEADING UP!!!
THERE THEY ARE!!!
SHOOO
ARG!
!!
YOU'VE GOT GOOD EYES!
I DIDN'T THINK EVEN YOU COULD TRACK ME AT THAT SPEED.
POP

READ THIS WAY

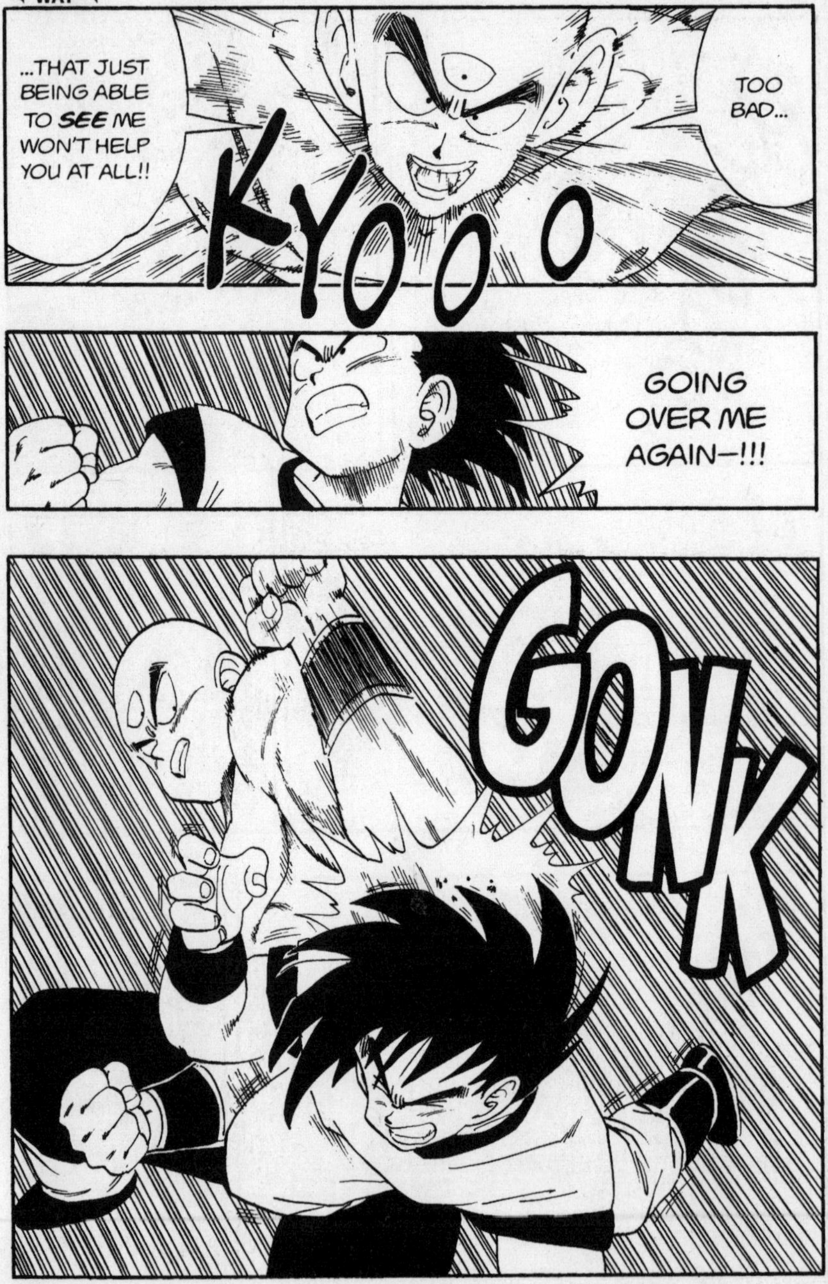
TOO BAD...
...THAT JUST BEING ABLE TO SEE ME WON'T HELP YOU AT ALL!!
KYOOO
GOING OVER ME AGAIN—!!!
GONK

READ THIS WAY

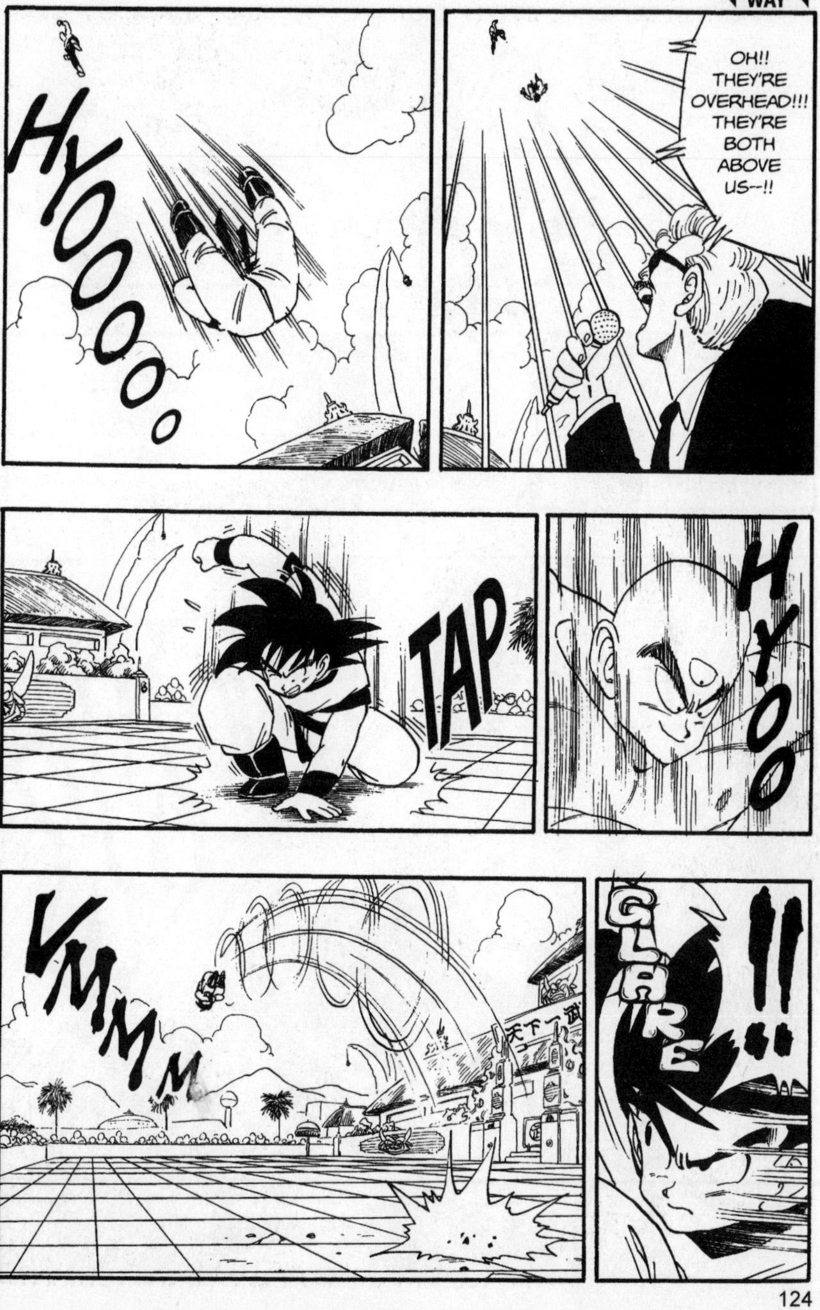

OH!! THEY'RE OVERHEAD!!! THEY'RE BOTH ABOVE US--!!
HYOOOo
HYOO
TAP
GLARE!!
VMMMM

READ THIS WAY

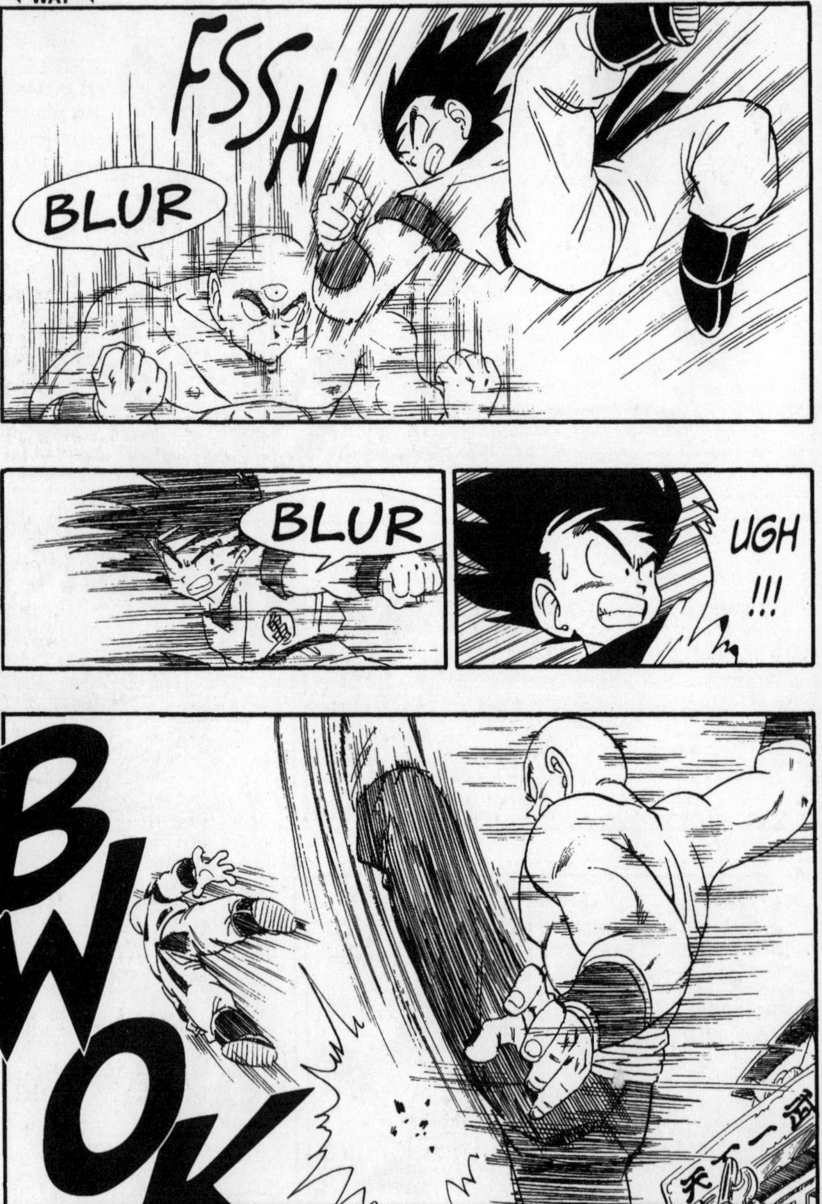
FSSH
BLUR
UGH !!!
BLUR
BWOK

READ THIS WAY

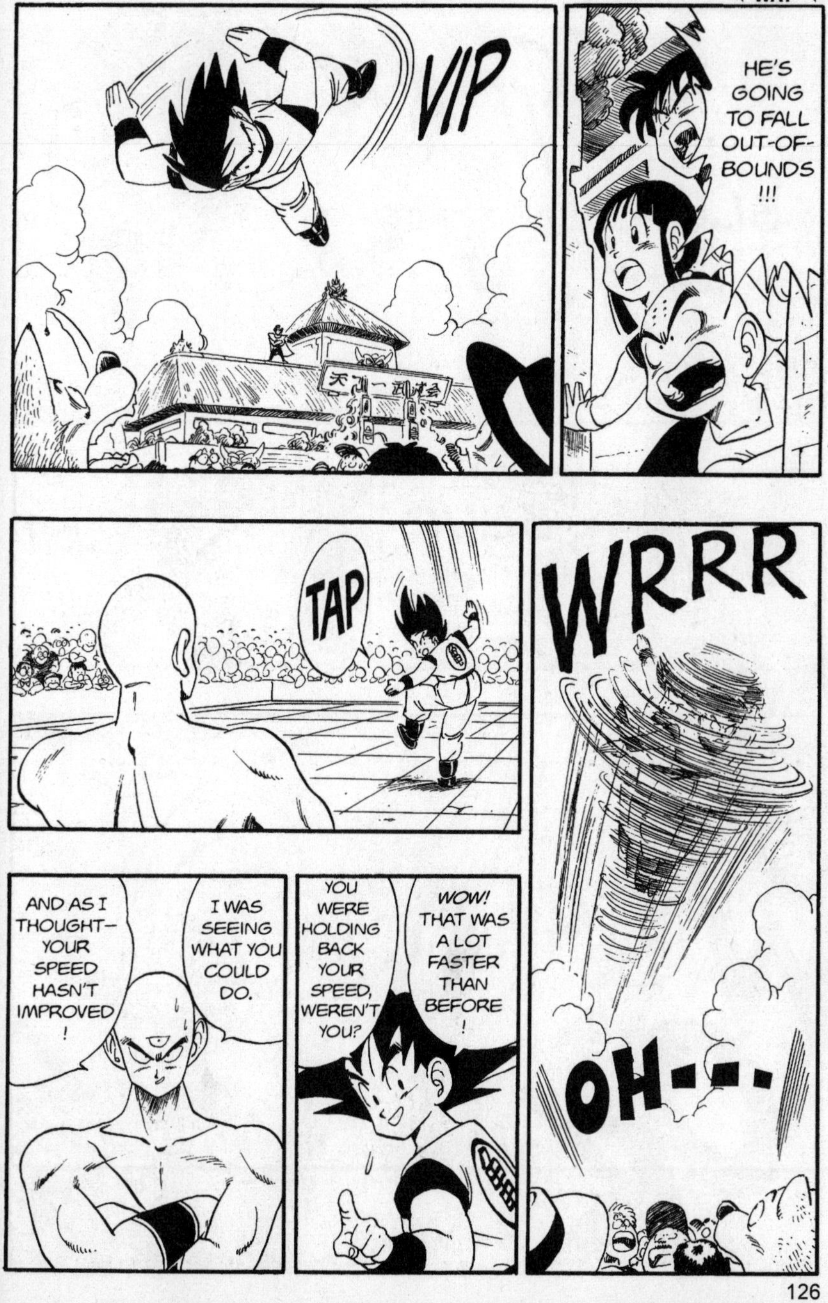

HE'S GOING TO FALL OUT-OF-BOUNDS !!!
VIP
WRRR
OH...
TAP
WOW! THAT WAS A LOT FASTER THAN BEFORE !
YOU WERE HOLDING BACK YOUR SPEED, WEREN'T YOU?
I WAS SEEING WHAT YOU COULD DO.
AND AS I THOUGHT— YOUR SPEED HASN'T IMPROVED !

READ THIS WAY

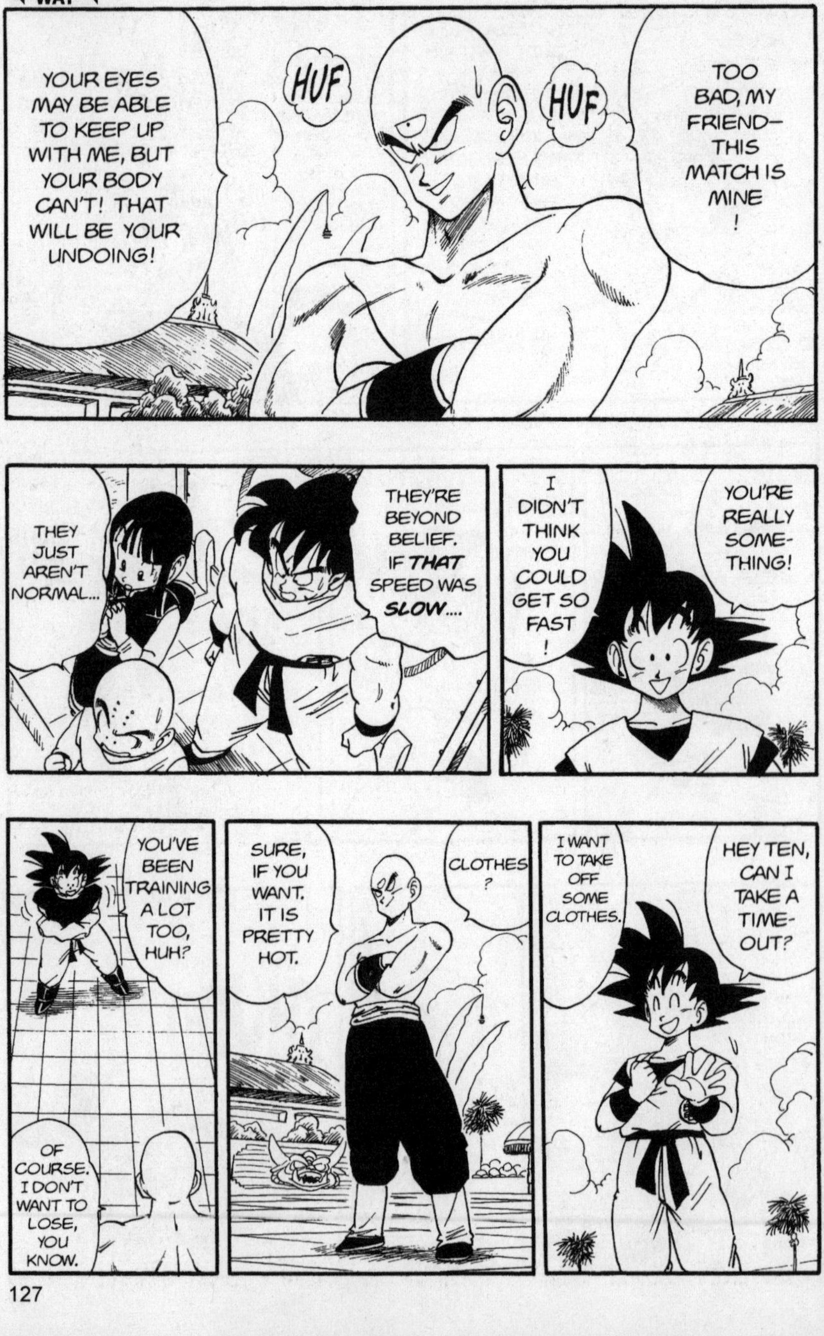

TOO BAD, MY FRIEND— THIS MATCH IS MINE!
HUF
HUF
YOUR EYES MAY BE ABLE TO KEEP UP WITH ME, BUT YOUR BODY CAN'T! THAT WILL BE YOUR UNDOING!
YOU'RE REALLY SOME-THING!
I DIDN'T THINK YOU COULD GET SO FAST!
THEY'RE BEYOND BELIEF. IF THAT SPEED WAS SLOW....
THEY JUST AREN'T NORMAL...
HEY TEN, CAN I TAKE A TIME-OUT?
I WANT TO TAKE OFF SOME CLOTHES.
CLOTHES?
SURE, IF YOU WANT. IT IS PRETTY HOT.
YOU'VE BEEN TRAINING A LOT TOO, HUH?
OF COURSE. I DON'T WANT TO LOSE, YOU KNOW.

READ THIS WAY

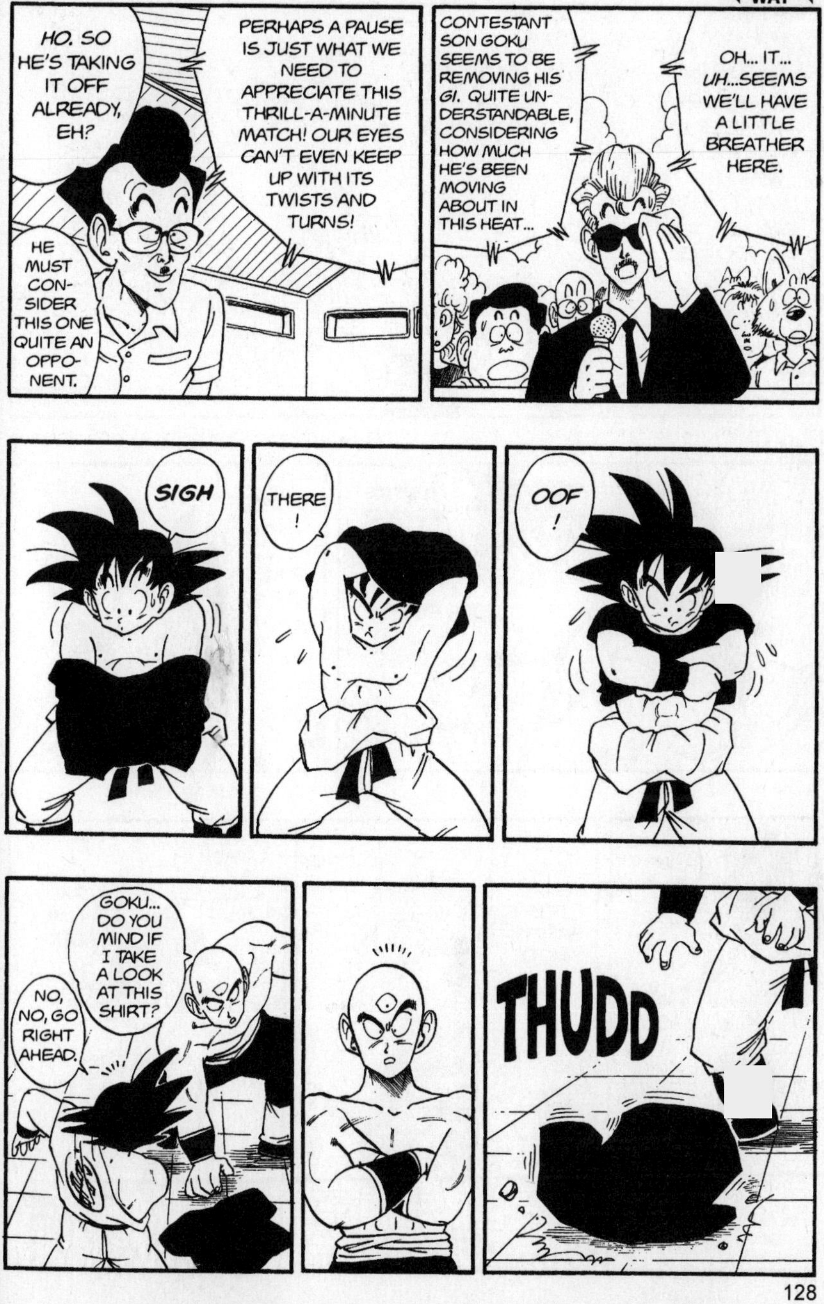

OH... IT... UH...SEEMS WE'LL HAVE A LITTLE BREATHER HERE.
CONTESTANT SON GOKU SEEMS TO BE REMOVING HIS GI. QUITE UNDERSTANDABLE, CONSIDERING HOW MUCH HE'S BEEN MOVING ABOUT IN THIS HEAT...
PERHAPS A PAUSE IS JUST WHAT WE NEED TO APPRECIATE THIS THRILL-A-MINUTE MATCH! OUR EYES CAN'T EVEN KEEP UP WITH ITS TWISTS AND TURNS!
HO. SO HE'S TAKING IT OFF ALREADY, EH?
HE MUST CONSIDER THIS ONE QUITE AN OPPONENT.
OOF!
THERE!
SIGH
THUDD
GOKU... DO YOU MIND IF I TAKE A LOOK AT THIS SHIRT?
NO, NO, GO RIGHT AHEAD.

READ THIS WAY

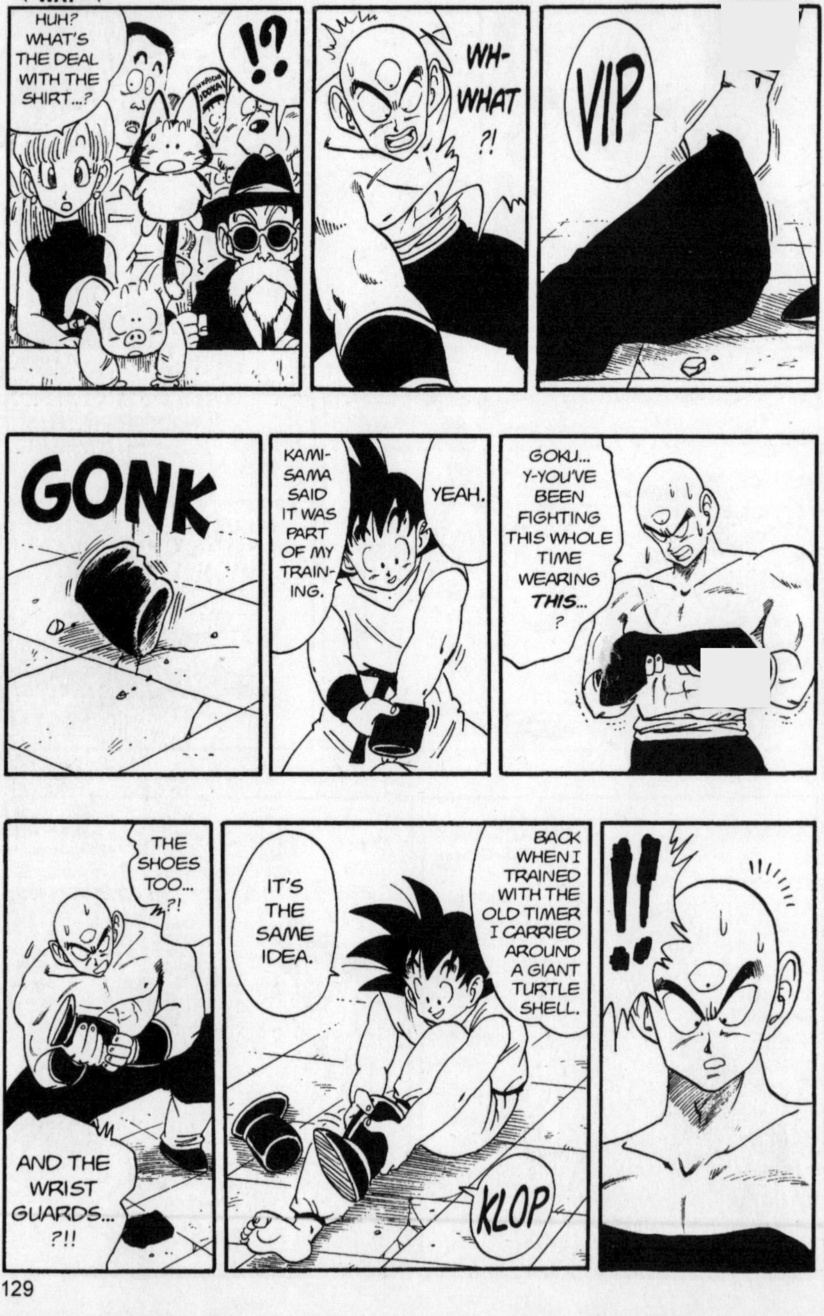
VIP
WH- WHAT ?!
!?
HUH? WHAT'S THE DEAL WITH THE SHIRT...?
GOKU... Y-YOU'VE BEEN FIGHTING THIS WHOLE TIME WEARING THIS...?
YEAH.
KAMI-SAMA SAID IT WAS PART OF MY TRAINING.
GONK
!!
BACK WHEN I TRAINED WITH THE OLD TIMER I CARRIED AROUND A GIANT TURTLE SHELL.
IT'S THE SAME IDEA.
KLOP
THE SHOES TOO...?!
AND THE WRIST GUARDS...?!!

READ THIS WAY

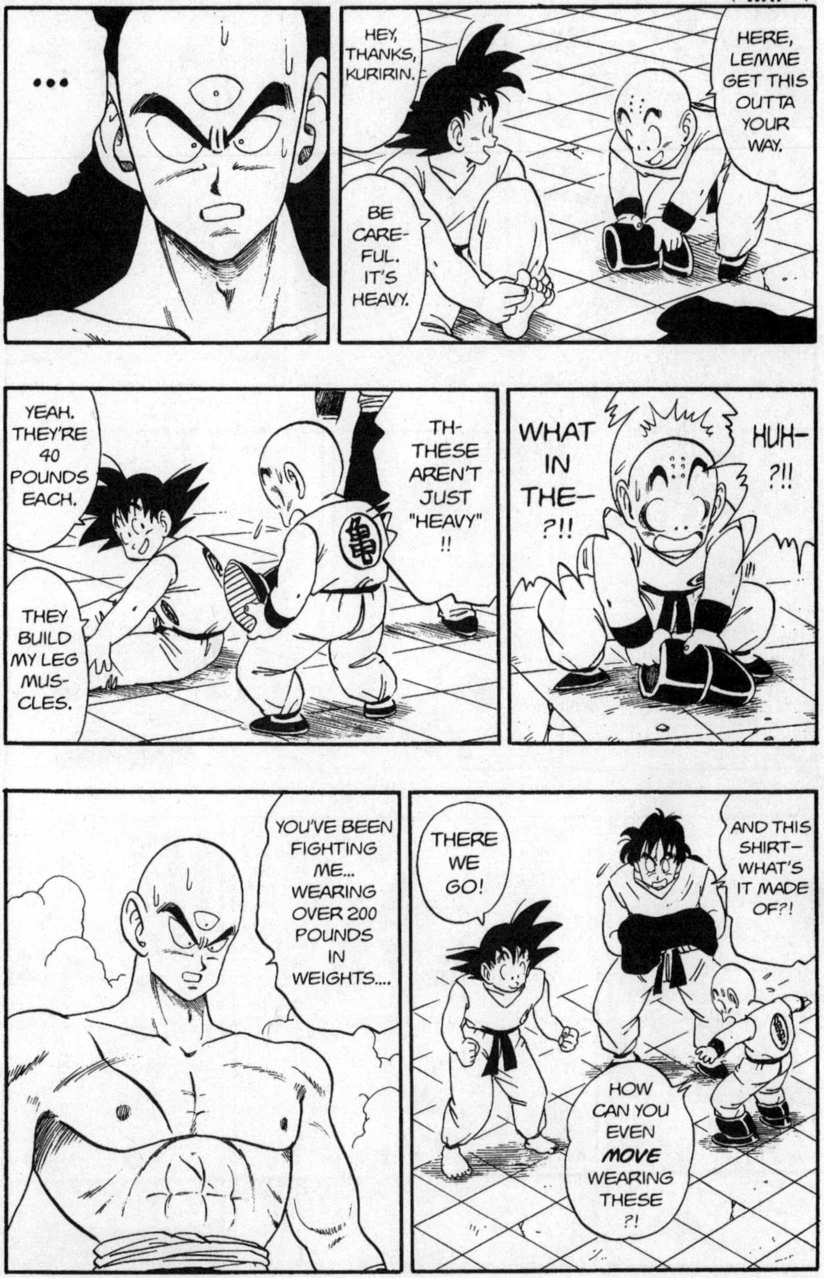

HERE, LEMME GET THIS OUTTA YOUR WAY.
HEY, THANKS, KURIRIN.
BE CARE-FUL. IT'S HEAVY.
...
HUH-?!!
WHAT IN THE-?!!
TH-THESE AREN'T JUST "HEAVY" !!
YEAH. THEY'RE 40 POUNDS EACH.
THEY BUILD MY LEG MUS-CLES.
AND THIS SHIRT—WHAT'S IT MADE OF?!
THERE WE GO!
HOW CAN YOU EVEN *MOVE* WEARING THESE?!
YOU'VE BEEN FIGHTING ME... WEARING OVER 200 POUNDS IN WEIGHTS....

READ THIS WAY

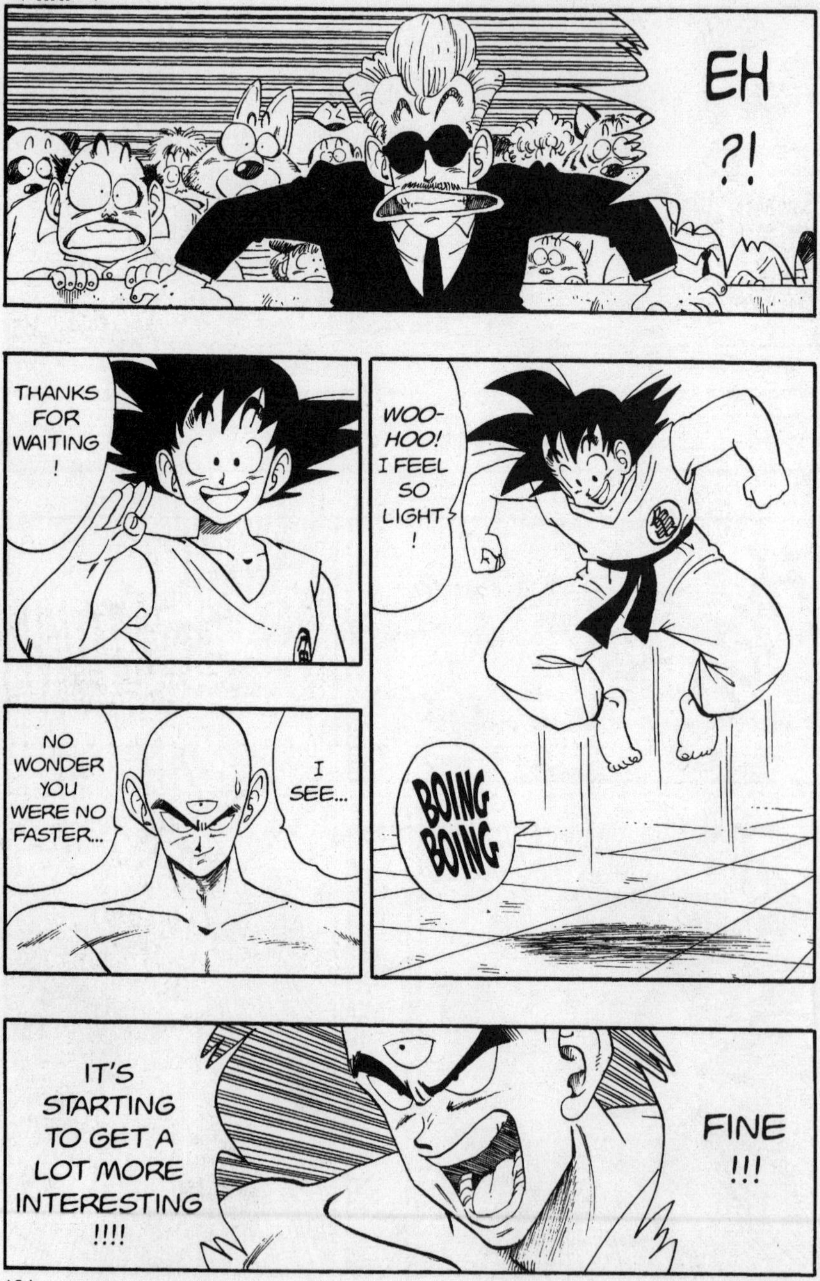

EH ?!
WOO-HOO! I FEEL SO LIGHT!
BOING BOING
THANKS FOR WAITING!
I SEE...
NO WONDER YOU WERE NO FASTER...
FINE!!!
IT'S STARTING TO GET A LOT MORE INTERESTING!!!!

READ THIS WAY

NOW SHOW ME HOW MUCH DIFFERENCE IT MAKES!
OK!
TSUAH!!!
HYOOO
SSS

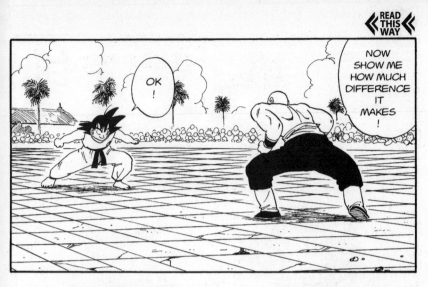

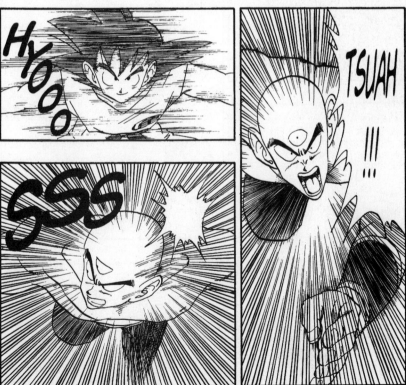

READ THIS WAY

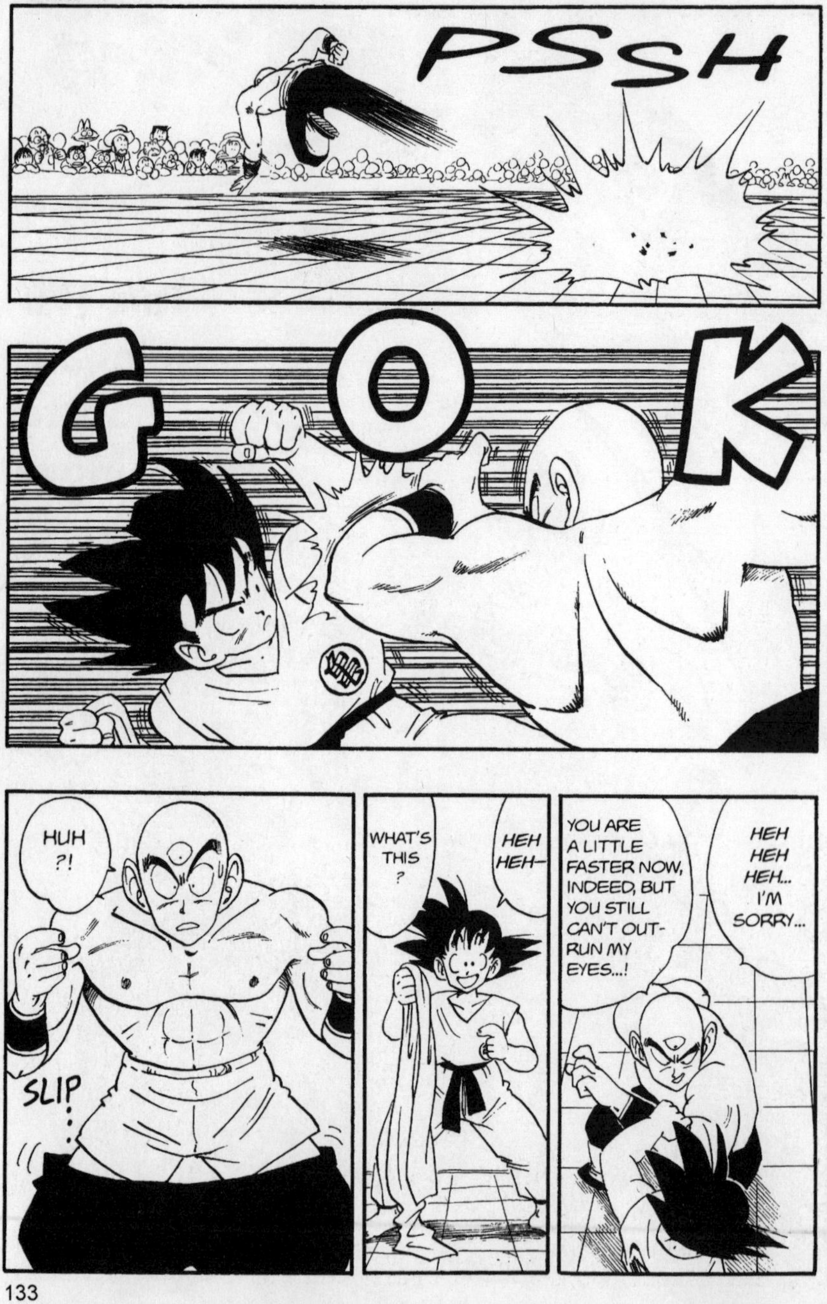
PSSH
GOK
HEH HEH HEH... I'M SORRY...
YOU ARE A LITTLE FASTER NOW, INDEED, BUT YOU STILL CAN'T OUT-RUN MY EYES...!
HEH HEH-
WHAT'S THIS ?
HUH ?!
SLIP...

Tale 178 · Tenshinhan's Secret Move!

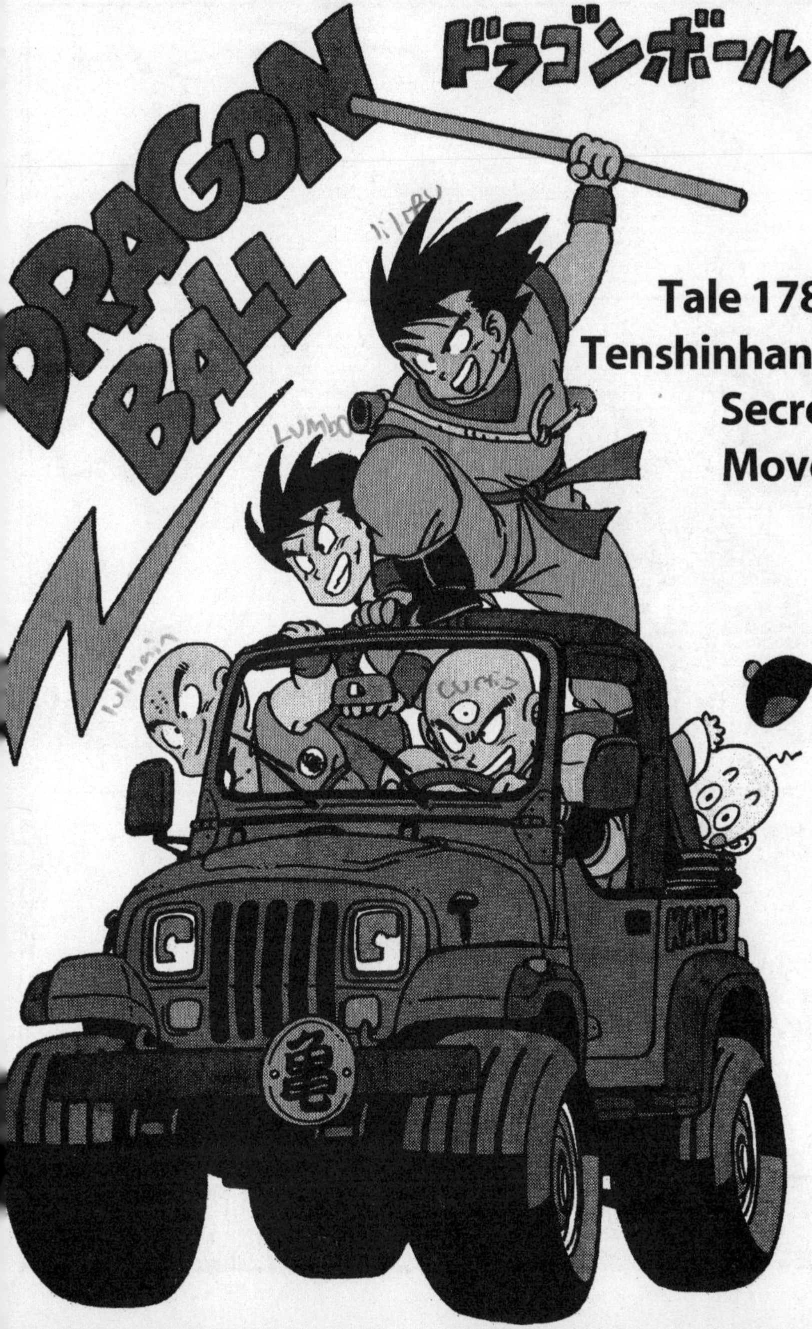
DRAGON BALL
ドラゴンボール
亀

READ THIS WAY

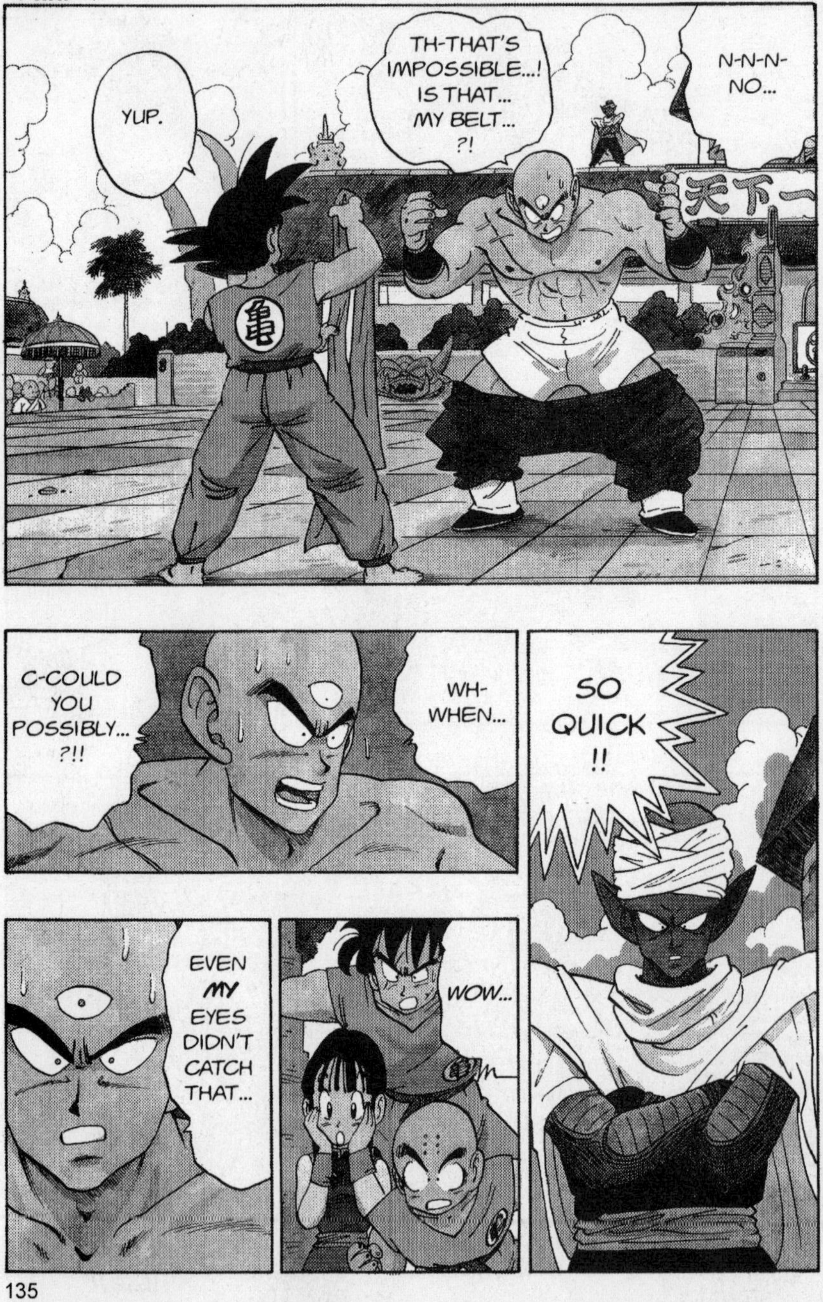
N-N-N-NO...
TH-THAT'S IMPOSSIBLE...! IS THAT... MY BELT...?!
YUP.
天下一
SO QUICK!!
WH-WHEN...
C-COULD YOU POSSIBLY...?!!
WOW...
EVEN MY EYES DIDN'T CATCH THAT...

READ THIS WAY

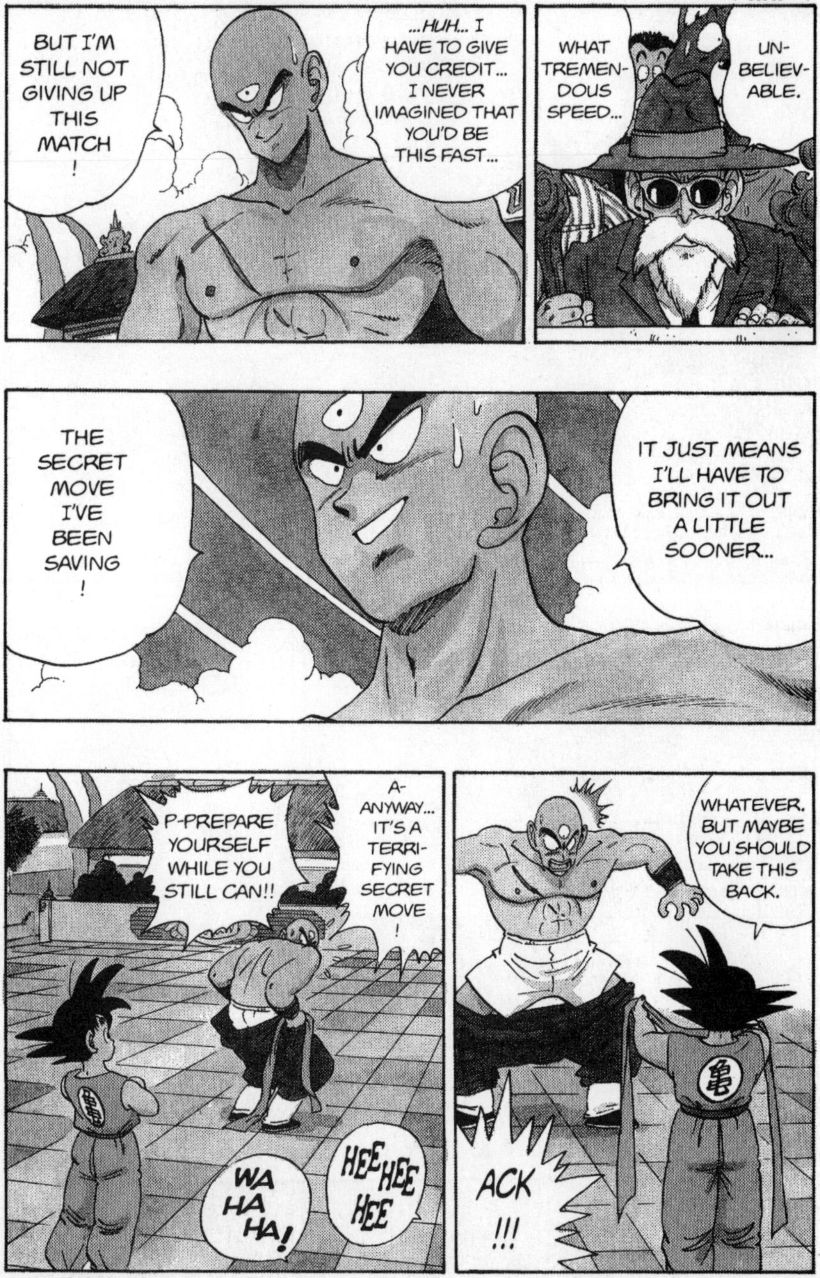

UNBELIEVABLE.
WHAT TREMENDOUS SPEED...
...HUH... I HAVE TO GIVE YOU CREDIT... I NEVER IMAGINED THAT YOU'D BE THIS FAST...
BUT I'M STILL NOT GIVING UP THIS MATCH!
IT JUST MEANS I'LL HAVE TO BRING IT OUT A LITTLE SOONER...
THE SECRET MOVE I'VE BEEN SAVING!
WHATEVER. BUT MAYBE YOU SHOULD TAKE THIS BACK.
ACK!!!
A-ANYWAY... IT'S A TERRIFYING SECRET MOVE!
P-PREPARE YOURSELF WHILE YOU STILL CAN!!
HEE HEE HEE
WA HA HA!

READ THIS WAY

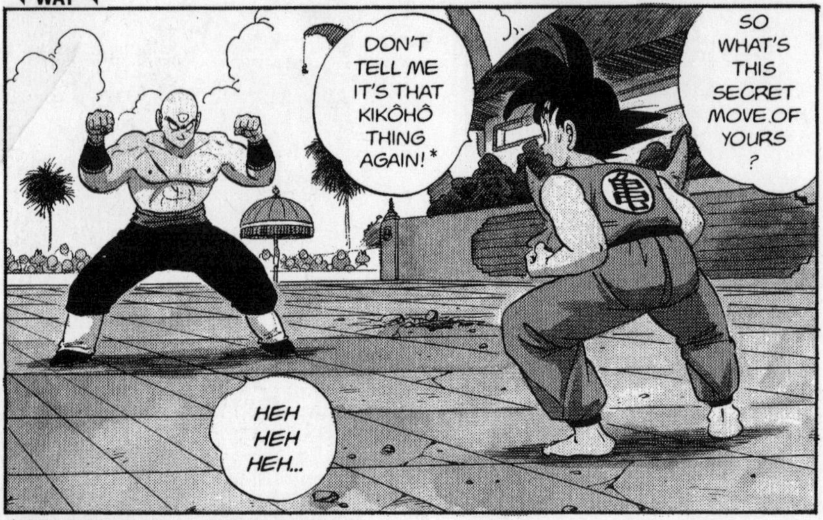
SO WHAT'S THIS SECRET MOVE OF YOURS ?
DON'T TELL ME IT'S THAT KIKÔHÔ THING AGAIN! *
HEH HEH HEH...

* SEE DRAGON BALL VOL. 12—EDITOR

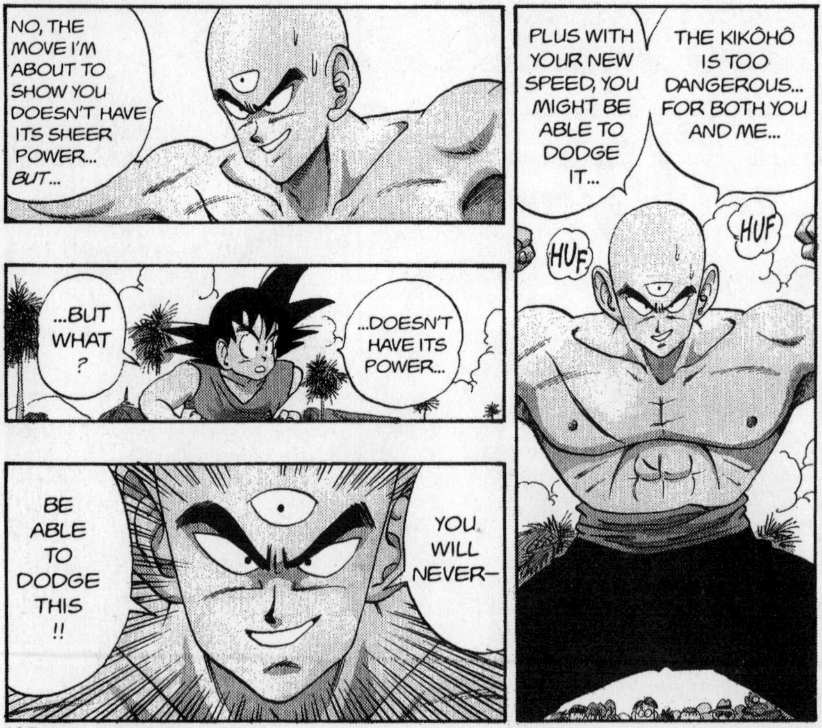
THE KIKÔHÔ IS TOO DANGEROUS... FOR BOTH YOU AND ME...
PLUS WITH YOUR NEW SPEED, YOU MIGHT BE ABLE TO DODGE IT...
HUF
HUF
NO, THE MOVE I'M ABOUT TO SHOW YOU DOESN'T HAVE ITS SHEER POWER... BUT...
...DOESN'T HAVE ITS POWER...
...BUT WHAT ?
YOU WILL NEVER—
BE ABLE TO DODGE THIS !!

READ THIS WAY

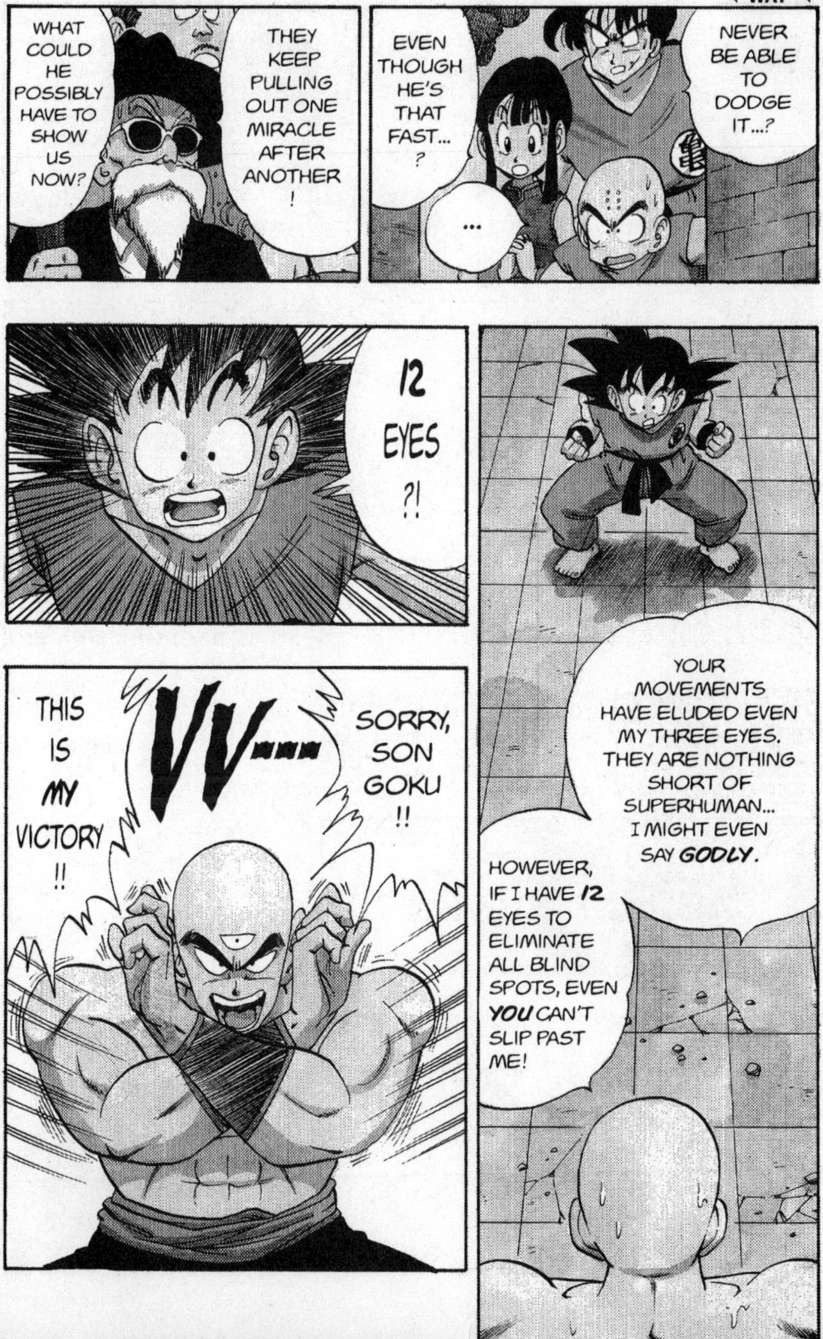
NEVER BE ABLE TO DODGE IT...?
EVEN THOUGH HE'S THAT FAST...?
...
THEY KEEP PULLING OUT ONE MIRACLE AFTER ANOTHER!
WHAT COULD HE POSSIBLY HAVE TO SHOW US NOW?
YOUR MOVEMENTS HAVE ELUDED EVEN MY THREE EYES. THEY ARE NOTHING SHORT OF SUPERHUMAN... I MIGHT EVEN SAY **GODLY**.
HOWEVER, IF I HAVE **12** EYES TO ELIMINATE ALL BLIND SPOTS, EVEN **YOU** CAN'T SLIP PAST ME!
12 EYES?!
SORRY, SON GOKU!!
VV----
THIS IS **MY** VICTORY!!

READ THIS WAY

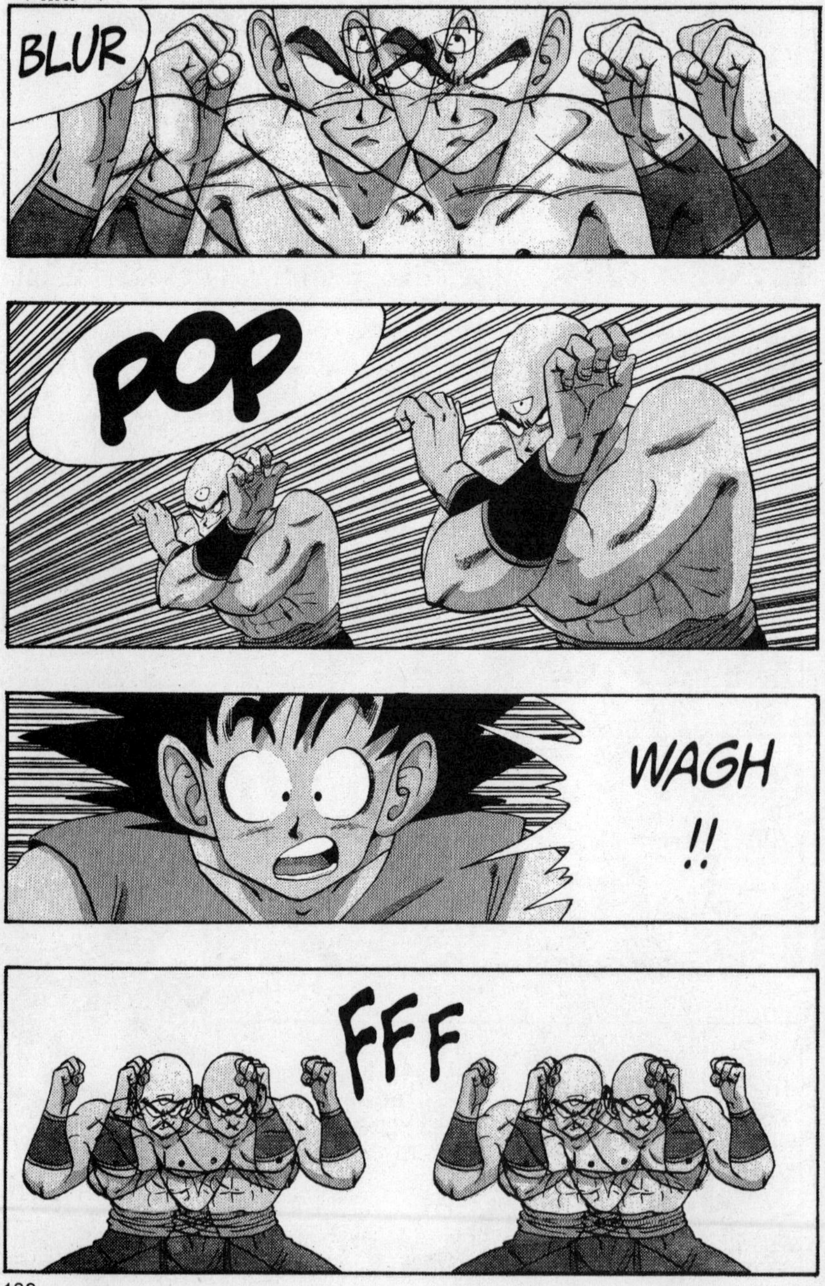
BLUR
POP
WAGH !!
FFF

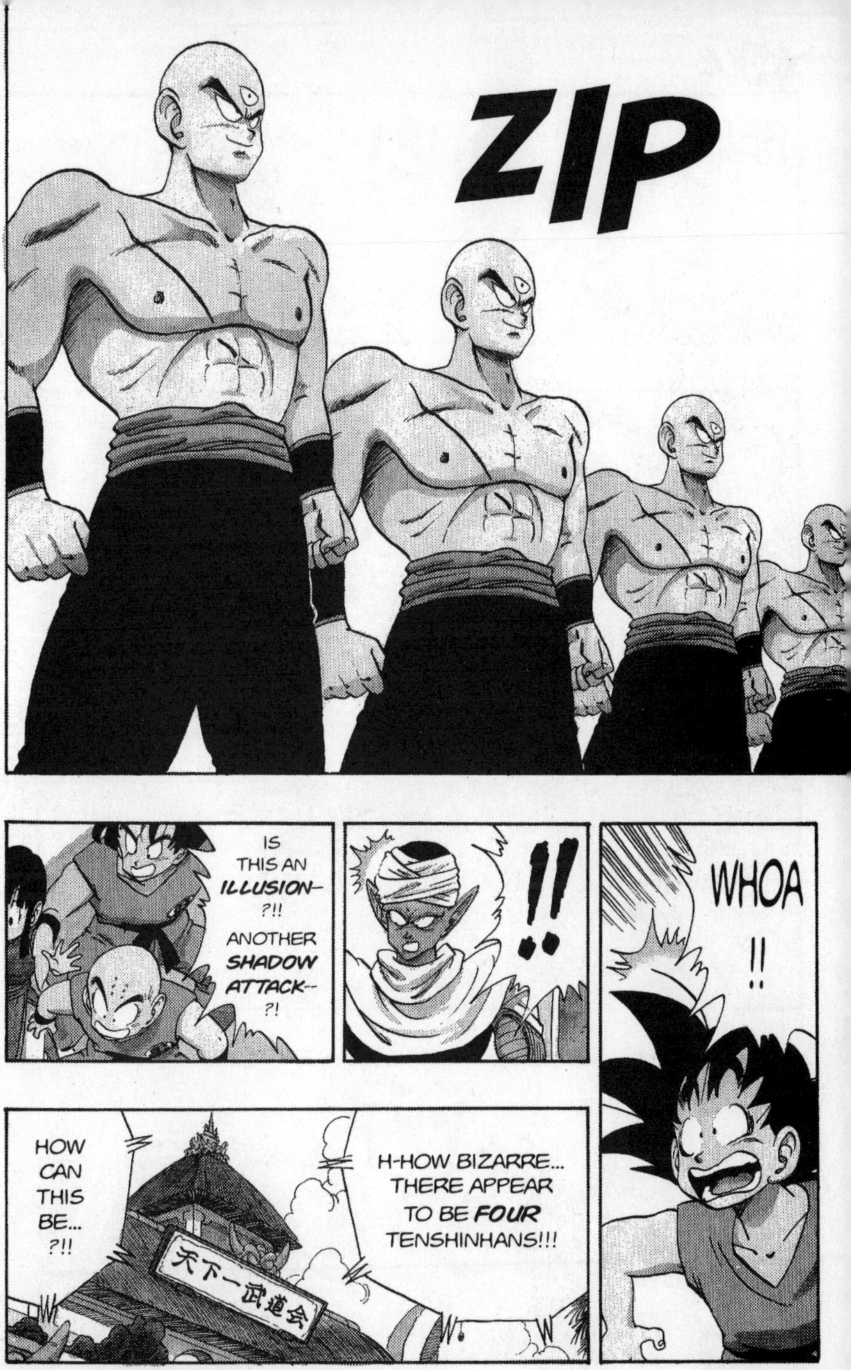
ZIP
WHOA !!
!!
IS THIS AN ILLUSION--?!!
ANOTHER SHADOW ATTACK--?!
H-HOW BIZARRE... THERE APPEAR TO BE FOUR TENSHINHANS!!!
HOW CAN THIS BE...?!!
天下一武道会

READ THIS WAY

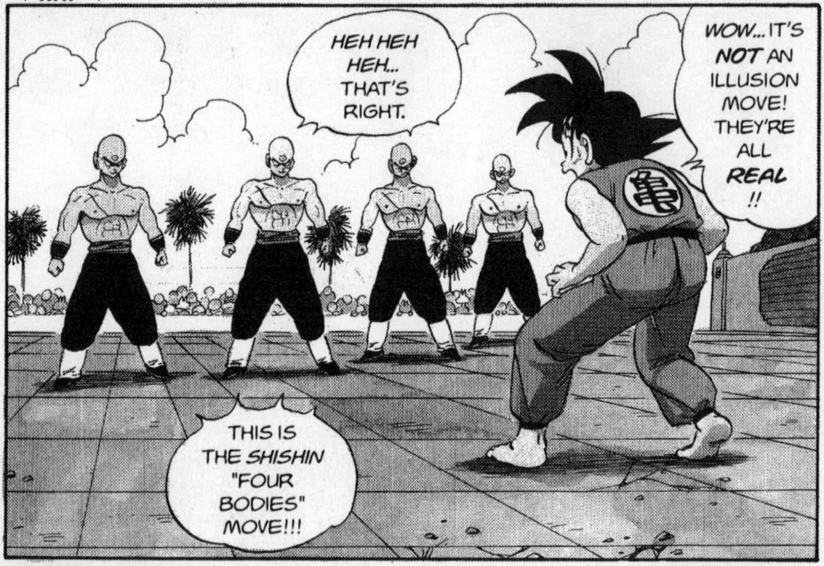
WOW... IT'S NOT AN ILLUSION MOVE! THEY'RE ALL REAL !!
HEH HEH HEH... THAT'S RIGHT.
THIS IS THE SHISHIN "FOUR BODIES" MOVE!!!

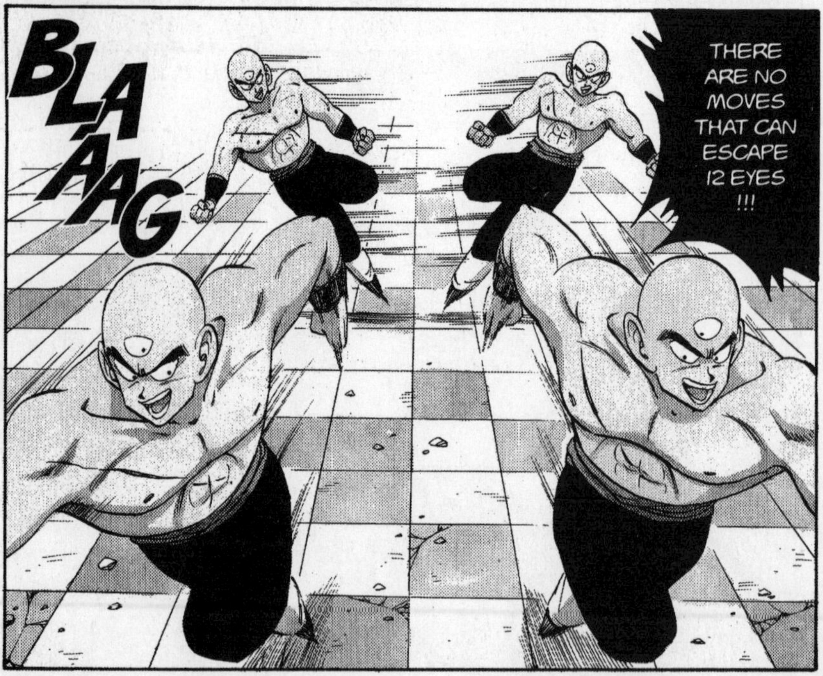
THERE ARE NO MOVES THAT CAN ESCAPE 12 EYES !!!
BLAAAG

READ THIS WAY

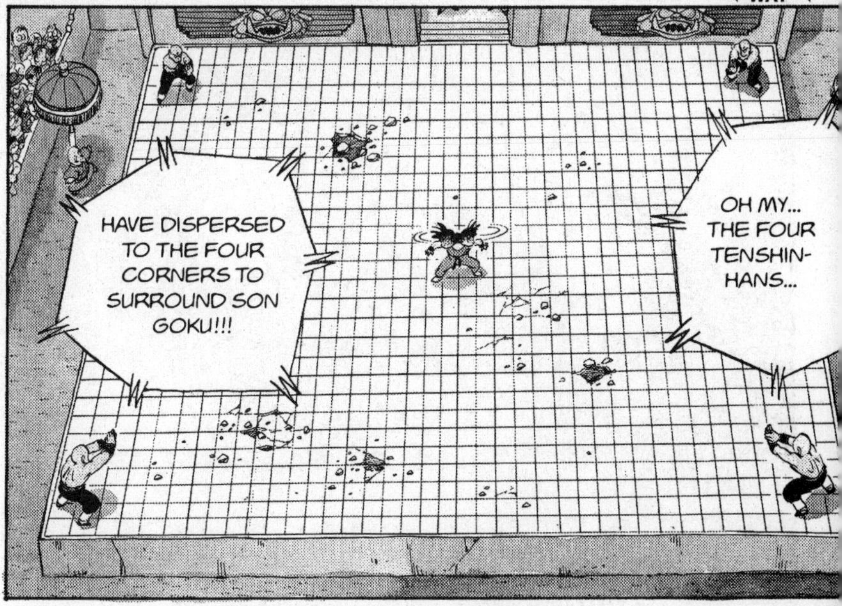
OH MY... THE FOUR TENSHIN-HANS...
HAVE DISPERSED TO THE FOUR CORNERS TO SURROUND SON GOKU!!!

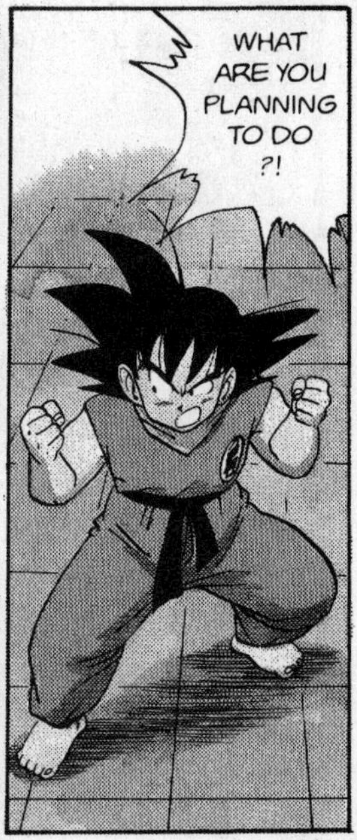
WHAT ARE YOU PLANNING TO DO ?!

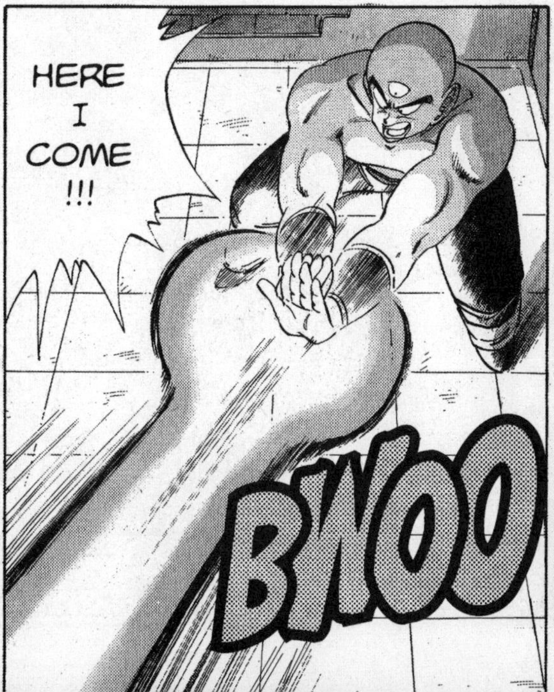
HERE I COME !!!
BWOO

READ THIS WAY

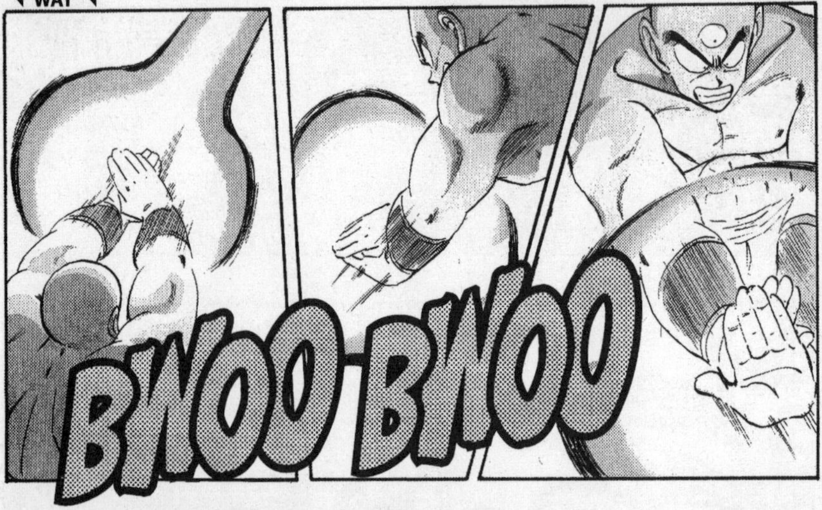
BWOO BWOO

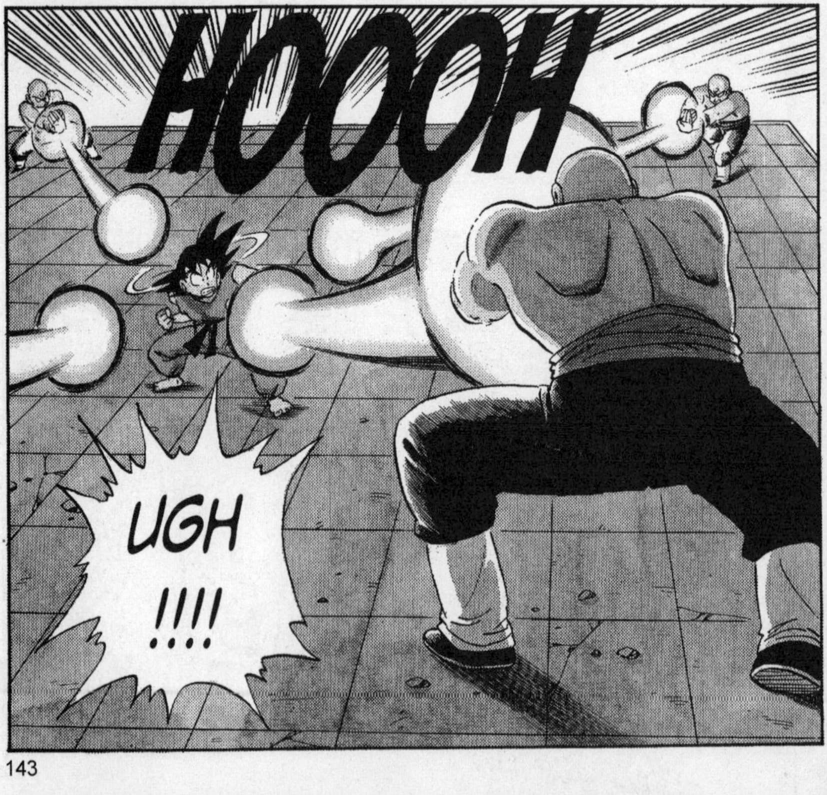
HOOOH
UGH !!!!

READ THIS WAY

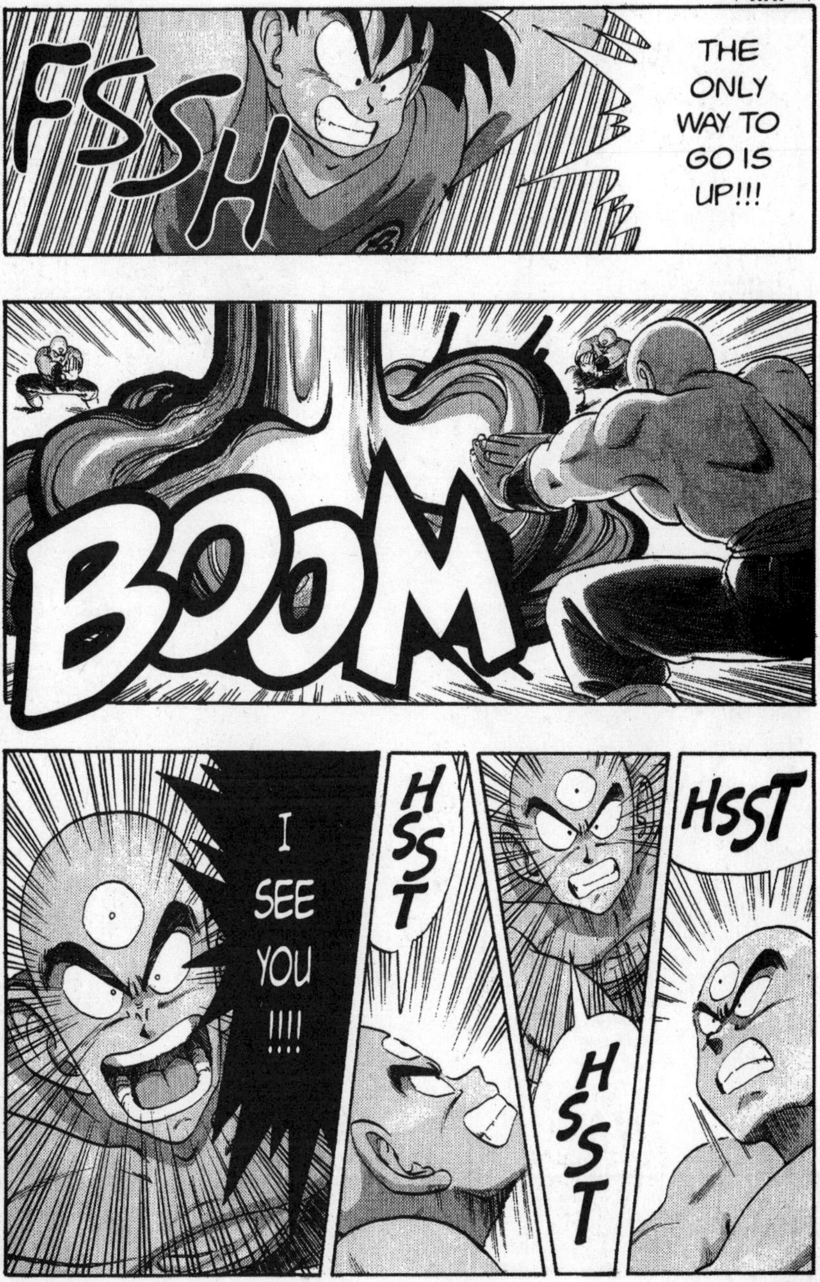

THE ONLY WAY TO GO IS UP!!!
FSSH
BOOM
HSST
HSST
HSST
I SEE YOU!!!!

READ THIS WAY

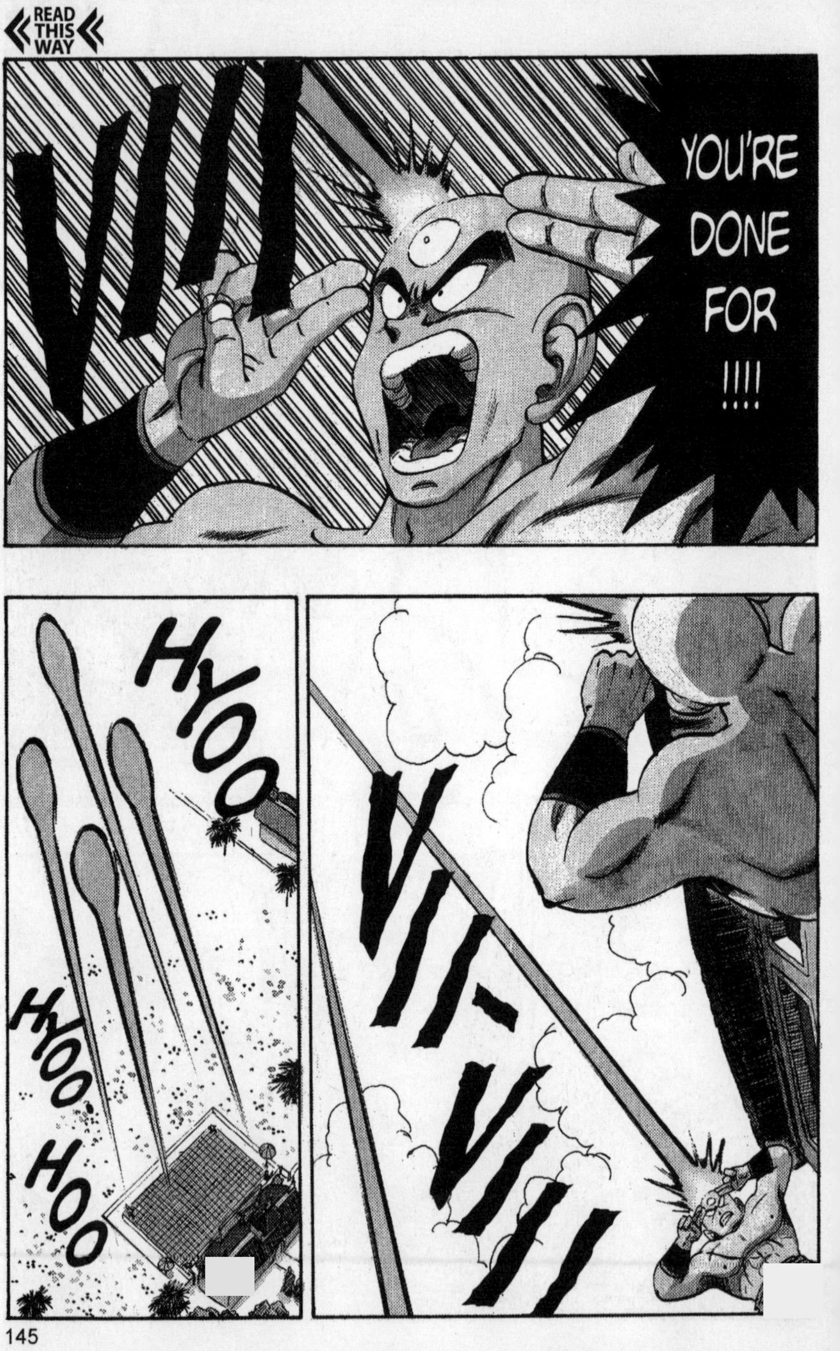
YOU'RE DONE FOR !!!!
VIII
VII-VIII
HYOO
HYOO
HOO
HOO

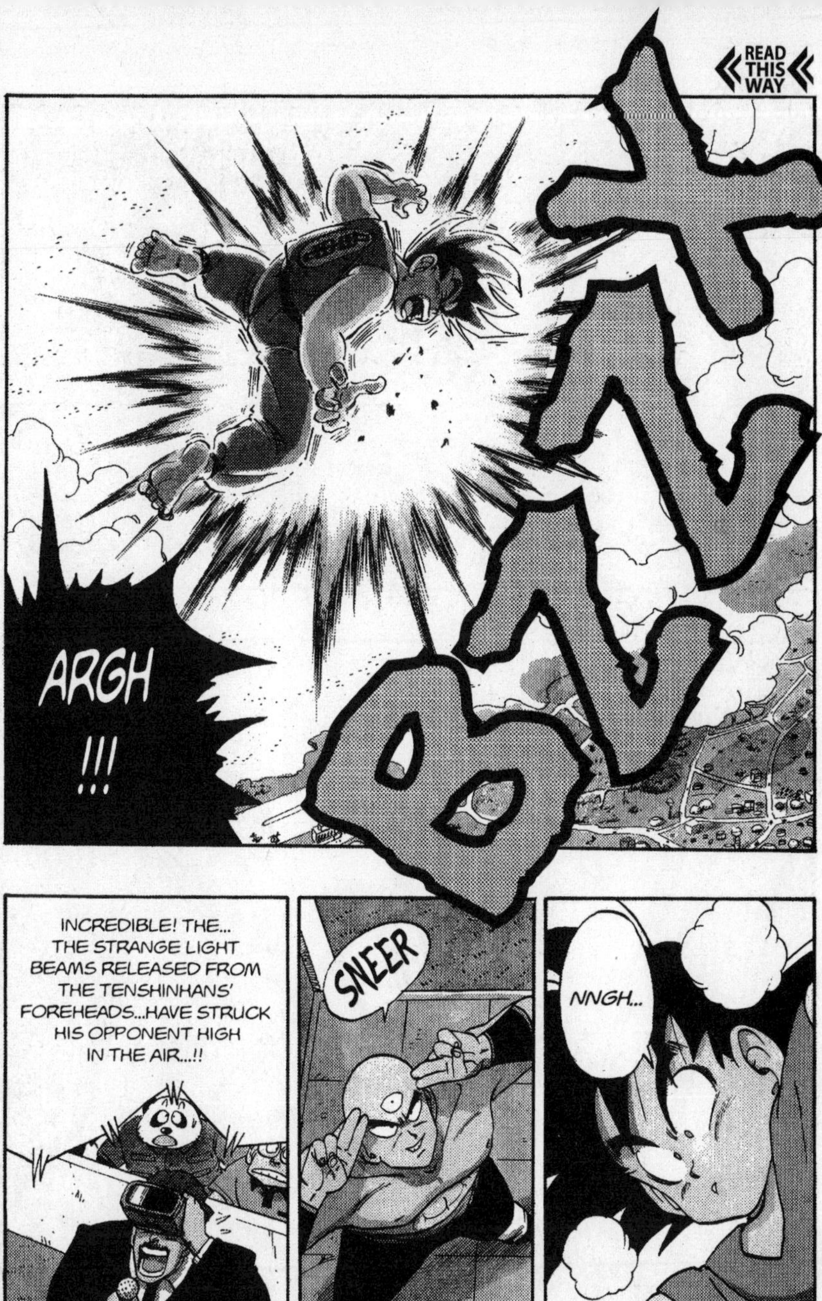
READ THIS WAY
ARGH !!!
NNGH...
SNEER
INCREDIBLE! THE... THE STRANGE LIGHT BEAMS RELEASED FROM THE TENSHINHANS' FOREHEADS...HAVE STRUCK HIS OPPONENT HIGH IN THE AIR...!!

READ THIS WAY

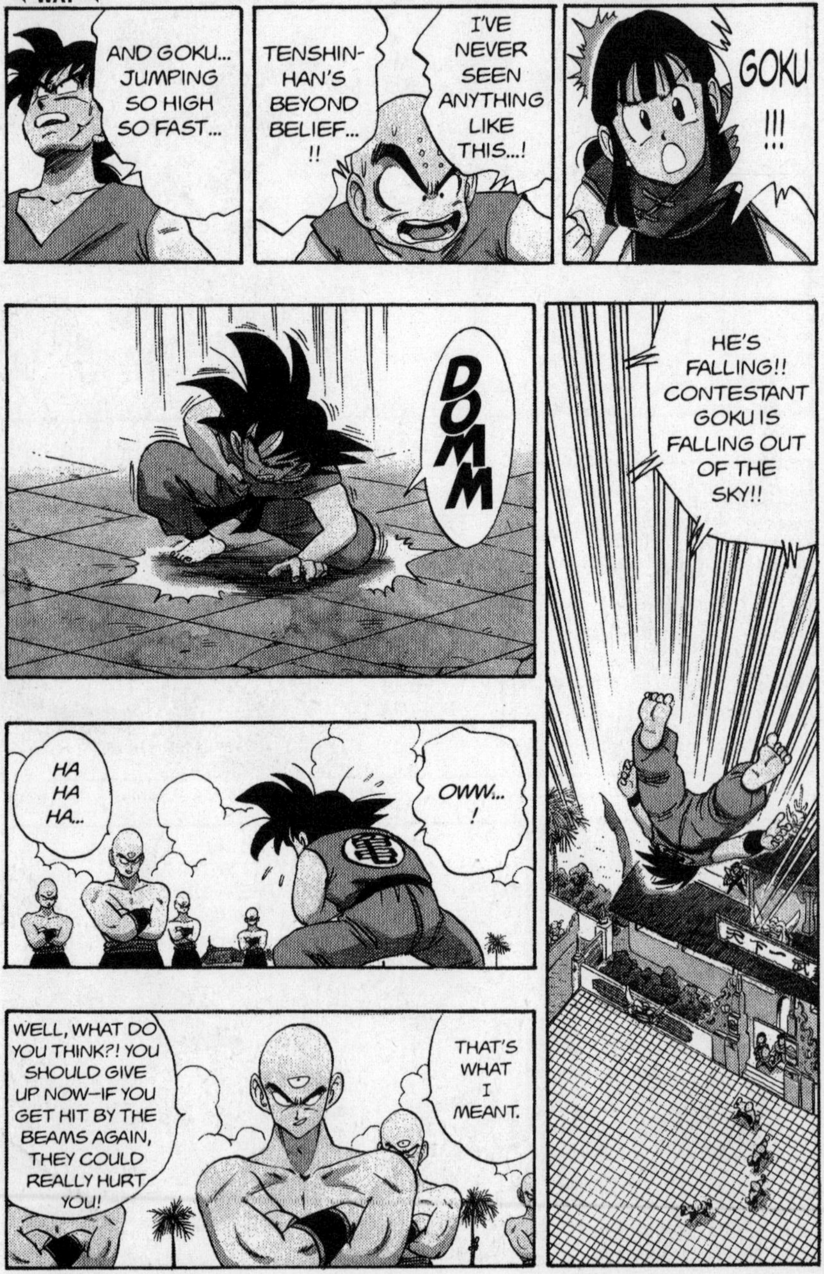
GOKU !!!
I'VE NEVER SEEN ANYTHING LIKE THIS...!
TENSHIN-HAN'S BEYOND BELIEF... !!
AND GOKU... JUMPING SO HIGH SO FAST...
HE'S FALLING!! CONTESTANT GOKU IS FALLING OUT OF THE SKY!!
DOMM
OWW... !
HA HA HA...
THAT'S WHAT I MEANT.
WELL, WHAT DO YOU THINK?! YOU SHOULD GIVE UP NOW—IF YOU GET HIT BY THE BEAMS AGAIN, THEY COULD REALLY HURT YOU!

READ THIS WAY

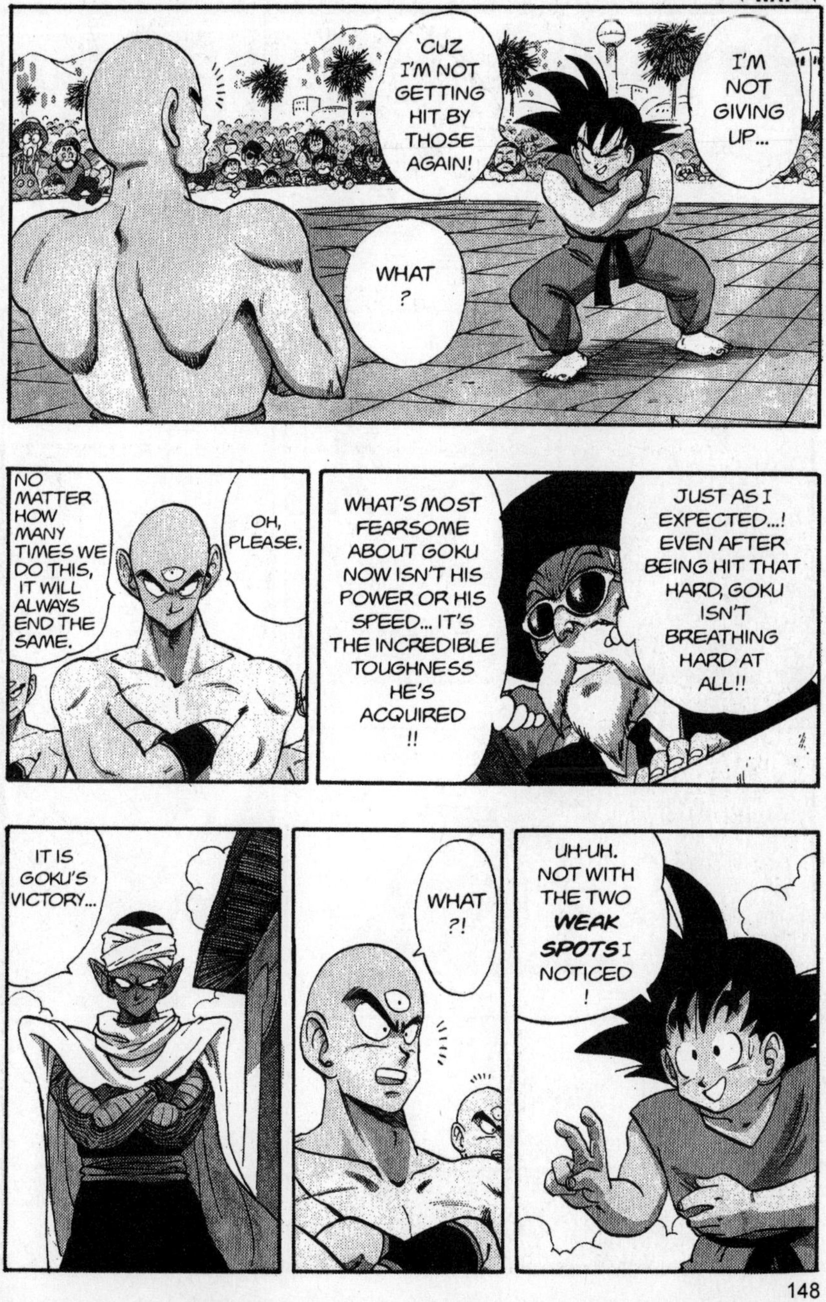
I'M NOT GIVING UP...
'CUZ I'M NOT GETTING HIT BY THOSE AGAIN!
WHAT ?
JUST AS I EXPECTED...! EVEN AFTER BEING HIT THAT HARD, GOKU ISN'T BREATHING HARD AT ALL!!
WHAT'S MOST FEARSOME ABOUT GOKU NOW ISN'T HIS POWER OR HIS SPEED... IT'S THE INCREDIBLE TOUGHNESS HE'S ACQUIRED !!
OH, PLEASE.
NO MATTER HOW MANY TIMES WE DO THIS, IT WILL ALWAYS END THE SAME.
UH-UH. NOT WITH THE TWO **WEAK SPOTS** I NOTICED !
WHAT ?!
IT IS GOKU'S VICTORY...

ドラゴンボール

DRAGON BALL

Tale 179
The Two Weak Points

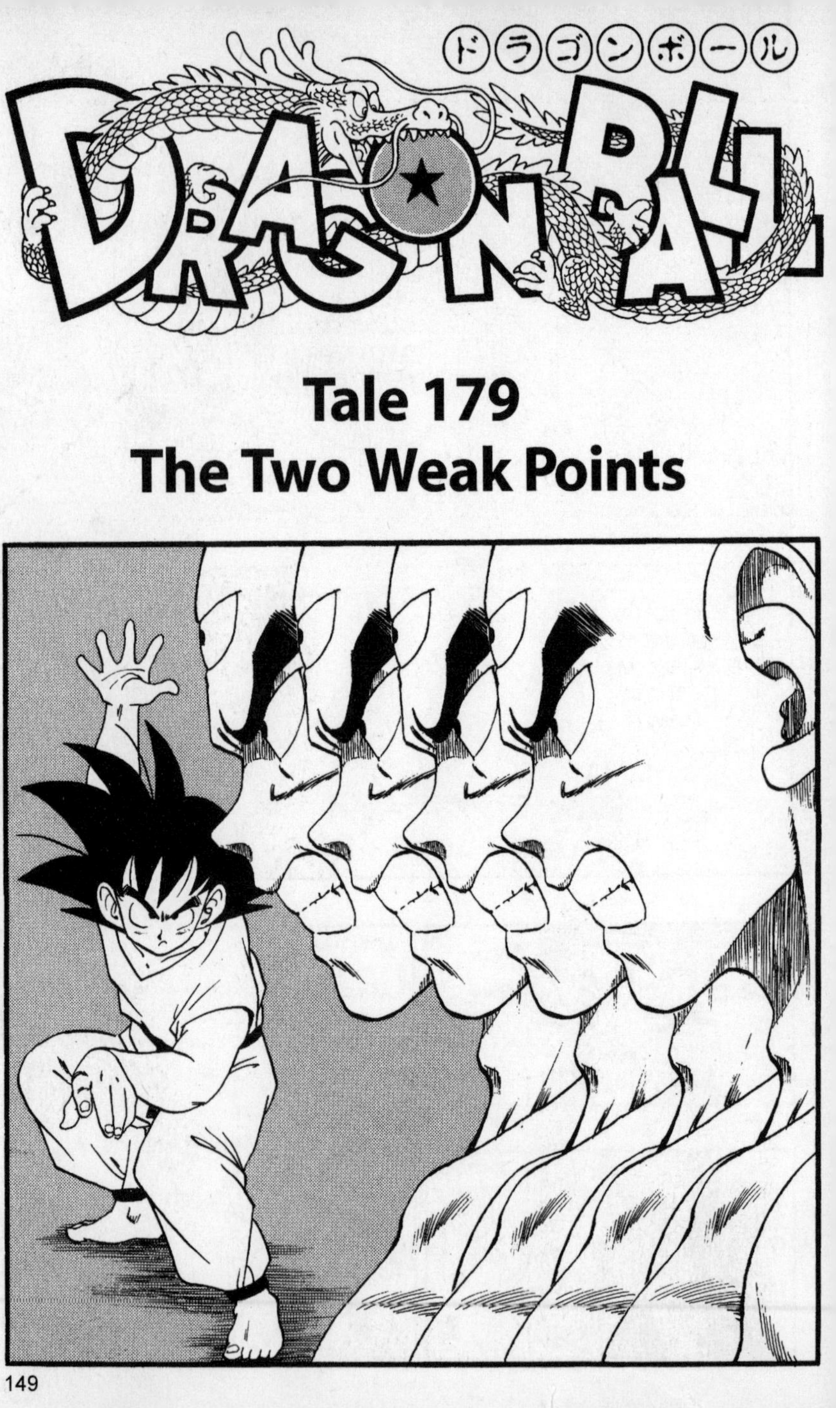

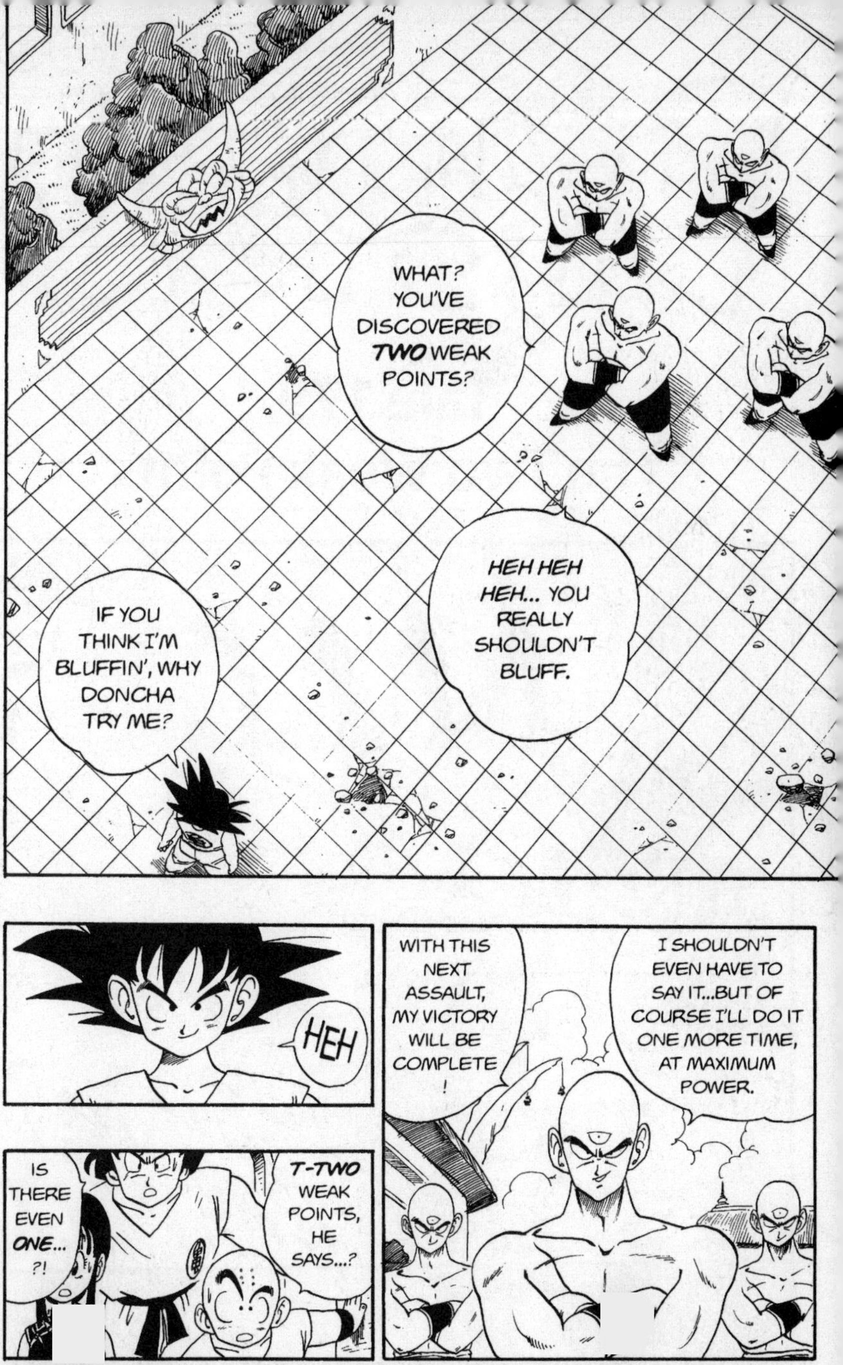
WHAT? YOU'VE DISCOVERED **TWO** WEAK POINTS?
HEH HEH HEH... YOU REALLY SHOULDN'T BLUFF.
IF YOU THINK I'M BLUFFIN', WHY DONCHA TRY ME?
I SHOULDN'T EVEN HAVE TO SAY IT...BUT OF COURSE I'LL DO IT ONE MORE TIME, AT MAXIMUM POWER.
WITH THIS NEXT ASSAULT, MY VICTORY WILL BE COMPLETE!
HEH
T-TWO WEAK POINTS, HE SAYS...?
IS THERE EVEN *ONE...*?!

READ THIS WAY

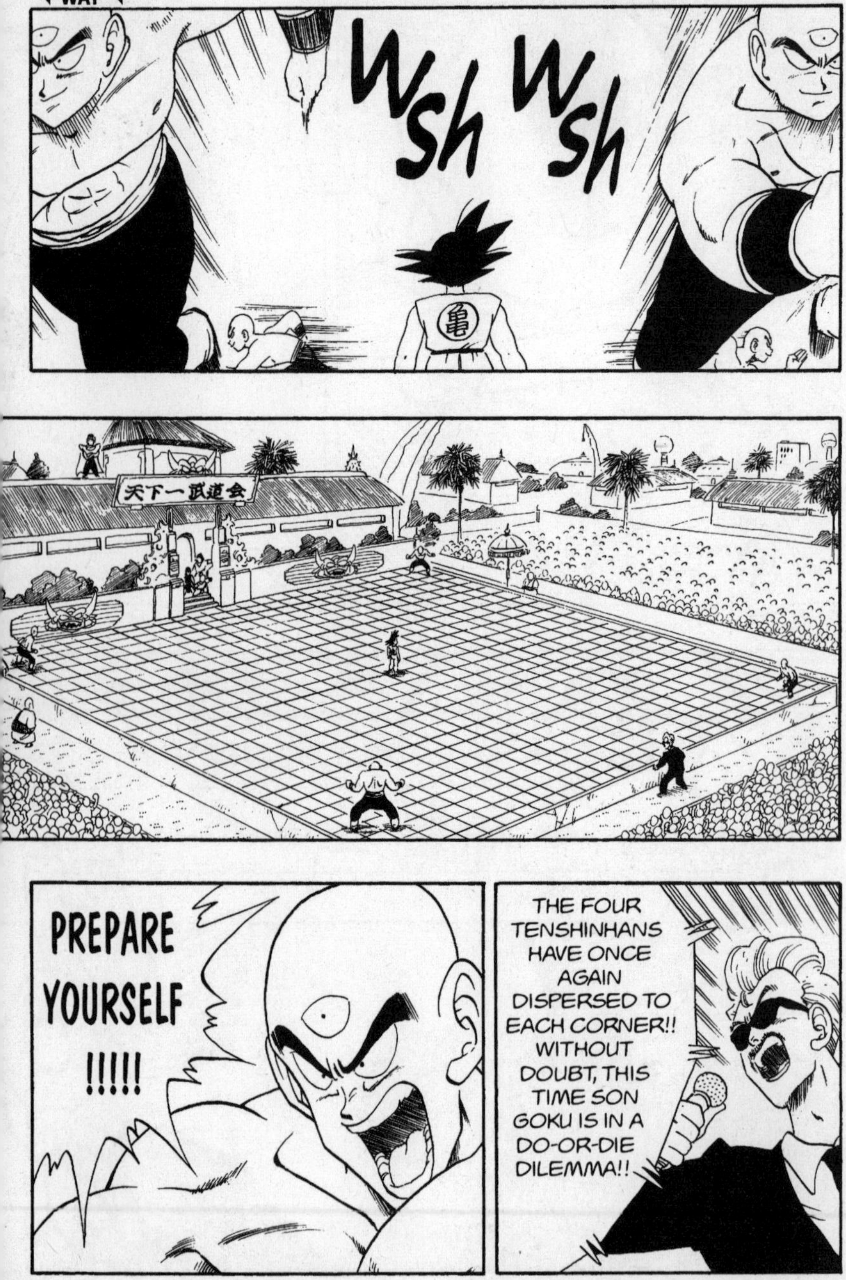

WSH WSH
天下一武道会
THE FOUR TENSHINHANS HAVE ONCE AGAIN DISPERSED TO EACH CORNER!! WITHOUT DOUBT, THIS TIME SON GOKU IS IN A DO-OR-DIE DILEMMA!!
PREPARE YOURSELF !!!!!

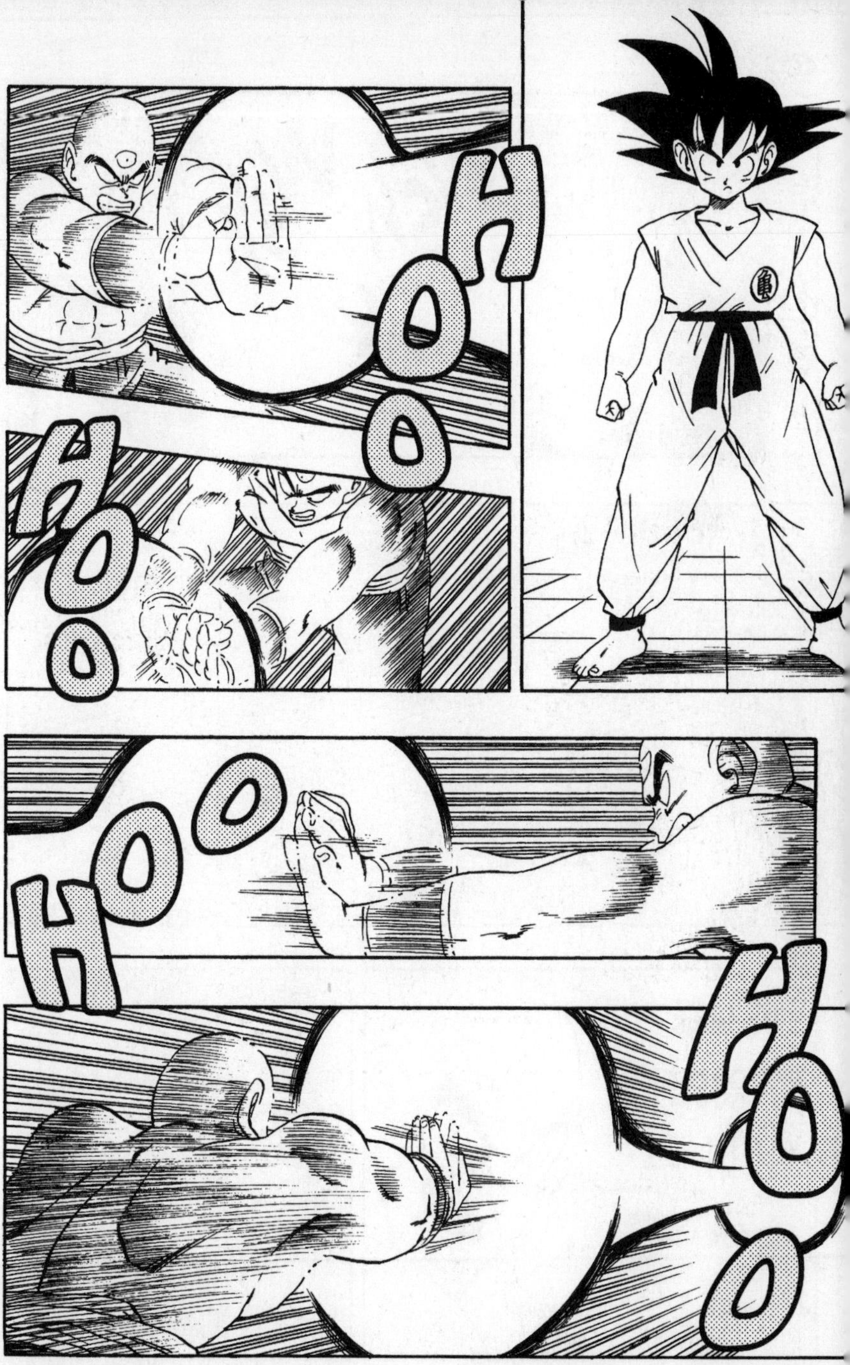
HOOO
HOOO
HOOO
HOOO

READ THIS WAY

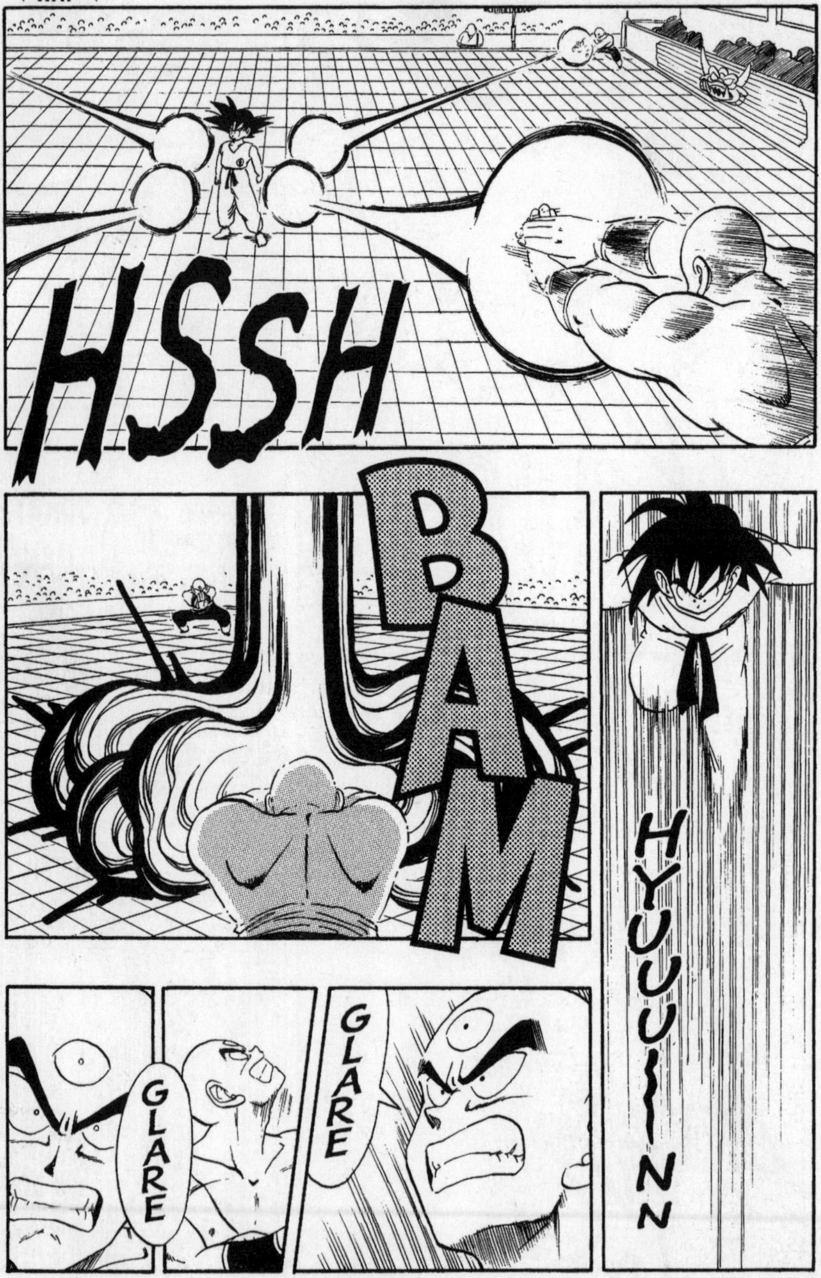
HSSH
HYUUUIINN
BAM
GLARE
GLARE

READ THIS WAY

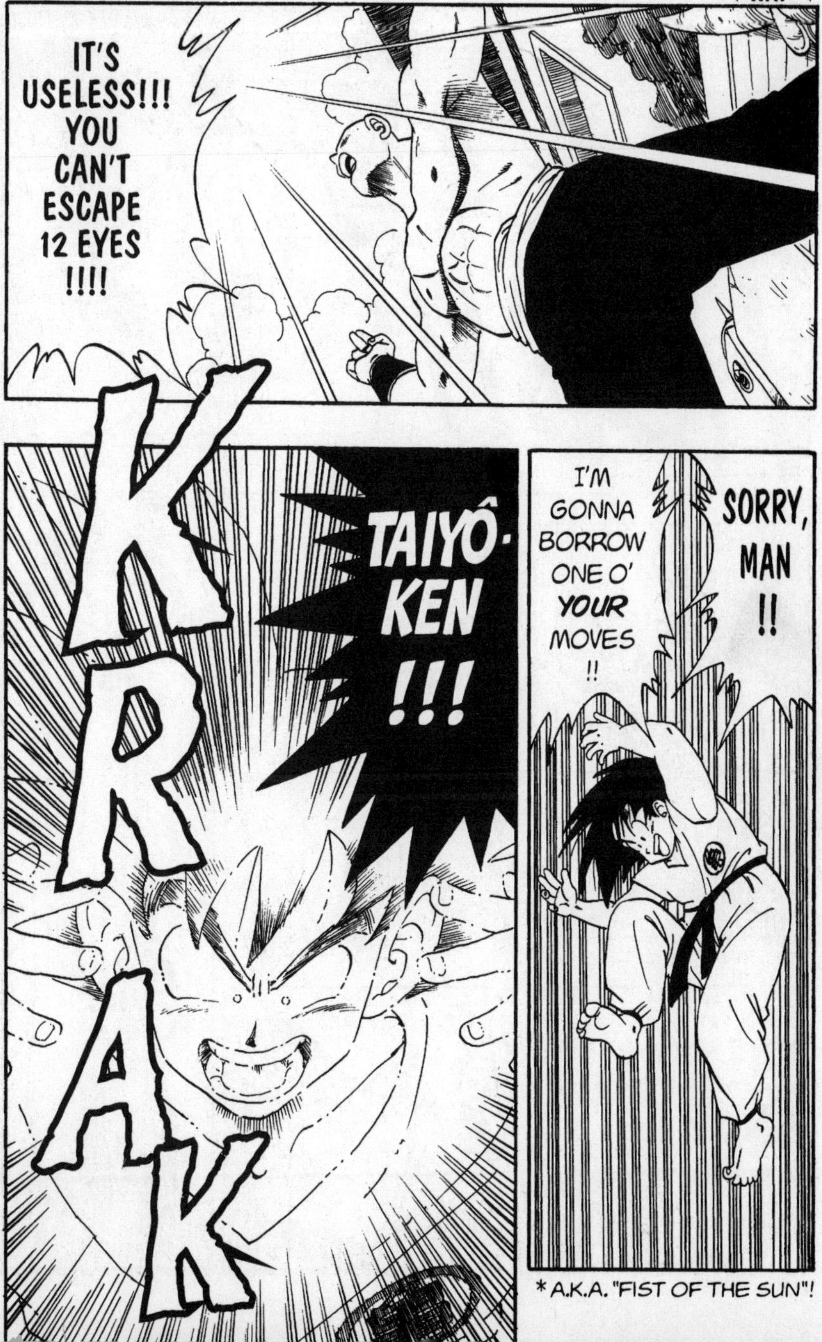
IT'S USELESS!!! YOU CAN'T ESCAPE 12 EYES !!!!
SORRY, MAN !!
I'M GONNA BORROW ONE O' YOUR MOVES !!
TAIYÔ-KEN !!!
KRAK

* A.K.A. "FIST OF THE SUN"!

READ THIS WAY

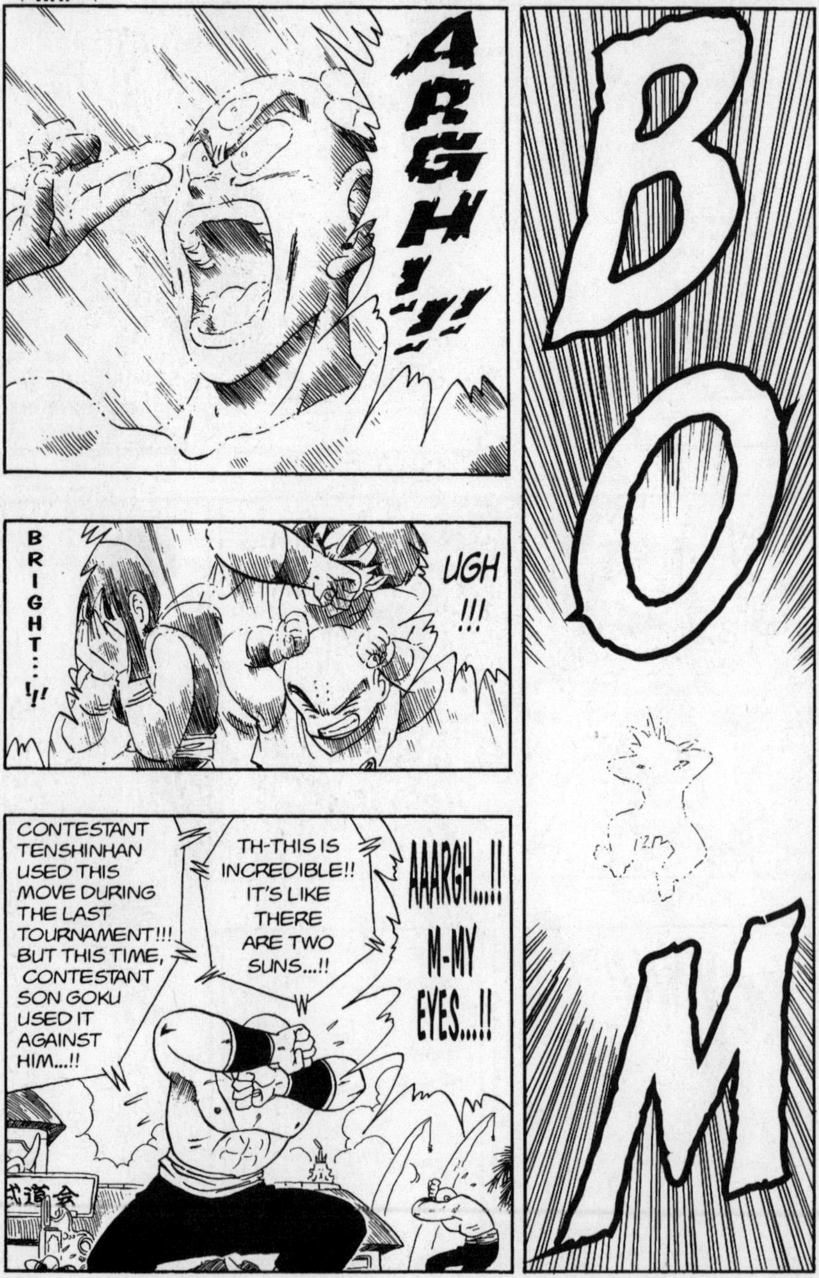
BOOM
ARGH!!!!
UGH!!!
BRIGHT...!!!
AAARGH...!! M-MY EYES...!!
TH-THIS IS INCREDIBLE!! IT'S LIKE THERE ARE TWO SUNS...!!
CONTESTANT TENSHINHAN USED THIS MOVE DURING THE LAST TOURNAMENT!!! BUT THIS TIME, CONTESTANT SON GOKU USED IT AGAINST HIM...!!
武道会

READ THIS WAY

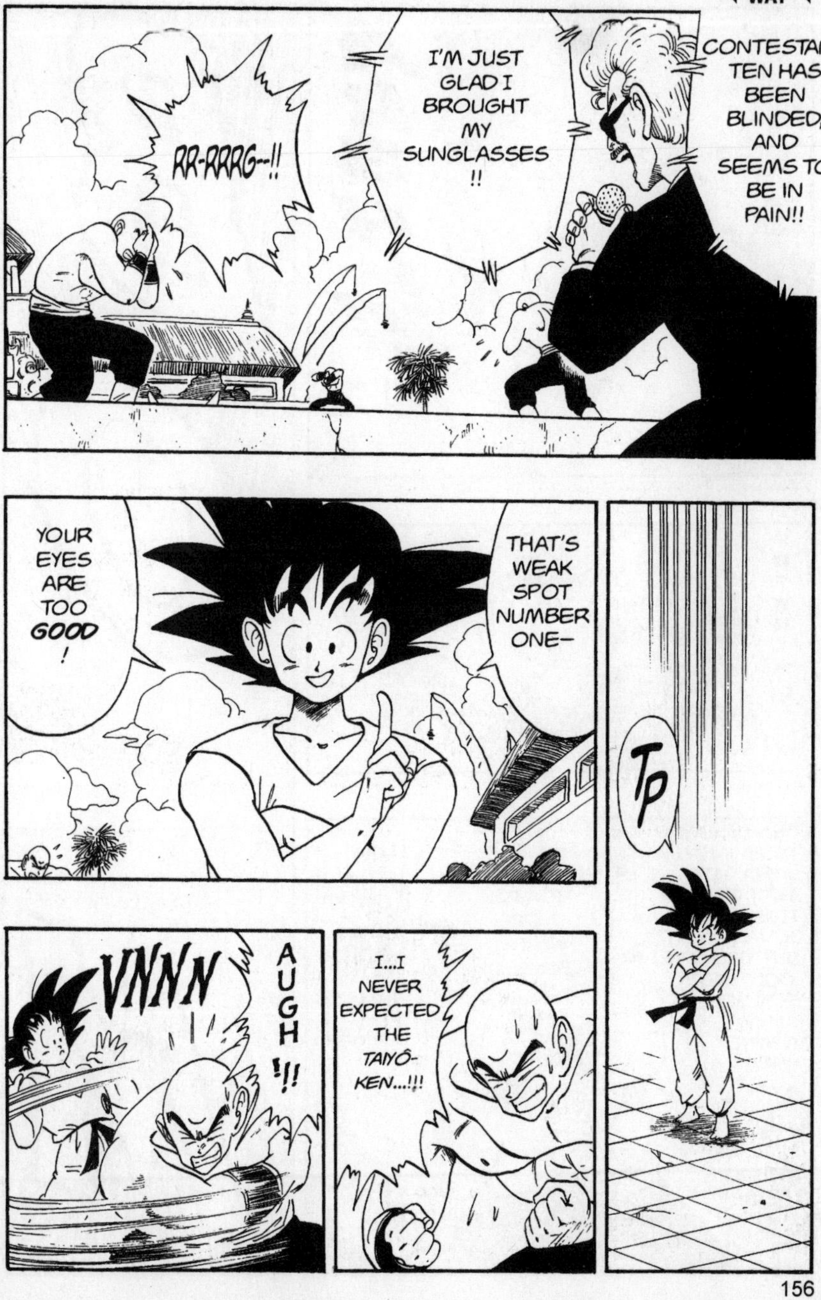
CONTESTANT TEN HAS BEEN BLINDED, AND SEEMS TO BE IN PAIN!!
I'M JUST GLAD I BROUGHT MY SUNGLASSES!!
RR-RRRG--!!
TP
THAT'S WEAK SPOT NUMBER ONE–
YOUR EYES ARE TOO *GOOD*!
I...I NEVER EXPECTED THE *TAIYÔ-KEN*...!!!
AUGH!!!
VNNN

READ THIS WAY

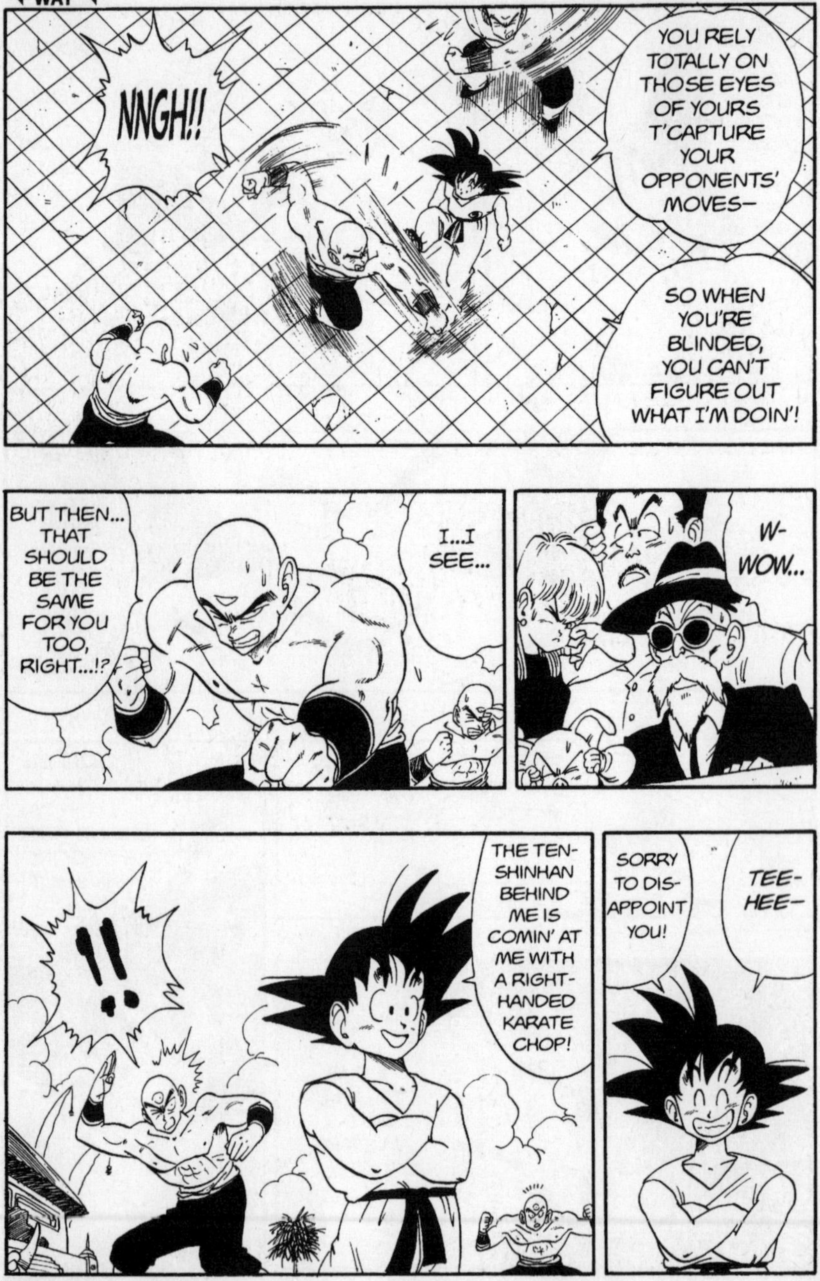

YOU RELY TOTALLY ON THOSE EYES OF YOURS T'CAPTURE YOUR OPPONENTS' MOVES–
SO WHEN YOU'RE BLINDED, YOU CAN'T FIGURE OUT WHAT I'M DOIN'!
NNGH!!
W-WOW...
I...I SEE...
BUT THEN... THAT SHOULD BE THE SAME FOR YOU TOO, RIGHT...!?
TEE-HEE–
SORRY TO DIS-APPOINT YOU!
THE TEN-SHINHAN BEHIND ME IS COMIN' AT ME WITH A RIGHT-HANDED KARATE CHOP!
!!

READ THIS WAY

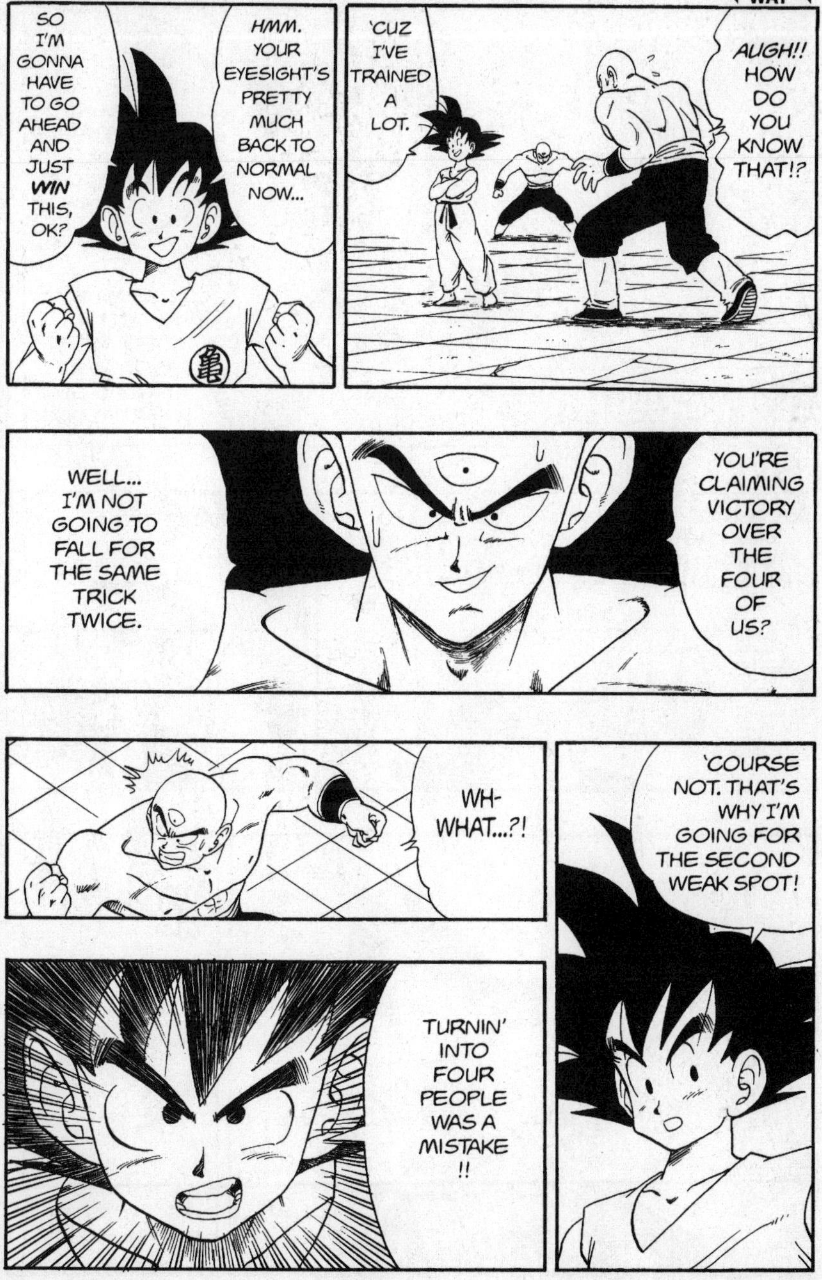
AUGH!! HOW DO YOU KNOW THAT!?
'CUZ I'VE TRAINED A LOT.
HMM. YOUR EYESIGHT'S PRETTY MUCH BACK TO NORMAL NOW...
SO I'M GONNA HAVE TO GO AHEAD AND JUST WIN THIS, OK?
YOU'RE CLAIMING VICTORY OVER THE FOUR OF US?
WELL... I'M NOT GOING TO FALL FOR THE SAME TRICK TWICE.
'COURSE NOT. THAT'S WHY I'M GOING FOR THE SECOND WEAK SPOT!
WH- WHAT...?!
TURNIN' INTO FOUR PEOPLE WAS A MISTAKE !!

READ THIS WAY

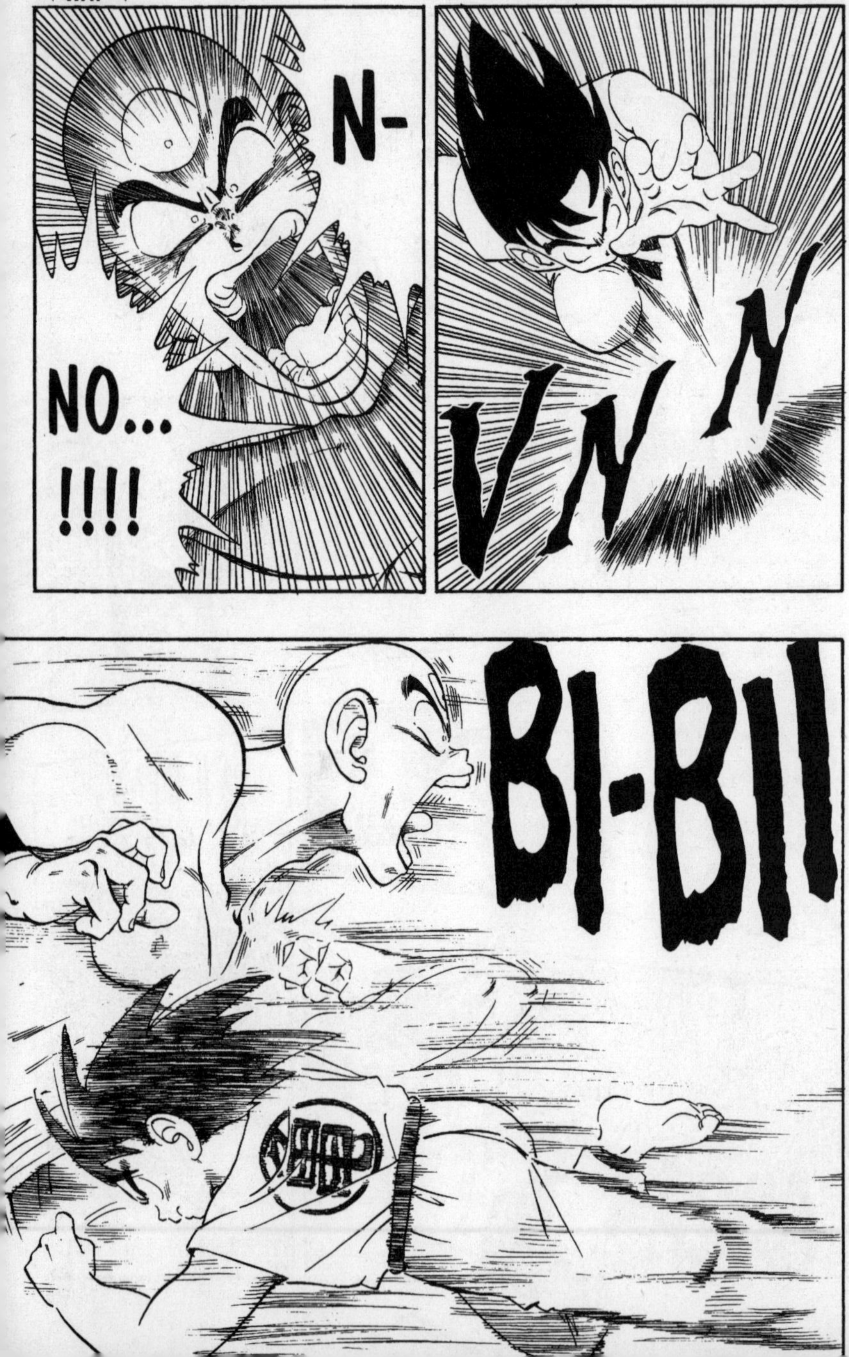

VNN
N-
NO...
!!!!
BI-BII

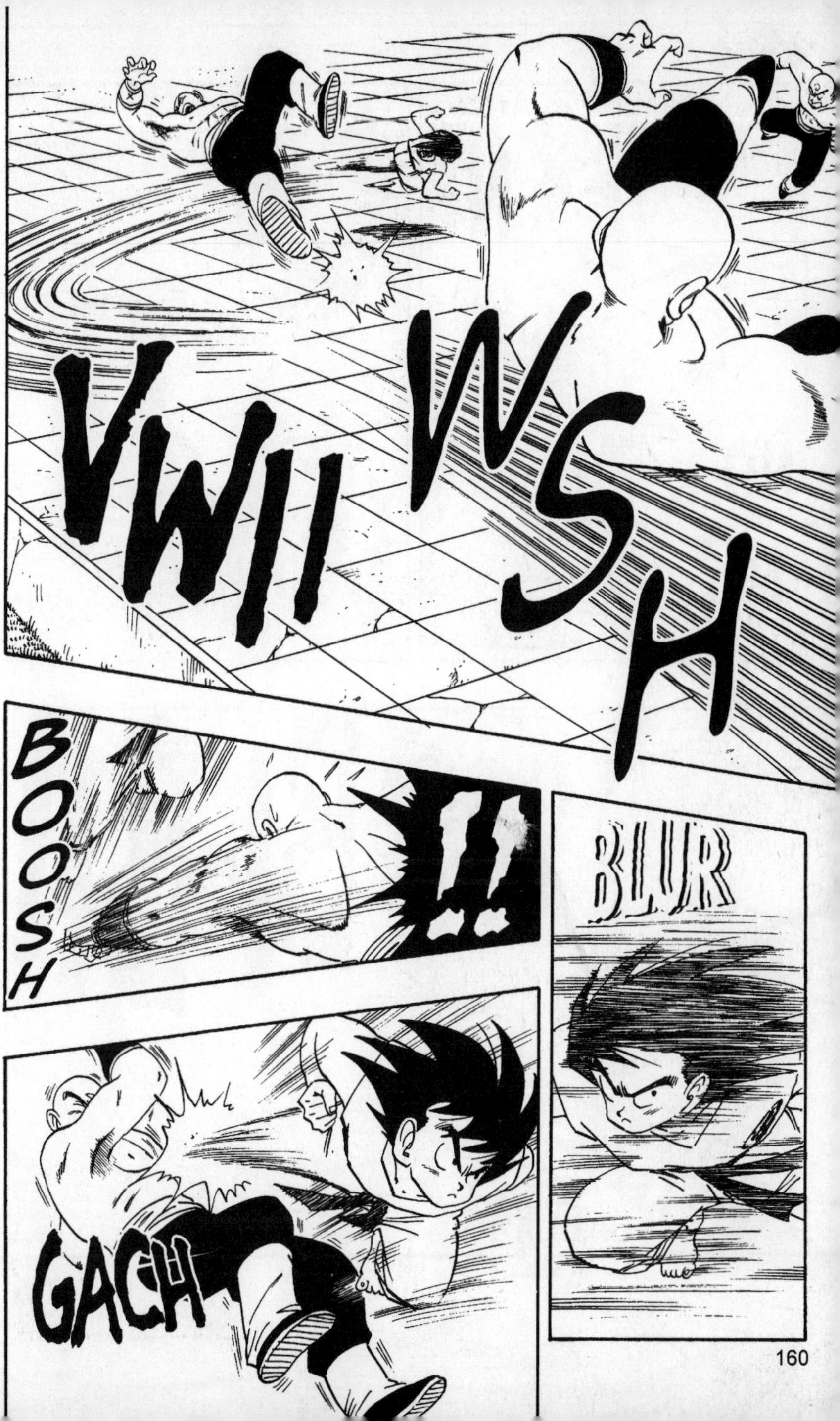
VWIISH
BOOSH
!!
BLUR
GACH

READ THIS WAY

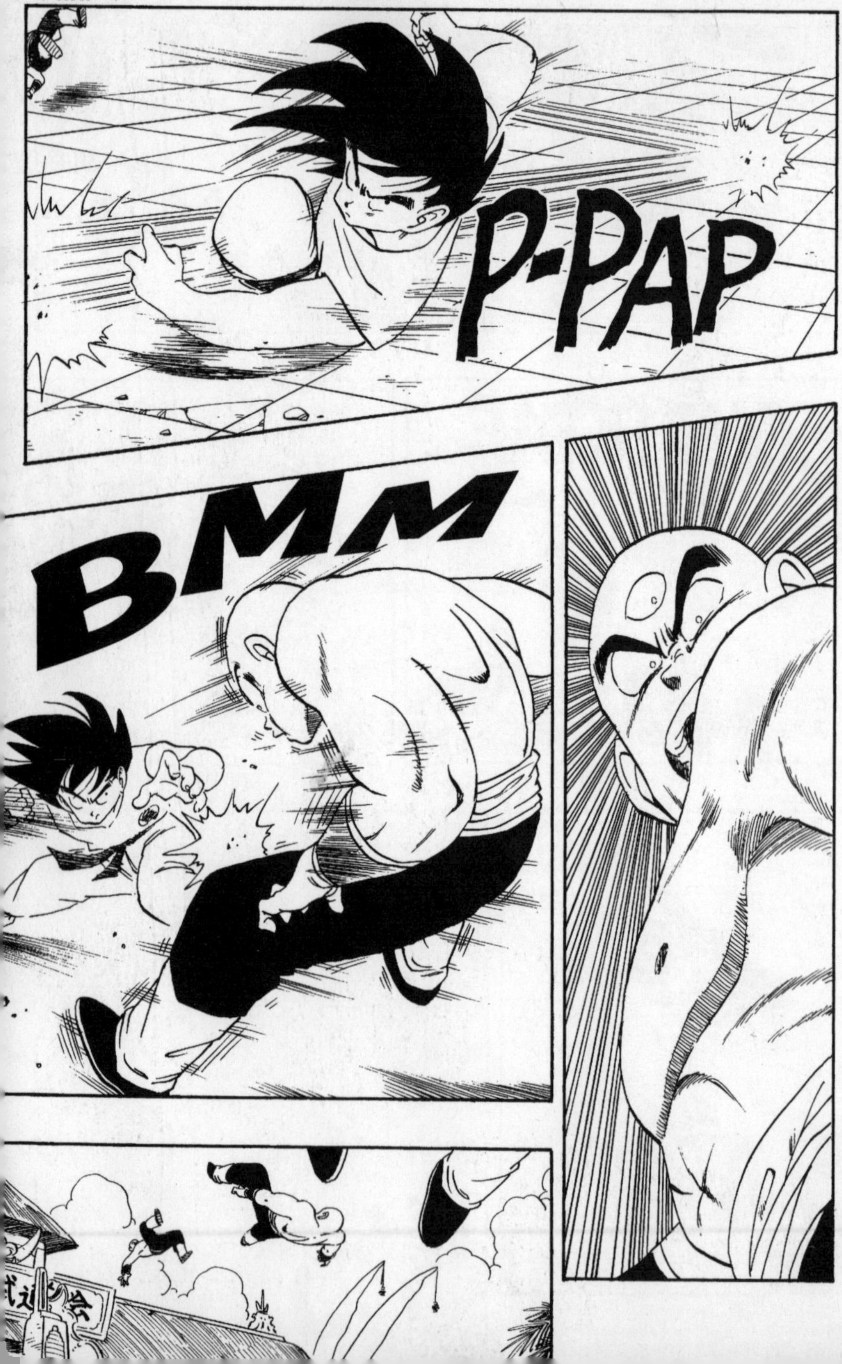
P-PAP
BMM

READ THIS WAY

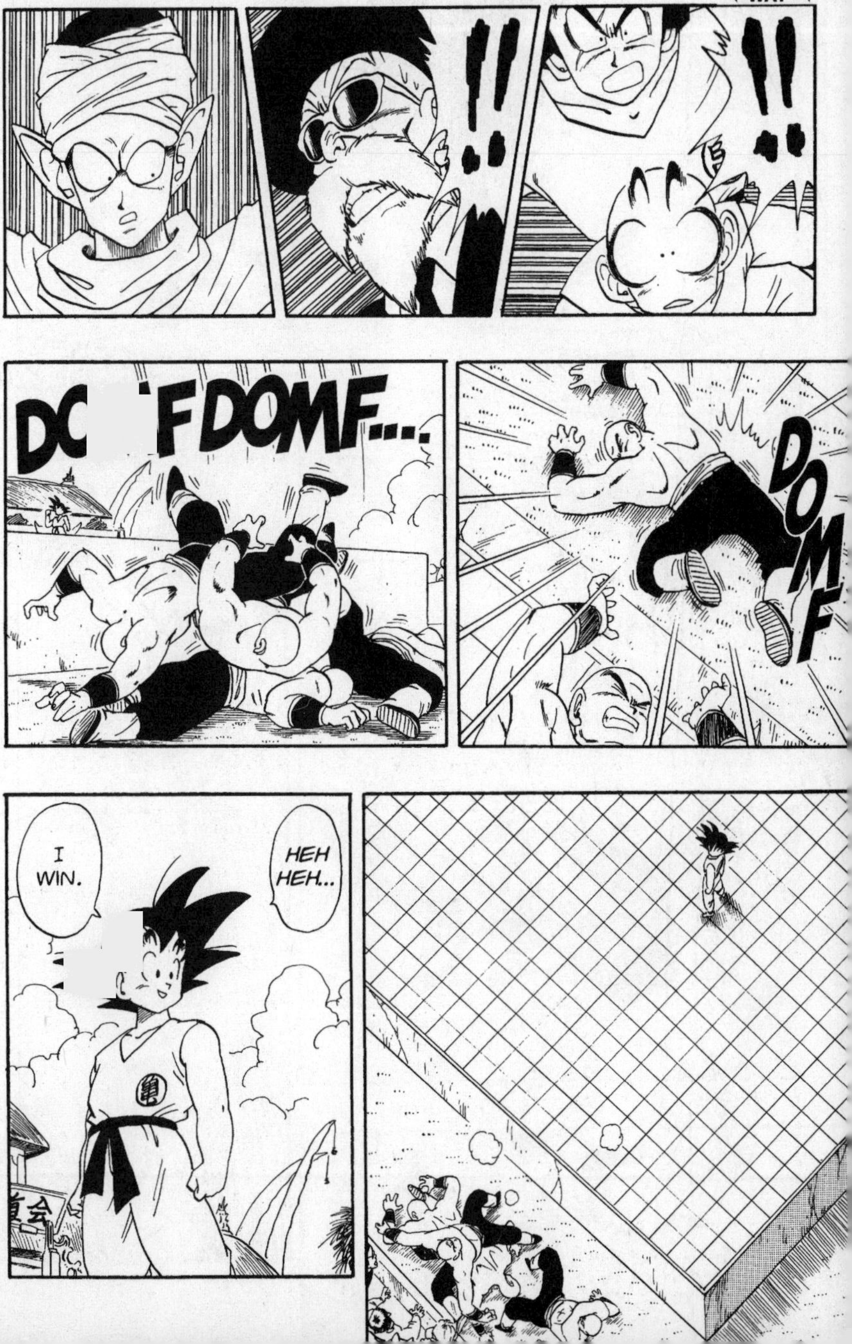

!!
!!
DOMF
DO F DOMF....
HEH HEH...
I WIN.

READ THIS WAY

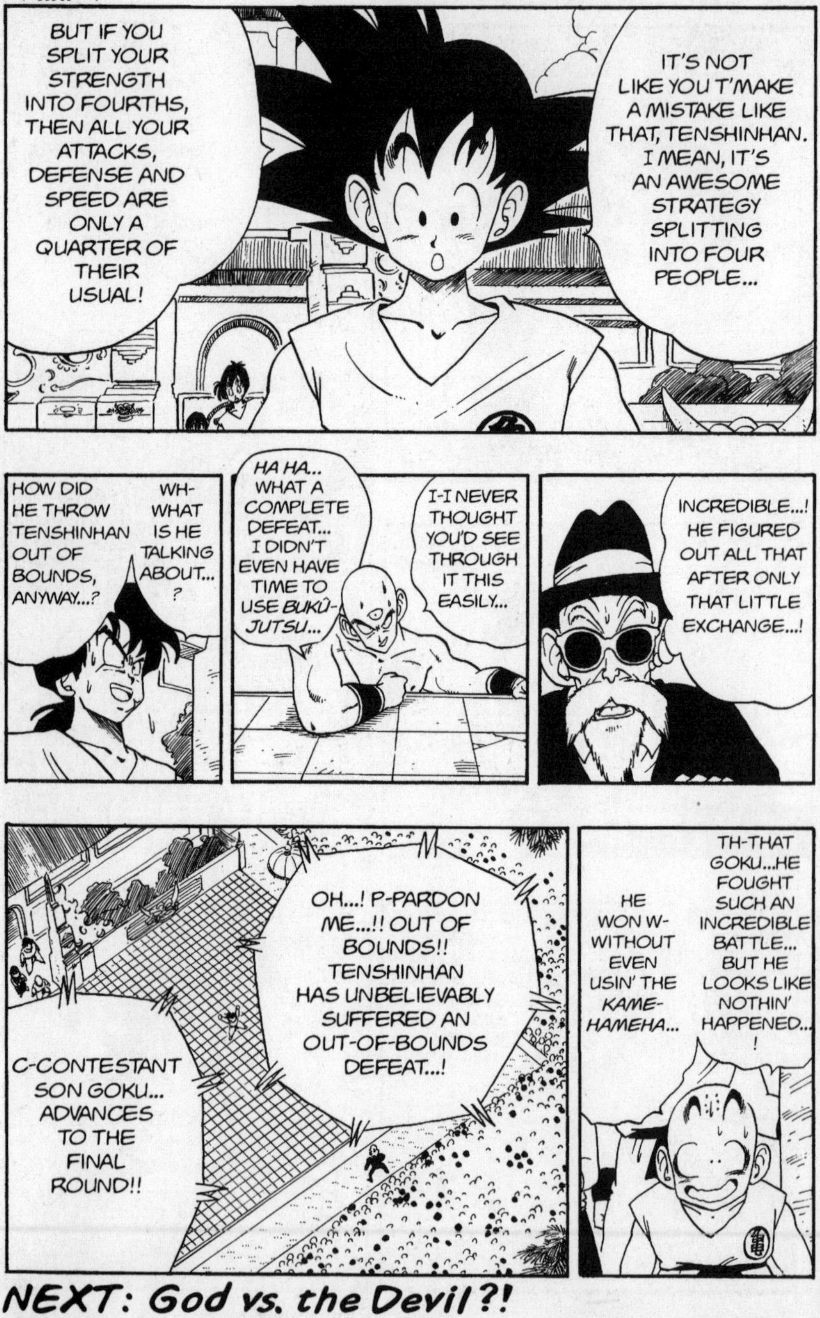

IT'S NOT LIKE YOU T'MAKE A MISTAKE LIKE THAT, TENSHINHAN. I MEAN, IT'S AN AWESOME STRATEGY SPLITTING INTO FOUR PEOPLE...
BUT IF YOU SPLIT YOUR STRENGTH INTO FOURTHS, THEN ALL YOUR ATTACKS, DEFENSE AND SPEED ARE ONLY A QUARTER OF THEIR USUAL!
INCREDIBLE...! HE FIGURED OUT ALL THAT AFTER ONLY THAT LITTLE EXCHANGE...!
I-I NEVER THOUGHT YOU'D SEE THROUGH IT THIS EASILY...
HA HA... WHAT A COMPLETE DEFEAT... I DIDN'T EVEN HAVE TIME TO USE *BUKŪ-JUTSU*...
WH-WHAT IS HE TALKING ABOUT...?
HOW DID HE THROW TENSHINHAN OUT OF BOUNDS, ANYWAY...?
TH-THAT GOKU...HE FOUGHT SUCH AN INCREDIBLE BATTLE... BUT HE LOOKS LIKE NOTHIN' HAPPENED...!
HE WON W-WITHOUT EVEN USIN' THE *KAME-HAMEHA*...
OH...! P-PARDON ME...!! OUT OF BOUNDS!! TENSHINHAN HAS UNBELIEVABLY SUFFERED AN OUT-OF-BOUNDS DEFEAT...!
C-CONTESTANT SON GOKU... ADVANCES TO THE FINAL ROUND!!

NEXT: God vs. the Devil?!

Tale 180 • Kami-Sama vs. The Demon King

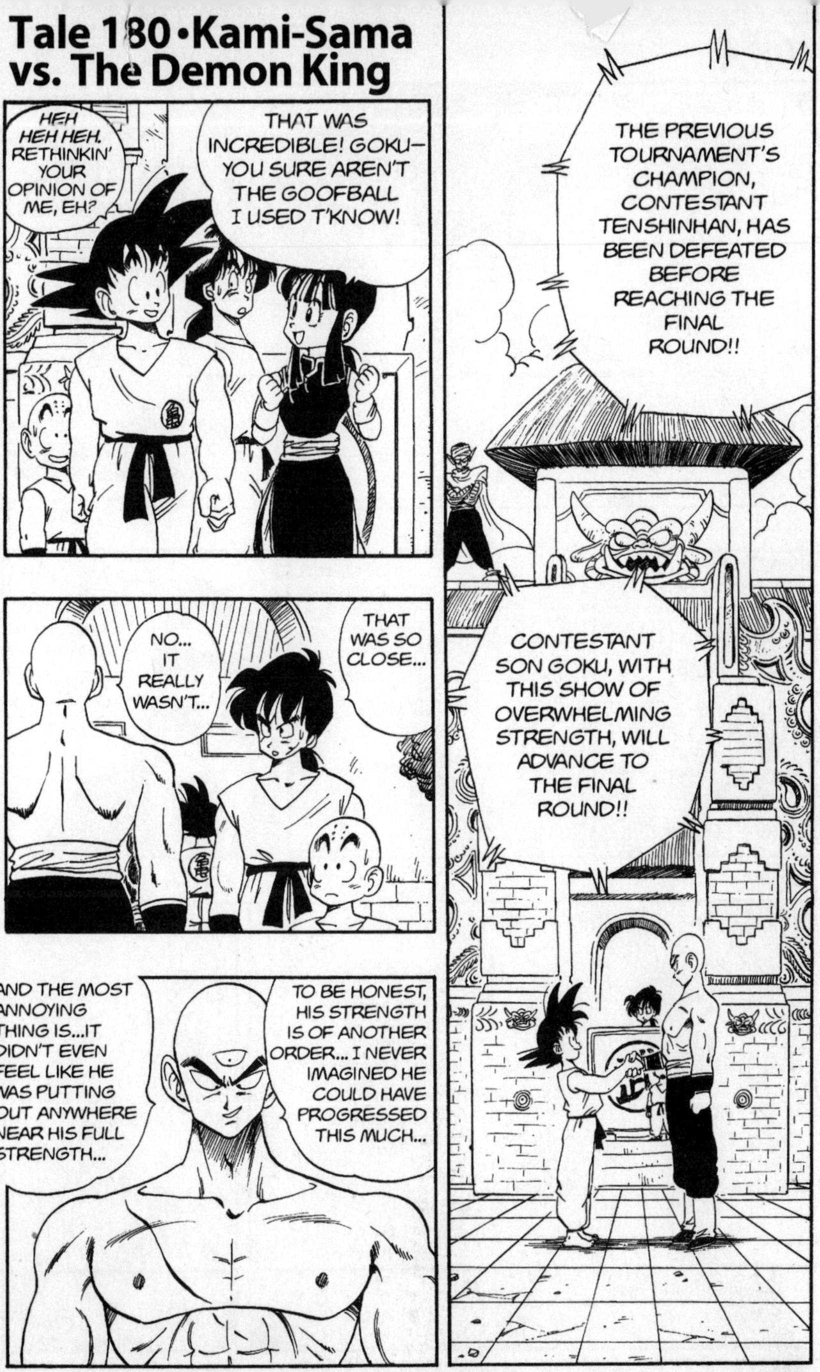
THE PREVIOUS TOURNAMENT'S CHAMPION, CONTESTANT TENSHINHAN, HAS BEEN DEFEATED BEFORE REACHING THE FINAL ROUND!!
CONTESTANT SON GOKU, WITH THIS SHOW OF OVERWHELMING STRENGTH, WILL ADVANCE TO THE FINAL ROUND!!
THAT WAS INCREDIBLE! GOKU— YOU SURE AREN'T THE GOOFBALL I USED T'KNOW!
HEH HEH HEH. RETHINKIN' YOUR OPINION OF ME, EH?
THAT WAS SO CLOSE...
NO... IT REALLY WASN'T...
TO BE HONEST, HIS STRENGTH IS OF ANOTHER ORDER... I NEVER IMAGINED HE COULD HAVE PROGRESSED THIS MUCH...
AND THE MOST ANNOYING THING IS...IT DIDN'T EVEN FEEL LIKE HE WAS PUTTING OUT ANYWHERE NEAR HIS FULL STRENGTH...

READ THIS WAY

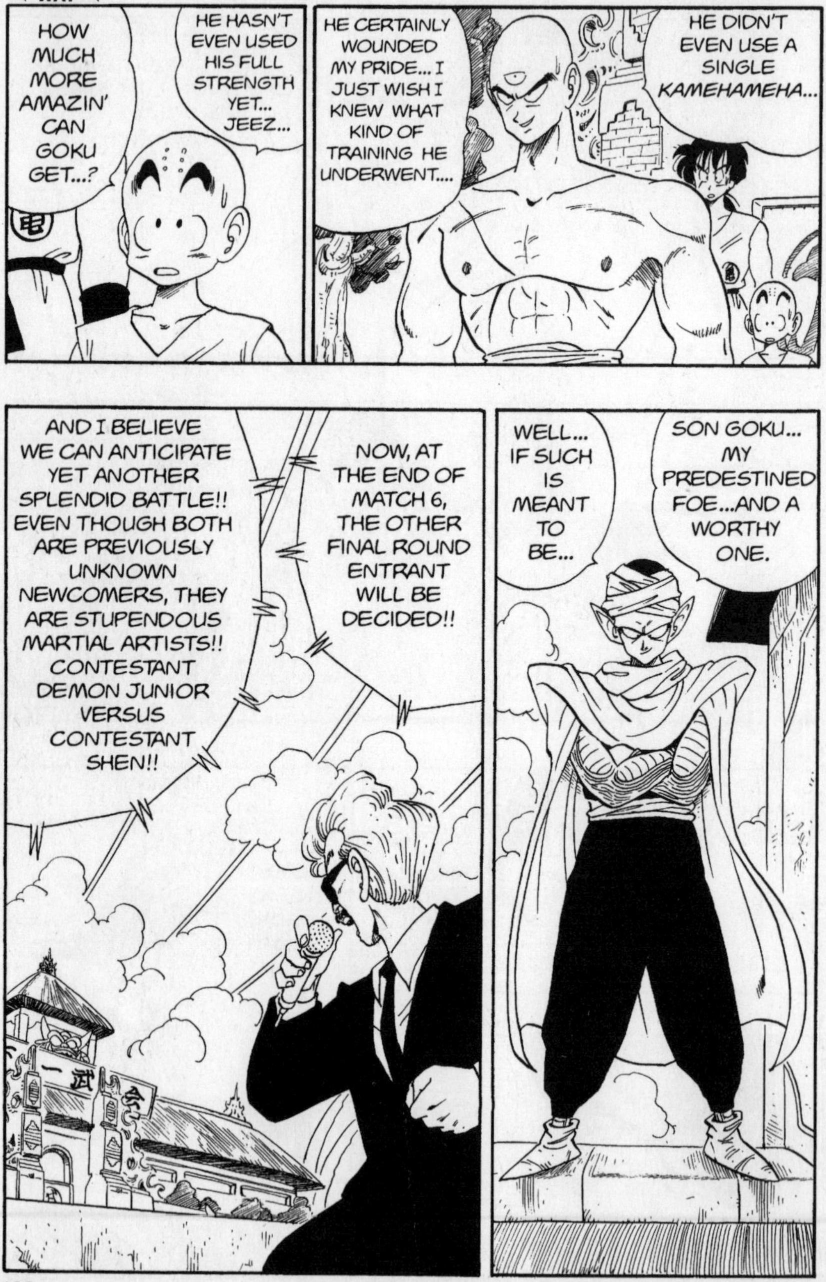
HE DIDN'T EVEN USE A SINGLE *KAMEHAMEHA*...
HE CERTAINLY WOUNDED MY PRIDE... I JUST WISH I KNEW WHAT KIND OF TRAINING HE UNDERWENT....
HE HASN'T EVEN USED HIS FULL STRENGTH YET... JEEZ...
HOW MUCH MORE AMAZIN' CAN GOKU GET...?
SON GOKU... MY PREDESTINED FOE...AND A WORTHY ONE.
WELL... IF SUCH IS MEANT TO BE...
NOW, AT THE END OF MATCH 6, THE OTHER FINAL ROUND ENTRANT WILL BE DECIDED!!
AND I BELIEVE WE CAN ANTICIPATE YET ANOTHER SPLENDID BATTLE!! EVEN THOUGH BOTH ARE PREVIOUSLY UNKNOWN NEWCOMERS, THEY ARE STUPENDOUS MARTIAL ARTISTS!! CONTESTANT DEMON JUNIOR VERSUS CONTESTANT SHEN!!

READ THIS WAY

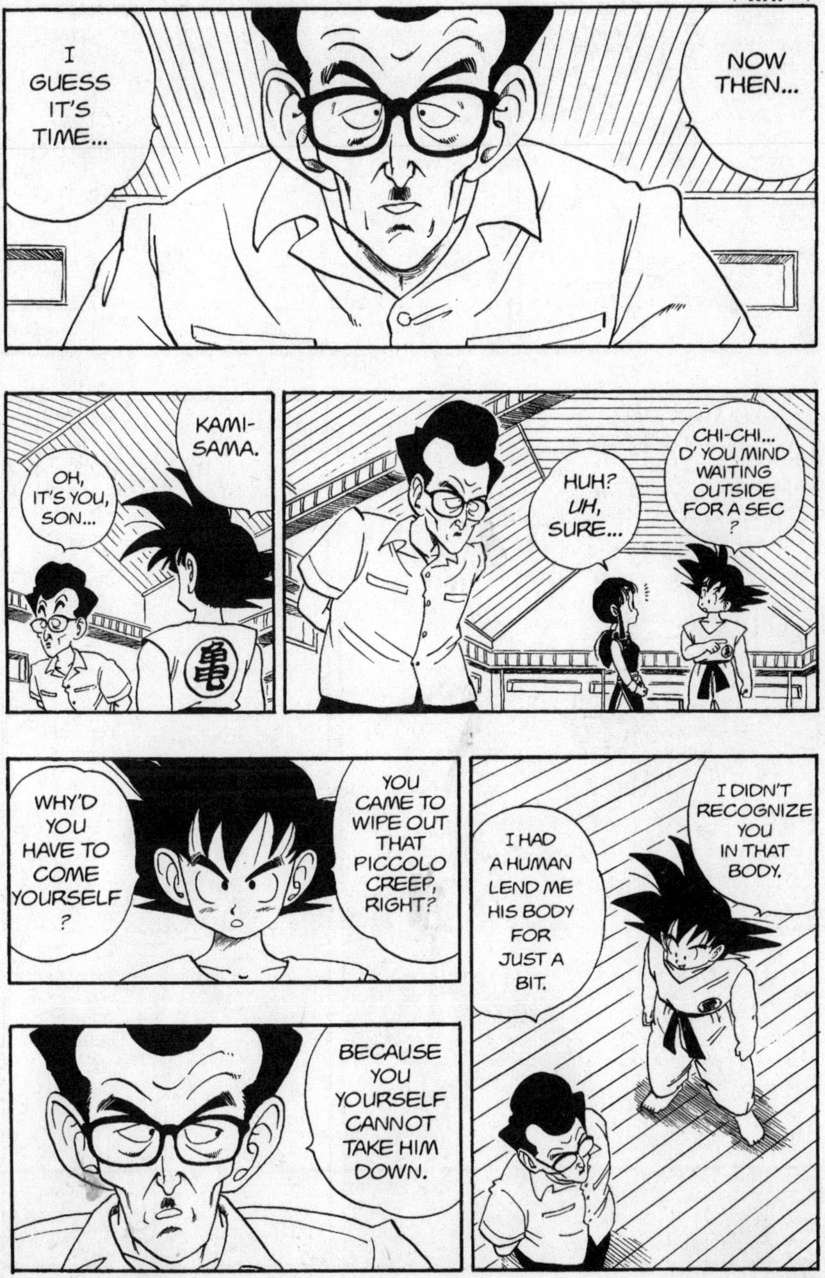

NOW THEN...
I GUESS IT'S TIME...
CHI-CHI... D' YOU MIND WAITING OUTSIDE FOR A SEC?
HUH? UH, SURE...
KAMI-SAMA.
OH, IT'S YOU, SON...
I DIDN'T RECOGNIZE YOU IN THAT BODY.
I HAD A HUMAN LEND ME HIS BODY FOR JUST A BIT.
YOU CAME TO WIPE OUT THAT PICCOLO CREEP, RIGHT?
WHY'D YOU HAVE TO COME YOURSELF?
BECAUSE YOU YOURSELF CANNOT TAKE HIM DOWN.

READ THIS WAY

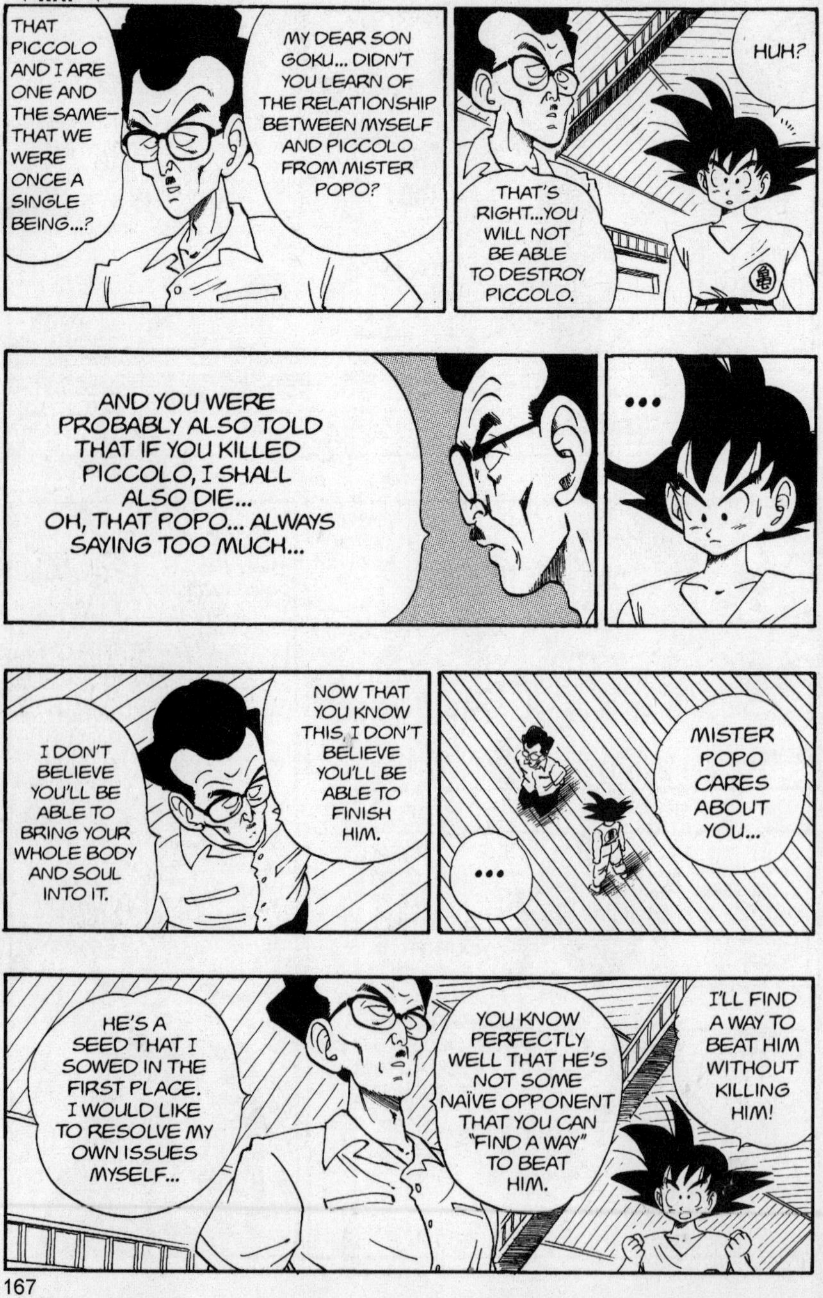
HUH?
THAT'S RIGHT...YOU WILL NOT BE ABLE TO DESTROY PICCOLO.
MY DEAR SON GOKU... DIDN'T YOU LEARN OF THE RELATIONSHIP BETWEEN MYSELF AND PICCOLO FROM MISTER POPO?
THAT PICCOLO AND I ARE ONE AND THE SAME— THAT WE WERE ONCE A SINGLE BEING...?
...
AND YOU WERE PROBABLY ALSO TOLD THAT IF YOU KILLED PICCOLO, I SHALL ALSO DIE... OH, THAT POPO... ALWAYS SAYING TOO MUCH...
MISTER POPO CARES ABOUT YOU...
...
NOW THAT YOU KNOW THIS, I DON'T BELIEVE YOU'LL BE ABLE TO FINISH HIM.
I DON'T BELIEVE YOU'LL BE ABLE TO BRING YOUR WHOLE BODY AND SOUL INTO IT.
I'LL FIND A WAY TO BEAT HIM WITHOUT KILLING HIM!
YOU KNOW PERFECTLY WELL THAT HE'S NOT SOME NAÏVE OPPONENT THAT YOU CAN "FIND A WAY" TO BEAT HIM.
HE'S A SEED THAT I SOWED IN THE FIRST PLACE. I WOULD LIKE TO RESOLVE MY OWN ISSUES MYSELF...

READ THIS WAY

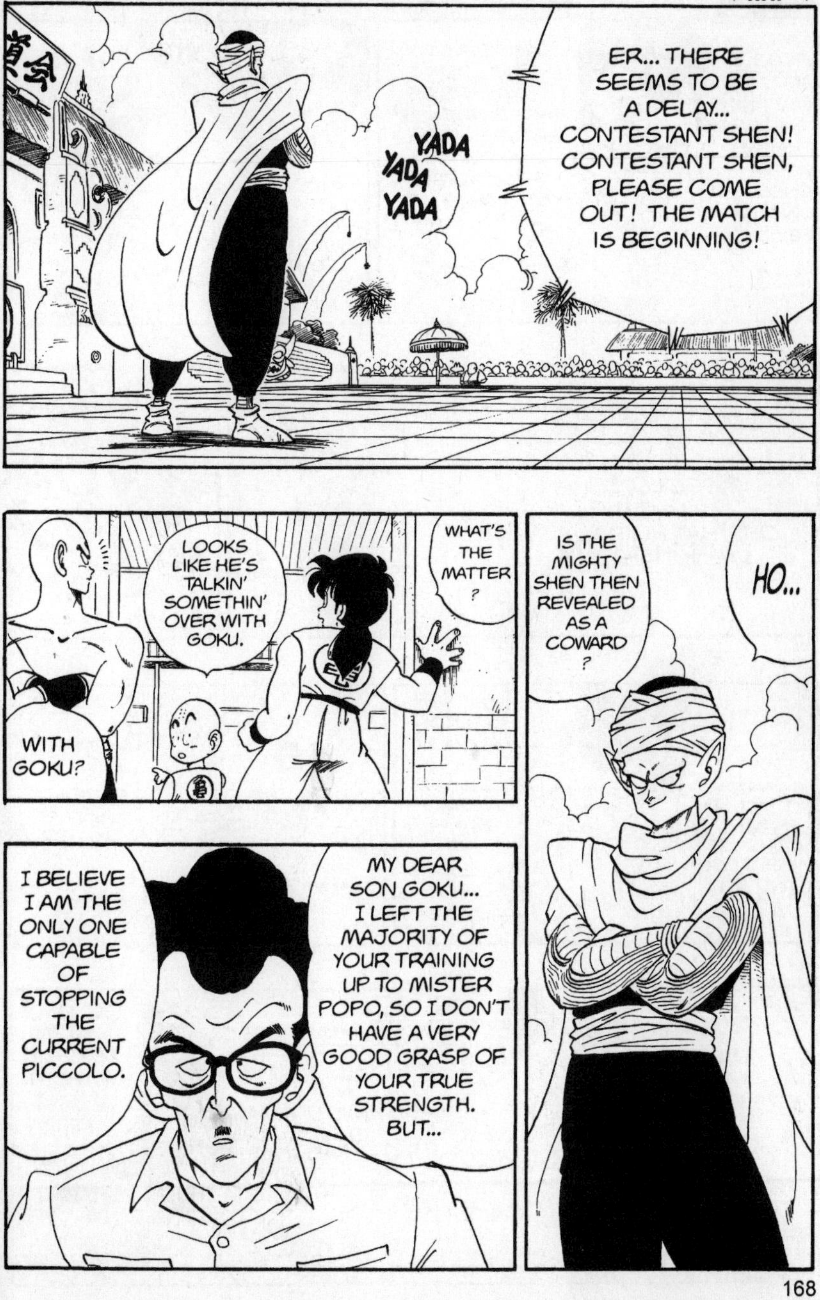

ER... THERE SEEMS TO BE A DELAY... CONTESTANT SHEN! CONTESTANT SHEN, PLEASE COME OUT! THE MATCH IS BEGINNING!
YADA YADA YADA
HO...
IS THE MIGHTY SHEN THEN REVEALED AS A COWARD?
WHAT'S THE MATTER?
LOOKS LIKE HE'S TALKIN' SOMETHIN' OVER WITH GOKU.
WITH GOKU?
MY DEAR SON GOKU... I LEFT THE MAJORITY OF YOUR TRAINING UP TO MISTER POPO, SO I DON'T HAVE A VERY GOOD GRASP OF YOUR TRUE STRENGTH. BUT...
I BELIEVE I AM THE ONLY ONE CAPABLE OF STOPPING THE CURRENT PICCOLO.

READ THIS WAY

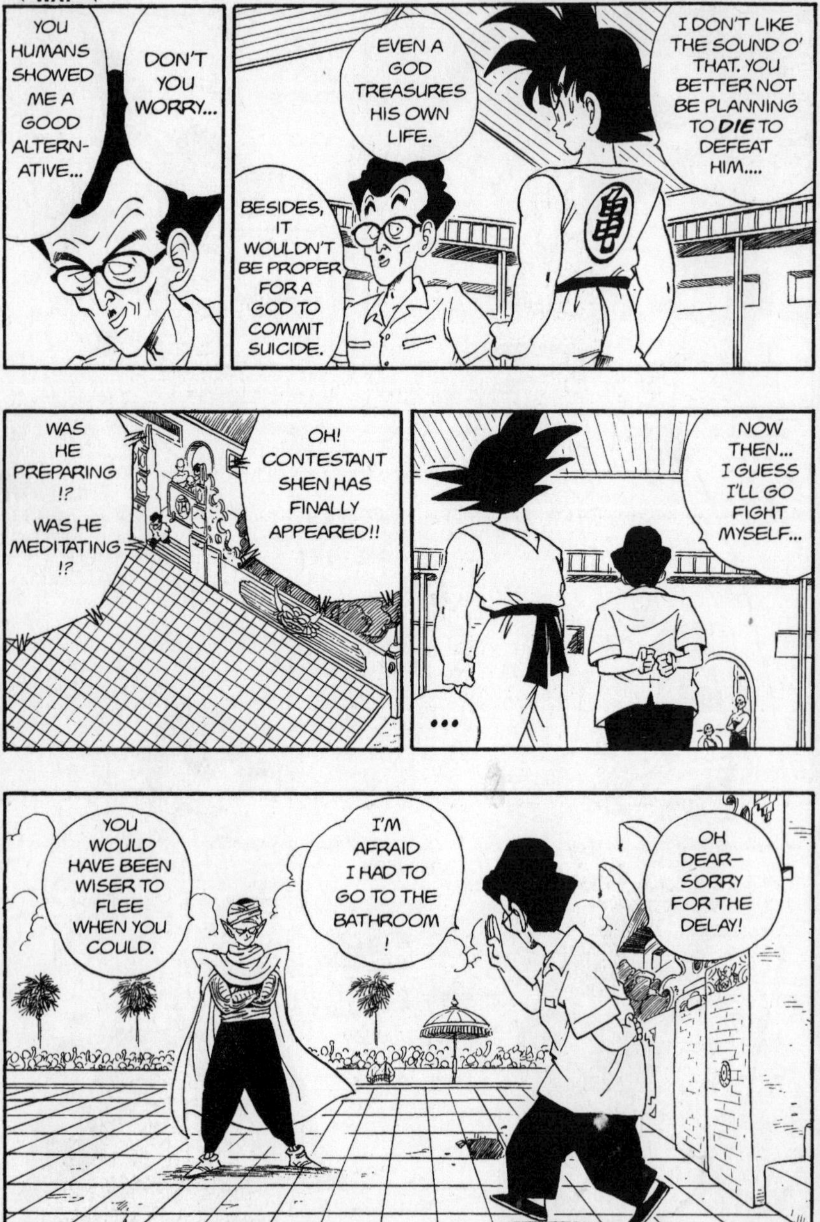
I DON'T LIKE THE SOUND O' THAT. YOU BETTER NOT BE PLANNING TO **DIE** TO DEFEAT HIM....
EVEN A GOD TREASURES HIS OWN LIFE.
BESIDES, IT WOULDN'T BE PROPER FOR A GOD TO COMMIT SUICIDE.
DON'T YOU WORRY...
YOU HUMANS SHOWED ME A GOOD ALTERN-ATIVE...
NOW THEN... I GUESS I'LL GO FIGHT MYSELF...
...
OH! CONTESTANT SHEN HAS FINALLY APPEARED!!
WAS HE PREPARING !?
WAS HE MEDITATING !?
OH DEAR- SORRY FOR THE DELAY!
I'M AFRAID I HAD TO GO TO THE BATHROOM !
YOU WOULD HAVE BEEN WISER TO FLEE WHEN YOU COULD.

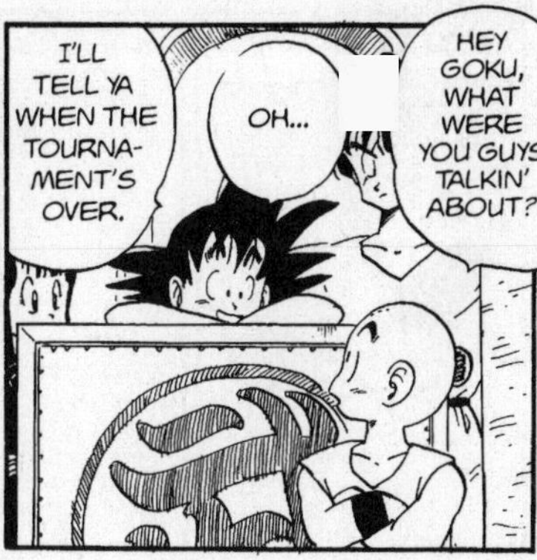
HEY GOKU, WHAT WERE YOU GUYS TALKIN' ABOUT?
OH...
I'LL TELL YA WHEN THE TOURNAMENT'S OVER.

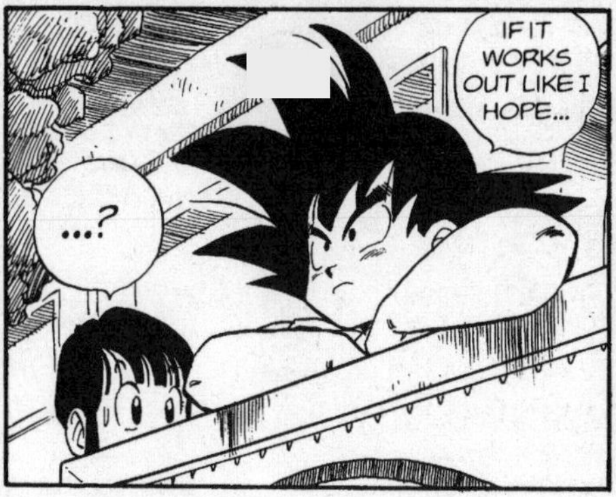
IF IT WORKS OUT LIKE I HOPE...
...?

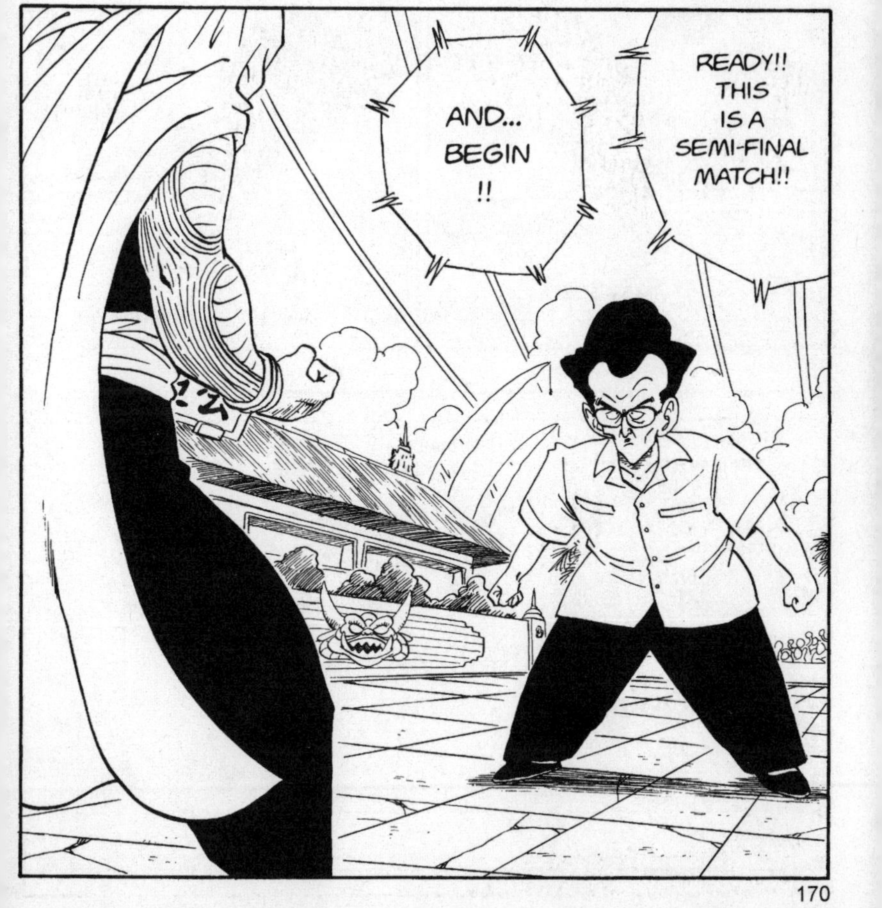
READY!! THIS IS A SEMI-FINAL MATCH!!
AND... BEGIN !!

READ THIS WAY

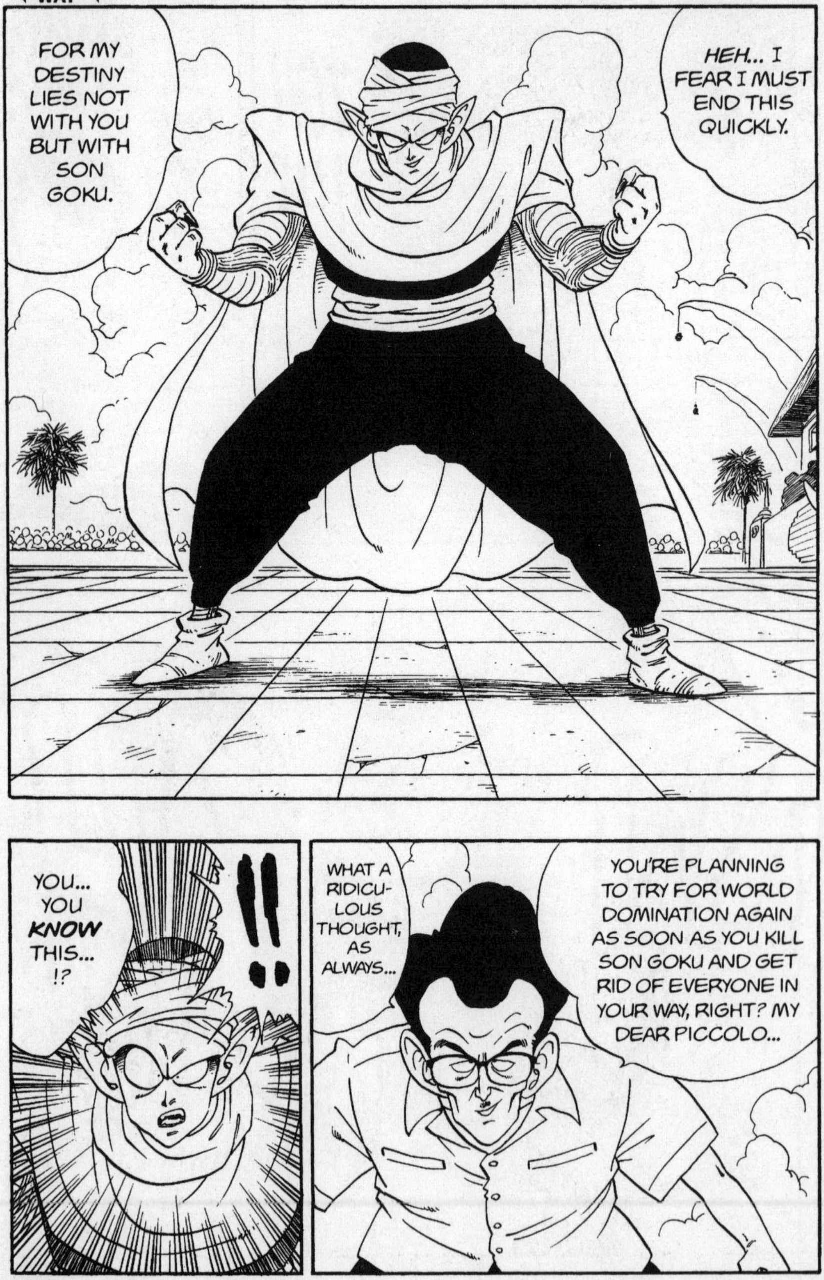

HEH... I FEAR I MUST END THIS QUICKLY.
FOR MY DESTINY LIES NOT WITH YOU BUT WITH SON GOKU.
YOU'RE PLANNING TO TRY FOR WORLD DOMINATION AGAIN AS SOON AS YOU KILL SON GOKU AND GET RID OF EVERYONE IN YOUR WAY, RIGHT? MY DEAR PICCOLO...
WHAT A RIDICU-LOUS THOUGHT, AS ALWAYS...
!!
YOU... YOU ***KNOW*** THIS... !?

READ THIS WAY

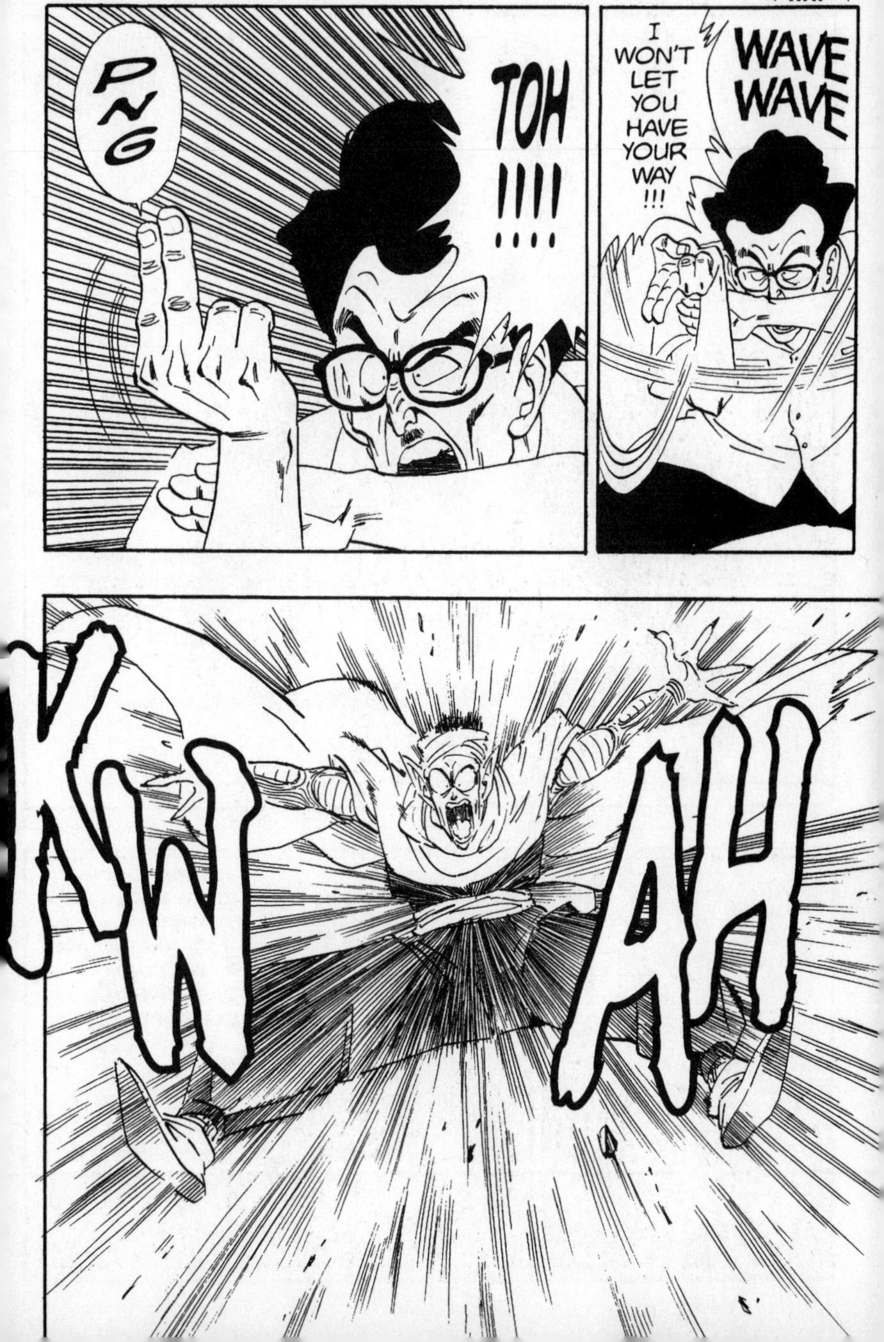
WAVE WAVE
I WON'T LET YOU HAVE YOUR WAY!!!
TOH!!!!....
PNG
KWAH

READ THIS WAY

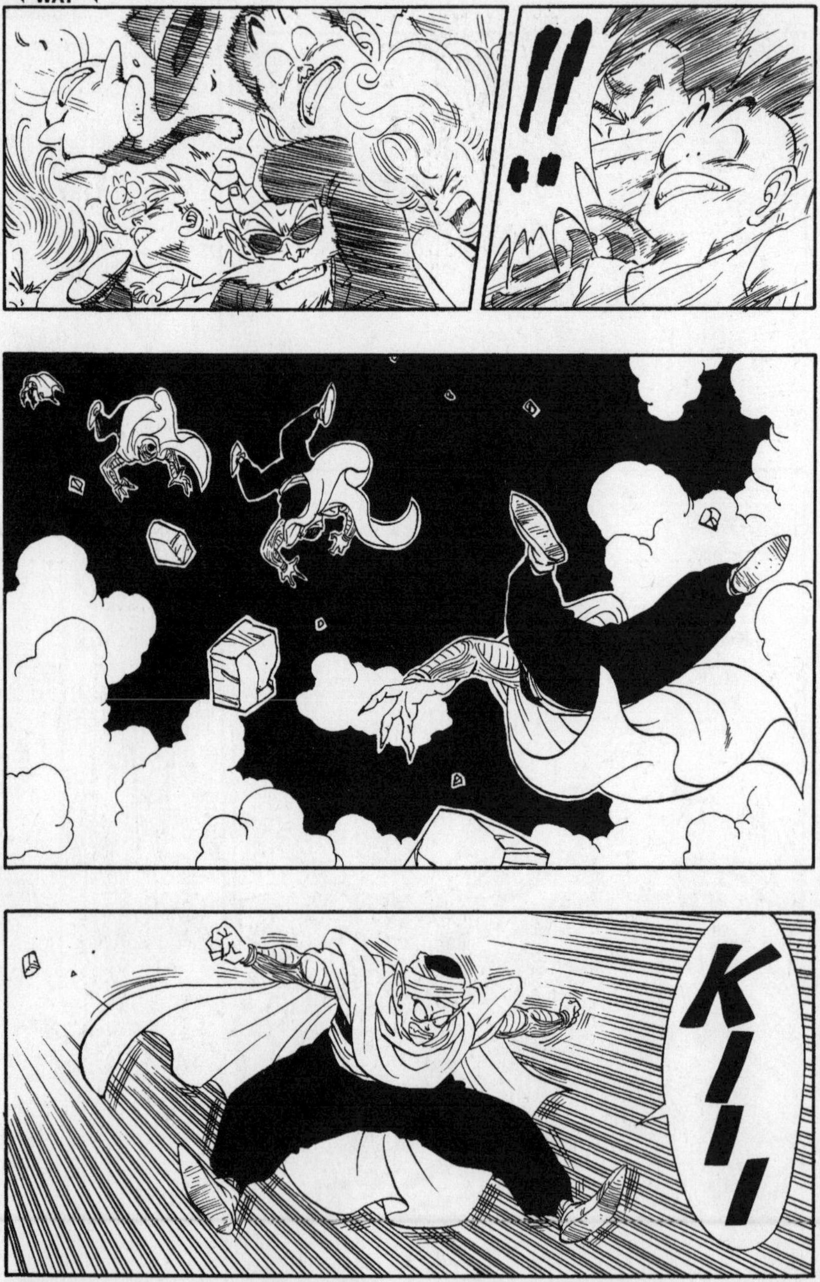
!!
KIII

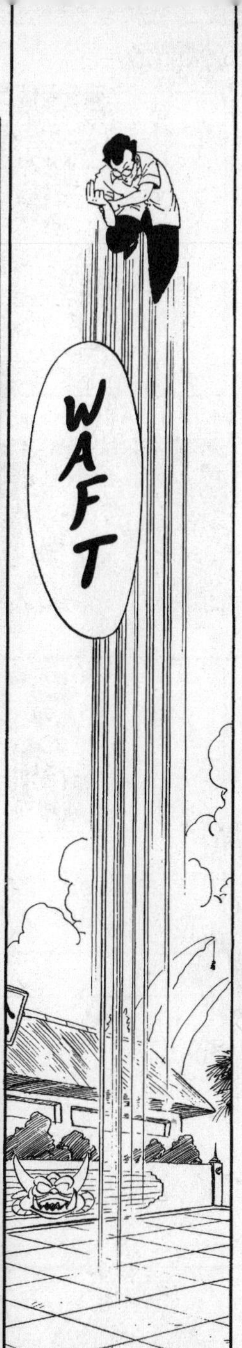
WAFT
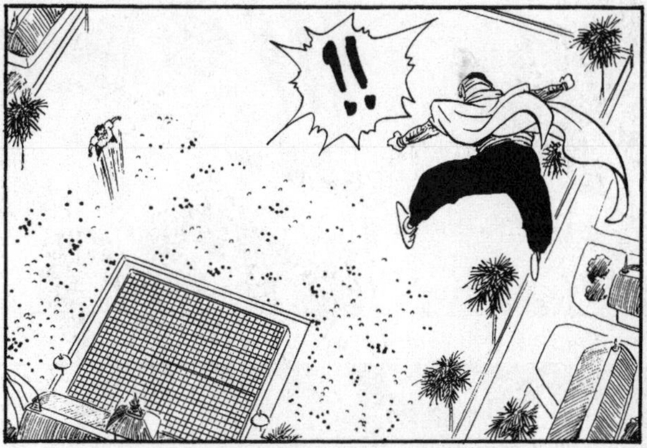
!!
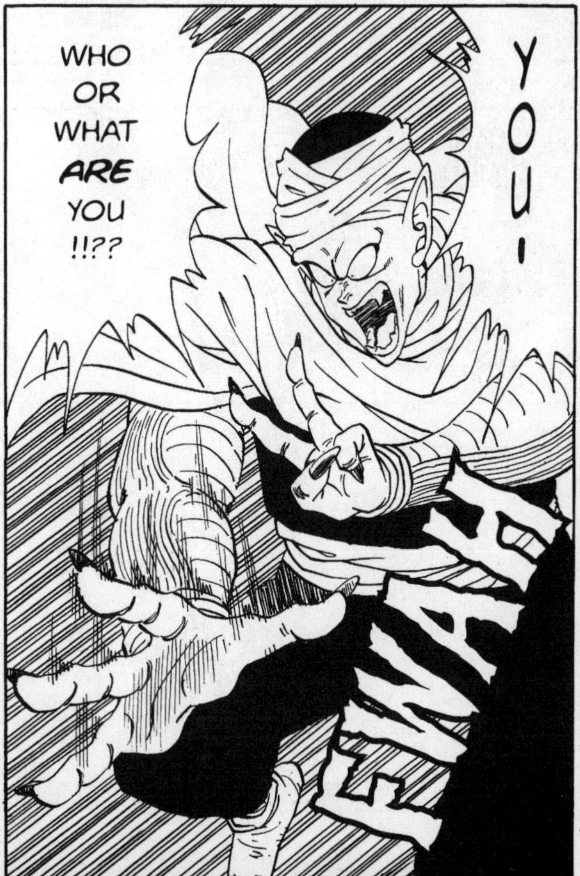
YOU!
WHO OR WHAT ARE YOU !!??
GWAH

READ THIS WAY

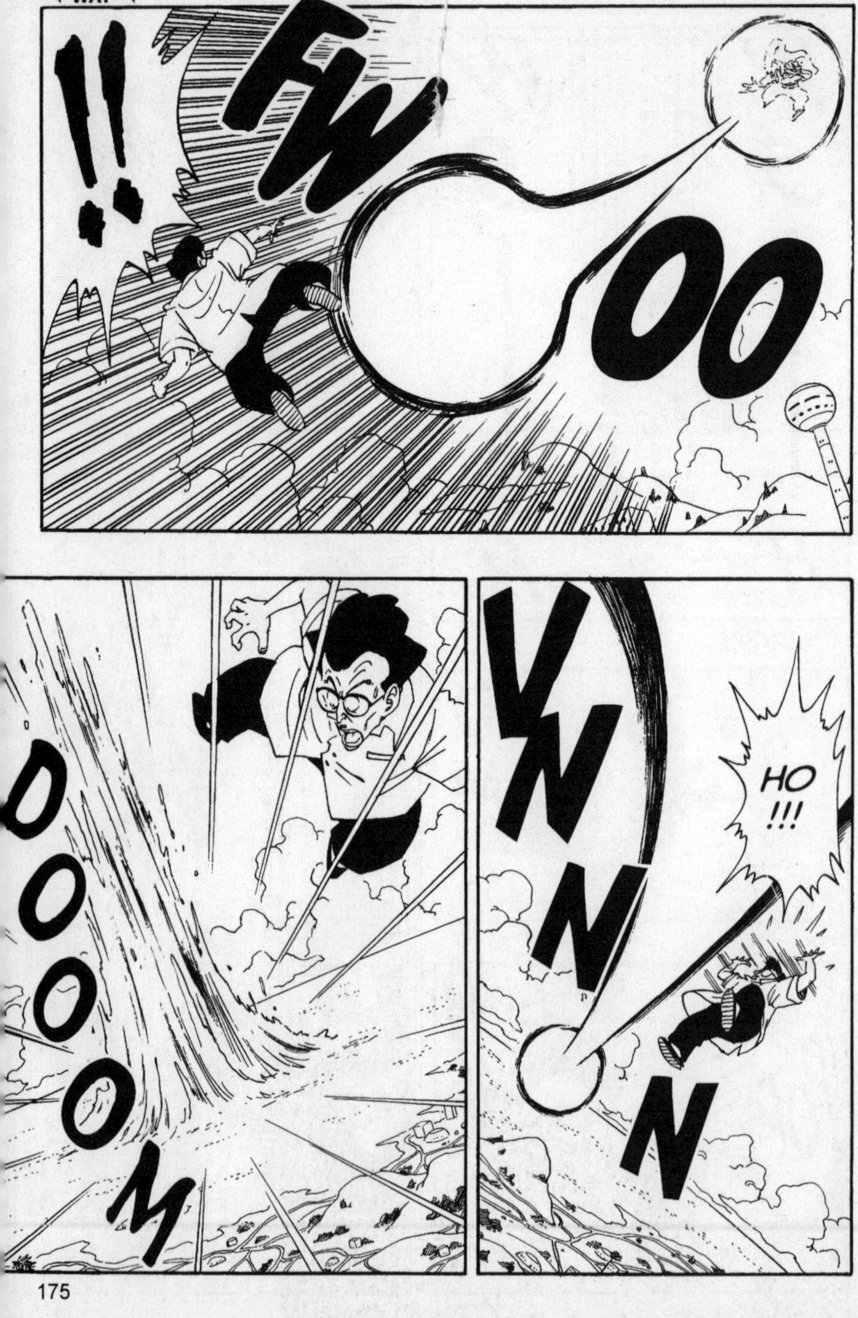
!!
FWOO
VNNN
HO !!!
DOOOM

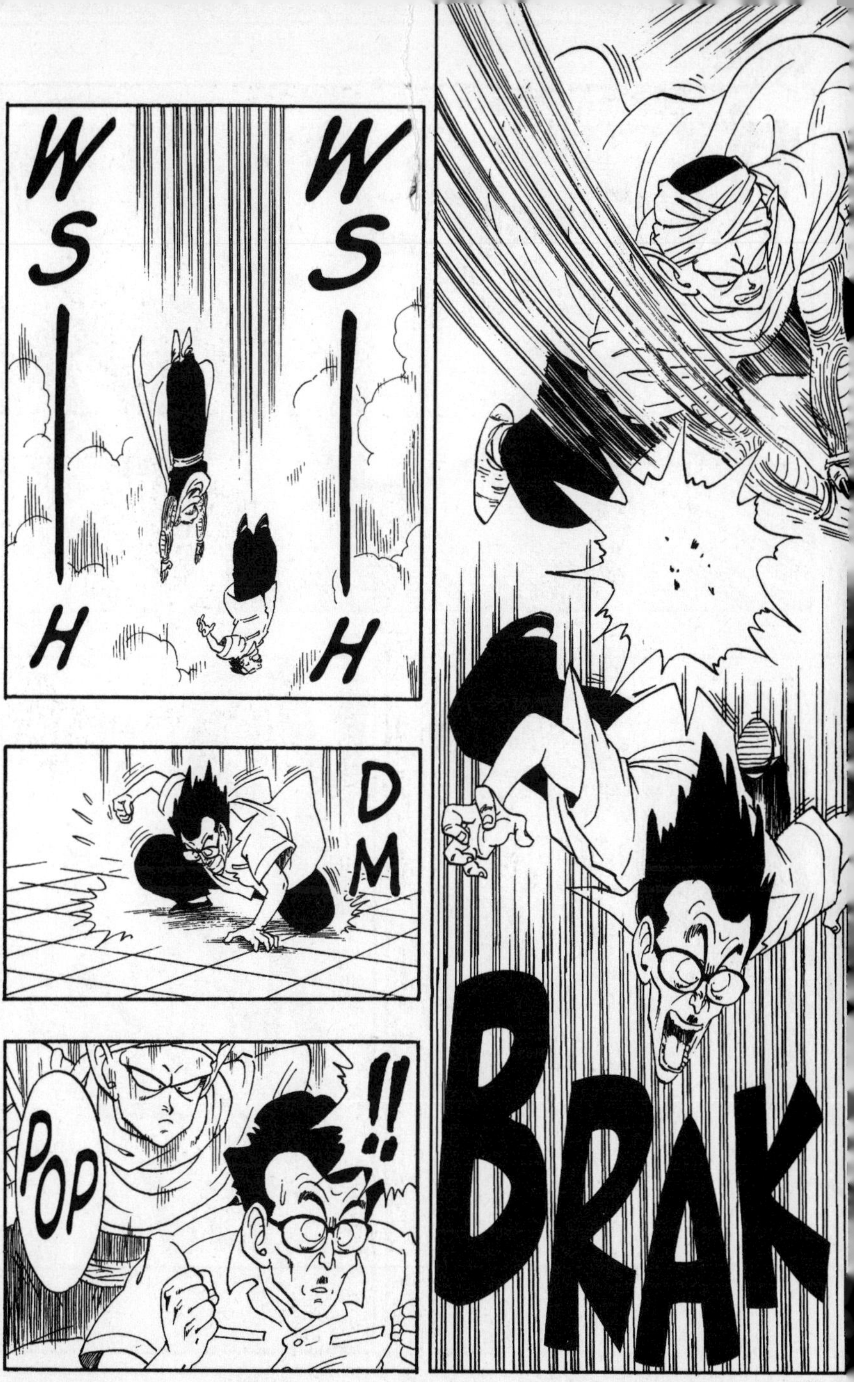
BRAK
WSSH
WSSH
DM
POP
!!

READ THIS WAY

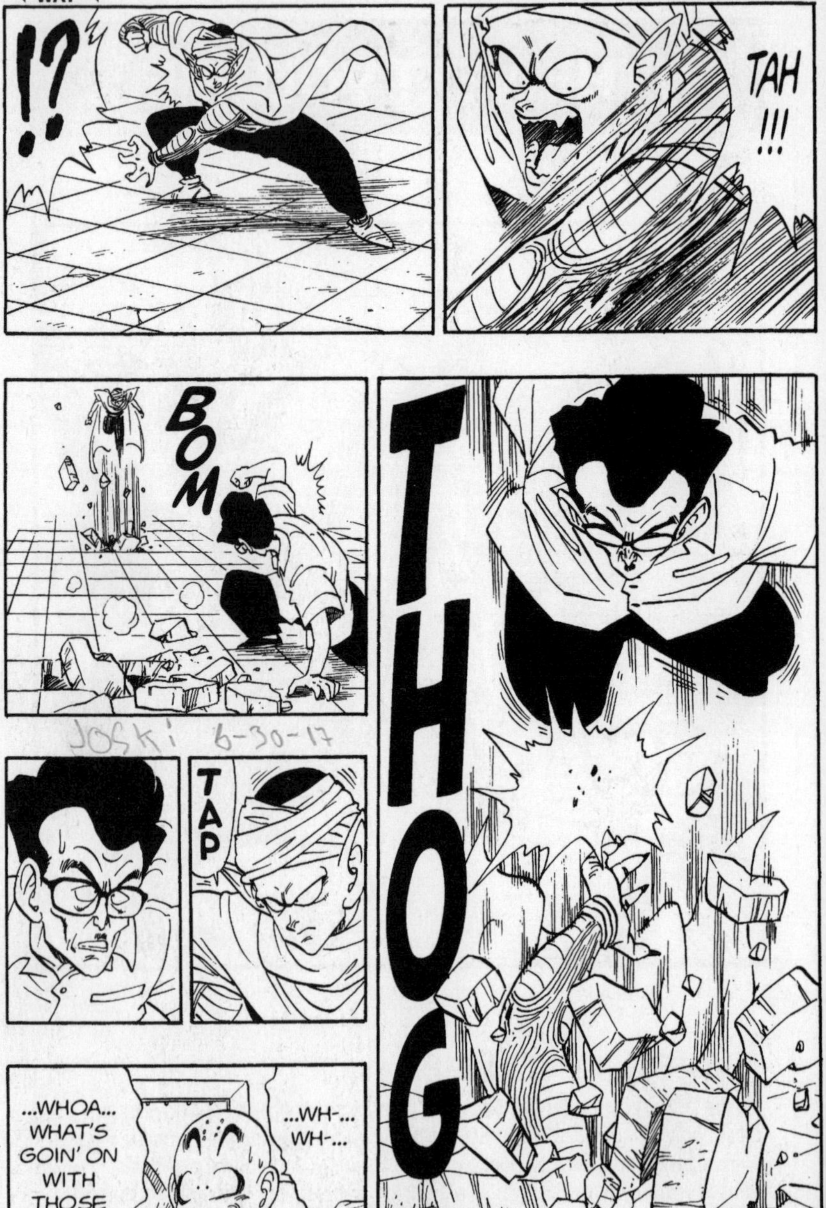

TAH !!!
!?
THOG
BOM
TAP
...WH-... WH-...
...WHOA... WHAT'S GOIN' ON WITH THOSE TWO...?

NEXT: The Rivalry of the Lords

IN THE NEXT VOLUME...

IN THE NEXT VOLUME...

As the "Strongest Under the Heavens" martial arts tournament draws to a close, only Goku, Piccolo and Shen—the disguised Kami-sama—remain! But even a god is no match for Piccolo's new powers, and soon Goku finds himself fighting in a battle which will decide not just who is strongest, but who or what will *rule the world!* The audience flees for their lives as the struggle shakes the heavens apart in the gripping conclusion of **Dragon Ball**!

TITLE PAGE GALLERY

These title pages were used when these chapters of **Dragon Ball** were originally published in Japan in 1988 in **Weekly Shonen Jump** magazine.

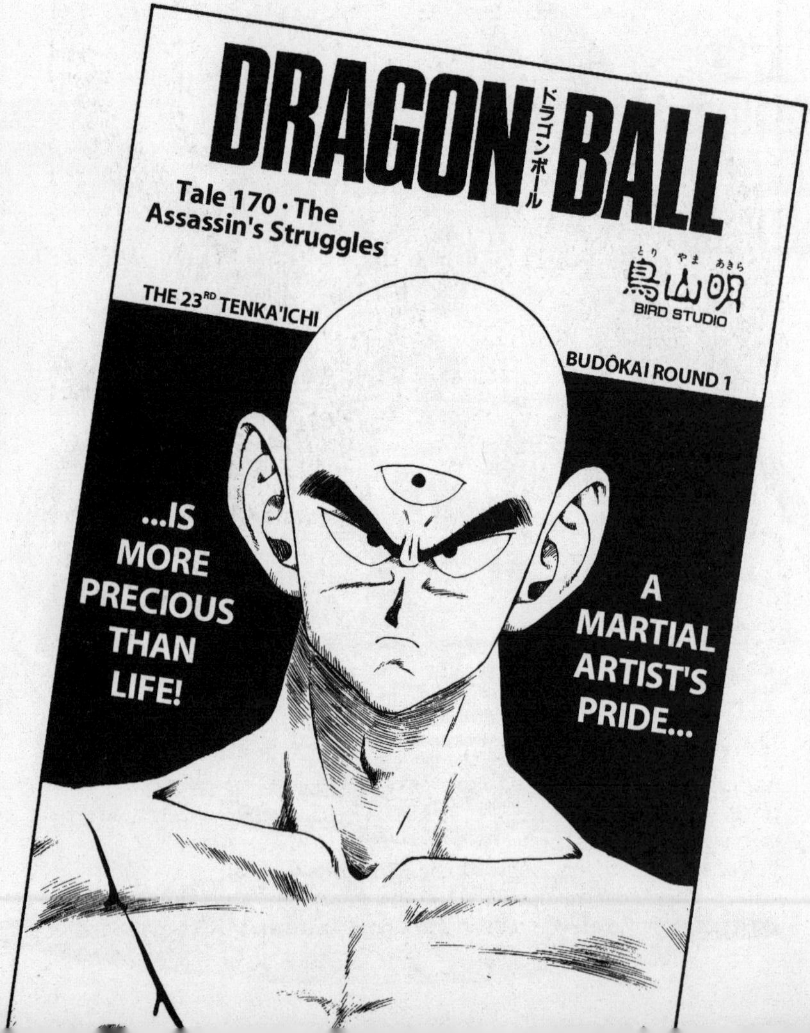
DRAGON BALL
ドラゴンボール
Tale 170 · The Assassin's Struggles
とりやまあきら
鳥山明
BIRD STUDIO
THE 23RD TENKA'ICHI
BUDÔKAI ROUND 1
A MARTIAL ARTIST'S PRIDE...
...IS MORE PRECIOUS THAN LIFE!

DRAGON BALL

ドラゴンボール

Tale 171•Goku Gets Married

とりやまあきら
鳥山明
BIRD STUDIO

♪

HERE COMES THE BRIDE...!

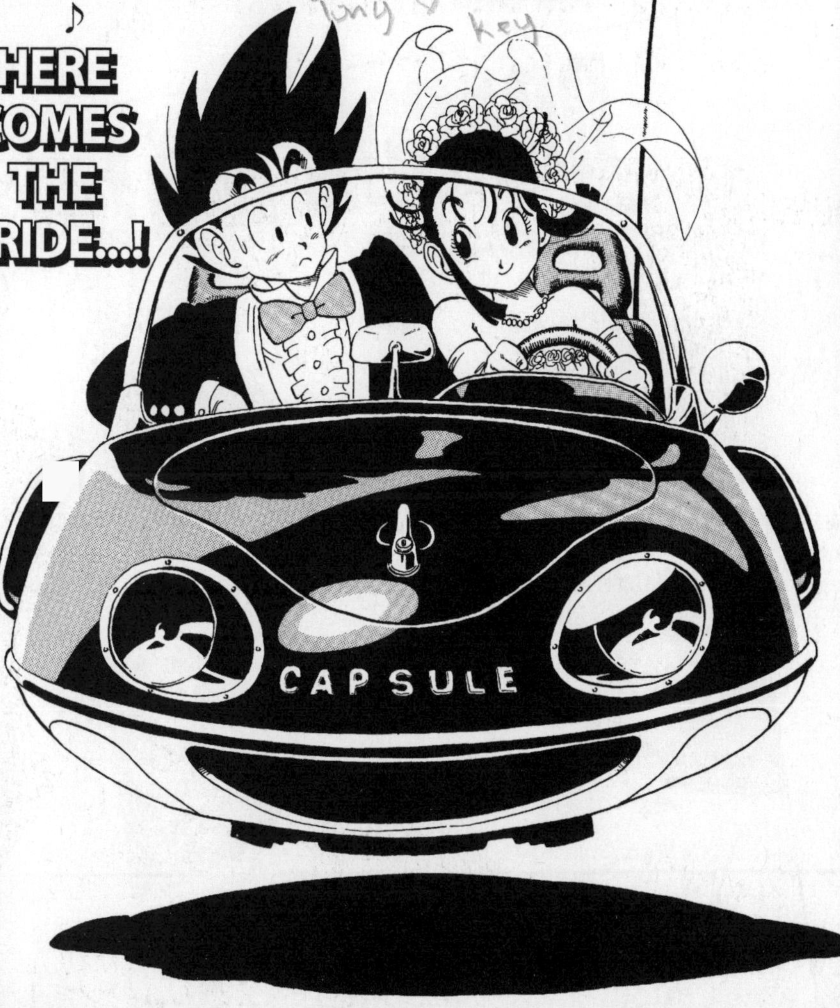
...
CAPSULE

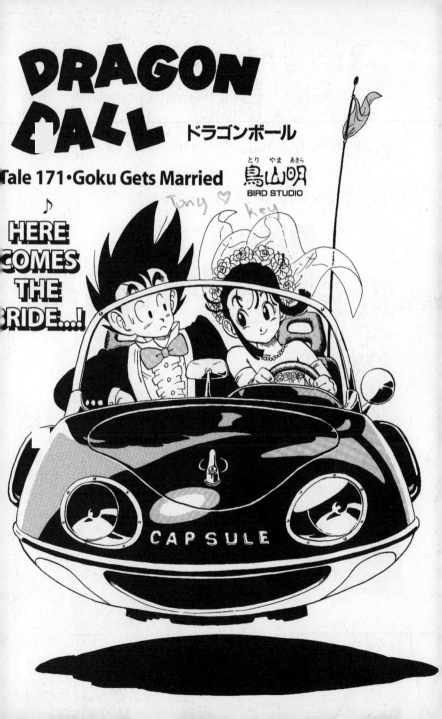

ドラゴンボール

DRAGON BALL

I'LL CRUSH YOU EASILY, YOU NOTHING!

Tale 172 • Kuririn vs. Demon Junior

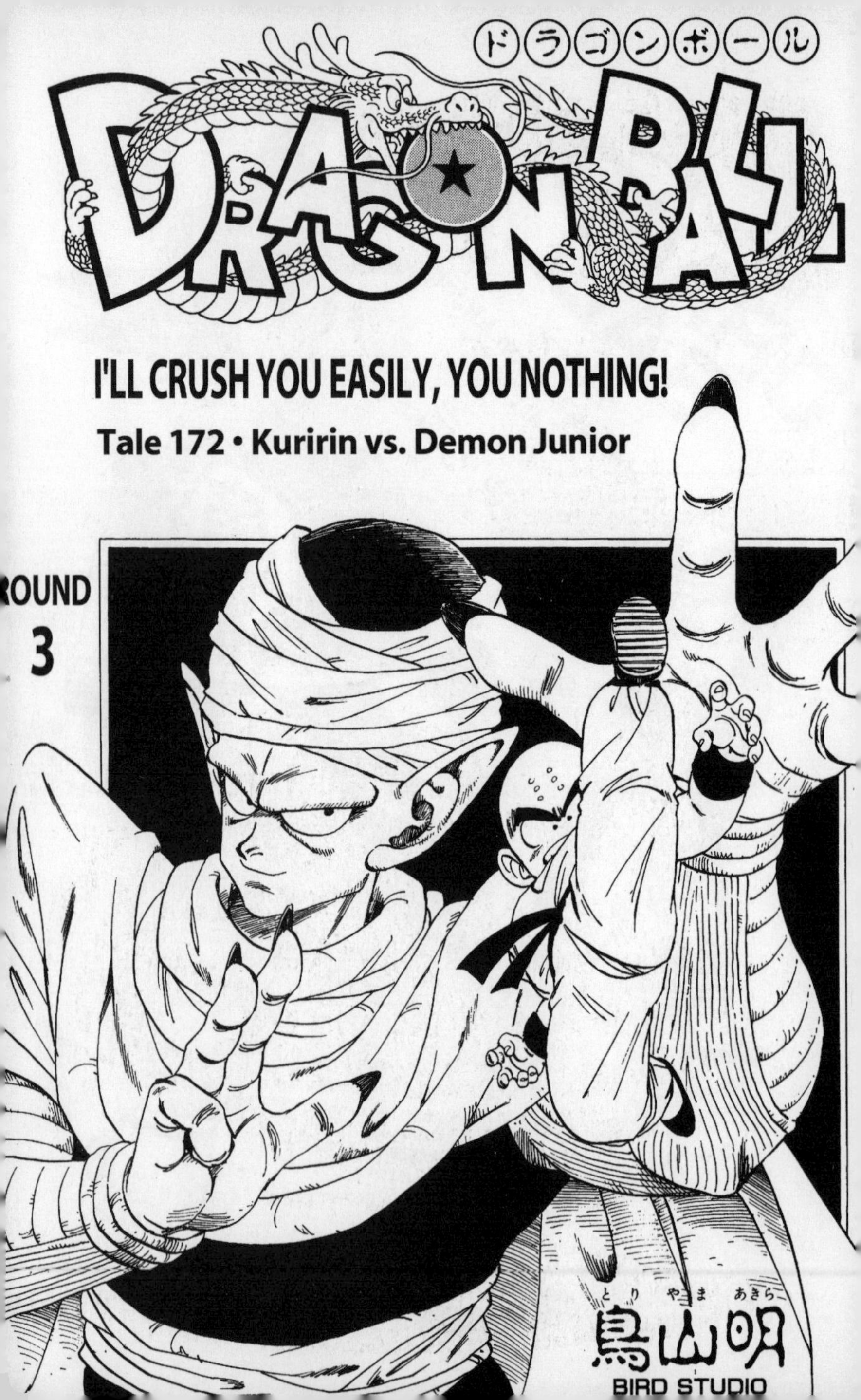
ROUND 3
とりやま あきら
鳥山明
BIRD STUDIO

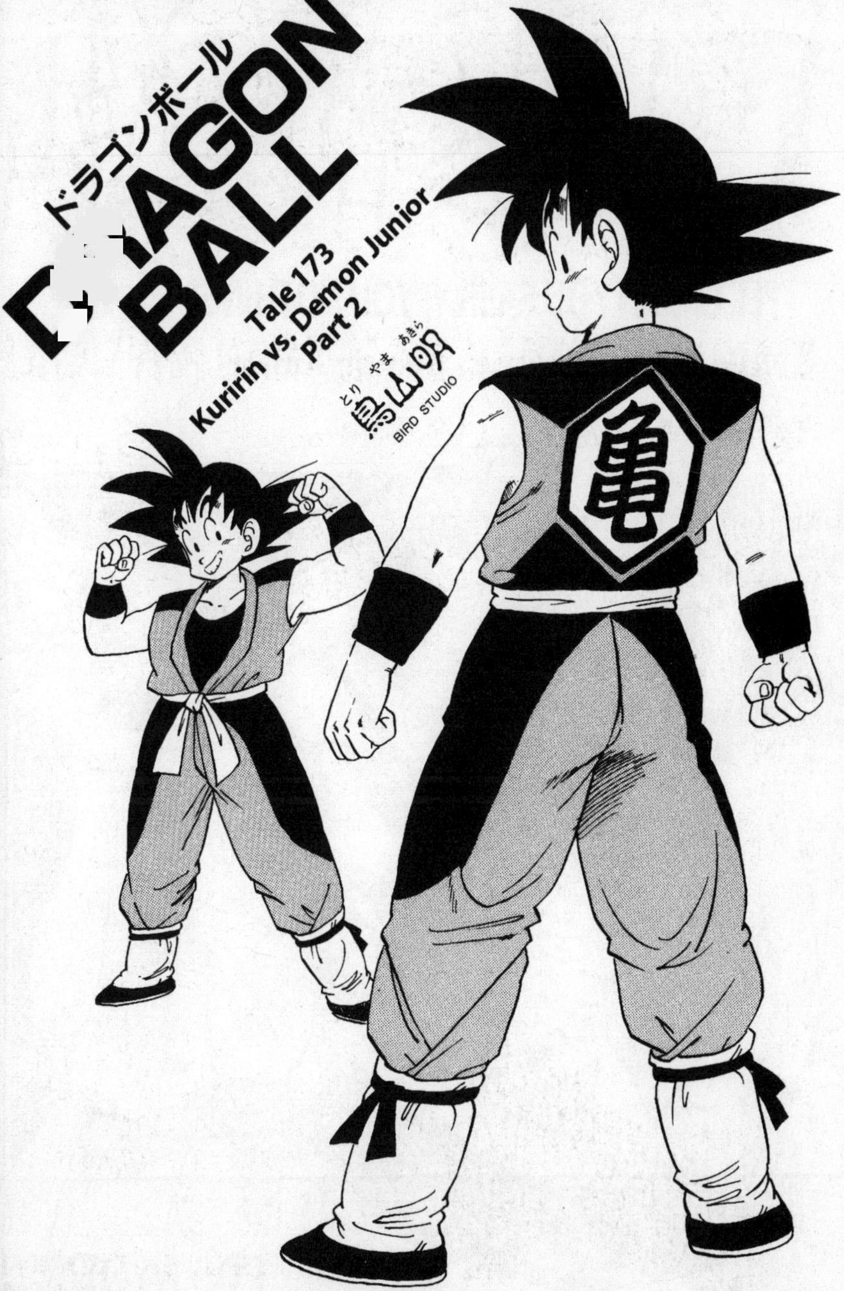
ドラゴンボール
AGON
BALL
Tale 173
Kuririn vs. Demon Junior
Part 2
鳥山明
BIRD STUDIO

ドラゴンボール

DRAGON BALL

TRUE STRENGTH IS MORE THAN PHYSICAL!

Tale 174 • Yamcha vs. Shen

とりやまあきら
鳥山明
BIRD STUDIO

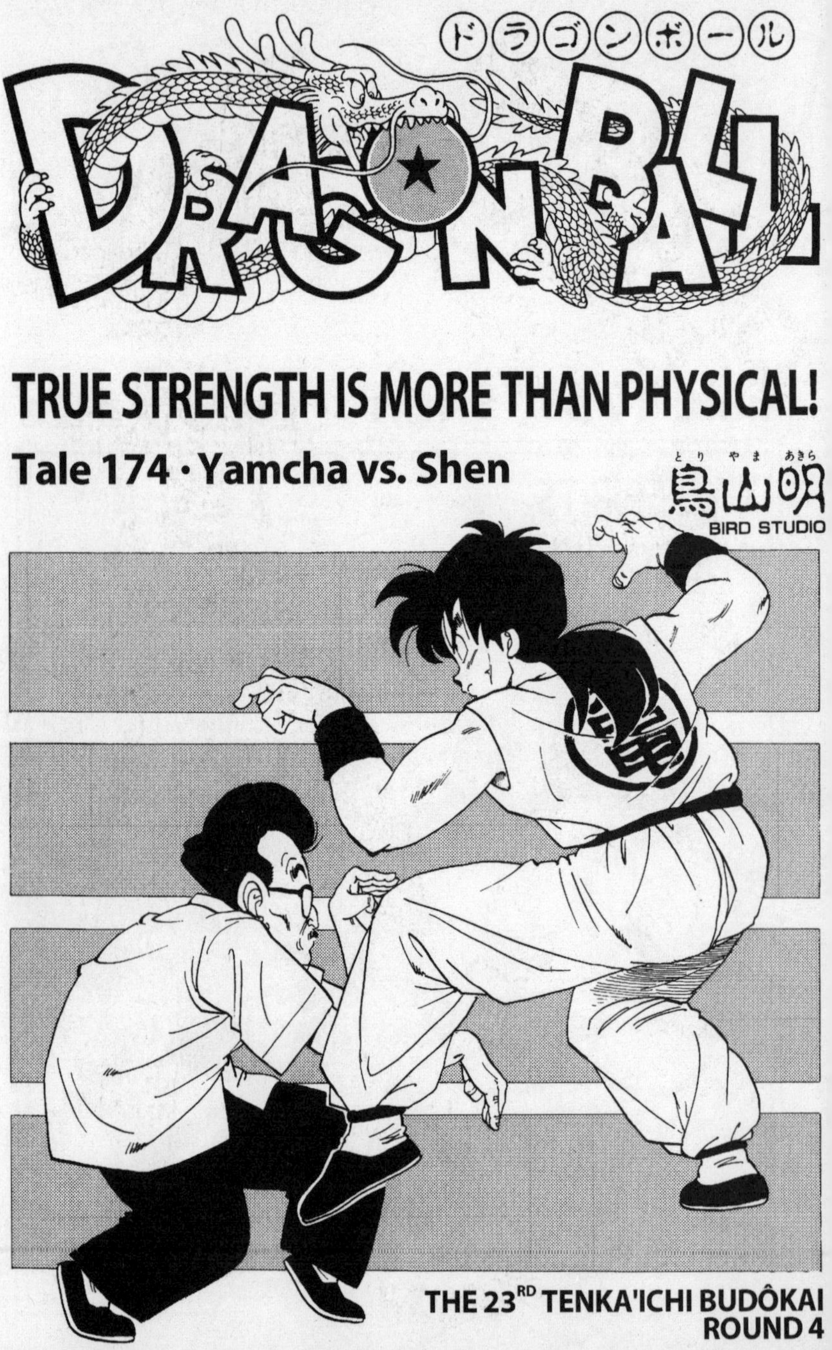

THE 23RD TENKA'ICHI BUDÔKAI
ROUND 4

ドラゴンボール

DRAGON BALL

HOW STRONG HAVE YOU BECOME?

Tale 176 • Goku vs. Tenshinhan

THE 23RD TENKA'ICHI BUDÔKAI SEMI-FINALS

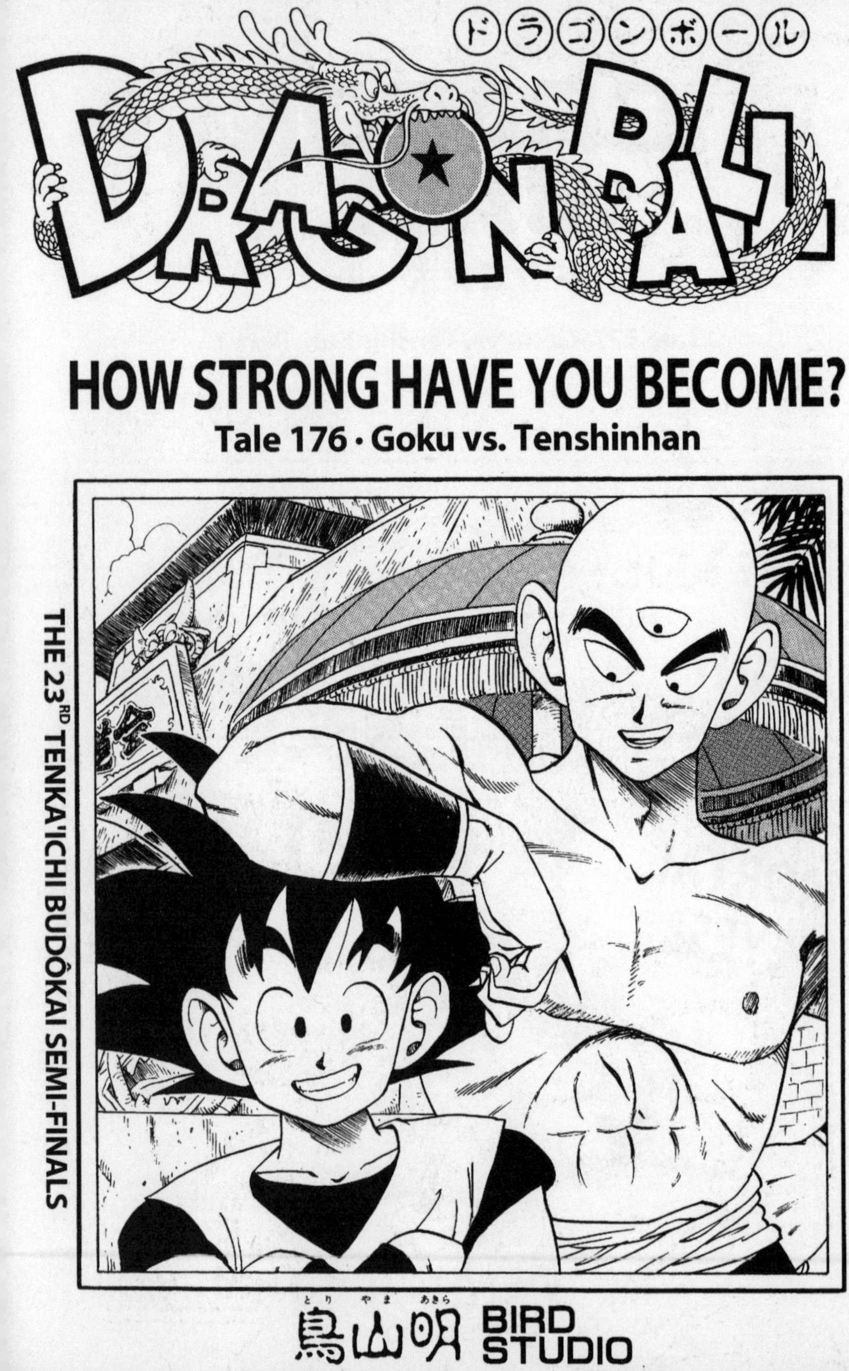

鳥山明 BIRD STUDIO

DRAGON BALL

ドラゴンボール

Tale 177 · Goku vs. Tenshinhan, Part 2

A FIGHT
TOO FAST
FOR
MORTAL
EYES!

THE 23RD
TENKA'ICHI
BUDÔKAI
SEMI-FINALS

とりやま あきら
鳥山明
BIRD STUDIO

ドラゴンボール

DRAGON BALL

GOD OR DEVIL – WHO IS STRONGER?

Tale 180 • Kami-sama vs. The Demon King

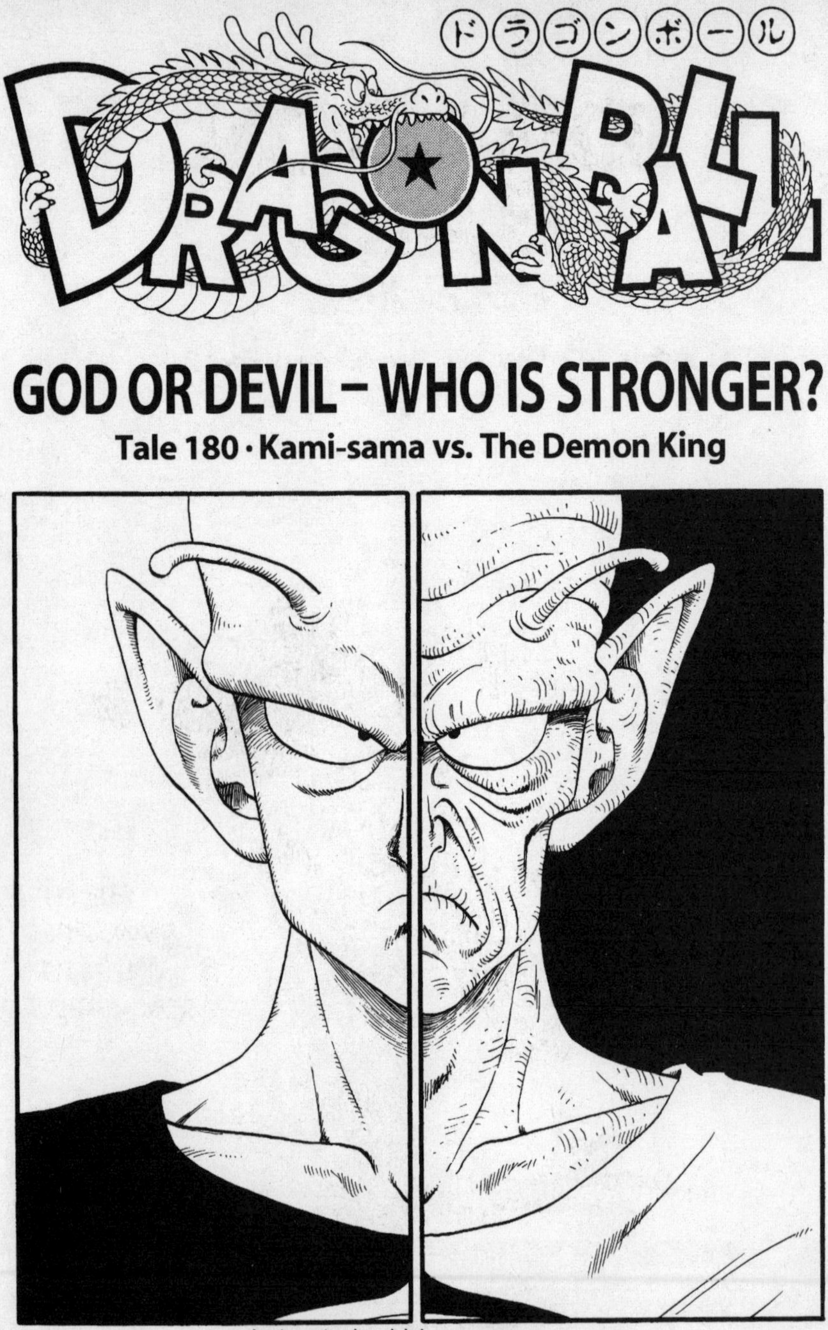

とりやま あきら
鳥山明 BIRD STUDIO